Region, religion and patronage

MANCHESTER
UNIVERSITY PRESS

Region, religion and patronage

Lancastrian Shakespeare

edited by
Richard Dutton,
Alison Findlay
and Richard Wilson

Manchester University Press

Manchester and New York

distributed exclusively in the USA by Palgrave

Published by Manchester University Press
Oxford Road, Manchester M13 9NR, UK
and Room 400, 175 Fifth Avenue, New York, NY 10010, USA
www.manchesteruniversitypress.co.uk

Distributed exclusively in the USA by
Palgrave, 175 Fifth Avenue, New York,
NY 10010, USA

Distributed exclusively in Canada by
UBC Press, University of British Columbia, 2029 West Mall,
Vancouver, BC, Canada V6T 1Z2

British Library Cataloguing-in-Publication Data
A catalogue record for this book is available from the British Library

Library of Congress Cataloging-in-Publication Data applied for

ISBN 0 7190 6368 X *hardback*
　　0 7190 6369 8 *paperback*

First published 2003

10 09 08 07 06 05 04 03　　10 9 8 7 6 5 4 3 2 1

Typeset in Sabon
by SNP Best-set Typesetter Ltd., Hong Kong
Printed in Great Britain by CPI Bath

Contents

Illustrations

Plates appear between pp. 194 and 195.

List of contributors

Philippa Berry is Fellow and Director of Studies in English at King's College, Cambridge. She is the author of *Of Chastity and Power: Elizabethan Literature and the Unmarried Queen* (Routledge, 1989), *Shakespeare's Feminine Endings: Disfiguring Death in the Tragedies* (Routledge, 1999) and is co-editor *of Shadow of Spirit: Postmodernism and Religion* (1992) and *Textures of Renaissance Knowledge* (forthcoming from Manchester University Press). She is currently completing another book on Shakespeare's comedies and preparing one entitled *Riddling the Renaissance*.

Mary A. Blackstone is a member of the Department of Theatre at the University of Regina. She has served as a dramaturg at the Globe Theatre and works independently with playwrights in the community on the development of new plays. She has published research concerning patronage of the performing arts in early modern England and the application of electronic geographical information systems to the study of performer itineraries, contributing most recently to *Shakespeare and Theatrical Patronage in Early Modern England*, edited by Suzanne Westfall and Paul Whitefield White (Cambridge University Press, 2002).

John Callow is a Lecturer in the History Dept., Goldsmiths College, University of London. He is author of *The Making of King James II* (Sutton, 2000) and *The King in Exile: James II: Soldier, King and Saint* (forthcoming, Sutton, 2003); and is joint author (with G. Scarre) of *Magic and Witchcraft in Sixteenth and Seventeenth Century Europe* (Palgrave, 2001). He has contributed 30 articles to the New Dictionary of National Biography.

Richard Dutton is Professor of English at Lancaster University, where he has taught since 1974. He has published widely on early modern drama, particularly on questions of censorship and authorship, in *Mastering the Revels: The Regulation and Censorship of English Renaissance Drama* (Macmillan, 1991) and *Licensing, Censorship and Authorship in Early Modern England: Buggeswords* (Palgrave, 2002). He has recently finished editing, with Jean E. Howard, four *Companion* volumes of new essays on Shakespeare's *Comedies, Tragedies, Histories* and *Problem Plays, Late Plays and Poems* (Blackwell, 2003). He is General Editor of the Palgrave Literary Lives Series and of the Revels Plays. He has recently edited Ben Jonson's *Epicene* (Manchester University Press, 2003) and is currently editing *Volpone* for the forthcoming new Cambridge Ben Jonson.

Alison Findlay is Reader in Renaissance Drama at Lancaster University. Her publications include *Illegitimate Power: Bastards in Renaissance Drama* (Manchester University Press, 1994), *A Feminist Perspective on Renaissance Drama* (Blackwell, 1998). She is co-director of an interdisciplinary research project on early modern women's drama, and co-author of *Women and Dramatic Production 1550–1700* (Longmans 2000). She has written on *Much Ado About Nothing* for the *Companion to Shakespeare: The Comedies*, edited by Richard Dutton and Jean E. Howard (Blackwell, 2003), and is currently working on *Women in Shakespeare* for the Athlone Shakespeare Dictionaries series.

David George is Professor of English at Urbana University, Ohio. He has edited *Shakespeare's First Playhouse* (Liffey Press, Dublin, 1981); *Records of Early English Drama: Lancashire* (Toronto University, 1991); and *Shakespeare: The Critical Heritage: Coriolanus* (Continuum Press, London, 2003). He has received grants and fellowships from the Huntington Library, the Harry Ransom Center, the Newberry Library, and the Folger Shakespeare Library in the course of co-editing (with Thomas Clayton) the New Variorum *Coriolanus* for the Modern Language Association.

Peter Greenfield is professor of English at the University of Puget Sound and editor of *Research Opportunities in Renaissance Drama*. He edited *Gloucestershire* for the Records of Early English Drama Series and is completing work on the records of Hampshire and Hertfordshire.

Phebe Jensen is an Associate Professor of English at Utah State University. She is working on a book on religion and festivity in the early modern period, and has published articles on these and other topics in journals including *Renaissance and Reformation, Shakespeare Quarterly, Reformation*, and *Criticism*.

Anne Lecercle is Professor of English Literature at the University of Paris at Nanterre, where she has taught since 1994. Since 1980 she has also lectured on Shakespeare at the *Ecole Normale Superieure* in Paris. She has published widely in French and English on early modern and modern theatre, and on literary and cultural theory. A book *Regard et Parole dans l'oeuvre de Pinter* is in press, and she is currently completing *Holbein's Ambassadors and the Transmission of Letters* before finalising another on *Shakespeare and Critical Theory (A French Point of View)*. A collection of essays by various authors on *Early Modern Cartographies of Difference* is also in the pipeline.

Sally-Beth MacLean is the Executive Editor for the Records of Early English Drama series and co-author, with Scott McMillin, of *The Queen's Men and Their Plays* (Cambridge University Press, 1998). Her most recent publication is 'Tracking Leicester's Men: the patronage of a performance troupe', in *Shakespeare and Theatrical Patronage in Early Modern England*, edited by Paul Whitfield White and Suzanne Westfall (Cambridge University Press, 2002).

Michael Mullett is Professor of Cultural and Religious History at the University of Lancaster, where he has taught for the last thirty-four years. He has published extensively in the field of religious history, including a study of John Bunyan, and in Catholic history, and is currently working on a new life of Martin Luther.

Suzanne Westfall is Professor of English and Theatre at Lafayette College, and has published extensively on patronage and household performance. She is author of *Patrons and Performance: Early Tudor Household Revels* (Clarendon Press, 1990) and has edited, with Paul W. White, *Shakespeare and Theatrical Patronage in Early Modern England* (Cambridge University Press, 2002). She has recently been working on a project entitled *Theatre and Court: Performances for Edward VI*.

Richard Wilson is Professor and Director of the Shakespeare Programme at Lancaster University. He has published numerous essays on Shakespeare and his contemporaries, and is author of *Will Power: Essays on Shakespearean Authority* (Harvester Wheatsheaf, 1993) and editor of *Christopher Marlowe* (Longman Critical Readers, Longman 1998). He co-edited *New Historicism and Renaissance Drama* (Longman, 1991) with Richard Dutton. His most recent research has been on Shakespeare, secrecy, and Catholicism.

Marion Wynne-Davies is Reader in English at the University of Dundee. She is the author of *Women and Arthurian Literature: Seizing the Sword* (Macmillan, 1996) and has edited, with S. P. Cerasano, *Renaissance Drama by Women: Texts and Documents* (Routledge, 1995).

Acknowledgements

We would like to thank Cambridge University Press for permission to reprint Suzanne Westfall's ' "The useless dearness of the diamond": Patronage Theatre and Households', from *Shakespeare and Theatrical Patronage in Modern England*, ed. Paul Whitfield White and Suzanne Westfall; Routledge Publishers for permission to reprint Richard Wilson's 'The Management of Mirth: Shakespeare *via* Bourdieu' from *Marxist Shakespeares*, ed. Jean E. Howard; Blackwell Publishers for permission to reprint Philippa Berry's 'Between Astrology and Idolatry: Modes of Temporal Repetition in *Romeo and Juliet*' from *Feminist Shakespeares*, ed. Dympna Callaghan; Ashgate Publishers for permission to reprint a revised version of Phebe Jensen's 'Recusancy, Festivity and Community: the Simpsons at Gowlthwaite Hall', from *Reformation*; and *Shakespeare Quarterly* for permission to reprint Richard Dutton's 'Shakespeare and Lancaster'.

We are grateful for the generosity of all those who assisted in the organisation of the 'Lancastrian Shakespeare' conference and exhibition at Hoghton Tower and the University of Lancaster in July 1999. In particular, we would like to thank Sir Bernard and Lady Rosanna de Hoghton, whose hospitality and enthusiasm made the conference such an outstanding success. For their invaluable support we are also indebted to the Council of the Duchy of Lancaster, and the Clerk of the Council, Mr M. K. Ridley; the late David Fraser and Granada Television; Peter Robinson and the members of the Blackburn Partnership; Gary Bates and Paul Heathcote of Heathcote's Restaurant; the music director and staff of Lancaster Priory; Professor Pierre Iselin and the Sorbonne Scholars; Anthony Holden; Dr Robert Poole; Tristram Quinn and the BBC *Newsnight* team; Lindsay Newman and the Librarians of Lancaster University; and Matthew Frost and Manchester University Press.

Introduction

The starting point of the conference from which this book and its companion volume *Theatre and Religion: Lancastrian Shakespeare* derive was, of course, the possibility that Shakespeare was the 'William Shakeshafte' who received forty shillings in Alexander Hoghton's 1581 will. Hoghton bequeathed play clothes and instruments, and recommended William Shakeshafte and the actor Fulk Gillom 'now dwelling with me' to Sir Thomas Hesketh, asking him 'either to take them unto his service or else help them to some good master'.[1] This history of the 'lost years' places the young Shakespeare in a world of country houses, provincial theatre and Catholic recusant circles. Aside from its obvious interest for Shakespeare scholars, seen in the work of Professor Ernst Honigmann and others, it opens up wider areas of early modern culture which oblige us to rethink our ideas of Elizabethan England and its theatre. Chapters in this volume explore the relatively neglected culture of the recusant provinces such as Lancashire, which had strong links with the vibrant world of Counter-Reformation Europe, and the country households which were little (and sometimes not so little) courts unto themselves, linked through intermarriage, local politics and religious sympathies. The business of playing, an increasingly important mode of cultural exchange in this world, is the focus of other diverse yet complementary chapters on the 1570s, 1580s and 1590s, when Shakespeare was growing up and learning his trade. These examine a range of primarily regional theatrical practices which challenge the assumption that the construction of the purpose-built London theatres was necessarily the development which had most impact on the profession in the period, or loomed as large in its priorities as it has in subsequent theatre history.

Households

Unless more evidence is forthcoming, we will not know whether Shakespeare was indeed the Shakeshafte mentioned in Alexander Hoghton's will, whether he was a member of one of the great Lancashire households, or of the patronized playing companies that toured there, such as Lord Strange's Men who are recorded as having performed *Titus Andronicus*.[2] Nevertheless, an examination of the households and their connections to Shakespeare's work makes this an intriguing possibility, as well as revealing a community with its own playing spaces and micro-politics, linked to religious households on the Continent and to the wider European politics of the Counter-Reformation.

Shakespeare's experiences of the noble household echo through his drama, sometimes obviously as in the staged domestic performances at Elsinore, Duke Theseus's Court, or Timon's house; sometimes more subtly, as in Bolingbroke's anger that his parks and forests have been spoiled, his 'household coat' torn from 'mine own windows', thus erasing his gentlemanly status (*Richard II* 3.1.23–5).[3] When Rumour speaks at the beginning of 2 *Henry IV*, however, the domestic household has been replaced by the commercial playhouse. Rumour addresses spectators here, 'among my household' (Induction 23–4). This metropolitan arena resonates with democratic opportunities, but Richard II's dream of a feudal magnate who 'every day under his household roof / Did keep ten thousand men' (4.1.272–3) exerts a powerful nostalgic appeal, as Richard Wilson's chapter explores. Even when Shakespeare was working at the centre of commercial and governmental power, he may have been artistically, emotionally and spiritually connected to a provincial alternative which deconstructed the monolithic and absolutist rhetoric of Elizabethan government.

It is with the Hoghton, Hesketh and Stanley households that Shakespeare's Lancashire apprenticeship is associated. Alexander Hoghton's bequest of play clothes and instruments to Thomas Hesketh suggests a theatrical troupe and 'Sir Thomas Hesketh plaiers' are recorded in the Earl of Derby's household book for 1587, a significant entry since the most likely 'good master' to whom Hesketh would have helped Shakeshafte, if he followed the spirit of the will, was either Henry, Fourth Earl (1531–93), or his son Ferdinando, Lord Strange (c.1559–94). The relationship between these households was not simply hierarchical, since, as Suzanne Westfall points out, 'patrons shifted their relationships with those above and those below them' (Chapter 2 below, p. 37). In 1567 close links between the Hesketh and the Stanley families were cemented by the marriage of Thomas's heir Robert (1560–1620) and Mary Stanley, daughter of Derby's cousin, Sir George of Cross Hall. The Heskeths had a strong sense of their powerful family connections. The author of the *Henry VI* plays or *Richard II* need have looked no further than the Hesketh family as inspiration for his images of dynastic succession. A beautiful illustrated family tree, composed c.1594, displayed the Heskeths' claims to alliance with not only the local Hoghtons, Ashtons and Stanleys, but to Elizabeth Woodville 'married unto King Edward the forthe', the Earls of Arundel and even the Plantagenets, by the female line.[4] The extract illustrated in Plate I shows flourishing branches and leaves, the male line represented as oak and the many different female lines from the Hesketh, Fleming, and Stanley families, shown by rose and laurel, the Derby family line running down the right-hand side of the document to be grafted on to the Heskeths via Mary Stanley.[5] It is intriguing to consider that if Shakespeare had been on tour to Lancashire with Lord Strange's Men in 1593–94, as David George suggests, this family tree with its intertwined foliage might have inspired *Richard II*'s horticultural references, including the 'seven fair branches springing from one root' (1.2.13). On a humbler level, perhaps the activities of Robert Hesketh's brother Thomas (1561–1613), whom John Gerard, the herbalist, acknowledged as a 'diligent searcher of Simples', may lie behind the Friar who trusts in the 'powerful grace that lies / In plants, herbs, stones and their true qualities' (*Romeo and Juliet* 2.2.15–16). Thomas Hesketh was a physician rather than a priest and supplied specimens to Gerard, a son of the nearby Gerard family of Ince, marked with a cross on Lord Burghley's 1590 map of Lancashire recusants.[6]

Patronage by Thomas Hesketh or 'some other good master' of an even more powerful Lancashire family, such as the Earl of Derby or Lord Strange, would have represented an important asset to a young actor and dramatist such as Shakespeare. In the case of Lord Strange's Men, it meant preferment at Court, as records of 1580–88 and 1592–93 show. Appearances in London were only part of a much bigger picture however. Sally-Beth MacLean's and David George's chapters make the important point that households such as those of the Earls of Derby were networks of power, patronage and culture which rivalled those of the capital. Writers, artists and actors commonly moved between the two, taking them equally seriously. When playing was forbidden in London because of the plague, the companies knew there was a world elsewhere in which they could practise their craft, and some of the most successful ones opted for that world even when there were no plague restrictions. The licence granted by the Privy Council to Lord Strange's Men on 6 May 1593, to play in other venues beyond seven miles of London, gives us a glimpse of these:

> They shal and maie in regard of the service by them don and to be don at the court exercize their qualitie of playing comodies, tragedies and such like in anie other cities, tounes and corporaction, where the infection is not … that they maie be in the better readines hereafter for her majesty's service whensoever they shall be thereto called.[7]

Although the Privy Council inevitably sees all other performances as rehearsals for those at Court, the *Records of Early English Drama* show that touring was a significant part of the companies' itineraries. Patronage meant equally important preferment in the provinces, and not just within the immediate area of the patron's country estates. Companies benefited from their patron's wider influence in that local area and in other counties on the touring routes. For a patron, the benefits of patronizing a touring company, a superfluous luxury which apparently made little contribution to the household, seem more intangible. However, as Suzanne Westfall's chapter points out, players were their patron's cultural ambassadors across the counties of England, promoting his public persona and ideologies. Their reception by local authorities and local patrons was therefore indicative of a much wider social network.

At the centre of these wider opportunities for preferment was the patron's household. Although records suggest that Tudor companies of players spent very little of the year in residence at their Lord's home or homes, this household did function in the metaphorical and ideological sense as a base. Architecture, household records and details from legal documents can give us some sense of the cultural space in which Shakespeare, as Shakeshafte, might have begun work in the theatre. To appreciate the dynamics of household performance, we must abandon twentieth-century perspectives on what constitutes theatre (or a theatre) and begin to think of the whole property as a stage with members of the household, including the designated players, participating as both spectators and performers at different stages of the revels. At festival times, processions to and from designated areas, into a chapel or a banqueting hall, whether to serve or to be served, were an integral part of the spectacle.[8] The architecture of Hoghton Tower, with its chapel linked to the great hall via an adjoining room, would have allowed for such processional performance. The great hall of a noble household, such as that at Hoghton Tower, offered a very different architectural and psychological space from those of the public theatres. Bruce Smith has pointed out that the medieval hall or open space constituted the viewer as part of an organic whole while the Roman theatre located the spectator within a geometrical grid that obliged him to 'place himself' self-consciously in relation to the surrounding space, with more detachment.[9] In the public theatres, open thrust stages offered opportunities for blurring boundaries between actors and performers, like the medieval mode. However, the commercial structure of those theatres, partitioned by galleries and different entrance prices, more closely resembled the Roman model and belied the illusion of an organic 'Globe'. A different dynamic operated in the household. Within the great hall, the hierarchical organization of space around the principal spectator, the patron, meant there could be no doubt about the differences between members. Nevertheless, actors and spectators, nobles and servants were incorporated as parts of a whole within the communal space.

We have little physical sense of the Stanley houses in which Shakespeare might have performed since New Park and Lathom no longer exist and Knowsley has been much rebuilt, but, in addition to Hoghton Tower, the Hesketh household offers evidence of a distinctly Catholic performance space into which Gillom and Shakeshafte would have been incorporated. The great hall at Rufford is constructed on a late medieval pattern which prevailed into the Tudor period, so was probably built by Sir Robert Hesketh, a bastard slip 'made capable', who triumphed over the inheritance claims of his three married sisters. (Unlike the daughters in *King Lear*, the sisters do not appear on the family pedigree.)[10] At one end of the great hall at Rufford, four entrances leading to the buttery, pantry, kitchen and staircase are concealed by a large heavy screen, providing an excellent range of entrance or exit opportunities for performers. The Heskeths' spiritual and worldly concerns sit side by side on the screen which is carved with angels and the arms of the Fitton and Banastre heiresses who married into the family. Powerful alliances are also advertised in carvings on the great hall's hammerbeam roof, whose armorial bosses include the 'eagle and child' crest of the Earls of Derby. The roof's most striking features ostentatiously declare the Hestkeths' Catholic sympathies. A wooden spandrel carving on the left presented an image of the five wounds of Christ to those who raised their eyes from the high table to give thanks. On each beam of the roof hovers a large wooden angel, 'unique in the secular architecture of Lancashire'.[11] Possibly brought from one of the suppressed monasteries, these figures must have been a hauntingly beautiful presence with their finely carved outstretched wings. Looking round, it is hard to resist the temptation that memories of the hall might have filtered through Horatio's epitaph to Hamlet. In *The Poetics of Space* Gaston Bachelard argues that the houses of our past, particularly our youth, return uncannily to us throughout our lives, shaping our consciousness of every subsequent room.[12] The powerful resonances of Catholic homes in Stratford and Lancashire may have echoed down the corridors of Shakespeare's consciousness to the Globe. The traces of household rituals and festivals are explored in more detail in the chapters on *Romeo and Juliet* by Philippa Berry and on *Twelfth Night* by Anne Lecercle.

The more sinister aspects of recusant household life are recalled by the presence of a suspended 'secret chamber' behind the canopy above the high table in the Rufford Old Hall, possibly a priest's hole.[13] The problem of recusancy in Lancashire heightened the pressure of household politics. For an apprentice dramatist such as Shakespeare, the blessing of patronage must have been a turbulent experience. Although Henry VI thinks that 'notes of household harmony' would make caged birds 'quite forget their loss of liberty' (*3 Henry VI* 4.7.12–15), the realities of life in the houses of Hoghton or Hesketh were far from harmonious. Priests were caged in secret cells to escape pursuivants while recusant householders were frequently presented before the Earl of Derby, as the perhaps equivocal representative of the Queen, and suffered loss of liberty themselves. After Campion's arrest in 1581, the Privy Council sent letters to Sir John Biron, Sir Edmund Trafford and the Earl of Derby asking them to interrogate all suspected Catholic sympathizers 'whether the said Campion hathe ben there or no', and 'further to cause the said houses to be searched for bookes and other superstitious stuffe'.[14] In 1581 and then again in 1584 Sir Thomas Hesketh was arrested by Trafford as a disaffected papist, though for how long we do not know. If Shakespeare was still in his employ in 1584, when Hesketh was betrayed by an unscrupulous kinsman in London, this second offence may have provoked Shakespeare's move to 'some other good master' at the Derby household and the first step away from an unequivocally Catholic household.

Hesketh secured his release in 1584 by appealing to the Earl of Leicester. He excused himself from the 'material matter' of recusancy, claiming that his only fault had been in failing to police other members of his household, and promised to 'see the reformation of some in his family'.[15] If Thomas Hesketh was a church papist who did attend services, as his appeal suggests, his policy of shifting the dangerous burden of nonconformity on to the less public family figures, women and children, was typical. Marie Rowlands has pointed out that women were often responsible for upholding the structures of Catholicism behind the closed doors of the household while their husbands presented a public appearance of conformity.[16] This was certainly true of Lancashire where, as J. A. Hilton points out, Catholicism remained 'a predominantly female community'.[17] Dame Alice Hesketh, lady of the house when Shakeshafte was recommended to Sir Thomas, continued to live openly as recusant when she was widowed in 1588, harbouring Catholic priests at Martholme.[18] The 1590 'Vewe of Lancashire' noted numerous cases of nonconformity amongst female family members. Of Edward Scarisbrick, it reported 'conformable he, but his wife is a recusant', and the 1591 'Summarie Information of the State of Lancashire' complained 'his children [were] trayned up in Popery, and his daughters never come to church'. Sir Richard Shireburne of Stonyhurst was another head of family who paid lip service to parish services while 'his wife, children and famylie, for the most parte, seldome come to churche, and never communycate, and some of his daughters married and not knowne by whome, but suspect by masse priests'.[19]

By 1593 the Privy Council identified a sisterhood of 'very many widdowes and others of accompt' as a distinct problem in prosecuting recusancy under the new legislation. Their Lordships complained that the Lancashire women 'obstinatly continewing Recuzancy do absent themselves, by which means they remayn stil at libertie to the manifest contempt of aucthoritie and good government'. In order to tighten the power of the patriarchal state, on 5 June 1593 the Privy Council commanded the Earl of Derby to apprehend 'Mistress Anne Hoghton of the Tower', widow to Alexander's half-brother Thomas. Exasperated by 'her removing from place to place', they ordered her to London and tried to destroy her peculiarly female powers of non-accountability by charging her new husband,

Mr Shireburne (son of the troublesome Sir Richard), with responsibility to 'see her forthcoming'. When Mistress Hoghton refused on account of pregnancy, they insisted 'she presentlie be sent up unto us' mounted or in a coach and accompanied by Shireburne. Their insistence indicates just how much of a threat she posed: 'her staie in the countrie maie be daungerous in that her example and endeavours heareotofore have perverted and confirmed many in their obstinacy'.[20] Like truly modern, enlightened rulers, the Privy Councillors wished not to harm Anne Hoghton physically but to convert her into a docile subject. Anne's promise to renounce her 'contemptius behaviour' and attend church, rather than travel to London, was greeted with pleasure. As agents of the Queen's mercy, the Privy Council ventriloquized Her Majesty's gracious delight, that 'those her subjectes which have bene seduced maie by anie meanes be brought to acknowledge theire duties towardes God and her Majestie'. To Derby they pointed out that since Mistress Hoghton's example 'when she was perverselie given hath done great hurt' in Lancashire, 'so this her conformytie maie doe good yf she shall performe it in deede'.[21]

The Privy Council's attempt to break up a wall of female recusant solidarity was perhaps motivated as much by the growth of a religious sisterhood as by a wish to enforce the law. While women such as Anne Hoghton flaunted their recusancy at home, and in some cases were imprisoned for it, others were building up strong religious orders on the Continent. Thomas Tydersley's widow Elizabeth, of Myerschough Lodge in Lancaster, was reported to Lord Burghley to be 'one of the most obstinate' recusants in 1598 and Elizabeth, one of her daughters, became the Abbess of the Poor Clares at Gravelines. Two daughters of the Allen family of Rossall Hall, nieces to Cardinal Allen, became Augustinian nuns at Louvain.[22] Marion Wynne-Davies's chapter points out the importance of family connections to English nuns sent abroad to Continental convents. Scholastica Houghton is represented as 'a Lady highly distinguished in the World by her descent from an Antient and good family'.[23] However, Wynne-Davies shows that by 1656–57 the women's spiritual households and sisterhoods had become their new families: 'The genealogical relationships that generated the dialogic lines of the last century and a half had, by the mid-seventeenth century, been replaced with spiritual ties in which faith replaced blood' (Chapter 7 below, p. 133).

The shift from family pedigree to spiritual community was an important one, connecting Lancashire to a much wider Counter-Reformation movement. The county was, according to the Privy Council, 'the very sink of popery, where more unlawful acts have been committed and more unlawful persons holden in secret than in any other part of the realm'.[24] Catholic households across England were united by common experiences of faith, fear and persecution, particularly if they harboured priests from the Jesuit mission. In Lancashire, the Talbots of Salesbury Hall suffered because

'William Allen hath divers tymes been in his house', for example. John Talbot's name appeared in the list of Lancashire gentry allegedly revealed by Campion on the rack, and, when Richard Simpson stayed with Talbot in 1581, the house was raided by pursuivants.[25] John Callow and Michael Mullet's chapter offers a detailed reading of the Shireburne family's attempts to balance the demands of loyalty to their faith and to the state, ultimately sacrificing the latter in favour of maintaining their loyalty to a Catholic community in England and abroad. Many Lancashire families were connected by marriage ties anyway, but the community may have been catholic in more senses than one, bringing into its fold temporary household members such as Shakespeare. The more fluid 'cultural neighbourhoods' which existed between groups of players and Catholic sympathizers are analysed in Mary Blackstone's important chapter.

The Stanley household occupied a different position in the religious cultural geography of Lancashire. The Earls' of Derby extensive power meant that, in effect, it functioned as a northern equivalent to the royal Court, its household riches 'at such proud rate that it outspeaks / Possession of a subject', like Cardinal Wolsey's household in *Henry VIII* (3.2.126–9). If Shakespeare spent some of the 'lost years' in Lord Strange's Men, or visited the Stanley household as part of another touring company, he would have experienced a site where people of Catholic, Anglican and Puritan sympathies were brought together. The extended family, the permanent staff and the prominent clergymen who visited to preach were by no means uniform in the faith, or conformity to the state religion. This entry in the *Derby Household Book* for 31 December to 5 January 1588–89 shows the variety of people a visiting player could have encountered during a week's residence in the household:

> On Tvsedaye the reste of my L.[ordship's] Cownsill & also Sr Jhon Savadge, & at nyght a Playe was had in the Halle, & the same nyghte my L. Strandge came home; on Wednesdaye Mr ffletewood pretched, and the same daye yong Mr Halsoll & his wiffe came; on Thursdaye Mr Irelande of the Hutte came; Fryday Sr Jhon Savadge dep[ar]ted, & the same daye Mr Hesketh, Mr Anderton, & Mr Assheton came, & also my L. Bushoppe & Sr Jhon Byron.
> Sondaye Mr Caldewall pretched, & that nyght the Plaiers plaied.[26]

Members of the Stanley family range from immediate (Lord Strange) to more distant relations such as Sir John Savage, descended from the First Earl of Derby's sister. Also represented are illegitimate branches such as 'yong Mr Halsoll', a bastard son of Richard Hallsal who married Dorothy, an illegitimate daughter of Henry Earl of Derby.[27] Members of the local nobility are present, many of them holding important positions such as Sir John Byron, Sheriff of Lancashire, magistrates such as 'Mr Irelande of the Hutte', George Ireland of Hale. George Ireland, Mr Hesketh, Mr Asheton and Mr Anderton were all members of families marked on Burghley's map as suspected recusants. Mr Fleetwood, Rector of Wigan, and Mr Caldwell were two of the most zealous Puritans in the locality. The Sunday on which Mr Caldwell preached in the morning and the players performed in the evening symbolized what appeared to be a remarkably catholic community of differences.

The Stanleys' own recent family history showed diametrically opposed religious sympathies. Sir Thomas and Sir William Stanley, brothers to Henry, Fourth Earl of Derby, had been implicated in the Ridolfi plot to help Mary Queen of Scots escape from Chatsworth House and flee to the Isle of Man in 1570. Henry, however, had been one of the commissioners responsible for overseeing Mary's execution in 1587. On 1 December 1581 the Privy Council had thanked the Earl of Derby for offering his house 'to serve for the safe keping of the Recusantes in their Diocese'.[28] In spite of the visits of leading Puritan divines such as Caldwell and Fleetwood at his houses, however, Henry's religious sympathies were still a cause of concern. In 1587 Fleetwood wrote to Lord Burghley, concerned about the religious sympathies of some of Derby's councillors and cautioning him not to nourish in the Earl 'that humour of carelesse securitie in tolleratinge and no way sowndly reforminge the notoriows backwardnesse of his whole Company in religion, and chefely of the chefest abowte him'.[29] In the late 1580s and 1590s Henry's cousin Sir William Stanley was involved in planning invasions from Ireland, Anglesey and Scotland into Lancashire to re-convert England to Catholicism. In 1592 Thomas Christopher reported to Burghley that Stanley recommended invading Lancashire 'neer unto Stanleyes owne Countrey where a great Parsonage would be readie to helpe and take parte with him'.[30] This person was Ferdinando, Lord Strange, who became Fifth Earl of Derby on Henry's death in 1593, the focus of further Jesuit conspiracies. In 1593 Richard Hesketh, a cousin to Sir Robert Hesketh, suggested that Ferdinando should usurp Elizabeth. Ferdinando revealed the plot and Hesketh was executed, but Ferdinando's own sudden death, in April 1594, roused suspicions that he had been poisoned by Catholic sympathizers.[31] Such a household and such patrons would have exposed Shakespeare to the bloody extremes of religious politics, on both a national and a local scale.

Similar though less bloody extremes jostle alongside each other in *Twelfth Night*, where the madonna and her steward, 'a kind of puritan' (2.3.125), rule over a somewhat disorderly household. According to a family tradition, William Farrington (1537–1609), the Steward of the Derby Household, was the inspiration for Shakespeare's Malvolio.[32] It was Farrington who recorded and catered for the comings and goings of players, Puritan preachers and recusant gentry such as Sir Thomas and Dame Alice Hesketh and Thomas and Mistress Ann Hoghton in the *Derby Household Book*. Farrington's wife and family were Catholic and he is marked on Burghley's map with a cross at Worden Hall in the parish of Leyland, but 'his outward actions were certainly not those of a Catholic'.[33] His 'Orders touching the Gov[ern]ment of my L. his house' set down in 1587 give a sense of how he could be viewed as 'a kind of puritan', a rigid embodiment of the law. They itemize, in fourteen notes, a strict regime requiring the attendance of himself, the Steward or Comptroller, over weekends 'for the bett[er] gov[ern]ment of his Lo. house' and supervision of every inferior officer. 'Acates' or cakes are to be precisely accounted for at the end of the week, and the final item in the list could serve as a warning to any waiting woman tempted to anticipate Maria's behaviour: 'my Lo. his chiefe officers make a weeklie viewe & take Ord. that noe vagrant p[er]sons or maister-les men be fostered and kept aboute the house and that noe househould S[er]vante of any degree bee p[er]mitted to carie forth of the house or gates any maner of victualls, bread or drinke'.[34] William Farrington's picture, painted in 1593, offers an early sketch of Malvolio. Over his plain rich russet doublet, he wears a large three-banded chain of linked gold. His silver-headed cane was probably his staff of office. As F. R. Raines, the editor of the *Derby Household Book*, points out, 'he looks like a man who has been more accustomed to rule than to obey'.[35]

It would have been over the Christmas and Twelfth Night festivities that Farrington, and subsequent Stewards of the household, were busiest catering for visitors and the players. Ferdinando's brother William (c.1561–1642) and William's successor, James (1607–51), continued the patronage of household performance, and in 1640 Shakespeare's dramatization of a battle between a festive catholicism and Puritan return to work is rewritten as part of a Stanley family tradition. 'A Masque' was presented before 'ye Lord Strange his at Knowsley on Twelfth Night' in 1640–41, written by Sir Thomas Salusbury, grandson of the Sir John Salusbury who married Ursula Stanley (an illegitimate daughter of Henry, Fourth Earl) and was the dedicatee of *Love's Martyr* (1601) in which Shakespeare's 'The Phoenix and the Turtle' was published.[36] In Thomas Salusbury's masque, Christmas, whose first entrance bears close resemblance to that of Falstaff in *2 Henry IV*, proclaims that he has never felt better, but the Doctor borrows Romeo's lines (5.3.87–90) to inform Christmas that this merriment is 'a lightning before death' (p. 255, l. 32).[37] The Doctor warns that by tomorrow 'the whininge schoole boy', making his way miserably to school no doubt, 'shall with his satchell on his backe lament / ye losse of Christmas' (p. 256, ll. 11–13). Christmas resolves (like Hotspur in *I Henry IV* 4.2.135) to 'dy merrilie' (p. 256, l. 20), but 'Leane' ghost-like apparitions 'of fasting dayes' appear in an antemasque to frighten him, in the manner of Richard III's night before Bosworth (p. 256, ll. 26–32). After a dance, the lenten ghosts carry off the personifications of 'ye hollidayes', leaving Christmas to moralize the scene in a specifically religious way. Christmas looks back to a tradition of Stanley hospitality, 'with soe magnificent solemnities' (p. 257, l. 33) but fears for the future:

        least my poore successors
with all theyre troopes of hollidayes bee bannasht
for ever hence to Roome: & heere esteem'd
as superstitious raggs of popery. (p. 257, ll. 19–22)

However, after a song of priests and priestesses in the Temple of the New Year, the Earl's son, Mr Stanley, promises that although states and kingdoms change, the 'Auncient plentie, Mirth and happines' performed before by his 'great Ancestors' will continue (p. 262, ll. 30–4). To give substance to the promise, the months of the year are then represented by members of the household and friends, including Mrs Farrington, wife or daughter of the present William Farrington (grandson of the Steward, and now Officer to the current Earl). Even though Lord and lady Strange were committed Protestants, this much later Twelfth Night celebration re-presents a Catholic festivity whose privileged performance conditions protected it from Puritan anti-theatricality or the alterations in national politics. If Shakespeare had been at a Derby household as part of a theatre company, his memories of that household would surely have endured just as strongly, even in a world of secular commercial performance where 'what's to come is still unsure' (2.3.45).

Journeyman players ambling by a play-wagon

We would love to know how, when and where William Shakespeare entered the theatrical profession. We would love to know what troupes he worked with, before emerging into the dubious light of the written record of such things in March 1595 – already a leading figure, one who received payment for two performances of the new Lord Chamberlain's company at Court the previous Christmas.[38] But the fact is that we do not. There has, of course, been endless speculation, much of it focusing on troupes that are known to have visited Stratford-upon-Avon at plausible times, notably the Earl of Leicester's Men and the Queen's Men.[39] The *Lancastrian Shakespeare* conference inevitably foregrounded the possibility that he might have spent at least some time with Lord Strange's Men, the most successful of all Lancashire-based troupes in the era, patronized by the heir of the Earl of Derby from his northern seats at New Park, Lathom and Knowsley.

If definitive answers to these questions are elusive, we need nevertheless to keep asking them afresh, in the light of new information and perspectives. By far the most important new perspectives on early modern theatre in recent years have emerged from the *Records of Early English Drama* project, based at the University of Toronto. Sally-Beth MacLean, Peter Greenfield and David George have all contributed to that project, and their chapters here develop insights from it. Those by Suzanne Westfall and Mary Blackstone more broadly raise the kinds of questions we now need to ask to make coherent sense of such insights, to relate them to our wider understanding of that culture. There is a degree of irony in the fact that a project which deliberately set its face against the Shakespeare-centredness of so much early modern theatre history should now be invoked to allow us to rethink Shakespeare.

How anyone, let alone Shakespeare, entered the Elizabethan theatrical profession is a matter about which we know far less than we would like. How a few of those in the profession then contrived to join its most prestigious companies is equally, for the most part, a matter of guesswork and conjecture. It has not helped us to understand the little we do know about recruitment to the profession that, until very recently, so much of our thinking has been so Shakespeare-centred and London-centred, focused on the period post-1590, where the information is more fully (if not necessarily representatively) available: as if it was self-evidently the case that playing in the capital was the ultimate goal of serious actors and that theatre there (particularly as reflected in Henslowe's *Diary*) was professionally in a different league from anything going on in the rest of the country. G. E. Bentley's magisterial *The Profession of Dramatist in Shakespeare's Time, 1590–1642* (Princeton, 1971) is entirely representative in these respects. Perhaps by the time, say, of the building of the Globe in 1599 this was the reality (though in terms of sheer quantity there was always far more theatrical activity outside the capital than was ever sanctioned in the city, albeit largely anonymous and barely recorded). Earlier than that, however, as Shakespeare was growing up and becoming involved with theatre, the actuality was far less London-focused than we have commonly supposed, and some features of it (such as its patronage by the gentry and aristocracy) had little to do with urban working conditions which implicitly dominate those perspectives of which Henslowe and Bentley are differently representative. Moreover, as we have already seen, the non-urban, non-metropolitan and even non-courtly dimensions of playing continued to have a bearing on Shakesepeare's working life, even after its centre of gravity was securely in London.

To illustrate some of these issues, let us consider what we know of the careers of two leading actors in the 1580s, the brothers John and Laurence Dutton. (Since one of the editors is himself a Dutton of Dutton, albeit of a distinctly cadet branch of the family, we should acknowledge an element of personal interest. But their case does illustrate, and suggests connections between, many of the key issues here.) Firstly, where did they come from and how did they become actors? We do not know, though their name gives rise to the very reasonable speculation that they were related to the Duttons of Dutton in Cheshire, who since medieval times had held the authority to license minstrelsy in that county palatine. Every Parliamentary Act against vagrancy in the Elizabethan or Jacobean period (which of course had particular resonances for travelling players) contained a clause declaring that it did not infringe the authority of the house of Dutton.[40] Tempting and plausible though this connection is, and even though we know that John and Laurence were names in the family, no precise candidates have ever been identified, despite the best efforts of E. K Chambers or, more recently, of the Mormon Genealogical Index. Like the Hoghton Tower connection for Shakespeare, which implies a similar geographical translation some have found implausible in the era, it remains an intriguing and not unreasonable hypothesis.

'It is curious', as Chambers observes, 'that a John and a Laurence Dutton also appear as Court Messengers' (*ES*, II, p. 314). Indeed, the very first record of a Laurence Dutton in this time frame finds him paid at Court for 'sondry jorneys' in 1561–62; the only reference to a John Dutton in this context was for carrying letters to Antwerp in May 1578, three years after a player of that name was first recorded. Laurence was also a regular Messenger of the Chamber from 1576 to 1582, serving the Privy Council. Were these men also the players? Was it possible to combine two such employments? Again, we do not know. As with Shakeshafte and Shakespeare, the fact of similar (or even identical) names is no guarantee of identity. The most pressing argument against their being so is that in May 1580 the actor Laurence had been jailed for an affray, at the same time as his namesake was serving as a Messenger. But the one does not entirely preclude the other: the status and connections of the Court messenger might have effected the release of the fractious actor, pending the hearing of the case. William Ingram, in a recent article that casts much new light on the affairs of the two brothers, argues that 'Dutton the messenger was often away from London when our Laurence was demonstrably present; and no record yet found speaks of [him] as having any connection with the court', yet the evidence remains, in ways I have suggested, just sufficiently muddy to make it unwise for us to rule out the identity categorically.[41] In favour of the identity of the two sets of men is indeed their status. The Dutton players, as we shall see, had pretensions to be gentry, which might derive in part from Court appointments, and these in turn might have been secured by their derivation from a substantial north-country family. It is, in truth, no more than speculation. But the possibility that the Dutton actors were indeed scions of the lesser gentry, rather than 'common players', provides a link of sorts between many of the 'facts' we know about them, and so may cast some light on the business of playing in their era.

This would need to be squared with something that Ingram has clearly established: that one of the actor Duttons (Laurence) was a freemen of the Company of Weavers, at least as early as the 1570s, and that his brother was probably one too. How they came to hold those positions, and whether they were ever active weavers, is less clear: 'It may well be that the Duttons acquired their freedom by patrimony rather than apprenticeship, in which case they may well have known nothing about the actual craft of weaving'.[42] A Dutton is mentioned in the scanty company records in 1553, who was presumably a Londoner and could have been their father: if so, this would

seem to reduce the possibility of strong and immediate links with the Cheshire Duttons. Yet kinship links ran deep at this time, and the one connection need not entirely preclude the other. Is it possible that the actors Laurence and John were, at least by derivation, Cheshire Duttons, freemen of the Company of Weavers, *and* court messengers? The odds are against their being all of these. But the most frustrating feature of this array of possibilities is that none of them offers us a very convincing explanation as to how they might have become involved with the theatre.

The first we hear of them as players is when Laurence is recorded as receiving payment on behalf of Sir Robert Lane's Men for two performances at Court in the Christmas season of 1571–72 (*ES*, II, p. 96). As with Shakespeare and the Lord Chamberlain's Men in 1595, this suggests that he was already recognized as a senior figure. If he was indeed from the Cheshire family, we have to ask how and why he moved so far south; if he was ever an apprenticed weaver, how he came to leave his trade and the city: Sir Robert Lane's estate was in Horton, Northamptonshire. Conceivably, opportunities as a Court messenger came first, and the theatrical connections developed later – theatre seems to have attracted numerous opportunists away from other, more conventional and respectable careers.[43] Sir Robert is not a particularly notable figure, though his adventurer brother, Sir Ralph, went on to be first governor of Virginia. But his players travelled at least as far as Bristol (August 1570) and were one of the very last troupes not under aristocratic patronage to perform at Court. They then disappeared, almost certainly because the anti-vagrancy statute of 1572 required that all actors travelling professionally must have an *aristocratic* patron. This was the first of several decisions made at Westminster in the period (in this instance by Parliament rather than the Privy Council) which significantly impacted on the profession. It seems hardly to have affected things at the most local levels, since troupes from neighbouring and related households (for whom acting was probably never a full-time profession) continued to visit at the customary times.[44] But for the permanent, professional troupes the required fact of aristocratic patronage had important implications, breaking down some existing patronage relationships and more widely disrupting the laws of supply and demand. It prompted some aristocrats who had never been serious patrons of the drama before to adopt this form of self-promotion, which fuelled a degree of competition for symbolic capital among them – to be represented in the country at large, and perhaps also at Court, by the most notable actors, as the careers of the Duttons demonstrate.

In June 1572 we can establish that the brothers were jointly engaged in the theatre, since they and Thomas Goughe, who was also with Lane's Men, 'contracted with one Rowland Broughton for the delivery of eighteen playscripts over the course of the ensuing thirty months, the plays to be performed by a company of boys who were to be under the supervision of the Duttons and Gough'.[45] This is a fascinating sidelight on another question about which we know very little: how did the actors of this period acquire their scripts? Did they have members of the company who would write for them, or were there other Broughtons prepared to deliver wholesale? Broughton, in fact, failed to deliver (which is why we know about the contract), nor do we know if the children's company was ever formed. We might hazard a guess, however, that the whole venture was a provisional way round the problem caused by the anti-vagrancy legislation, since that would not affect boy companies as it did the adults. In the event, the Duttons did not need to pursue that option, since they found aristocratic patronage.

Laurence Dutton next appears in the record at Christmas 1572–73, as the leader of the Lord Admiral's Men (patron Edward de Clinton, created Earl of Lincoln in May 1572, and so perhaps looking for ways of flaunting his new status), when they performed at Court. It seems reasonable to infer that this was essentially Lane's Men under new patronage, though it would be interesting to know whether their translation to a more impressive livery affected the size of the troupe. Sir Robert might resent this change, but could hardly blame his players for it. It also seems reasonable to infer that this was again the same company, still led by Laurence Dutton, which performed three times at Court at Christmas, 1574–75, but now under the patronage of Lord Clinton, the Lord Admiral's son. Here family loyalties remained the same, and we may suppose that this was intended to enhance the prestige (or reflect the particular interests) of the son and heir, a more modest expedient than that employed by the even grander Stanleys who, between 1576 and 1582, patronized two separate troupes, the Earl of Derby's and Lord Strange's Men.

But this arrangement evidently did not suit Laurence Dutton, who at Christmas 1575–76 is to be found collecting payment at Court for the Earl of Warwick's Men; another of the payees was his brother, John, who had perhaps remained with him all along, although unrecorded. What exactly happened? It is not that the Clintons ceased patronizing players, since their company toured in Bristol, Coventry and Southampton in 1576–77. But they never again performed at Court. What is chicken here and what is egg? Did the Duttons leave because they knew they had lost their entrée at Court, which presumably did not augur well for future business? Or did the company lose their entrée at Court because they no longer had the (presumably impressive) services of the Duttons and any actors who went with them? That is, did the lesser status of the younger Clinton as a patron lose him talented players, or did the loss of talented players diminish his status? We would dearly love to know the political economics of such patronage relations.

An intriguing secondary question is whether Laurence Dutton (and, probably, others) transferred to another pre-existing company, or in effect created a new one with his defection. Although the Earl of Warwick had patronized players in the 1560s, we then hear of no players in his livery until a Court performance on 14 February 1575 – about six weeks after Clinton's Men had last performed there. No names are attached to that performance: the Duttons appear only as payees the following Christmas. But it is entirely possible that negotiations between Laurence Dutton and the Earl of Warwick in January/February 1575 led to the creation of the instantly successful new company. Would it have been diplomatically necessary for Warwick to seek the blessing of the Clintons for this? Or was there ultimately bad blood? The next chapter of the saga suggests that this was quite likely.

No names appear in the records, but it seems certain that the Duttons remained with Warwick's Men (who were called to perform at Court in each of the next four Christmases) until 1580: because the transfer of the whole company that year to the Earl of Oxford's patronage provoked outrage which was levelled personally at the Duttons. This is where their social pretensions become an overt issue. Contemporary verses earthily mock their claim to be on a par with gentry. The printed text explains: 'The Duttons and theyr fellow-players forsakyng the Erle of Warwycke theyr mayster, became followers of the Erle of Oxford, and wrot themselves his COMOEDIANS, which certayne Gentlemen altered and made CAMOELIANS [i.e. chameleons]. The Duttons, angry with that, compared themselves to any gentleman; therefore these armes were devysed for them . . .' (*ES*, II, p. 98). There is no knowing how representative this resentment was, much less whether Warwick felt this way about the affair. But it tells us something that someone felt strongly enough to put pen to paper – the verses are quite inventive, if hardly decorous. Another intriguing dimension to all of this is the 1577 testimony of one John Shawe, a manager of bawdy houses, to the effect that Laurence Dutton had taken one of his working girls, little Margaret Goldsmith, and set her up in business at an inn; moreover 'he is a player; there is two brethren and by report both their wives are whores'.[46] Whatever the 'report' of their wives, it seems certain that Laurence, at least, was combining the business of theatre, under aristocratic patronage, with the trade of whoremaster. In and of itself, however, this need not be incompatible with pretensions to be of the lesser gentry.

In some minds at least, the status of actors as liveried servants of a noble patron was not simply one of commercial convenience, as London-focused narratives often suggest; at around the time we may suppose Shakespeare left school, actors were still thought to owe their patron genuine allegiance as members of the extended family household. Hence the outrage at what is seen in the satirical verses as dishonourable, commercially minded treachery. It is tempting to suppose (but totally unprovable) that this outrage lay behind the affray on 13 April 1580 between Laurence Dutton and Robert Leveson, both servants of Oxford, and certain gentlemen of the Inns of

Court, for which the Privy Council committed the actors to the Marshalsea.[47] Yet if Warwick himself resented what his players had done, he either had no recourse against them or chose not to use it. He seems never again to have patronized players in any significant way.

But why should the Duttons and their fellow players have made this move – and at a time when they seem to have been establishing a London base, since one of them, Jerome Savage, was involved in setting up the Newington Butts playhouse about then?[48] It is entirely comprehensible that they should have transferred from Clinton to Warwick if they (correctly) anticipated a stronger entrée at Court. But what did the Earl of Oxford have to offer that Warwick did not? If they anticipated even greater Court favour, they miscalculated badly, since no Oxford troupe performed at Court until 1584, and by then John (if not also Laurence) had already left them. It is impossible to say whether Oxford's prestige as a member of the old aristocracy (Seventeenth Earl and hereditary Lord Great Chamberlain) outweighed Warwick's more immediate status as a Privy Councillor and brother of the great favourite, Leicester. All that can really be said is that Oxford, who had no record of patronizing players before this, developed a strong interest in things theatrical at around this date. He appeared himself in a Court device in 1579 and by 1598 Francis Meres was to describe him as a playwright, indeed 'one of the best for comedy among us'. The likely inference is that (as the Sixth Earl of Derby after him is said to have done) he wrote plays for the companies he himself patronized.[49]

Is it possible, then, that Oxford sought out the Duttons (as among the most successful players of the era) and made them a compelling offer of some kind, in his new enthusiasm to enhance his prestige through this form of patronage? At the same time he created a boys' company ('the Earl of Oxenfordes lads', as they are recorded at Norwich in 1580–81), so outgoing even the Stanleys in maintaining two troupes in his own name. As far as the adult company was concerned, however, he was thwarted on more than one front. They failed at first to receive an entrée at Court, and even (despite the intervention of Burleigh, Oxford's father-in-law, as Chancellor of the University) failed to break the usual ban on playing in Cambridge, though they received a payment in lieu (*ES*, II, p. 100). Then in 1583 they suffered (like their leading competitors, Leicester's, Sussex's and – in all probability – Derby's Men) when leading personnel were taken by the Master of the Revels, Edmund Tilney, to create the Queen's Men – a development whose wider implications we discuss below.[50] John Dutton, at least, is recorded in the earliest list of the Queen's Men, from December that year, as again in a list drawn up on 30 June 1588. Oxford's Men did not, however, go out of existence as, for a time, Leicester's, Sussex's and Derby's Men all did; indeed in 1584 they appeared twice at Court, against the general trend in which the Queen's Men eclipsed all the other adult companies there, as they had partly been designed to do. But they did not appear there again, though they continued as a touring company (and in 1587 were reported as posting their bills in London) until the end of the decade (*ES*, II, p. 101; *SPC*, 309). Oxford's boy company also flourished for a time under John Lyly, until it apparently amalgamated with Paul's Boys and the Children of the Chapel, losing a specific association with Oxford. Where Laurence Dutton was in all this, we cannot say. He disappears altogether until the late 1580s, when he is associated with John once more, this time among the leadership of the Queen's Men.

Strictly speaking, Laurence disappears until 1589, when he and John were among the company's leaders in Nottingham; and on 7 March 1591 they were both payees for the company for performances at Court.[51] But there are also intriguing details in the record of the Queen's Men's visits to Stanley properties in Lancashire, which were quite frequent around this time. On 31 October 1588 they visited New Park, on 5 July 1589 Lathom House and on 6 and 7 September 1589, and again 24 June 1590, Knowsley Hall. On the first and last of these occasions a 'Mr. Dutton' is reported as having been present when the actors were; this can hardly have been accidental, though we have no information as to the relationship between the visitor and the troupe. He might be either of the actors, if their pretensions to gentry warranted the honorific 'Mr.', though Laurence as the senior is marginally more likely. Or he might be one of the Duttons of Dutton, from just beyond the county border, timing his visit to coincide with performances by the leading troupe in the land – who just happened to be led by what may well have been two family members. In either case, this association lends some substance to the possibility that the actors were at least related to gentry. In September 1589 that there was a flurry of diplomatic activity to track the company down, to try to comply with King James's request that they should visit Scotland to perform at his marriage to Anna of Denmark. They were eventually located at Knowsley and did indeed go to Edinburgh, though adverse winds prevented the bride's arrival during the month they stayed.[52] There is thus no record of actual performances, though it seems unlikely that they would have gone so far and not performed. If they did, one or both of the Duttons presumably led the first troupe to entertain both monarchs in Britain, both the monarchs that Shakespeare's plays were to entertain.

The company, and the Duttons, had reached the height of their success. The winter of 1591–92 shows the Queen's Men losing their predominant position at Court, where they were to perform for the last time in 1594. Almost the last we hear of either of the Duttons in the theatre is, rather typically, another altercation. In September 1592 the Queen's Men attempted to perform at Chesterton, near Cambridge. The University authorities (as with Oxford's Men in 1580) forbade it but, encouraged by Lord North and the constables of Chesterton, the performance went ahead. The Vice-Chancellor and Heads of Houses complained to the Privy Council, citing 'one Dutton' as 'a principale'.[53] It is a fitting epitaph. But it is not quite the end of their theatrical associations; in the touring of 1592/3, both brothers are named twice as payees at Lyme Regis, at a time when John at least also had significant other interests.

From 1951, John's name suddenly begins to appear regularly in the surviving records of the Company of Weavers, and he was elected warden in both 1591 and 1592, having held none of the minor offices which usually preceded that senior position, and first bailiff (effectively master) in 1595; he held responsible office repeatedly down to 1608. Perhaps with the deaths of the key sponsors of the Queen's Men, Leicester and Walsingham, he saw that change was inevitable and looked to exploit other possibilities, even if he did continue to tour at times. He was also proprietor of the Dolphin inn, in Bishopsgate, the parish where he had lived for many years, and seems to have flourished until his death in 1614.[54] Apart from a highly questionable association with the Duke of Lennox's Men around 1608, he was never again linked with the theatre.[55]

Nor was Laurence, whose fortunes declined markedly. He took out a loan in 1591, and failure to pay it (and subsequent loans) off haunted him for years, putting him in bad odour with an expanding list of creditors. In 1594 he obtained a new position as one of the City of London's Keepers of Register Books, but still owed money. The following year, 'Dutton was involved with, and for at least part of the time ringleader of, a group of persons . . . who were involved in money changing, some of them actively'. As William Ingram puts it: 'One or more versions of Dutton's role can be teased out . . . the likeliest, I suspect, is that the activities of this group were self-serving, that the enterprise was a carefully documented sting operation that failed when it was discovered, and that the participants hastily converted it, rhetorically, into a service being performed for the Crown'.[56] It is all very dubious, and still failed to relieve his debts. By 1596 these saw him in gaol, firstly in the Counter, then in Ludgate. He was released, partly on the surety of one of his fellow Keepers, Anthony Marlowe, a goldsmith, and promptly decamped, leaving various debts to be paid by his colleagues and indeed his brother.[57] On that ignominious note, he fades the following year altogether from the record. Both the apparent prosperity of John and the debt-ridden dubious dealing of Laurence beg the question why neither seems to have returned to the theatre after 1593. Possibly the major reorganisation of the companies that followed the heavy plague of 1593/4 effectively squeezed them out, and never offered them a way back in. It is surely a significant part of the whole picture that both of them maintained interests and connections outside the theatre, perhaps throughout their acting lives – John his inn and associations with the Company of Weavers (which paid off with handsome respectability in his later years), Laurence his brothel and whatever patronage made him a Keeper of Register Books (which should have been lucrative, but somehow wasn't). Perhaps even for the most successful actors of their day, it was only ever a provisional or part-time profession, one in which it made sense to keep alternative possibilities open. Here, as in so much else, the 1593/4 watershed may, at least for a favoured few, have marked a significant change.

The wider significance of the Duttons' involvement with the Queen's Men cannot be divorced from the unique features of that troupe. As McMillin and MacLean have conclusively shown, in their important study of *The Queen's Men and Their Plays*, the company's formation was explicitly a political act, and it developed a style, a repertoire and working practices which were designed to further the political agenda, not exactly of the Privy Council as a whole, but of two of its more Puritan-minded members, Walsingham and Leicester. It flourished while they were alive, but declined markedly (at least in terms of access to Court) after their deaths. During its ascendancy, the company was large enough to have two separate troupes which, among other things, makes it difficult to read anything into the absence of Laurence Dutton's name from most of the records: they may reflect only part of the company. On the other hand, it is equally possible that he did not join them (perhaps staying with Oxford's Men) until later, a likely vacancy occuring when the incomparable Richard Tarleton died in 1588. By this phase of the company's life it is unclear whether changes of personnel would have been driven by strictly business considerations, or whether Tilney would have kept a proprietary control of their affairs. (He was certainly their licenser, but also performed that role for other troupes with a Court entrée.)

But, while they flourished, the Queen's Men's two-pronged business agenda remained clear: they drew on their wealth of talent and sheer numbers to dominate theatrical life at Court, largely putting an end to the contestation for entrée there between various companies and their patrons – precisely the kinds of contestation we have seen in the earlier groups with which the Duttons were associated. But when they were not at Court, they were almost always on the road: it was part of their remit to carry the royal livery (and celebrations of patriotic Protestantism, which feature strongly in their repertoire) as widely as possible around the kingdom, and even beyond – they went to Ireland, as well as Scotland, in 1590. They are known to have played in London occasionally, but this seems usually to have been in preparation for Court performances, the two halves of the company perhaps reuniting for that purpose.

This turns on its head our usual understanding that London was the natural goal for anyone with aspirations in the theatre business, and that touring was always a second-best option, the recourse of those denied a base in the capital or driven away by plague – an attitude summed up in Samuel Schoenbaum's graphic assertion that 'the troupes could hardly maintain themselves intact through a seemingly endless banishment to the hand-to-mouth existence of provincial barnstorming'.[58] For the Queen's

Men touring was, admittedly, the consequence of a political fiat, but it is difficult to believe that it would have succeeded, or for so long, if it flew in the face either of economic realities or of the pronounced preferences of leading actors such as the Duttons. The central prize here – all the way from Sir Ralph Lane's Men to the Queen's Men – seems to have been performance at Court, rather than simply in London. When the Queen's Men themselves lost political backing, and the entrée to Court that went with it, they fell back on touring alone and seem to have survived quite effectively in that mode until the end of Elizabeth's reign – but perhaps not effectively enough to satisfy the Duttons for long.

What we also see explicitly in the case of the Queen's Men, but may suppose was implicitly so for all other troupes, is the complex interrelationship of politics (in its broadest senses) and business in the theatre of the day. Patronage was not just a fig-leaf to make playing socially acceptable. It involved a genuine relationship with a patron, whose public face in important ways the actors were, though its precise nature remains elusive. Sally-Beth MacLean observes of Derby's Men in the late 1570s that their 'touring routes seem less likely to have been motivated by their patron's need to promote his political or landed interests, by comparison with others at Court, such as the earl of Leicester'.[59] But in the context of early modern culture, where power and prestige mirrored each other very closely, how securely can we distinguish between the self-display represented by the patronage of liveried actors and the promotion of 'political or landed interests'? It was surely at most a matter of style or emphasis, hardly of substance. This would explain why the question of an actor's loyalty to his patron might arouse such strong passions.

But patronage itself could wax and wane, being affected at various times by the direct intervention of Parliament or of the Privy Council, or by the death or whim of a patron. The sudden enthusiasms of an Earl of Oxford, or the apparently enhanced interest of a Lord Strange in the late 1580s or early 1590s might also upset the theatrical economy. Whether allegiances between players and their lord (for whom they certainly prayed at the end of public performances) might extend to commissioning and performing material specifically attuned to his interests is yet another of those questions to which we wish we had more concrete answers. In the case of the Queen's Men it clearly did, though in this unique instance we must regard Leicester and Walsingham as the patrons rather than the monarch whose livery they wore: but this came with a commercial price. The 'jigging veins of rhyming mother wits' scorned in the prologue to Marlowe's *Tamburlaine* are surely those of the Queen's Men, whose playwrights commonly wrote in the old-style rhyming fourteeners, an unsubtle but effective medium. Marlowe and his Stratford contemporary, conversely, pioneered the dramatic use of blank verse, which proved to be the medium of the future.

How and why that came about is another question which would repay further study. Part of the answer would seem to be that blank verse plays featured strongly in the repertoire of Lord Strange's Men (including works by both Marlowe and Shakespeare) at the time of their meteoric rise in the late 1580s, culminating in an unprecedented six performances at Court in 1591–92 and a further three performances the following year (*SPC*, pp. 259–61). But blank verse alone is unlikely to have secured their success: it may have been equally significant, for example, that they were, by the early 1590s, a notably large company and one which specialized in the use of pyrotechnics in their shows – something distinctive and different.[60] So that the eclipsing of the Queen's Men may have owed something to changing and competing fashions, as well as to the critical loss of patronage. Moreover, success bred success: by 1591 Strange's Men had the services of the leading serious actor of the time, Edward Alleyn.[61] It is impossible to determine the primary cause of their (brief) success, but it is important to remember that multiple issues were in play.

Tracing the career of the Duttons through the period when Shakespeare was somewhere learning his trade emphasizes just how hybrid a profession theatre was at the time, complexly torn between quasi-feudal patronage relations and commercial competition, between local household customs and a nationwide professional business. And it would be a mistake to suppose that this changed overnight in 1594–95. Clearly the prolonged closure of the London theatres by plague in 1593–94 created crises which resulted in multiple break-ups and amalgamations for some of the leading companies, a measure perhaps of how important London was becoming in the theatrical economy. But it is almost certainly a mistake to see commercial considerations as the sole motor driving these changes. There is good reason to suppose that the most critical outcome, the emergence of two newly formed companies patronized by the Lord Chamberlain and Lord Admiral, who between them had the only entrées at Court for several years, was in the broadest sense a new political arrangement. The Queen's Men and their backers had had their day; the Lords Hunsdon and Howard, closely related by marriage and both first cousins of the Queen, had determined on a new phase of Privy Council policy towards Court theatre, and brought it under their own personal patronage.[62] They may even have called on the Master of the Revels to determine the personnel in each troupe, as he had that of the Queen's Men: a significant number of the Chamberlain's Men (Richard Burbage, George Bryan, John Heminges, Will Kemp, Augustine Phillips and Thomas Pope of the principals, and Will Sly, Richard Cowley and John Sincler of lesser players) had previously been with Strange's (*SPC*, pp. 279–80). But where the Queen's Men had, Court duties apart, largely been expected to travel (which they continued to do), the Chamberlain's and Admiral's Men seem from the start to have been expected to maintain regular bases in London – perhaps a political remit, as much as a commercial decision. Other companies were not precluded from performing there, and many doubtless did so on an occasional basis, but these companies dominated the market by their almost permanent presence and exclusive access to Court. When Pembroke's Men apparently tried to muscle in, in 1597, they were effectively put out of business by the *Isle of Dogs* affair. Derby's Men had some success between 1599 and 1601, even appearing at Court, but they failed to achieve permanent London status. Only a joint company of Worcester's and Oxford's Men succeeded, from 1601, in obtaining a status alongside that of the Chamberlain's and Admiral's Men, almost certainly on the strength of Worcester's own new prestige as a Privy Councillor and Master of the Horse.[63]

It has been usual to regard theatrical patronage at this juncture as rather notional, as a mechanism in effect for enforcing the wider Court interest in theatre (which in some respects it clearly was). But it would be a mistake to write off the old ways and the old assumptions too quickly. There is often resistance to the idea that a play such as *A Midsummer Night's Dream* or *The Merry Wives of Windsor* might have been written or revised to accommodate some form of Hunsdon family interest, on the grounds that this is not how commercial theatre works. But even now this was not *purely* commercial theatre, and the days when honest artisans strove to please their lord with a play in the hope of sixpence a day for life (as Bottom, Quince and company do) were not yet entirely in the realms of nostalgia. The two modes clearly overlapped for a time, in ways we do well to try to understand and discriminate between. As Richard Wilson has observed, the paradigm of performance in Shakespeare's own plays (even those clearly written for London presentation) is always that before a noble patron, at Court or at a country house, not in the commercial theatre. When we try to imagine Shakespeare's journey from Stratford-upon-Avon to that payment at Court in March 1595, we need to do so in this context of often competing practices and pressures: country household theatricals, and their local interconnections; the patronage and prestige of aristrocratic grandees projected on a much wider scale; the growth of a different kind of urban market in London; interventions of different kinds from Westminster. Nothing quite like the situation that pertained in 1594–95 had existed before that date: it was almost certainly not an arrangement that Shakespeare and his fellows expected or planned for themselves, however well they made it work.

We have so far tried to imagine Shakespeare's way into the theatre through what we are coming to understand of the mechanisms of patronage, as they operated both locally and nationally, as they may to an extent have reflected religious sympathies, as they were compromised both by commercial pressures and by political interventions. But this ignores one other potentially useful source of information from what we know of early modern social practices: the nature of relations *within* the theatre (as distinct from the theatre's relationship with the social hierarchy). The players emerged from different parts of the country and different occupations, and had distinctive artisan-like ways of relating to each other, often apparently modelled on those of the trade guilds such as the Company of Weavers to which the Duttons belonged – the normal organizational superstructure for artisans in the period. Unusually, the two great rival tragedians of the age seem, in effect, to have been born to the stage and in London: Edward Alleyn's father owned an inn in Bishopsgate (not for from John Dutton's Dolphin), which we may surmise was used by the players; Richard Burbage's joiner father, James, built the Theatre in 1576 and later the second Blackfriars playhouse.[64] Ben Jonson, too, was London born and bred but (if Dekker's jibes in *Satiromastix* are to be believed) he made his way into the profession as 'a poore Iourneyman Player' who 'amble[d] (in leather pilch) by a play-wagon, in the high way, and took'st mad Ieronimoes part, to get service among the Mimickes'.[65] So simply *being* in London did not guarantee an entrée into its theatre, unless like Alleyn and Burbage you already had connections there. Even Londoners toured. In the case of the great comedian Richard Tarleton, tradition is split between his having been a swineherd in Condover, Shropshire, and an apprentice in London; actually both traditions might be true if he followed a similar path to his 'adopted son', Robert Armin, who was brought up in Norfolk then apprenticed to a London goldsmith. (The Duttons *may* have followed similar paths.) This gets them both to London, but does not explain how they became players. John Heminge, often thought of as the business manager of the Lord Chamberlain's or King's Men was apparently born in Worcester, though we know nothing about his journey to London or the stage.

There were no trade guilds for actors or their writers, and so no apprenticeships. But some players, like the Duttons and Armin, were freemen of *other* guilds (whether or not they ever practised that trade), which conferred upon them certain civic privileges and perhaps instilled in them certain assumptions about working relationships. Heminge was a member of the Grocers' Company, while Jonson continued to pay his dues to the Bricklayers' Company long after he gave up such work. Nor was this confined only to London, though the surviving records are much fuller there, and indeed by Stuart times the 'allowed' London-based troupes began to operate collectively somewhat like trade guilds, though never formally incorporated as such. The Simpsons of Egton, Yorkshire, whose performance at Gowlthwaite Hall in 1609 was later cited in the prosecution of its owner, Sir John Yorke, were cordwainers or shoemakers – a status which they tried to assert on occasions when they were accused of vagrancy.[66] There is no reason to suppose that they were unusual in this (some of their fellows when they were questioned in 1613 were weavers): the only thing unusual is that the information has survived.

It has been suggested, though this remains speculative, that such affiliations made it possible to recruit boy actors as their apprentices. Certainly, John Rice is first heard of as Heminge's 'boy' when he took part in an entertainment for King James provided by the Merchant Taylors in 1607. And Richard Brome, who was apparently an actor before he became a playwright, is described in the Induction to *Bartholomew Fair* as Jonson's 'man'.[67] In the case of the Simpsons, it was an apprentice of theirs, Thomas Pant, who was most helpful to the authorities when the 1609 performance came under close scrutiny, because he resented the fact that his apprenticeship had condemned him to the life of a travelling player.[68] This must have been one regular route into the profession. But there is no evidence to associate Shakespeare, unlike so many of his fellows, with any aspect of trade guild life, even though early on he may well have been apprenticed to his father as a glover or wittawer.

There is nothing, in fact, of the 'rude mechanical' (Puck's sneering description of Bottom, Quince and their fellows) in the surviving record of William Shakespeare. He is, rather, always 'gentle Shakespeare', a mark of social standing as much as it is a compliment to his character. As Henry Chettle puts it in 'To the Gentlemen Readers' prefacing *Kind-Heart's Dream*, one of our earliest accounts (1592–93) of Shakespeare, 'myself I have seen his demeanour no less civil than he excellent in the quality he possesses'.[69] Within two years of the 1595 payment, Shakespeare was seeking (in his father's name) a coat of arms, formal seal of the family's gentility. We recall the Duttons who 'compared themselves to any gentleman' and were rewarded with obscene verses for their pretension; that in turn brings to mind Robert Greene's famous death-bed sneer about Shakespeare as 'an upstart crow' – where at least part of the point (from a university-educated playwright) must be to mock someone with pretensions above his station.[70] If the majority of those associated with the theatre at this time were artisan-class, or even lower in the social scale, a small fraction of them at least liked to think of themselves as gentry. The Duttons seem to have hovered precariously in the middle.

The Duttons were almost certainly actors, but in Shakespeare's case (as in both Greene's and Chettle's comments, albeit from different perspectives) the status of gentry is commonly associated with the nature and quality of his writing *for* actors. And this is already an issue, we note, before the pivotal date of March 1595. How much of an actor was Shakespeare? The question is worth pursuing because so many records of who was with which troupe relate specifically to actors who were present at a particular venue or event. They would not necessarily tell the whole tale of personnel associated with a company, especially if someone was principally employed as a writer. This may help to explain Shakespeare's absence from the pre-1595 record, when we can trace the earlier paths of virtually everyone with him after that date. The prevailing wisdom, which makes of him a thorough-going man of the theatre, assumes that Shakespeare was regularly involved in productions, albeit perhaps not in the largest parts: anecdote connects him with the roles of Adam in *As You Like It* and the Ghost in *Hamlet*.[71] Yet as early as 1699 the antiquary James Wright observed that 'Shakespear ... was a much better poet, than player'.[72]

In fact the most concrete evidence for Shakespeare's acting is Jonson's inclusion of him, in the 1616 folio of his *Workes*, in the lists of principal players who first performed *Every Man In His Humour* and *Sejanus*. But Jonson does not include him in the lists for the other plays where we might expect to find his name, *Every Man Out of His Humour*, *Volpone* and *Catiline* – whereas other senior members of the company throughout this time, such as Burbage and Heminge, are in every list. This may suggest that Shakespeare picked and chose his roles, rather than appearing in everything. Yet however much playing he did, by 1595 his principal value to the Lord Chamberlain's Men was surely already that of a writer of plays; for over a decade he would write at least two a year for them, regulary enough to suggest that this was a contractual arrangement with the company rather than fortuitous inspiration.

Henslowe's *Diary* inevitably implies that the standard model of Elizabethan play-writing was akin to that of Hollywood screenwriting in the 1930s and 1940s, with teams of writers commissioned to write pre-scribed sections of a given plot, or to rework an existing script. Indeed, it has become something of a modern orthodoxy to celebrate such collabo-rative writing rather than to castigate it, as traditional canonical thinking did (elevating Marlowe, Shakespeare and Jonson in good part because they were deemed so little tainted by it).[73] But just how much was the precise Henslowe model – hiring in writers who otherwise had no stake in the acting company – ever the *norm*? Were there Henslowe-style writing fac-tories for Warwick's Men or Derby's Men back in the 1570s and 1580s, even though they had no permanent London base? Were there many Rowland Broughtons prepared to contract to supply eighteen scripts in thirty months? Again, the Queen's Men are an instructive model. When Tilney put them together in 1583 he made a point of including both Richard Tarleton (formerly with Sussex's Men) and Robert Wilson (formerly with Leicester's Men) – both leading comic actors, but both also accomplished playwrights.[74] That is, in as much as we can trace such matters back, it was common – perhaps indeed the norm – for troupes to have a writer *con-tractually* within the company, a shareholder, though more often than not even their names (like their plays) have been lost to posterity. He would not, of course, be the only person to write plays for them, but his work would be a bedrock for the company's repertoire. This is precisely the posi-tion that Shakespeare seems to have held in the Lord Chamberlain's Men, probably devoting the majority of his professional time to it. It may already have seemed a somewhat old-fashioned arrangement. After Shakespeare, the company retained John Fletcher and then Philip Massinger as their 'ordinary poets', probably on a similar basis to that experienced by Richard Brome with the 1630s Salisbury Court company, the only such relationship where any of the contractual details have survived.[75] But these men were only ever writers for their companies, bound by contract but not actors or shareholders. Indeed, the only other man in the post-1595 era who enjoyed a situation anything like Shakespeare's was Thomas Heywood, as an actor, playwright and shareholder for Queen Anne's Men.

Shakespeare thus emerges into the dubious light of the written theatrical record in 1595 in what, with hindsight, we can see as an almost unique pivotal role. Like the companies of the 1580s, the Lord Chamberlain's Men had an 'ordinary poet' who was also a shareholder, though probably one with a diminished acting presence compared with Tarleton and Wilson. In the earlier era, when touring predominated, there was less need for a constant turnover of new scripts: the same limited repertoire would serve a city such as Norwich or a great house such as Lathom, especially if plays written with the particular interests of a patron in mind (such as many have supposed *Love's Labour's Lost* to be for Ferdinando, Lord Strange; or *A Midsummer Night's Dream* and *The Merry Wives of Windsor* for the Hunsdons) were sufficiently robust to serve equally on public stages. London, with its fixed audience, constantly demanded novelty – a demand which Henslowe-style arrangements helped to meet. After Shakespeare, his fellow King's Men continued to recognize the value of an 'ordinary poet', but on a commercial contractual basis rather than as one of themselves, as a shareholder.

Shakespeare, as a shareholder 'ordinary poet', also wore his patron's livery and must have recognized the quasi-feudal loyalties it entaileds He was in every sense a product of that 1570s and 1580s world we explored via the Duttons, but also the man who – more than any other – bridged the way to the more overtly capitalist and contract-led commercialism of London in the Stuart era. If we seek to track him, we have some way yet to go to disentangle the disparate waxing and waning constituencies to which he was attached.

Notes

1 E. A. J. Honigmann, *Shakespeare: The 'Lost Years'*, second edition (Manchester: Manchester University Press, 1998), pp. 136–7.
2 The title-page of the 1594 Quarto of *Titus Andronicus* says that it 'was played by the Right Honourable Earl of Derby, Earl of Pembroke and Earl of Sussex their Servants' and Honigmann points out that this must have been Lord Strange's Men: *Shakespeare: The 'Lost Years'*, pp. 59–60.
3 All Shakespeare quotations are from *The Norton Shakespeare*, eds Stephen Greenblatt, Jean E. Howard, Katherine Eisaman Maus and Walter Cohen (New York: Norton 1997).

4 The family tree, British Library Add 44026, states that the Hoghtons, Ashtons of Croston and Heskeths share common ancestors in the Dallamore family. Alexander Hoghton's second wife Elizabeth was a daughter of Gabriel Hesketh of Aughton, whose pedigree is detailed as an insert to the Hesketh of Rufford family tree on the top left-hand side of the document. The Woodville connection, inserted into the family tree within in a blue border on folio 6, is traced via Elizabeth Fleming who married Sir Thomas Hesketh (c.1465–1523) in 1471, though she was later divorced from him.

5 See Rev. W. G. Proctor, 'Notes on the Hesketh Pedigree', *Transactions of the Historic Society of Lancashire and Cheshire for the Year 1910*, New Series, Volume XXVI (Liverpool: Historic Society of Lancashire and Cheshire, 1911), pp. 58–66.

6 John Gerard's *Herbal* (London, 1633) includes *Primula veris Heskethi*, named after Thomas Hesketh who discovered it. It is not known whether the herbalist was related to the contemporary Jesuit John Gerard, though both were born in Lancashire. The herbalist was employed by Lord Burghley in his gardens in the Strand and at Theobalds, and dedicated the first edition of *Herbal* (1597) to him.

7 *Acts of the Privy Council*, New Series XXIV, eds John Roche (Nendeln and Liechtenstein: Kraus Thomson Organization, 1974), p. 212.

8 See Suzanne Westfall, ' "A Commonty a Christmas gambold or a tumbling trick": Household Theater', in *A New History of Early English Drama*, eds John D. Cox and David Scott Kastan (New York: Columbia University Press, 1997), pp. 39–58.

9 Bruce R. Smith, *Ancient Scripts & Modern Experience on the English Stage 1500–1700* (Princeton: Princeton University Press, 1988), pp. 61–2.

10 Rufford Old Hall is owned by the National Trust. Richard Dean, *Rufford Old Hall: Lancashire* (London: National Trust, 1999), p. 37.

11 *Ibid.*, p. 11.

12 Gaston Bachelard, *The Poetics of Space: The Classic Look at How We Experience Intimate Spaces*, trans. Maria Jolas (Boston: Beacon Press, 1994), pp. 14, 53.

13 Dean, *Rufford Old Hall*, p. 11.

14 *Acts of the Privy Council 1580–1*, Vol. XII, New Series, ed. John Roche Dasent (London: HMSO 1896), p. 149.

15 Honigmann, *Shakespeare: The 'lost years'*, p. 35.

16 Marie Rowlands, 'Recusant Women 1560–1640', in *Women and English Society 1500–1800*, ed. Mary Prior (London: Routledge, 1985), pp. 149–80.

17 J. A. Hilton, *Catholic Lancashire: From Reformation to Renewal 1559–1991* (Chichester: Phillimore Press, 1994), p. 12.

18 Dean, *Rufford Old Hall*, p. 40.

19 Joseph Gillow, *Lord Burghley's Map of Lancashire 1590*, Publications of the Catholic Record Society, Being an Excerpt from Vol. IV (London: Catholic Record Society, 1907), p. 33, p. 17.

20 *Acts of the Privy Council*, New Series, Vol. XXIV, ed. John Roche Dasent (London: HMSO, 1901), p. 234. p. 281, p. 334.

21 *Ibid.*, p. 410.

22 Gillow, *Lord Burghley's Map*, pp. 10, 13.

23 *Catholic Record Society*, volume XIII. *Miscellanea VIII* (London: Catholic Record Society), p. 81.
24 Privy Council to the Earl of Derby, 1574, cited in Christopher Haigh's very detailed analysis of Catholicism in the region, *Reformation and Resistance in Tudor Lancashire* (Cambridge: Cambridge University Press, 1975), p. 223.
25 Gillow, *Lord Burgley's Map*, p. 21.
26 William Farrington, *The Derby Household Book*, ed. Rev. F. R. Raines (Manchester: Chetham Society, 1853), pp. 56–7.
27 *Ibid.*, pp. 144–7.
28 *Acts of the Privy Council 1580–1*, Vol. XII, New Series, ed. John Roche Dasent (London: HMSO, 1896), p. 270.
29 British Library Cotton Titus B.ii, ff. 239–40, cited in David George, ed., *Lancashire*: Records of Early English Drama (Toronto: University of Toronto Press, 1991), p. 223.
30 Letter of Thomas Christopher to Burghley, 24 August 1592, PRO SP 12/238/163, cited in Barry Coward, *The Stanleys, Lords Stanley and Earls of Derby 1385–1672* (Manchester: Manchester University Press, for the Chetham Society, 1983), p. 146.
31 *Ibid.*, p. 146.
32 William Farrington was Comptroller of the Household of Edward, Third Earl of Derby, Steward to the Fourth Earl of Derby from 1572 to 1593 and then Receiver General to Ferdinando, Fifth Earl. *Derby Household Book*, p. lxiii. Rev. Raines's introduction to the *Household Book* gives a detailed biography of William Farrington. I am grateful to Stephen Sartin, Curator of Art, Lancashire County Museum Service, for information about the family tradition.
33 Gillow, *Lord Burgley's Map*, p. 31–2, p. 21.
34 Farrington, *Derby Household Book*, pp. 20–2.
35 *Ibid.*, p. xcvi. The painting is at the Museum of Lancashire Life, Preston. It is probably by Gheerhaerts.
36 See Honigmann, *Shakespeare: The 'lost years'*, Chapter IX, for the theory that 'The Phoenix and the Turtle' may have been composed as early as 1586 for Sir John and Ursula.
37 Sir Thomas Salusbury, 'A Masque as it was presented at y right honourable ye Lord Strange at his Knowsley on Twelfth night 1640', National Library of Wales MS5390D, pp. 35–45. Line numbers are to the text in George, ed., *Lancashire*, pp. 255–66.
38 See S. Schoenbaum, *William Shakespeare: A Compact Documentary Life*, rev. edn (Oxford: Oxford University Press, 1987), pp. 183ff.
39 *Ibid.*, pp. 115ff.
40 See E. K. Chambers, *The Medieval Stage* (2 vols; Oxford: Clarendon Press, 1903), II, p. 259, on the origins of this authority, and *The Elizabethan Stage* (4 vols; Oxford: Clarendon Press, 1923), I, p. 280n, on the reserving clauses. *The Elizabethan Stage* is hereafter cited parenthetically in the text as *ES*.
41 William Ingram, 'Laurence Dutton, Stage Player: Missing and Presumed Lost', *Medieval and Renaissance Drama in England*, 14 (2001), 122–43, p. 141 (Note 5).
42 Ingram, 'Laurence Dutton', p. 142 (Note 14).

43 It is, of course, equally possible that he was not from the north of England anyway. But possible associations with the Stanleys later in his career, as we shall see, suggest he might well have been.

44 On such localized travelling in and around Lancashire see Sally-Beth MacLean, 'A Road Less Travelled? Touring Performers in Medieval and Renaissance Lancashire', in *Porci ante Margaritum: Essays in Honour of Meg Twycross*, Sarah Carpenter, Pamela King and Peter Meredith, eds (Leeds: University of Leeds, 2001), pp. 321–43. The records of such visiting are exceptionally full for Gawthorpe Hall: see George, ed., *Lancashire*, pp. 166–79.

45 Ingram, 'Laurence Dutton', p. 124, citing R. Mark Benbow, 'Dutton and Goffe versus Broughton: A Disputed Contract for Plays in the 1570s', *Records of Early English Drama Newsletter* (1981:2), 3–9.

46 Ingram, 'Laurence Dutton', p. 123.

47 *Acts of the Privy Council of England*, eds J. R. Dasent (32 vols; London: HMSO, 1890–1907), XI, p. 445. This is the business which may preclude the actor and Court messenger Laurence Dutton being the same man, since the messenger was employed on 20 May, well before the matter was resolved. But it is far from impossible that Oxford intervened to effect a provisional release.

48 See William Ingram, 'The Playhouse at Newington Butts: a New Proposal', *Shakespeare Quarterly* 21 (1970), 385–98.

49 See Andrew Gurr, *The Shakespearian Playing Companies* (Oxford and New York: Clarendon Press, 1996), pp. 306ff. Hereafter cited parenthetically in the text as *SPC*.

50 See Scott McMillin and Sally-Beth MacLean, *The Queen's Men and Their Plays* (Cambridge: Cambridge University Press, 1998), pp. 11ff.; on the losses to Derby's Men see Sally-Beth MacLean, Chapter 11 below.

51 John also served in that capacity, with John Laneham but without Laurence, on 15 March 1590.

52 See McMillin and MacLean, *The Queen's Men and Their Plays*, p. 58; George, ed., *Lancashire*, pp. 182–3, 356.

53 *ES*, II, p. 113; McMillin and MacLean, *The Queen's Men and Their Plays*, pp. 66–7.

54 Ingram, 'Laurence Dutton', pp. 123, 125.

55 See Mark Eccles, 'Elizabethan Actors I: A–D', *Notes and Queries* (1991), 49.

56 Ingram, 'Laurence Dutton', pp. 130, 137.

57 It is tempting to associate Anthony Marlowe with the playwright, Christopher; but no documented family link has ever been established.

58 Schoenbaum, *Compact Documentary Life*, pp. 168–9.

59 Chapter 11 below (pp. 205–26).

60 Lawrence Manley considered this feature of their repertoire in an unpublished paper, 'Playing with Fire: From Strange's Men to Pembroke's Men', at the Shakespeare Association of America meeting in Miami, Easter 2001.

61 In a perplexing anomaly, which only underlines how little we really know about theatrical patronage, Alleyn somehow retained Lord Admiral Howard's livery while serving with Lord Strange's Men (*SPC*, p. 259).

62 See Andrew Gurr, 'Privy Councillors as Theater Patrons,' in *Shakespeare and Theatrical Patronage in Early Modern England*, eds Paul Whitfield White and Suzanne Westfall (Cambridge: Cambridge University Press, 2002), pp. 221–45.

63 Richard Dutton has discussed these developments in greater detail in *Licensing, Censorship and Authorship in Early Modern England* (Basingstoke: Palgrave, 2000), pp. 16–40.

64 Unless otherwise specified, information about actors derives from Edwin Nungezer, *A Dictionary of Actors* (New Haven: Yale University Press, 1929).

65 *Satiromastix* (4.1.128–32) in *The Dramatic Works of Thomas Dekker*, ed. Fredson Bowers, 4 vols, Vol. I (Cambridge: Cambridge University Press, 1962).

66 See Nungezer, *A Dictionary of Actors*, under John Heminges; on Jonson, W. David Kay, *Ben Jonson: A Literary Life* (Basingstoke: Macmillan, 1995), pp. 15 and 196, note 9; on the Simpsons, see *ES*, I, 304–5n and Phebe Jensen, Chapter 6 below.

67 Nungezer, *Dictionary*, under John Rice and Richard Brome. Someone also described as Jonson's 'man' was paid for work in relation to the *Entertainment at Britain's Burse* in 1609: see Scott McMillin, 'Jonson's Early Entertainments: New Information from Hatfield House', *Renaissance Drama*, n.s. 1 (1968), 153–66. If that too was Brome, his relationship with Jonson may well have gone back to his teenage years, when apprenticeships normally began.

68 See Jensen, Chapter 6 below.

69 Richard Dutton discusses the question of Shakespeare's 'gentility' in *Licensing, Censorship and Authorship in Early Modern England*, pp. 90–113. Chettle, incidentally, somehow got into writing for the theatre – he was Henslowe's most prolific playwright – from his trade as a printer.

70 See Schoenbaum, *Compact Documentary Life*, pp. 151ff.

71 *Ibid.*, pp. 200ff.

72 James Wright, *Historia Histrionica: An Historical Account of the English Stage* (London. 1699), p. 4.

73 See Jeffrey Masten, 'Playwrighting: Authorship and Collaboration', in Cox and Kastan, eds, *New History of Early English Drama*, pp. 357–82.

74 Nothing by Tarleton has survived, so this judgement is based on his reputation. But at least three plays by Wilson have survived: *The Three Ladies of London The Three Lords and Three Ladies of London* and *The Cobbler's Prophecy*.

75 See Ann Haaker, 'The Plague, the Theater, and the Poet', *Renaissance Drama*, n.s. 1 (1968), 283–306.

'The useless dearness of the diamond': patronage theatre and households

In an unpublished variant ending to Virginia Woolf's theatrical novel *Between the Acts*, Isa asks 'Is the play a failure . . . if we don't know the meaning? Who had written it? . . . that we have to act our parts?'[1] Woolf raises questions here that I have been facing as I investigate patronage and theatre in the great households of England during the early modern era. Up until recently, such entertainments have been marginalized precisely because we don't know who wrote them, what they meant to those who saw them and what they should mean to us today. We do not know what 'parts' the household members acted, as actors, audiences or some combination of the two. Private theatre, performed *gratis* for select audiences because it was subsidized by aristocratic, ecclesiastical and educational patrons, has been for some time an unexplored form, but the maps are changing. Looking at early modern theatre from the perspective of patronage and households allows us to re-evaluate the meaning and purpose of theatre, to understand better the power structures and hierarchies of Elizabethan England and to reassess noblemen's and particularly noblewomen's roles in creating Renaissance theatre.

If we believe most governmental budget offices, we do not need theatre, or any other art form for that matter. In the United States righteous citizens lobby Congress to destroy the National Endowment for the Arts, to end subsidies to arts that they neither participate in nor approve of. In Britain subsidized companies fight continual battles for their funds. Yet theatre, art and music historians have suggested that the impulse to create and receive art is ancient, fundamental, necessary to civilization; perhaps, as Freud believed, we sublimate our violent tendencies through the creation of beauty. Play, *spiel, ludentibus* – these are primary human instincts.

But how, in the sixteenth or the twenty-first century, do we account for the cost of such art? In a capitalist world, art must turn a profit or be damned – football yes, footlights, no. Yet in the fifteenth, sixteenth and seventeenth centuries account books of aristocrats, guilds, civic authorities and ecclesiastics show that financial support for the arts was generous, that many of these establishments retained resident performers and rewarded visitors with regularity. Surely there was some profit mixed with the pleasure. I'd like here to explore the profits and the costs of theatre, to examine how patronage works. Hence, my title 'The useless dearness of the diamond', a concept Foucault used to explore how and why a lovely but perfectly unnecessary bit of crystallized carbon could become such an numinous symbol, such a treasured object.

I am interested primarily in households because my research has shown that household auspices, from provincial courts to royal courts, from ecclesiastical halls to school halls, were frequent sites of theatrical activity for private audiences, a phenomenon ignored by literary critics for many years although theatre historians have been piling up references to these activities since E. K. Chamber's monumental works. As we have begun to explore the complex relationship between private and public theatre, however, we are finding that without household theatre, especially without troupes patronized by aristocrats, the Rose, the Theatre, the Red Lion, the Curtain, Newington Butts, the great Globe itself, might never have existed. Without Queen Elizabeth's taste for theatre, the Chapel Children at Blackfriars might never have inspired Hamlet's ire, the Queen's Men might never have consolidated to rule London theatre. By 1583 MacLean and McMillin have clearly shown that London theatre was an actor's, not a playwright's theatre.[2] Well before that (and in actuality well after that) I maintain it was a patron's theatre.

Precious little theory exists in the field of patron theatre, perhaps because for so many years theatre was considered a literary rather than an interdisciplinary art. During the thirty-odd years in which New Criticism was the predominant methodology, book after book analysed plays divorced from their staging, as absurd an enterprise as attempting to understand a folksong by reading the lyrics without hearing the music. Most critics turned their attention almost exclusively to dramatic rather than theatrical texts, which may have contributed significantly to *literary* history, but was almost disastrous for *theatrical* studies.[3] For many years theatrical activities that lacked dramatic text (such as pageantry, ceremony, folk dramas and rituals – even executions) were largely ignored, although some, such as Chambers, Wickham and Anglo, continued to analyse these forms.[4] Teachers focused on teaching Shakespeare's plays as poetry, or 'theatre of the mind', and scores of medieval plays (interludes, moral plays, mysteries, miracles and moralities) were (and continue to be) pronounced 'primitive' and 'boringly didactic', primarily because any cultural or performative context was utterly ignored in favour of textual analysis. Thus, most household theatre, which comprises specifically ceremonalia, interlude and masque, was dismissed.

With the antiquarians of the nineteenth century and early twentieth centuries, and especially since the 1970s, with the establishment of the *Records of Early English Drama* project, what Ron Vince has called the first stage of theatre history as an academic discipline ('the collection, organization, and description of data, selected on the basis of hypotheses or assumptions either conscious or unconscious') has made possible the second stage: 'the interpretation of data at the level of "cultural-historical integration" a concept drawn from the science of archaeology'.[5] The masses of valuable source information now available to scholars have enabled us to focus once again on the metatheatrical, on theatre in all its incarnations rather than solely on drama, the old cliché stage versus page. The tabulation of plays (Stratman), writers, acting companies (Murray and Gurr) and references to theatrical activities (Lancashire)[6] – present us with rich hoards that are mined in various ways by scholars interested in patronage studies, and have been instrumental in establishing households as an important venue for theatre.

But publishers continue to list books that concern patronage, even literary or theatrical patronage, under the category 'social history', that hybrid of history and sociology that gives a home to many cultural studies that have no other label to claim them. Reflecting (or perhaps causing?) this categorical displacement is the fact that the phenomenon of patronage continues to be approached from a great number of theoretical perspectives: biographical and historical critics have led the way while feminist, Marxist, new historicist, cultural materialist, semiotic, structuralist, deconstructionist and psychoanalytic critics have all made significant contributions. To complicate matters further, in Shakespeare's England patronage could originate from a number of different sources: aristocratic, ecclesiastical, educational and civic. All these groups had specific political agendas, and all used performance at different times in different ways and for different purposes.

Theatre is itself an interdisciplinary art, so it comprises several ideological binaries that necessitate a broad view. It is both public and private, text (sometimes) and context, literary art and plastic art, commodity and the labor that produces it – labour that encompasses the carpenters, tailors, writers, actors, designers and moneyed patrons. In addition, patronage theatre produces so much more 'product' than mere text; it also delivers spectacle, visual art, music, crowds called spectators, celebratory mood, and movement. By approaching early modern theatre from a cultural studies or anthropological perspective, we can better comprehend the conditions and contexts of 'patronage theatre', for the artists and patrons of the early modern period were engaged in an elaborate semiotic that reflected, reinforced and in a way created the power – or the illusion of power – for the aristocratic class.

Clifford Geertz explains that:

> At the political center of any complexly organized society (to narrow our
> focus now to that) there is both a governing elite and a set of symbolic forms

expressing the fact that it is in truth governing. No matter how democrati-
cally the members of the elite are chosen (usually not very) or how deeply
divided among themselves they may be (usually much more than outsiders
imagine), they justify their existence and order their actions in terms of a collection of stories, ceremonies, insignia, formalities and appurtenances that
they have either inherited or, in more revolutionary situations, invented. It is
these – crowns and coronations, limousines and conferences – that mark the
center and give what goes on there its aura of being not merely important but
in some odd fashion connected with the way the world is built. The gravity
of high politics and the solemnity of high worship spring from liker impulses
than might first appear.[7]

Though speaking as an anthropologist about the structures of cultures,
Geertz could well have been describing the way patronage and patronage
theatre functioned in Shakespeare's England. The structure of Elizabeth's
court affirms what Geertz notes – that, regardless of veiled factionalism, the
Tudor elite, and indeed the national culture, affected an image of patriotic
unity, and expressed this solidarity through various performative activities
that reaffirmed the hegemonic spirit. These representational encodings so
thoroughly permeated public life as to be inextricable from it. From the cult
of Diana, the virgin queen (so frequently invoked by John Lyly),[8] to the
ostentatious ceremonies of the Order of the Garter, to squabbles over
precedence at table (as enacted by those consummate actors Wolsey and
Buckingham at the Field of the Cloth of Gold), to the complex insignias of
the College of Heralds (which often provided a subtext to tournaments that
modern readers can barely discern), to civic ceremonies portraying political figures as gods, goddesses and holy virtues, to the fictional hierarchies
and royal characters of the Renaissance playwrights – early modern social
life was filled with what Sir Thomas More called 'kynges games, as it were
stage plays, and for the more part plaied vpon scafoldes'.[9]

I would not maintain, like Tillyard, that these hierarchies and unities
were inflexible and 'real'; as I say, they were performative and fluid, but
nevertheless they construct a social reality that many mistake for stability.
Theatrical patronage, in particular, must be explored from a variety of
perspectives, for the anthropologist views the patron–client relationship
through a very different lens than does the theatre historian. There is a difference (though perhaps not so great as we might think) between a Yoruba
villager and a seventeenth-century English craftsman, between Hrothgar the
ring-giver of *Beowulf* and the CEO of an American corporation. I want to
focus on ways in which theatrical patronage in Tudor England 'connected
with the way the world is built', as Geertz puts it. From the historical, biographical and bibliographic scholars who edited source documents at the
turn of our own century to the contemporary theorists and philosophers
who have given us the epistemological lenses through which to view the
subtexts (or the 'micropolitics' as Robert Evans calls it) of patronage

theatre, the parameters of patronage studies as a field of inquiry within cultural studies have changed considerably.

Early references, from the thirteenth-century *Sir Gawain* through Wycliffe, Lydgate and of course Spenser show that already patronage was thought of in terms of ownership and protection. Wycliffe seems to sound early a Protestant alarm that would remain unheard for three centuries when he cautioned that 'crist and his apostlis techen vs to lyue beter than thes patrouns of thes newe ordris'. A patron could also be thought of as one who 'supports a commercial undertaking', a meaning Ben Jonson had in mind when Volpone, disguised as a mountebank, salutes his audience as 'my worthy patrons'. By the latter half of the sixteenth century this meaning of 'patron' was becoming more and more important, as theatre became more and more commodified, as the public theatre claimed patronage from both aristocratic households and the shoemaker's holiday.[10]

We all know that Shakespeare was a member of the Lord Chamberlain's Men and later the King's Men, signalling for some critics a renewed interest in and commitment to theatre patronage in the royal household. But during the earlier part of this century, few literary critics were interested in pursuing *exactly* what such patronage entailed. It became commonplace for writers to acknowledge that virtually all players (or at least those who wished to be exempted from the acts against vagrancy) wore the livery of a patron, implying household service, but most did not speculate on precisely what that patronage meant either to the player or to the aristocrat who acted as patron. Did the relationship imply political protection? Guarantee of economic security? Provide a home? Require at least limited residency, as the household books of King Edward IV and Henry Algernon Percy, fifth Earl of Northumberland, state? Indicate simple largess?

From the historian's perspective Werner Gundersheimer states the case succinctly: 'The political and social orderings in European societies in the Renaissance are mirrored in their structures of patronage. Could Shakespeare's awareness of this point have led him to prefer the support of the London crowds to that of a single *patronus*?'[11] Guy Fitch Lytle is even more specific in his definition: 'Patronage in the sixteenth century was an inherited muster of laws, properties, obligations, social ligatures, ambitions, religious activities, and personal decisions that kept a complex society working.'[12] The words 'mirror' and 'muster' in the statements above is particularly interesting, for they once again suggest that these structures were sometimes vague and illusionistic – like the diamond, paradoxical and ostentatious.

But few theatre historians have been as bold as have social and political historians. For example, Gundersheimer, focusing on Italy, begins his article 'Patronage in the Renaissance: an Exploratory Approach' with the sweeping statement that 'Patronage, broadly defined as "the action of a patron in supporting, encouraging, or countenancing a person, institution, work, art, etc.," has been clearly established as one of the dominant social processes of pre-industrial Europe'. He further asks 'Can there be a Renaissance society without patronage?'[13] And we cannot forget the observations of a fundamental text in early modern social history, Machievelli's *The Prince*:

> A prince ought also to show himself a patron of ability, and to honour the proficient in every art . . . Further, he ought to entertain the people with festivals and spectacles at convenient seasons of the year; and as every city is divided into guilds or into societies, he ought to hold such bodies in esteem, and associate with them sometimes, and show himself an example of courtesy and liberality; nevertheless, always maintaining the majesty of his rank, for this he must never consent to abate in anything.[14]

More and more we are realizing that early modern England was indeed formed by shows, by interlocking patterns of patronage–client relationships: a network, as Linda Levy Peck and Richard Dutton have shown, that bound Privy Councillor to Queen, and local government to central.[15]

These patronage networks, weaving communities together from the kitchen scullions in the great households of noble men and women to the bishops in their palaces and the monarchs on their thrones, seem to create a hierarchy rather like that described by Tillyard in his *Elizabethan World Picture*, a work that has been widely discredited in the past thirty years. The intertwining system of patronage does indeed resemble a hierarchy, but Renaissance men and women did not assume the order to be either natural or divinely inspired, as Tillyard proposes. Rather, they understood this hierarchy to be fluid and reactive; patrons shift their relationships with those above and those below them, constantly adjusting system equilibrium. The creation of the Queen's Men from the *crème de la crème* of other competing companies in 1583, so ably explored by MacLean and McMillin, is a clear representation of such adjustment, with far-reaching causes and consequences.

Perhaps the most violent (in all senses of the word) example of the reorganization of patronage networks is the English Civil War, in which Oliver Cromwell's iconoclasts (I use the word in its original sense – destroyers of icons) demonstrated quite vividly their iconophobia, their contempt for the signs of patronage. Although most Protestant reformers, including Calvin and Luther, had supported social hierarchies while razing ecclesiastical ones, Cromwell's armies demolished and despoiled a variety of the artefacts of patronage, from noblemen themselves to their homes to religious artwork, visual and visceral manifestations of patronage of the arts as well as 'graven images'. And in their most revolutionary attack on the patronage systems that had entangled and oppressed them for so long, they 'defaced' the supreme icon, the fountainhead of patronage, the king.

Martin Butler has focused on this period, scrutinizing the theatre scene from 1632 to 1642, and pointing out that, far from retreating into fantasy entertainments (the 'useless' part of Foucault's 'dear diamonds') as has so often been thought, theatre during this period was in fact intensely political, and that various patrons with particular agendas at Court were using the theatre, as they had for so many years, as another front on the battlefield for the hearts and minds of the people, as another way of knitting country interests to Court. He is particularly interested in the heterogeneity of Caroline audiences, which he characterizes as 'crossed by a network of friendship and kinship the extraordinary complexity of which must have made the environment at once public and intimate'. Once again, this complexity mirrors the structure of the patronage system.[16]

We have learned that from the very beginning of the Tudor dynasty, as early as Henry VII's Burgundian wedding revels at his newly formed household,[17] theatre and theatre artists had been used by patrons and had themselves used patrons in a variety of complex fashions; both parties could, to use Stephen Greenblatt's term, 'self-fashion' through the sign systems of both theatrical art and socio-political ideologies. Indeed, the fundamental structures of patronage politics and maintenance were so intrinsic to the culture of Tudor England that all, from the servants to the sovereigns, were creatures of the paradigm, which, through overdeterminism rather than through the base/superstructure model suggested by Tillyard, forged their social and political relationships and penetrated their very psychology. In 'Politics and Community in Elizabethan London' Frank Foster points out that virtually all power and exchanges of wealth functioned through various strata of patronage.[18] Theatre in this period functions as what Althusser calls 'ideological state apparatuses', social institutions (ecclesiastical, familial, educational, legal and cultural) that legitimize the state and the sovereign, that predispose rather than coerce the public to ascribe to 'socially acceptable ideas',[19] making these ideas seem natural rather than constructed. But rather than one set of ISAs to create one hegemonic spirit, we have a series of competing paradigms, often depending on the patron's religious, social and ideological perspectives. These paradigms were sometimes in conflict (as, for example in the famous case of Essex using Shakespeare's *Richard II* to criticize Elizabeth), sometimes in concert, as in wedding celebrations and civic processions.

Even within the early modern period itself, the ideology of patronage in England changed greatly, suggested by the fact that an unpatronized player in the sixteenth century could be prosecuted under the vagrancy laws, yet by the eighteenth century Dr Johnson could complain to Lord Chesterfield that a patron was 'one who looks with unconcern on a man struggling for life in the water, and when he has reached ground encumbers him with help'.[20] Johnson's antipathy notwithstanding, patronage was, for seventeenth-century writers, a fundamental necessity. As Alvin Kernan puts it: 'Ninety percent of all published books appeared with a dedication to an actual or a prospective patron.'[21] Many artists, Jonson and Shakespeare among them, showed negative attitudes toward patronage; the patronized artists in *Timon of Athens* are parasites, as are Volpone's retained entertainers. And indeed, by the end of Charles I's reign, the patronage system had become so corrupt that it led to public disdain.[22]

One of the richest sources for patronage studies has been anthropological study; kinship systems and patron–client relationships have formed an integral part of anthropological and sociological literature, fundamental to the primal cultures and corporate structures they study. Up until the late 1960s, however, literary critics often overlooked this work, perhaps because they were reluctant to view so-called 'first-world' cultures such as the British and the American as analogous to the primal 'third-world' cultures that form most ethnographies. Potlatch, after all, is a far cry from largess or office politics. Or is it?

Studies such as S. N. Eisenstadt and L. Roniger's *Patrons, Clients, and Friends: Interpersonal Relations and the Structure of Trust in Society* tend to make many of the same observations about ancient and modern cultures in Europe, Asia, and South America that I make here about early modern England. Discussing the basic characteristics of patron–client relationships, for example, they note:

> The interaction on which these relations are based is characterized by the simultaneous exchange of different types of resources – above all, instrumental and economic as well as political ones (support loyalty, votes, protection) on the one hand, and promises of reciprocity, solidarity and loyalty on the other. Ideally, a strong element of unconditionality and of long-range credit is built into these relations . . . It is often very strongly related to conceptions of personal identity (above all of personal honour, personal value or face-saving) and of obligations, and it is also evident in the presumed existence in such relations of some, even if very ambivalent, personal 'spiritual' attachment between patron and clients. At the same time, relations established between patron and clients are not fully legal or contractual; they are often opposed to the official laws of the country and they are based much more on 'informal' – although very strongly binding – understandings. Despite their seemingly binding, long-range, almost (in their ideal portrayal) life-long, endurance, patron–client relations are entered into, at least in principle, voluntarily, and can, officially at least, be abandoned voluntarily . . . Last and not least patron–client relations are based on a very strong element of inequality and of differences in power between patrons and clients.[23]

It seems to me that Eisenstadt and Roniger are clearly describing the qualities of a household in early modern England – that corporation, tribe or family who lived and worked together under the protection or control of a secular or ecclesiastical aristocrat. This definition of patronage also clearly applies to the relationships among the monarch, the ruling classes and their maintained servants, both noble and common, as I have described in detail elsewhere.[24] Household patrons exchanged money and/or protection for art, and prided themselves on the number and quality of retainers they maintained, a pride that frequently led to excessive ostentation, and for which they were sometimes called to account when the monarch perceived a threat or opportunity for informal taxation, of which 'Morton's Fork' is perhaps the best example.[25] Further, as Paul Whitfield White has demonstrated, the patron–client relationship was also often characterized by shared political and religious beliefs.[26] Household entertainers provided polemical and propagandistic art, courier services and espionage.[27] And, of course, the relationships were fluid, as artists negotiated for more generous or powerful patrons, served multiple households or abandoned those whose star had fallen. For example, when Essex fell from the Queen's grace, those he maintained in his offices and through his power quickly scrambled for safe ground, joining other households in an attempt to re-stabilize their own lives. Robert Greene tried sixteen different patrons in his seventeen published books, while Thomas Lodge tried twelve in the span of twelve years.[28] On the other side of the contract, aristocratic patrons would seek to attract men and women who could serve them well, gathering more power as they gathered more retainers within their spheres of influence. In some cases, successful artists could play patrons off against one another. The Bassanno family gathered as much as they could from Henry VIII (including residence in the Charterhouse, which had been harvested by the King at the dissolution), before heading back to more lucrative and prestigious employment with the Doge of Venice, then returning after Henry granted the family a monopoly for trading in Gascon wine.[29]

To refine the anthropological approach to patronage, Grace E. Goodell distinguishes between paternalism, which robs clients of freedom, autonomy, choice and responsibility (a type of patronage that seems to characterize British behaviour towards colonial populations), and patronage *per se*, which offers 'mutually binding obligations, [in which] the patron and client can hold one another accountable'. This sense of patronage seems more useful in the theatrical context, when we are considering not only the market value of the artefact but also the increasing autonomy of the artists in the later Tudor period as they acquired public as well as private patrons. In addition, Goodell believes that this reciprocity allows the client to 'initiate service to his patron, obligating the latter to respond. This gives the client political leverage.' Later Goodell echoes Eisenstadt's perception that 'the patron is accessible to his client; the latter plays off patrons, shops around for new ones, if need be, goes over one patron's head to *his* patron, or acquires more leverage by becoming a patron to others himself'.[30]

Goodell's explanation of potlatch as a 'redistributive mechanism' that 'hinges on common values' which 'enables it to bind giver and receiver, who cosponsor the giving' seems to describe accurately the social concept of largess; she goes on to discuss more altruistic giving (analogous to almsgiving in the noble households) and the boasting associated with potlatch, which recalls the flyting matches of the court, and certainly pertains to aristocratic jockeying for position and precedence.[31] In *Cultural Aesthetics: Renaissance Literature and the Practice of Social Ornament* Patricia Fumerton connects this redistribution of wealth more concretely to early modern England and to art. Through her analysis of all sorts of interhousehold gift-giving, from miniatures to banquet foods to children in marriage, Fumerton shows that

> The confusion here of objects, values, contracts, and sexes (establishing the further etymological link between 'generosity' and 'gender') characterizes all systems of gift. For the gift ring is a complete cultural experience ... that through the act of donation at once generates, expresses, and contains every aspect of the community: economic, legal, social, political, religious, and – not the least – aesthetic.[32]

Ideologies, hegemonies, alliances, political hierarchies – all these are served by networks of patron–client gift exchange among households, as, for example when the Duke of Buckingham's entertainers were rewarded more highly than others by his brother-in-law the Earl of Northumberland, who recorded a scale of payments depending upon the rank of the entertainer's patron.[33]

The words of Clifford Geertz, with which I began this inquiry, suggest how conflicted and problematic the relationships between artists and their patrons tended to be, and how dependent all were on the symbols and icons of power to convey to audiences a specific aesthetic or ideology, whether idiosyncratic to a particular patron or general to prevailing philosophies of the Crown. In their quest to convince all sorts of audiences that 'whatever is, is right', both patrons and artists conjured political, aesthetic and economic power (what Foucault calls the 'three great functions') to strut and fret upon the stage. And here the 'whatever' could indeed be a particularly loose and floating signifier, from the religious polemics of John Bale's *Kynge Johan* (for the household of Thomas Cromwell) to the consequences of regicide in Shakespeare's *Macbeth* (surely a particularly resonant issue for James I), to the divine right of hierarchy in Heywood's seemingly innocuous *Play of the Weather* (for the household of Henry VIII). For early modern theatre was almost always both didactic and conspicuously consumptive, the embodiment of the 'useless dearness of the diamond'.[34]

Geertz further challenges us in his essay 'Blurred Genres: The Refiguration of Social Thought', the title alone of which indicates the predominant methodology and aim of patronage studies for the last twenty years. Writing about the increasingly interdisciplinary methodologies of his own discipline, Geertz suggests that

> some of those fit to judge work of this kind [analysing cultures as 'theatre states'] ought to be humanists who reputedly know something about what theatre and mimesis and rhetoric are, and not just with respect to my work

but to that of the whole steadily broadening stream of social analysis in which the drama analogy is, in one form or another, governing. At a time when social scientists are chattering about actors, scenes, plots, performances, and personae, and humanists are mumbling about motives, authority, persuasion, exchange and hierarchy, the line between the two, however comforting to the puritan on the one side and the cavalier on the other, seems uncertain indeed.[35]

The invitation Geertz extends here, even in his allusion to the English Civil War, that violent intermission in the pageant of English theatre history, calls attention to the uniqueness of performance and the ubiquity of theatrical metaphors.

Until recently, however, many critics, foregrounding the diagetic, considered the mimesis of which Geertz speaks as ancillary rather than essential to the drama; and, unfortunately, many still labour under this misconception. Many also assume that the absence of dramatic *text* indicates the absence of drama, and fail to seek sources and resources that might indicate the conditions and contexts of performances. In this respect, the work of theatre historians resembles that of social, art and music historians. We find evidence for our reconstructions not in scripts alone but also in many artefacts belonging to household auspices: financial accounts, chronicles, archaeological digs, letters, biographies, local histories, legal documents, paintings and sculpture. In addition, because of the visual, aural and kinesthetic nature of performance, we must also consider music and dance history, as well as the arts of engineering and science, since all of these contribute toward the *mise en scène* and the physical production.

Furthermore, theatre differs from literature in the ephemeral and intensely social nature of the stage. It is certainly understandable that literary critics would feel discomforted by the elusive nature of theatre, by the fact that the conditions of performance, from commission to reception, cannot be (and are, indeed, not meant to be) reproduced. Though some argue that this historicity affects literary texts as well, it is undeniable that the printed literary text is the primary artefact, while the primary theatrical text, written on the wind as it were, leaves no tangible trace. In addition, while the literary artefact may be privately shared between patron and patron artist, the theatrical *event*, from beginning to end, is a communal, social occasion. Although a household entertainment may be written by one person, it may not be fully realized without the assistance of many artists and the reception of an audience.

In fact many social rituals require no written script, but are nevertheless essential to the theatre historian, particularly in studies of household theatre and patronage. Ceremonies (such as weddings, coronations, elevations to nobility, funerals), religious and civic processions, military parades, folk pageants and dances all comprise theatre. Many of these occasions require the participation of theatre artists and technicians to build, costume, manage, enact and design (if not compose or script) the event. Most of these occasions manipulate audience expectations and responses to create the same suspense, wonder and catharsis that more traditional plays of the public stage affect. And, as critic after critic has shown, these social and ceremonial occasions feed structures, styles, and ideas back into the public theatre in a symbiotic relationship. The most common instance of this recursive flow is perhaps Oberon's 'fair vestal' speech (2.1.146–74) as a remembrance of Queen Elizabeth's visit to the Earl of Hertford in 1591, when she went on progress to his estate at Elvetham.[36]

Theatre scholarship entails not only the reconstruction of the performance but also reconstructions of the venues and auspices, as well as the social and political conditions of production. Since we also include audience reception and response, we must conclude that no performance is recoverable, that each and every production of a script is a unique event, a different play. Theatre, paratheatre, metatheatre – all these must inform the work of theatre historians.

Interdisciplinary interests have led to many fresh approaches to our disciplines – Marxist, psychoanalytic, anthropological, semiotic, new historical and feminist theories adapt, inspire and test alternative approaches from wider perspectives; scholars have begun to contextualize materials to consider not only the productions but also the people who produced and received them. And it is here that the study of household theatre really comes into its own, for in addition to the all-important play and playwright, such subjects as patrons, venues, occasions, money, contracts, costume stocks, musicians and visual artists began to take centre stage in critical and theoretical work. That prolific playwright 'Anon' becomes more and more interesting as a clear signal that authority rested not just in authorship during the early modern period but also in households – aristocratic, ecclesiastical, educational and civic – as creators of theatrical art. Consequently, critics and historians began investigating auspices and political allegory as clues to the workings of theatrical patronage.[37]

Now that the dramatic text has to share the limelight with the performance text, various structuralist and post-structuralist theorists give us the language with which to talk about the non-linguistic systems of the stage and to encourage the exploration of various other 'texts' from finances to fashions. Clothes (or masks, or sets, or roles, or venues) do indeed 'make' the man, as the tradition of doubling parts by changing costumes indicates. We are indeed what we *seem* to be, and the theatre analogies so common to our lives are found to be more than 'mere shows', as Geertz suggests, but rather ritualistic enactments of the social constructions of reality.

We have to go further afield in the history of literary theory to note the philosophers who began formulating aesthetic theories that would be more useful to theatre theorists, some of whom base their analyses solely on social phenomenons and patterns that inform theatre but remain without scripts.[38]

Mikhail Bakhtin's *Rabelais and His World* (published in Russian in 1965, and translated into English in 1968), and later *The Dialogic Imagination* (which appeared originally in 1975) got us thinking about *carnivale* and the socio-political implications of comic performance. Jesters, clowns, the Feast of Fools and Boy Bishop, to which E. K. Chambers had collected references in the 1920s, were raised in status from marginalized players (ironically, household accounts are brimming with payments to people like these) to ritual actors in the social contract. Bakhtin's work challenges us to think more seriously about the political construction and exploitation of transgressive performances, which should finally put to rest what I call the 'big bang' theory of the development of medieval theatre – that the ecclesiastical authorities, once thought of as the monolith of theatrical patronage, expelled theatre from the nave to the marketplace because of its excessive use of the comic. Rather, recently published records have shown that household patrons, including aristocrats, schools and civic organizations, had long served as suppliers of theatre, and perhaps it was the increasing competition among patrons, the beginnings of the replacement of the feudal system with incipient capitalism based heavily on patronage politics, that encouraged actors to market their commodities in more lucrative and rewarding ways.

Ann Jennalie Cook, for example, in *The Privileged Playgoers of Shakespeare's London*, conveniently summarizes the socio-historical approaches that focus on patronage and patriarchy as it applies to Elizabethan theatre.[39] Feminist criticism has also inspired some of the most refreshing discoveries in household patronage, for it has restored women to a vital role in artistic production in early modern England. We have known for a long time that women were forbidden to act on the stage, except at the two social extremes – as vaudeville-type travelling entertainers and Court fools,[40] or as noble dancers in masques and disguisings; all of these were exclusively household entertainments. We have also never identified, until Aphra Behn, a woman playwright who earned her living through her art. But we do know that several women, including six queens (Catherine of Aragon, Anne Boleyn, Jane Seymour, Mary I, Anne and later Henrietta Maria), served as patrons to artists and playwrights who created household entertainments. Queen Elizabeth's tastes were certainly taken into account by artists destined to perform for her (or at least by the patrons of those artists who had their own patron–client interests to consider), as countless complimentary prologues and epilogues preserve. David Bergeron has identified, through dedications of dramatic texts, at least fourteen women who served as patrons.[41] David Roberts has continued this exploration in *The Ladies: Female Patronage of Restoration Drama*,[42] showing that the tradition of female patronage was strong enough to outlast the interregnum interlude. Through the power of their households, through patronage and purse strings, women did indeed have a say in the theatrical art of their era. And in more indirect fashion, women in the audiences, both public and private household, served as patrons, a situation satirized in quite controversial style in *The Knight of the Burning Pestle*.

As Richard Dutton has made quite clear in *Mastering the Revels*, patronage systems to a great extent *formed* the Elizabethan government, from the patron-based alliances of the countryside gentry, through those of the Privy Councillors, directly to the Queen. Through a detailed study of source documents, Dutton suggests a very complex relationship among the royal household, the aristocratic patrons, the Master of the Revels and the theatre producers and writers.[43] Rather than reproducing the traditional portrait of the Privy Council as a bunch of censors determined to control theatres and persecute playwrights, Dutton argues quite reasonably that the Master of the Revels and the producers of theatre enjoyed a comfortable and lucrative relationship; it was neither profitable nor productive for either party to antagonize the other. The complex lines of patronage served not just as channels of artistic discourse but also as the warp and woof of political life. Consequently theatrical patronage, rather than being some serendipitous arrangement to escape legal prosecutions and provide aristocrats with a hobby, formed an integral part of the socio-political fabric of the sixteenth and seventeenth centuries. Linda Levy Peck goes so far as to state that 'historians have emphasized the importance of patronage practices to the stability of monarchy', and to speculate that the Civil War may have been brought on by James I's inability to maintain and manage the patronage networks properly.[44]

As I have discussed in *Patrons and Performance*, theatre was a prominent form of largess and education (perhaps to the point of propaganda), and a means of ensuring political and aesthetic control through household lines. By Shakespeare's time, theatre was rapidly becomming commodified, and patronage began to shift more solidly from the upper strata of society to include the general public, although the public had, to a certain extent, been patrons since the first touring actor was received in an innyard. I do not mean to suggest that theatre happens only from the top down. Throughout these times we also see an intertwining line of popular theatre, as Michael Bristol has pointed out in *Theatre and Carnival*, a line that frequently intersects patronized theatre in such activities as the Feast of Fools and the various 'vaudeville' entertainers at any aristocratic fête. By the end of the sixteenth century, obviously, these lines had intertwined so that companies such as Shakespeare's clearly had two patrons – the King *and* the paying public. In some cases these two patrons worked at cross-purposes, but in most cases they appeared to be quite comfortable as bedfellows, implying that aristocratic patronage offered perquisites that the public could not, and that the public offered economic rewards that the patrons were (if we can believe, for example, in Queen Elizabeth's frugal habit of getting others to pay for her entertainment) reluctant to distribute.[45]

Studies of theatrical patronage recontextualize all the labour and motivation that created the theatre of the sixteenth and seventeenth centuries,
and begin to explore the intriguing connections between theatrical art
and the people who produced and consumed it. The infinite variety of
approaches to patronage that I have merely outlined here maps a rich and
varied topography of power and art in the period, one that will no doubt
grow sharper and more complex as we discover new source materials and
new ways to analyse them. Every year the *Records of Early English Drama*
adds new features to our landscape, and every year we learn to read more
clearly where the roads are taking us.

Notes

1 Berg Collection of English and American Literature, M7: Virginia Woolf,
  Between the Acts: typescript of end of projected longer version, p. 238.
2 Scott McMillin and Sally-Beth MacLean, *The Queen's Men and Their Plays*
  (Cambridge: Cambridge University Press, 1998), pp. 1–18.
3 I distinguish here between 'drama', the *page*, and 'theatre', the *stage*. More and
  more over the past two decades it has become obvious that many theatrical
  activities were unscripted, and consequently we have to refer to sorts of documents other than dramatic texts in order to analyse these activities. Ceremonies,
  disguisings, the offerings of tumblers, minstrels and fools – all these constitute
  theatre and are crucial to our understanding of early modern culture, yet none
  of them can be documented by scripts, and few of them were even described by
  audience members.
4 E. K. Chambers, *The Elizabethan Stage*, 4 vols (Oxford: Clarendon Press, 1923)
  and *The Mediaeval Stage*, 2 vols (Oxford: Clarendon Press, 1903); Glynne
  Wickham, *Early English Stages*, 3 vols in 4 (London: Routledge and Kegan Paul,
  1959) and Sydney Anglo, *Spectacle, Pageantry, and Early Tudor Policy* (Oxford:
  Clarendon Press, 1969).
5 R. W. Vince, 'Theatre History as an Academlic Discipline', in *Interpreting the
  Theatrical Past*, eds Thomas Postlewait and Bruce A. McConachie (Iowa City:
  University of Iowa Press, 1989), pp. 1–18; 14–15.
6 See, for example, Ian Lancashire, *Dramatic Texts and Records of Britain: A
  Chronological Topography to 1558* (Toronto: University of Toronto Press,
  1984); Carl J. Stratman, *Bibliography of English Printed Tragedy, 1565–1900*
  (Carbondale: Southern Illinois University Press, 1966), and his *Bibliography
  of Medieval Drama*, 2nd edn, 2 vols (New York: Frederick Ungar, 1972);
  John Tucker Murray, *English Dramatic Companies, 1558–1642* (New York:
  Houghton Mifflin Co., 1910); and Andrew Gurr, *The Shakespearian Playing
  Companies* (Oxford and New York: Oxford University Press, 1996).
7 Clifford Geertz, *Local Knowledge* (New York: Harper Collins, 1983), p. 124.
8 For a recent overview of royal court entertainments see Graham Parry, 'Entertainment at Court', in *A New History of Early English Drama*, eds John D. Cox
  and David Scott Kastan (New York: Columbia University Press, 1997). Parry
  discusses Lyly on pages 197–8.

9 Thomas More, *The History of Richard III*, Vol. 2 of *The Complete Works of Sir Thomas More*, ed. Richard Sylvester (New Haven: Yale University Press, 1963), pp. 80–1.

10 See the *Oxford English Dictionary*, and the chapters by Michael Shapiro and Sandy Leggatt in Paul Whitfield White and Suzanne Westfall, eds, *Shakespeare and Theatrical Patronage in Modern England* (Cambridge: Cambridge University Press, 2002).

11 Werner Gundersheimer, 'Patronage in the Renaissance: an Exploratory Approach', in *Patronage in the Renaissance*, eds Guy Fitch Lytle and Stephen Orgel (Princeton: Princeton University Press, 1981), pp. 3–23, 23.

12 Guy Fitch Lytle, 'Religion and the Lay Patron in Reformation England', in *Patronage in the Renaissance*, eds Lytle and Orgel, pp. 65–114.

13 Gundersheimer, 'Patranage in the Renaissance', pp. 3–4.

14 Niccolo Machievelli, *The Prince*, ed. and trans. Peter Bondanella (Oxford: Oxford University Press, 1984), p. 76.

15 Linda Levy Peck, 'Court Patronage and Government Policy: the Jacobean Dilemma', in *Patronage in the Renaissance*, eds Lytle and Orgel, p. 31. Richard Dutton, *Mastering the Revels: The Regulation and Censorship of English Renaissance Drama* (University City: University of Iowa Press, 1991).

16 Martin Butler, *Theatre and Crisis 1632–42* (Cambridge, Cambridge University Press, 1984), p. 133. For detailed explorations of these ideas see Paul Whitfield White's *Theatre and Reformation: Protestantism, Patronage and Playing in Tudor England* (Cambridge: Cambridge University Press, 1993), and the chapters in *Shakespeare and Theatrical Patronage*.

17 Anglo *Spectacle, Pageantry, and Early Tudor Policy* provides a thorough and thought-provoking survey of royal entertainments at the turn of the sixteenth century, combined with a cultural studies approach that demonstrates clearly how theatre and ideology have been, since the earliest Tudor entertainments, comfortable bedfellows. See also Alistair Fox, *Politics and Literature in the Reigns of Henry VII and Henry VIII* (Oxford: Blackwell, 1989).

18 Frank Foster, 'Politics and Community in Elizabethan London', in *The Rich, the Well Born, and the Powerful: Elites and Upper Classes in History*, ed. Frederick Cople Jaher (Chicago: University of Illinois Press, 1993).

19 Louis Althusser, 'Ideology and Ideological State Apparatuses', in *Lenin and Philosophy and Other Essays* (London: New Left Books, 1971), pp. 127–86.

20 Robert Boswell, *Life of Johnson*, 2 vols (Oxford: Oxford University Press, 1924). Unlike Jonson, Johnson had nothing positive to say about patronage. In *Vanity of Human Wishes* he includes patrons in the 'ills the scholar's life assails', and in the preface to his *Dictionary* defines a patron as 'commonly a wretch who supports with insolence and is paid with flattery'.

21 What Evans did for Ben Jonson as a 'patronage poet', Alvin Kernan does for William Shakespeare in *The Playwright as Magician* (New Haven: Yale University Press, 1979) and more recently in *Shakespeare, the King's Playwright: Theater in the Stuart Court 1603–1613* (New Haven: Yale Universty Press, 1995). While Kernan is decidedly anti-New-Historicist, he nevertheless concurs with most scholars about the recursive nature of patronage, that it shapes and is in turn shaped by political realities (see pp. 184–5). Donna B. Hamilton also focuses on patronage in *Shakespeare and the Politics of Protestant England*

(Lexington: University Press of Kentucky, 1992). Of the many books about Jonson's life, art and relationship with the Court, a few very important works focus extensively on the function of patronage in Jonson's career. See, for example, Stephen Orgel, *The Jonsonian Masque* (Cambridge, Mass.: Harvard University Press, 1965) or *The Illusion of Power: Political Theater in the English Renaissance* (Berkeley: University of California Press, 1975) or, with Roy Strong, *The Theatre of the Stuart Court; Including the Complete Designs for Productions at Court, for the most part in the Collection of the Duke of Devonshire, together with their Texts and Historical Documentation* (Berkeley: University of California Press, 1973); Leah Marcus, *The Politics of Mirth: Jonson, Herrick, Milton, Marvell and the Defense of Old Holiday Pastimes* (Chicago: University of Chicago Press, 1986); John Gordon Sweeney, *Jonson and the Psychology of Public Theater: To Coin the Spirit, Spend the Soul* (Princeton: Princeton University Press, 1985); Jonathan Haynes, *The Social Relations of Jonson's Theatre* (New York: Cambridge University Press, 1992); David Scott Kastan and Peter Stallybrass, eds, *Staging the Renaissance: Reinterpretations of Elizabethan and Jacobean Drama* (New York: Routledge, 1991); J. R. Mulryne and Margaret Shewring, eds, *Theatre and Government Under the Early Stuarts* (Cambridge: Cambridge University Press, 1993). Kernan, *Shakespeare*, p. 171.

22 Jaher, ed., *The Rich*, pp. 111, 163. This volume provides a particularly valuable study of the patronage network and its abuses from an historic and sociological perspective.
23 S. N. Eisenstadt and L. Roniger, *Patrons, Clients, and Friends: Interpersonal Relations and the Structure of Trust in Society* (Cambridge: Cambridge University Press, 1984), pp. 48–9.
24 Suzanne Westfall, *Patrons and Performance: Early Tudor Household Revels* (Oxford: Clarendon Press, 1990), p. 87. White and Westfall, eds, *Shakespeare and Theatrical Patronage*.
25 'Morton's Fork' refers to the policy of John Morton, Cardinal and Archbishop of Canterbury, who procured 'loans' for Henry VII by forcing the ostentatious aristocracy to contribute because they could clearly afford to, and the frugal aristocracy because they clearly were hoarding huge sums. Thus, no one could escape. Henry VII once fined the Earl of Northumberland for extravagant display during the wedding progress of his daughter Margaret to Scotland, as I discuss in *Patrons and Performance*.
26 White, *Theatre and Reformation*.
27 Ian Arthurson, 'Espionage and Intelligence from the Wars of the Roses to the Reformation', *Nottingham Mediaeval Studies* 35 (1991), 134–54.
28 Kernan, *Shakespeare*, p. 171.
29 Westfall, *Patrons and Performance*, p. 87.
30 Grace E. Goodell, 'Paternalism, Patronage, and Potlatch: the Dynamics of Giving and Being Given To', *Current Anthropology* 26:2 (April 1985), 247–66, pp. 252–3.
31 *Ibid.*, 256–7.
32 Patricia Fumerton, *Cultural Aesthetics: Renaissance Literature and the Practice of Social Ornament* (Chicago: University of Chicago Press, 1991), p. 35.
33 Westfall, *Patrons and Performance* pp. 91–2.

34 Michel Foucault discusses the interplay of '*Basileus, Philosophos*, and *Metalli-cos*' as fundamental to the organic structure of art in *The Order of Things* (New York: Vintage Books, 1970), pp. 167, 173.

35 Geertz, *Local Knowledge*, p. 30.

36 For a convenient edition see Alfred F. Kinney, ed., *Renaissance Drama: An Anthology of Plays and Entertainments* (Oxford: Blackwells, 1999).

37 See, for example, Thomas W. Craik's 'The Political Interpretation of Two Tudor Interludes: *Temperence* and *Humility and Wealth and Health*', *Review of English Studies* 4 (1953), 98–108, and *The Tudor Interlude* (Leicester: Leicester University Press, 1958); William Harris, 'Wolsey and Skelton's *Magnyfy-cence*', *Studies in Philology* 57 (1960), 99–122; Gwen Ann Jones, 'The Political Significance of the Play of *Albion Knight*', *Journal of English and German Philology* 17 (1918), 267–80; Ian Lancashire, 'The Auspices of *The World and the Child*', *Renaissance and Reformation* 12 (1976), 96–105, 'Orders for Twelfth Day and Night circa 1515 in the Second Northumberland Household Book', *English Literary Renaissance* 10 (Winter 1980), 7–45, and *Two Tudor Interludes: 'The Interlude of Youth'*, '*Hick Scorner*' (Manchester: Manchester University Press, 1980).

38 Roy Strong's illustration-rich *Art and Power* (Berkeley: Unversity of California Press, 1973) is a particularly good representation of an analysis of non-textual performances.

39 Ann Jennalie Cook, *The Privileged Playgoers of Shakespeare's London 1576–1642* (Princeton: Princeton University Press, 1981).

40 Westfall, *Patrons and Performance*, p. 91.

41 David Bergeron, 'Women as Patrons of English Renaissance Drama', in *Patronage in the Renaissance*, eds Lytle and Orgel, pp. 274–90. See also Barbara Lewalski, 'Re-writing Patriarchy and Patronage: Margaret Clifford, Anne Clifford, and Aemilia Lanyer', in *Patronage, Politics and Literary Traditions in England: 1558–1658*, ed. Cedric C. Brown (Detroit: Wayne Stage University Press, 1991), pp. 59–78.

42 David Roberts. *The Ladies: Female Patronage of Restoration Drama* (Oxford: Clarendon Press, 1989).

43 Dutton, *Mastering the Revels*.

44 Peck, 'Court Patronage', 27–46, p. 27.

45 Kathleen E. McLuskie and Felicity Dunsworth, 'Patronage and the Economics of Theatre', in Cox and Kastan, eds, *A New History of Early English Drama*, pp. 423–40.

The management of mirth: Shakespeare *via* Bourdieu

The Elizabethan playhouse at Knowsley, near Liverpool, remains one of the dark secrets of Shakespearean England. Very few commentators are aware of even the existence of this theatre, built by the Stewards of Henry Stanley, Earl of Derby, on the site of his cockpit, some time in the 1580s. Though the records of the Lancashire playhouse were collated from county archives in 1951,[1] the Shakespeare industry has ignored this building, which survived as late as 1902 as Flatiron House, so called from its shape, sixty foot deep and with a stage about thirty foot wide: almost exactly the dimensions of an auditorium such as the Cockpit-in-Court. Like the Yorkshire troupe which toured the Dales with *King Lear* and *Pericles* in 1609, the purpose-built theatre that operated until that year on the estate of a northern territorial magnate does not fit the dominant narrative of the Shakespearean stage, with its fixation on the bourgeois city and the commercial amphitheatre. Provincial stages are supposed to have been improvised in halls, inn yards or barns; but the Earl of Derby's Lancastrian theatre was a permanent structure expensively equipped for professional performance, and its quarter-century history offers a glimpse of an alternative itinerary to that of Stratford and Southwark, and a route not taken by the critics: away from Bankside, along with the diaspora to which, according to Peter Burke, early modern 'European popular culture owed its unity . . . the mass of the acting profession . . . who spent their lives on the move from town to town, and were no respecters of political frontiers'.[2] And facilities created for the players at petty courts such as that of the so-called 'King of Lancashire' might also help to explain one outstanding mystery of Shakespearean drama: which is that London's most successful commercial entertainment occludes its actual locale, by consistently staging scenes of aristocratic patronage, rather than holding a realistic mirror up to its 'barren spectators' (*Hamlet* 3.2.41) in the metropolitan playhouse.

On 20 September 1589 the Governor of Carlisle notified the English embassy in Edinburgh that on learning of King James's 'earnest desire to have Her Majesty's players repair unto Scotland to His Grace, I did forthwith despatch a servant unto them where they were in furthest Lancashire'. The Queen's Men were at Knowsley, where they acted in Derby's playhouse on 12 and 13 September; but a month later they were being 'used with great kindness and all courtesy' by the Earl of Bothwell in Edinburgh, while James escorted his bride, Anna of Denmark, from Elsinore. There her father had become the first Continental monarch to host English actors, a band of Derby's stars, whom the Danish King passed on to the Elector of Saxony. So, whether or not Bothwell enticed the Queen's Men to Scotland to rehabilitate himself after an abortive coup,[3] these journeys north all beg the question posed by Hamlet when 'the tragedians of the city' likewise beat a path to Elsinore: 'How chances it they travel', when 'Their residence, both in reputation and profit, was better both ways' in the metropolis? The surprising answer supplied by Jerzy Limon in his revelatory survey of 'English players in Central and Eastern Europe', *Gentlemen of a Company*, is not, as Rosencrantz complains, that performers were forced from the city by competition, when rival troupes, like the 'little eyases', were 'tyrannically clapped', nor that plague or prohibition drove them; but that 'The best actors in the world' found the grandiose production values in aristocratic courts so superior to those of 'the common stages' in London (*Hamlet* 2.2.326–92). The Europe of principalities described by Limon was a paradise for players, not because livery protected them from politics but because it transported their productions out of the bearpit of economic necessity. As the composer John Dowland testified, Continental patronage was embraced by performers because its extravagance defied the mercenary logic of the marketplace:

> When I came to the Duke of Brunswick he gave me a rich chain of gold, £23 in money, with velvet and satin and gold lace to make apparel, and a promise that if I would serve him he would reward me with as much as any prince in the world. From whence I went to the Landgrave of Hesse, who gave me the greatest welcome that might be for one of my quality, who sent a ring to my wife valued at £20, and gave me a great cup with a gilt cover, full of dollars, with many great offers for my service.[4]

'Motley's the only wear ... O that I were a fool! I am ambitious for a motley coat': though it is 'a charter as the wind, / To blow on whom I please', which attracts Jarques to ducal livery (*As You Like It* 2.7.34–49), the liberty aristocratic service offered the performers, Limon believes, was as much from commerce as from censorship. For as Stephen Greenblatt argues, when they accepted old clothes from new rulers in post-Reformation Europe, theatrical companies 'received more than an atttractive, cut-rate wardrobe; they acquired the charisma that clung to the old vestments'.[5] What this aura involved, when, for example, the Landgrave of Hesse 'ordered old apparel, weapons, armour and clothes despatched for the performance of a comedy about ancient potentates', had more to do with fantasy than profit. As Limon suggests, by loading them with 'silk suits for the entire company of nineteen players and sixteen musicians', coaches, banquets, painted clouds, and multiple changes of scenery, these princelings elevated 'the English comedians' who 'strut in collars set with pearls', on to an aesthetic plane where they became living signifiers of the arbitrariness of state consumption.[6] Thus, at a time when, as Kathleen McLuskie records, English dramatists were lamenting 'the shift from patronage to commerce',[7] their Continental passports secured them entry into the new cultural order which would supplant the old patronage system and reach its apex at Versailles. Recent scholars have traced the 'English comedians' on a circuit that took them to Lille, Ghent, Leiden, Frankfurt, Cologne, Stuttgart, Nuremberg, Heidelburg, Munich and Vienna, and as far east as Prague, Graz and Gdansk, all the time ratcheting higher rates of pay.[8] So, the court theatre named the *Ottoneum* built by Landgrave Moritz at Kassel in 1604 on the plan of the Fortune Playhouse in London, or the Royal Theatre designed by Italian architects in Warsaw in 1637, were arenas where a select few English actors came closest to a system Burke has termed the new state 'bureaucratisation' of art;[9] yet it is a central paradox of Shakespeare's drama that, despite the very small numbers employed, it is this absolutist regime of warrants, subsidies, annuities, committees and intendants, supervised by some enlightened Duke, which haunts the plays he wrote for his paying London public as the imaginary matrix of their own production:

> Come now, what masques, what dances shall we have,
> To wear away this long age of three hours
> Between our after-supper and bed-time?
> Where is our usual manager of mirth?
> What revels are in hand? Is there no play
> To ease the anguish of a torturing hour?
> Call Philostrate.   (*A Midsummer Night's Dream* 5.1.32–8)

In Shakespeare's ideal theatre it is a noble patron who welcomes the troupers, chooses the play to be 'preferred' (4.2.34), provides the 'rabble' with 'glistering apparel' (*The Tempest* 4.1.37; SD 193), and underwrites the production by commanding his 'usual manager of mirth' to 'Stir up the youth . . . to merriments' (*Dream* 1.1.12). It is then his master of ceremonies who counts the words of the script, edits its 'abridgement' and keeps the 'revels in hand' by overseeing rehearsals (5.1.39–70). Meanwhile, if his Court chamberlain censors 'the argument' to ensure there is 'no offence in it', it is this officer who is also charged with seeing the players 'well bestowed' and housed after his 'own honour and dignity' (*Hamlet* 3.2.242; 2.2.520–30). In Shakespearean fantasy, the lord will even 'give instructions' about stage business, such as how to provoke tears with 'an onion . . . in a napkin' (*The Taming of the Shrew* Ind.1.122–7); or direct a run-through, to the extent of inserting 'some dozen or sixteen lines' of his own into the playtext (*Hamlet* 2.2.538); and during the action it is the aristocrat who ordains 'No tongue! All eyes! Be silent!' (*The Tempest* 4.1.59); warns the audience to 'stay themselves from laughter' (*Shrew* Ind.1.132); instructs the stage-manager when to 'draw aside the curtain and discover' the scene (*The Merchant of Venice* 2.7.1); prompts when lines dry (*Love's Labour's Lost* 5.2.663); is 'as good as a chorus' glossing the plot (*Hamlet* 3.2.254); and may act a part himself to ensure 'we will not have our audience disappointed' (*The Book of Sir Thomas More* 4.1.257). It is the prince who defends even 'the worst' actors from the critics (*Dream* 5.1.210); pretends that 'That sport best pleases that doth least know how' (*Love's* 5.2.514); and promises that 'if art fail, we'll inch it out with love' (*Sir Thomas More* 4.1.117). And it is the great man who cues the comedians when to 'play on' or repeat 'That old and antique song' (*Twelfth Night* 1.1.1; 2.4.3); who tells them, 'Well done! Avoid! No more!' (*The Tempest* 4.1.142); announces whether to hear an epilogue (*Dream* 5.1.345); and at the end gives the order to 'Play, music' (*As You Like It* 5.4.175), or to 'Strike up pipers' (*Much Ado About Nothing* 5.4.125). Finally, it is the nobleman who decides whether to award the players pensions, like the 'sixpence a day for playing Pyramus' anticipated for Bottom (*Dream* 4.2.20). As Alvin Kernan comments, Shakespeare's dream of patronage is as far as possible from 'the rough actualities of production on Bankside', for his imaginary theatre is monopolized by a 'ruler as the source of all benefits and the wielder of all powers'.[10]

Shakespeare's monarchical theatre projects the cultural bureaucracy that was developing in the absolutist courts of Europe and was perhaps envisaged for England with the accession of the Stuarts. Thus, Richard Dutton has described the jockeying to upgrade the haphazard Elizabethan role of Master of the Revels into an authoritative post 'along lines of a Master of Ceremonies who would supervise grand occasions'; yet he goes on to relate how, even when the Court was modernized in 1603, 'Stuart autocratic ambitions (at least in theatrical matters) were matched by incompetence'.[11] For what is striking about Shakespeare's wishful thinking on princely orchestration of 'triumphs, mirth, and rare solemnity' (*Two Gentlemen of Verona* 5.4.162) is its inconsistency with English practice. Though 'The actors entered wholeheartedly into the fiction' that they existed 'to serve the King and Crown', as Kernan argues, he concedes that the reality was that 'court theatre was shaped by professionals working in public theatres', and that 'the official court view was that the king, and not the play, was the thing' at centre stage.[12] Elizabethan and Jacobean government was clearly neither as coercive nor conducive to players as Shakespeare's artistic dictators imply. Elizabeth's parsimony and James's attention-span militated against the royal involvement in theatricals assumed by new historicism; while, as Dutton concludes, 'the Masters of the Revels, though ostensibly representing an absolute authority . . . were products of a factional system . . . and likely to foster the relatively free expression that went with it'.[13] Such was Shakespeare's disillusion with the poverty of patron-age, Kernan believes, that he wrote his sonnets as 'a description of a failed patronage relationship', and never forgot how his real income derived from 'public means which public manners breeds' (*Sonnets* 111). That he shared contemporary cynicism towards actors who 'pretend to have a royal master', when 'their wages prove them to be the servants of the people',[14] and impatience with a patronage system that supplied, at most, a mere 10 per cent of his company's income, only highlights the anomaly, therefore, that 'When Shakespeare portrayed a theatre, he did not imagine a public theatre' but always a stage in 'a court or noble house', where 'the players are as base as the audience is noble'.[15]

The discrepancy between Shakespeare's ideal patrician audience and his real plebeian one seems so structural and self-evident – once it is pointed out – that what is surprising is that it has scarcely ever been discussed. The aberration that 'The great house dominated the representation of players in Shakespeare's plays, even as it disappeared from their lives', and that the dramatist who created more fictional players than any other confined them to 'a series of "great house plays"; neither established in the city, nor travelling independently . . . [but] dependent on aristocratic hospitality', has recently been diagnosed by Meredith Anne Skura, however, as symp-tomatic of a profound insecurity. Unfortunately, it is the thesis of *Shakespeare the Actor and the Purposes of Playing* that the reason why 'Shakespeare's players all conform to the outdated image of the player as a beggar living on alms', even though 'his own experience lay on the up-to-date public stage', is that he was thereby expressing stage-fright as a performer abreacting 'the narcissistic pleasure of exhibiting himself' for approval or rejection by his parents. Thus, rather than staging his actual conditions, 'Shakespeare accentuated the inferiority implied by patronage', and portrayed actors as 'childlike dependents' of noblemen, Skura infers, in a compulsive repetition of 'the infant's narcissistic wound . . . an anni-hilating terror of deprivation'.[16] What such vulgar Freudianism proves, of course, is the need for a true sociology of Shakespearean production, and one which takes account of evidence that players did not merely evade economics but actually 'increased their touring activities as they achieved pre-eminence in London'. A simple explanation proposed by Alan Somerset for this conflict between deference and self-interest is that touring under patronage was one of 'the expected duties, as was entertaining the monarch'.[17] This is a suggestion that helps to situate Shakespeare, not as some psychotic genius but as originator of a project defined precisely by its relations to power and profit. *Putting Shakespeare in his place* in this way involves reconstructing the author's intentions through a methodol-ogy that, unlike naive biographical criticism, locates his position within his entire universe of creative production. And it is just such an analysis that has been made possible by the theory of the literary field developed by Pierre Bourdieu.

For Bourdieu the literary field is a space 'in which one discusses what it means to be a writer', in the way that all social practices are organised as spaces of objective relationships endowed with greater or lesser autonomy in interaction with other fields, and crucially those of power and money.[18] It is the *relational* mode of this critique which distinguishes Bourdieu's concept of the field from both internal methods of analysis, such as formalism or deconstructionism, and external methods, such as 'old' historicism or Marxism. In particular, such a theory allows criticism to go beyond the reflection model of Marxists such as Lukács and Goldmann, which by reducing works to expression of class interests, and the writer to the medium of a mental structure or world view, neglected the *relative autonomy* of the literary field and so obliterated its literary specificity. By contrast, Bourdieu's crucial insight – 'that there are immaterial forms of capital, as well as an economic form, and that it is possible to convert one of these into another'[19] – offers what some see as 'not only the best, but the only ... tool for analysis of production, text, and audience in culture studies'.[20] What Bourdieu adds to Marxism is the recognition that 'a much wider range of labour is productive of capital than Marx suggested', though what he has been slow to develop is any explanation of the historical determinants of the convertibility of different kinds of value. Yet, as his commentators remark, it is the very convertibility of capital that distinguishes different historical epochs, as 'A high level of convertibility is characteristic of complex, market-based, and above-all capitalist societies', which are driven by 'a logic of increasing convertibility'.[21] So, though he has rarely written about it, Bourdieu implicitly affirms the importance assigned the Renaissance by new historicism, as the age when art starts to be differentiated from money and prestige, as much as from prayer or propaganda. Greenblatt's dictum that Shakespeare's playhouse 'escapes from the network of social practices that govern' it, because the stage 'would seem to be of no *use* to its audience', derives, in fact (as he acknowledges), directly from a reading of Bourdieu:

> The triumphant cunning of this theatre is to make its spectators forget that they are participating in a practical activity. Shakespeare's theatre is powerful and effective precisely to the extent that the audience believes it to be nonuseful and hence nonpractical.[22]

Like new historicism, Bourdieu's sociology of culture has been simultaneously branded by detractors 'a kind of Marxism' and a form of 'postmodern relativism',[23] and it is easy to see why a theory of the disinterestedness of art, that yet insists on the interest of the disinterested, should seem confusing to American and British readers. Such post-Marxist evasion of all 'false antinomies' of agency and society, culture and economy, or text and context, looks to Anglo-Saxon eyes very much a genuflection to the *Grande Ecoles* that inculcated the triangulating mentality not only of de Gaulle's *enarques* but also of Barthes, Derrida or Piaget.[24] None the less, it is Bourdieu's axiom that 'the work of art is a product of a negotiation between a creator or class of creators, equipped with a communally shared repertoire of conventions, and the institutions and practices of society', which is adopted by Greenblatt to explain the primacy of the Shakespearean theatre as the prototypical site of this 'mutually profitable exchange'.[25] Likewise, though never quoted, it is Bourdieu's concept of symbolic capital that informs Svetlana Alpers's interpretation, in *Rembrandt's Enterprise: The Studio and the Market*, of the one painter who, along with the dramatist, became most identified with the pricelessness of art, and whose lust for gold had less to do with accumulation of wealth than with the aesthetic liberties he took at the expense of patrons and public.[26] Thus, if autonomization of art is for Bourdieu a condition of capitalism, it is the Shakespearean era, his admirers infer, which is the threshold of modernity. And though he pays lip service to the structuralist taboo against 'the idol of origins', Bourdieu is happy to go along with this periodization, conceding how it was in the seventeenth century that the cultural field 'began to define itself in opposition to the economic, political and religious powers'.[27] Autonomization turns out, for Bourdieu, to be highly historically specific.

For one who is accused of treating all interests as if they were transhistorical and invariant, Bourdieu offers a surprisingly definite account of the Renaissance as the period when art 'gradually came to be organized into a field as creative artists began to liberate themselves economically from the patronage of the aristocracy and the Church and their ethical and aesthetic values'.[28] The relevance of this analysis to Shakespearean culture has been demonstrated, moreover, by Alain Viala in his 1985 study, *Naissance de l'écrivain*, a 'Sociology of literature in the classical age', which traces the emergence of a literary field in France to the rule of Richelieu, when the autonomy of art was first instituted in foundations such as the Académie Française.[29] And Bourdieu himself notes that freedom of expression and liberation from the external legitimizing authority of the nobility was accelerated in the case of Elizabethan drama owing to 'the demands of theatre managers and, through them, to entrance fees paid by a public of increasingly diverse origin'.[30] But, as he also points out, 'for a long time this process remained ambiguous, to the extent that artists paid with a statutory dependence on the state for the recognition it accorded them'.[31] It is this solidarity between art and power which concerns Christian Jouhard, who is intrigued that 'If there is autonomy . . . it does not establish itself at the expense of power, which, on the contrary, sustains it'. To Jouhard, then, what is striking about the literary field is that it was initiated not in defiance but deference to patronage; and it is his identification of an 'association between power and literature, profitable to both', that supplies a solution to the puzzle of Shakespeare's self-subjection. For on this view, early modern patronage was just as much an operation of mutual exchange as the capitalist art market, and never a relationship of crude appropriation: 'The new values of purism from which the profession of writer began to define itself, were produced in the context of a dependence on power which became the initial condition of the construction of the first literary field.'[32]

In his solitary comment on the dramatist, Bourdieu observes that the character of Shakespeare's who seems to argue most adamantly for the autonomy of art, when he 'instructs the actors like an experienced director', is in fact a royal patron and arts administrator. *Hamlet*, Bourdieu remarks, is a play that reminds us that 'the artist did not always display towards external restraints the impatience which for us appears to define the creative project', and that the playwright himself addressed his own patron as one who 'In other's works dost but mend the style . . . But dost advance / As high as learning my rude ignorance' (*Sonnets* 78). Thus, in an era when 'the writer for the stage was no longer dependent on the good-will of a single patron', Shakespeare deferred to the aristocracy not from nostalgia but as 'the group most anxious to distinguish itself' from the bourgeois.[33] This is the context, according to Bourdieu, of the Prince's notes to the Players to 'speak the speech . . . as I pronounced it to you, trippingly', and to 'suit the action to the word', in respect of the 'necessary question of the play'. For what emerges from this rehearsal is that the integrity of the artistic project will be contingent on the freedom from any 'pitiful ambition' to please 'the groundlings' that is a privilege of 'the judicious' (3.2.1–45). Already, then, at the dawn of absolutism, the contract struck by an enlightened despotism will be to 'make the market disappear' by liberating art from consumer expectations. Thus, what Bourdieu calls 'the symbolic revolution through which artists free themselves from bourgeois demand by refusing any master except their art' commences in the Shakespearean text as a strategy to exchange the economic capital earned in the public playhouse for the cultural capital awarded by the princely patron. *Hamlet's* neoclassical decree, when itemizing the Players' crowd-pleasing, to 'reform it altogether' (37), marks the aesthetic price demanded, on this view, of Europe's state academicians, whose emancipation from economics is made conditional on their submission to the esotericism and humanistic ideals of those who clothe them in their 'motley' costume.[34]

'Like iron filings', shaken between power and the public, Bourdieu remarks, those committed to the construction of the literary field were forced to 'slide towards whichever pole' seemed, from their position, to be momentarily strong.[35] Thus, in the Elizabethan theatre, as McLuskie shows, a utopian solution might be that afforded by the Universities, according to the Parnassus plays, where the true artist could 'scorn each Midas of this age, / Each earthly peasant and each drossy clown',[36] but a writer such as

Jonson, torn 'between the need to earn a living and refusal to compromise the poet's vocation', was forced by abhorrence of the bourgeois and attraction to the pole of power to 'divide his public into tiers, with the theatre audience at the bottom, and at the height, the enlightened aristocrat who had the status to make him an appropriate patron.' Trapped within this 'contradiction between the material need for employment and an ideology in which art and money were opposed', dramatists such as Middleton and Marston either dedicated works insultingly or to the 'most honourably renowned Nobody', as though 'they had no language with which to address' their customers; while, by contrast, it was the market that magnetized Dekker, who savaged Jonson for prostration to his patrons.[37] Between a political pole of attraction and economic pole of repulsion, the force field of Elizabethan drama corresponded closely, therefore, in this analysis, to the literary field of nineteenth-century France that is the subject of Bourdieu's recent book *The Rules of Art*. There he recounts how the autonomization of literature that began in the time of Shakespeare was finalized by Flaubert as the project of 'art for art's sake' in resistance to 'a bourgeois world that had never before asserted so bluntly its pretension to control the domain of culture'. Thus, just as Jonson protested how it was impossible 'in these Times, and to such Auditors, to observe the splendour of Dramatic Poems with preservation of any popular delight',[38] so 'Everything was false', Flaubert declared, 'The moment was disastrous for verse. Imagination was flattened by a public that was not disposed to permit independence of mind'.[39] From the instant of the Renaissance inception to the nineteenth-century completion of the process, then, the rupture with the bourgeois was accomplished by cultural producers negating the economic pole with the pole of power:

> A challenge to all economism, the literary order presents itself as an inverted economic world: those who enter it have an interest in disinterestedness. But this does not mean there is no economic logic in this charismatic economy founded upon a social miracle . . . the field of cultural production occupies a dominated position within the field of power.[40]

'The economic world turned upside down' might be the title of Shakespeare's first intervention in this process, the Induction to *The Taming of the Shrew*, where a 'charismatic economy founded upon a social miracle' is instituted by the Lord with all the scorn for plebeian reality that distinguishes Limon's nobility. It would be possible to connect the structure of this play with the takeover that occurred after the probable assassination in April 1594 of Shakespeare's theatre patron, Ferdinando, Lord Derby, when his players, based at Knowsley and the Rose, were reincorporated under the control of the Lord Chamberlain, Lord Hunsdon. Derby's (or Strange's) Company had been unique, Scott McMillin claims, for its ruinous size and subversiveness:[41] luxuries it owed to Ferdinando; and the on-stage audience for *The Shrew*, dropped half-way through, looks like a relic of his unsustainable standards of sponsorship. 'Struggles in the political field may best serve the interest of writers most concerned about literary independence', Bourdieu remarks,[42] and, whether devised before or after his death, the Induction to this comedy is itself a display of the exorbitance the Earl funded and that is its subject. When the Lord orders the drunken tinker, Sly, to be 'convey'd to bed, / wrapp'd in sweet clothes, rings put upon his fingers, / A most delicious banquet by his bed, / And brave attendants near him when he wakes', this 'flattering dream or worthless fancy' (1.35–42) therefore literalizes what Bourdieu takes to be a founding principle of the world of art, which is its denegation of commerce, since 'The game of art is, from the point of view of business, a game of "loser takes all"'. Viewed in this way, the evanescence of Sly's 'dream' cruelly obeys the dictate that 'In this economic world turned upside down, one cannot conquer money, honours, women', since 'The law of this *paradoxical* game is that the love of art is a crazed love':[43] like the love of Kate and Petruchio acted to amuse the beggar. We can only guess how this loser will react when he finds his 'lady' is a boy; but meanwhile the Players succeed, according to the rules of the game, precisely to the extent that they efface his real plebeian presence:

> There is a lord will hear your play tonight;
> But I am doubtful of your modesties,
> Lest over-eyeing of his odd behaviour –
> For yet his honour never heard a play –
> You break into some merry passion
> And so offend him; for I tell you, sirs,
> If you should smile, he grows impatient.
> *First Player*   Fear not, my Lord, we can contain ourselves,
> Were he the veriest antic in the world.   (Ind.1.91–9)

With its dense references to the Stratford locality, the Induction to *The Taming of the Shrew* is usually interpreted as Shakespeare's rite of passage from his social origins. As the Arden editor comments, 'The whole atmosphere is redolent of Warwickshire, which he left for London in the 1580s. No other play refers so specifically to the county of his birth. It may be that he was making dramatic capital out of personal nostalgia.'[44] It is important, however, to recognize what is involved in this production of 'dramatic capital' out of social marginality, as it typifies not only the ruse by which, as Bourdieu proposes, intellectuals or artists, such as actors, acquire cultural capital by becoming 'dominated dominators within the field of dominant power' but also the way in which Shakespeare, like Flaubert, inscribes the dynamics of his own social trajectory into his artistic project.[45] Robert Greene notoriously reviled him as an 'upstart crow beautified with our feathers'; but seen in the light of Bourdieu's theory, it was Shakespeare's

self-awareness of his *arriviste* status, as a provincial glover's son, without
elite education, who became a 'gentleman born' (*The Winter's Tale* 5.2.132)
only by gatecrashing the field of cultural production, which determined
both his famous capacity to 'contain himself' in his creative work –
the 'habitus', in Bourdieu's terms, which Henry Chettle praised as 'his
demeanour no less civil than he excellent in the quality he professes' – and
his representation of those of the petite-bourgeoisie, commencing with Sly,
who 'beautify' themselves in borrowed feathers.⁴⁶ For while 'old Sly's son
of Burton-heath' enters the art world with meagre cultural capital, being
'by birth a pedlar, by education a card-maker, by transmutation a bear-herd,
and by present profession a tinker' (2.18), its rules dictate that so long as
he submits with *goodwill* to the 'dream' (which Bourdieu calls the *illusion*)
of its legitimacy and autonomy, he will be exalted as 'the lord indeed' (73)
for whom it is produced. Nothing could be further, therefore, from the
Parnassian contempt for 'each earthly peasant' than the *distinction* conde-
scendingly conferred by his cultural consumption on 'this simple peasant'
(1.133), who (as Bourdieu notes of the middle-brow) struggles with such a
mixture of 'anxiety and avidity' to close 'the gap between his knowledge
and recognition'.⁴⁷

> *Sly*:   Is not a comonty
>   A Christmas gambol or a tumbling trick?
> *Page*: No, my good lord, it is more pleasing stuff.
> *Sly*:   What, household stuff?
> *Page*:   It is a kind of history.
> *Sly*:   Well, we'll see't. Come, madam wife, sit by my side
>   And let the world slip; we shall ne'er be younger. (2.137–42)

Sly's question about its household utility leads editors to suspect that he
takes comedy not for a 'comonty' but a *commodity*; and the emendment is
appealing since the commodification of art is confronted by Shakespeare
with a self-reflexivity alien to other Elizabethan dramatists, who, as
McLuskie notes, unanimously despise those who buy their culture like
clothes: 'haunting theatres, to sit there like a popinjay, only to learn
speeches which afterward they furnish to maintain table talk'; or spouting
'nothing but pure Shakespeare and shreds of poetry gathered at theatres'.⁴⁸
By contrast, from the moment when Sly lets his world slip into theatrical
illusion, Shakespearean culture will advertise itself as a product that transforms the paying public into private patrons, dignifying the playhouse spectators, in the words of the Prologue to *Henry V*, as 'gentles all' (8). As Louis
Montrose concurs, throughout the plays 'the status of the popular audience
is elevated in acknowledgement of the imaginative authority theatre con-
fers upon them . . . gentility is conferred upon those empowered to judge
the play . . . and in each play power to confer such gentility resides in the
players themselves'.⁴⁹ So, when, at the beginning of his career, Puck invites

the audience to 'Give me your hands, if we be friends' (*Dream* 5.1.423); or when, at the end, the Prologue of *Henry VIII* pledges that 'The first and happiest hearers of the town' will 'see away their shilling' as intimates of 'the very persons of our noble story' (12; 26), Shakespeare's strategy is to gentrify his playgoers as interlopers at exclusive celebrations in houses of nobility, like the Lord who commissions the comedy for Sly. Thus, in an era when theatre entrepreneurs were accruing huge fortunes from the modern world's first mass medium, Shakespearean drama inverted its economic conditions by representing itself to both its producers and consumers as a disinterested benefaction of some Maecenas, such as a Prince of Wales, King of France or Navarre, or Duke of Milan, Vienna, Illyria, Messina, Verona, Ephesus or Athens: 'All I will tell you is, that the Duke hath dined. Get your apparel together, good strings to your beards, new ribbons to your pumps; meet presently at the palace. Every man look to his part: for the short and the long of it is, our play is preferred' (*Dream* 4.2.32–7).

Mediating between the egalitarian playhouse, where professional entertainers purvey their cultural product, as Montrose says, according to a commercial contract 'freely entered into by the parties', and 'a royal court or noble hall, where the retainers perform in homage to their betters',[50] Shakespearean theatre invites its consumers to insinuate themselves with the actors on their entry to the palace. For David Wiles, there is something literally *patronizing* about this inducement of the paying public to intrude themselves 'as fellow commoners alongside the players, granted through their visit to the playhouse vicarious access to an elite gathering to which they would not normally be admitted', which he interprets as proof of how intimately Shakespearean drama is 'integrated with upper-class celebration'.[51] Yet this adoption of what Bourdieu characterizes as 'Thersites' viewpoint' risks missing what he insists is the function of the art game, which is as the field in which the upwardly mobile 'cash-in' economic capital to obtain cultural capital for themselves and their descendants.[52] It overlooks, in this sense, how Shakespeare's theatre was shaped by the very rules of the field his plays helped to produce, when they metadramatized themselves not as consecrations of nobility but as opportunities for social struggle and advancement. In nineteenth-century Paris, according to Bourdieu, 'art for art's sake' was the creed of those who wore their culture, like a dandy's costume, in denial of all sordid commercialism, asserting, with Flaubert, that 'Nobody is rich enough to pay us. A work of art has no commercial value.'[53] Likewise in Elizabethan London, Shakespeare's difference, it seems, was to ironize his labour as 'No more yielding than a dream' to those 'Gentles' who did 'not reprehend' its 'weak and idle theme' as their commercial loss (*Dream* 5.1.413–15). Thus, art was autonomized by this dramatist as a priceless 'court cloak' on that journey from the province to the palace of which his own career was the prototype and pattern:

See you these clothes? Say you see them not and think me no gentleman born: you were best say these robes were not gentlemen born: give me the lie; do; and try whether I am not now a gentleman born . . . and have been so any time these four hours. (*The Winter's Tale* 5.2.131–7)

Meeting a troupe of actors twice on the same road, Ratsey, the high-wayman hero of a 1605 pamphlet, is scandalized that they purport to 'serve such an honourable Personage' one day and another the next. Taking back the forty shillings he paid them, the gangster therefore lectures them to give up their deceit of patronage and make an 'honest profession' of themselves in town, where they will become good businessmen playing roles like Hamlet, 'for I have heard of some that have gone to London very meanly, and have come to be exceedingly wealthy'. 'Rise up, Sir Simon Two Shares and a Half', Ratsey therefore jokes, as he dubs their leader 'the first Knight that ever was Player in England'.[54] The gibe is thought to be aimed at managers such as Edward Alleyn as much as at shareholders such as Shakespeare; yet Ratsey's advice to renounce the figment of patronage betrays a classic *misrecognition* of the inverted economics of Shakespearean theatre, which would, of course, actually carry so many Hamlets to their knight-hoods. Licensed under the flag of convenience of some 'Baron or other honourable personage,' Shakespeare's drama was legitimated precisely by pretending to the gratuitousness of an aristocratic gift, oblivious of its routine dependence on groundlings 'capable of nothing but inexplicable dumb-shows and noise' (*Hamlet* 3.2.11). As Fredric Jameson writes, the moment of Shakespearean theatre was when 'nostalgia for an organic social order opposed the phantasmagoria of "imagination" to the bustling commercial activity all around it'.[55] It was when profits began to pile up from the Globe after 1600 that the contradiction became acute between this pretence of *noblesse oblige* and a reality where, in Andrew Gurr's words, 'companies were not doing what pleasure-loving lord commanded, but what brought most money'.[56] Then, Shakespeare's staging of the ruin of the nobility in *King Lear*, *Coriolanus* and *Antony and Cleopatra* provoked revulsion from those 'mechanic slaves / With greasy aprons' (5.2.208) before whom the crisis was displayed; while in *Timon of Athens* the actual bankruptcy of the patronage system cued a curse on the 'slaves and peasants' of the 'detestable town' who had feasted on the show (2.2.165; 4.1.33). But until Prospero at last untied the 'art to enchant' from the field of power, the fiction was maintained that Shakespearean theatre was indeed what this Duke asserts: some arbitrary 'provision' or 'vanity of mine art', which, having been created *ex nihilo* by princely fiat, would as soon be withdrawn from its tantalized consumers – like the 'great globe itself' – to 'Leave not a rack behind' (*The Tempest* Epi.14; 1.2.28; 4.1.41; 156).

'Graves at my command / Have wak'd their sleepers . . .' boasts Prospero, 'By my so potent Art' (5.1.48); and, as Stephen Orgel claims, it does seem that *The Tempest* brings to a climax the Renaissance idea of an art, not for art, still less for its audience, but for aristocracy, and that the masque within the play is 'Shakespeare's essay on the power of the royal imagination, unique in that its creator is the monarch at its centre'. Shakespeare's depiction of Prospero as a royal illusionist 'derives from profound understanding of court theatre', Orgel states; yet it is exactly at this moment, when 'the last of the great house lords' attains absolute control of the stage,[57] that the play envisages an art freed from power as much as economics. For if Ariel is indeed, as critics suppose, 'a celebration of the boy player', and his 'rabble' of 'meaner fellows' (4.1.35–6) Shakespeare's fantasy of the 'quality' of the acting profession (1.2.193), it is the end of patronage when the actor who has played a nymph and harpy and 'presented Ceres' (4.1.167) is set free, 'like an apprentice bound in indentures and chafing to be released'.[58] Prospero's abjuration of his 'rough magic' (5.1.50) – the 'courtly aesthetic' that hinged, as Gary Schmidgall writes, on scenery, lighting, dance and music[59] – can be read, in this light, only as the renunciation by power of its claim on art as homage. For while 'the King remained the patron of his acting troupe', and his plays 'fitted smoothly into court life', even Kernan admits that 'Shakespeare's patronage art always transcended his immediate occasion', and that 'Nowhere does Renaissance art speak of its powers with more confidence' than here, where it is implied that 'art is now at least as interesting as the political power it is paid to serve'. By releasing Ariel, then, 'Shakespeare claims a value for his theatrical art' beyond its service to the mighty, like the value attached to 'the "absolute" work of art' by painters such as Vasari.[60] Yet the fact that this enfranchisement occurs only with Prospero's consent underlines the paradox that it is in the courts of princes that the autonomy of art is first conceived, and that, even as Shakespeare writes, it is power which both licenses the literary field and renders it fraught with fragility and contradiction.

'Gentle breath of yours my sails / Must fill, or else my project fails' (Epi.11): conventionally interpreted as 'the supreme moment of balance, when art can protest its own right to exist, immune to the sceptical challenge of the world',[61] the ending of *The Tempest* in fact situates this project of autonomization historically as a compact between power and the public within the early modern market for symbolic goods. Shakespeare's 'prime duke' will be relieved of his responsibility for legitimating the 'liberal arts', of which he has been guarantor during their Renaissance development (1.2.72), in return for their future liberation from those mercenary bonds that chain them to consumer demand and expectation. Thus, Prospero begs the new commercial public to prove its gentility, and 'release me from my bands / With the help of your good hands' (Epilogue 9), in a negotiation that exactly foretells the process outlined by Bourdieu, when with 'the ending of dependence on a patron . . . artists and writers notice that this liberty is no more than submission to the laws of the market', and so affirm

'the irreducibility of a work of art to the status of merchandise'.[62] This is
a transaction that thereby suggests how, rather than investing aesthetic
value in Shakespearean drama, we should see that drama as the origin of
our valuation of the aesthetic. In Bourdieu's account, the invention of a
pure aesthetic progressed at different rates, 'according to the society and
artistic field in question'. In France it was the absolute monarchy that ultimately prevented cultural producers from escaping the pole of power; but
the abdication of Shakespeare's Duke explains why, under pretext of protection by a nominal prince, his playhouse was able to anticipate 'art for
art's sake' by over two centuries.[63] For the mutual 'indulgence' Prospero
craves – 'As you from crimes would pardoned be' (19) – is nothing less than
that 'pure gaze' of aesthetic appreciation which comes when art is at last
emancipated from the imperatives of both patronage and profit.

'It shapes the fantasies by which it is shaped', declared a celebrated new
historicist chiasmus of Shakespearean drama, 'begets that by which it is
begotten';[64] and Bourdieu's study of *The Rules of Art* suggests how this
aphorism might allow literary criticism 'to bypass the opposition between
internal and external analysis' when articulated by his history of the literary field as 'a world apart, subject to its own laws'. New historicism has
been much concerned to explore both the privileged poetics of Shakespeare's playtexts and the privileged conditions of his playgoers; but
Bourdieu proposes that it is through his notion 'of a homology between
the space of works defined by their symbolic content and the space of their
positions in the field of production' that this 'opposition between structure
and history will be overcome'.[65] After the new historicism, therefore,
Bourdieu helps us to grasp how by dreaming of 'cloud-capped towers' and
'gorgeous palaces' (4.1.152) at Elsinore or Knowsley in playhouses on
Bankside, Shakespeare's theatre was 'stripped of mercantile traces', as
Stephen Mullaney images 'the place of the stage' in *Pericles*, 'including its
designation as a marketplace'.[66] For the long road to artistic freedom that
took the dramatist from Stratford to Southwark via the Earl of Derby's
Lancashire household was replicated in each of his plays, by this account,
in their negation of the pole of commerce by the pole of power. In this
way they fulfilled their function as symbolic goods – in a market where
Ann Jennalie Cook confirms that 'quality of plays and players was equated
with quality of audience'[67] of demarcating the distinction between their
'gentle hearers' and 'they / That come to hear a merry bawdy play . . . with
such a show / As fool and fight is' (*Henry VIII* Pro.13–19). Bourdieu would
argue that it is by reason of his reflexivity about this exchange of economic
for cultural capital that, like Flaubert, Shakespeare is the truest analyst of
Shakespeare. For though they present themselves as art for art, by marrying patrician patron with paying public, his plays in fact remind us that
'over that art' which they say 'adds' to commerce, is an art that commerce
makes:

This is an art
Which does mend nature – change it rather – but
The art itself is nature.   (*The Winter's Tale* 4.4.95–7)

Notes

1 F. A. Bailey, 'The Elizabethan Playhouse at Prescot, Lancashire', *Transactions of the Historical Society of Lancashire and Cheshire* 103 (1951), 69–81.
2 P. Burke, *Popular Culture in Early Modern Europe* (London: Temple Smith, 1978, 97.
3 K. P. Wentersdorf, 'The Queen's Company in Scotland in 1589', *Theatre Research International* 6 (Winter 1980), 33–6.
4 Jerzy Limon, *Gentlemen of a Company: English Players in Central and Easter Europe, 1590–1660* (Cambridge: Cambridge University Press, 1985), p. 20.
5 S. Greenblatt, *Learning to Curse: Essays in Early Modern Culture* (London: Routledge, 1990), p. 62.
6 Limon, *Gentlemen of a Company*, p. 20.
7 K. McLuskie, 'The Poets' Royal Exchange: Patronage and Commerce in Early Modern Drama', in *Patronage, Politics and Literary Traditions in England, 1558–1658*, ed. Cedric C. Brown (Detroit: Wayne State University Press, 1991), p. 126.
8 June, Schlueter, 'English Actors in Kassel, Germany, during Shakespeare's Time', in *Medieval and Renaissance Drama in England*, ed. John Pitcher 10 (Madison: Fairleigh Dickinson University Press, 1998), pp. 245–7.
9 P. Burke, *The Fabrication of Louis XIV* (New Haven: Yale University Press, 1992), p. 58.
10 A. Kernan, *Shakespeare, the King's Playwright: Theater in the Stuart Court, 1603–1613* (New Haven: Yale University Press, 1995), p. 161.
11 R. Dutton, *Mastering the Revels: The Regulation and Censorship of English Renaissance Drama* (Basingstoke: Macmillan, 1991), p. 312.
12 Kernan, *Shakespeare*, pp. 5, 14, 190.
13 Dutton, *Mastering the Revels*, p. 145.
14 E. K. Chambers, *The Elizabethan Stage* (Oxford: Clavendon Press, 1923), IV, p. 256.
15 Kernan, *Shakespeare*, pp. 178, 180, 195.
16 M. A. Skura, *Shakespeare the Actor and the Purposes of Playing* (Chicago: Chicago University Press, 1993), pp. 18, 30, 85.
17 A. Somerset, 'How Chances It They Travel: Provincial Touring, Playing Places, and the King's Men', *Shakespeare Survey* 47 (Cambridge: Cambridge University Press, 1994), p. 54.
18 P. Bourdieu, 'Intellectual Field and Creative Project', trans. S. France, in *Knowledge and Control: New Directions for the Sociology of Education*, ed. M. Young (London: Collier-Macmillan, 1971).
19 C. Calhoun, 'Habitus, Field and Capital: the Question of Historical Specificity', in *Bourdieu: Critical Perspectives*, eds C. Calhoun, E. LiPuma and M. Postone (Cambridge: Polity Press, 1993), p. 68.
20 S. Lash, 'Pierre Bourdieu: Cultural Economy and Social Change', in *ibid.*, p. 193.

21 Calhoun, 'Habitus, Field and Capital', p. 68.
22 S. Greenblatt, *Shakespearean Negotiations: The Circulation of Social Energy in Renaissance England* (Oxford: Oxford University Press, 1990), p. 18.
23 L. J. D. Wacquant, 'Bourdieu in America: Notes on the Transatlantic Importation of Social Theory', in *Pierre Bourdieu: Critical Perspectives*, eds C. Calhoun, E. LiPuma and M. Postone (Cambridge: Polity Press, 1993), p. 237.
24 R. Brubaker, 'Social Theory as Habitus', in *ibid.*, p. 162.
25 S. Greenblatt, 'Towards a Poetics of Culture', in *The New Historicism*, ed. A. Veeser (London: Routledge, 1989), p. 12.
26 S. Alpers, *Rembrandt's Enterprise: The Studio and the Market* (Chicago: Chicago University Press, 1998), pp. 94, 100.
27 Bourdieu, 'Intellectual Field and Creative Project', p. 162.
28 *Ibid.*
29 A. Viala, *Naissance de l'écrivain: Sociologie de la littérature à l'âge classique* (Paris: Minuit, 1985).
30 Bourdieu, 'Intellectual Field and Creative Project', p. 162.
31 P. Bourdieu, *The Rules of Art: Genesis and Structure in the Literary Field*, trans. S. Emmanuel (Cambridge: Polity Press, 1996), p. 367, n. 1.
32 C. Jouhard, 'Power and Literature: the Terms of the Exchange, 1624–42', in *The Administration of Aesthetics: Censorship, Political Criticism, and the Public Sphere*, ed. R. Burt (Minneapolis: University of Minnesota Press, 1994), p. 34.
33 Bourdieu, 'Intellectual Field and Creative Project', p. 163.
34 Bourdieu, *Rules of Art*, pp. 61, 81.
35 *Ibid.*, p. 58.
36 W. D. Macray (ed.) *The Pilgrimage to Parnassus* (Oxford: Clarendon Press, 1986), p. 54.
37 J. Marston, *The First Part of Antonio and Mellida*, ed. G. K. Hunter (London: Edward Arnold, 1965), p. 3; McLuskie, 'The Poets', pp. 130–3.
38 Ben, Jonson, *Sejanus His Fall*, ed. W. F. Bolton (London: Ernest Benn, 1996), p. 5.
39 Bourdieu, *Rules of Art*, p. 58.
40 *Ibid.*, p. 215.
41 S. McMillin, *The Elizabethan Theatre and 'The Book of Sir Thomas More'* (Ithaca: Cornell University Press, 1987), pp. 57, 71.
42 Bourdieu, *Rules of Art*, p. 52.
43 *Ibid.*, p. 21.
44 W. Shakespeare, *The Arden Shakespeare: The Taming of the Shrew*, ed. B. Morris (London: Methuen, 1981), p. 63.
45 P. Bourdieu, *The Field of Cultural Production*, trans. R. Johnson (Cambridge: Polity Press, 1993), p. 37.
46 S. Schoenbaum, *William Shakespeare: A Documentary Life* (Oxford: Oxford University Press, 1975), pp. 115–19.
47 P. Bourdieu, *Distinction: A Social Critique of the Judgement of Taste*, trans. Anon. (London: Routledge, 1984), pp. 315, 327.
48 T. Dekker, *The Gull's Hornbook*, ed. E. D. Pendry (London: Edward Arnold, 1967), p. 73; Macray, *Pilgrimage to Parnassus*, p. 56; McLuskie, 'The Poets', p. 128.

49 L. Montrose, *The Purpose of Playing: Shakespeare and the Politics of the Elizabethan Theatre* (Chicago: Chicago University Press, 1996), p. 201.

50 *Ibid.*

51 D. Wiles, 'The Carnivalesque in "A Midsummer Night's Dream"', in *After Bakhtin: Shakespeare and the Politics of Carnival,* eds C. Brown and R. Knowles (London: Macmillan, 1998), pp. 67, 78.

52 Bourdieu, *Rules of Art,* p. 191; Bourdieu, *Distinction,* p. 125.

53 Bourdieu, *Rules of Art,* p. 81.

54 J. Munro, *The Shakespeare Allusion Book* (London: Chatto & Windus, 1909), p. 154.

55 F. Jameson, *The Political Unconscious: Narrative as a Socially Symbolic Act* (Ithaca: Cornell University Press, 1981), p. 148.

56 A. Gurr, *The Shakespearean Stage: 1574–1642* (Cambridge: Cambridge University Press, 1980), p. 29.

57 S. Orgel, *The Illusion of Power: Political Theater in the English Renaissance* (Berkeley: University of California Press, 1975), p. 45; Skura, *Shakespeare the Actor,* p. 201.

58 D. Mann, *The Elizabethan Player: Contemporary Stage Representation* (London: Routledge, 1991), p. 41.

59 G. Schmidgall, *Shakespeare and the Courtly Aesthetic* (Berkeley: University of California Press, 1981).

60 Kernan, *Shakespeare,* pp. 159, 181, 185, 201.

61 P. Edwards, *Shakespeare and the Confines of Art* (London: Methuen, 1968), p. 153.

62 Bourdieu, *Field of Cultural Production,* p. 112.

63 *Ibid.,* p. 113.

64 L. Montrose, '"A Midsummer Night's Dream" and the Shaping Fantasies of Elizabethan Culture', in *New Historicism and Renaissance Drama,* eds R. Dutton and R. Wilson (London: Longman, 1992), p. 130.

65 Bourdieu, *Rules of Art,* p. 205.

66 S. Mullaney, *The Place of the Stage: License, Play, and Power in Renaissance England* (Chicago: Chicago University Press, 1988), p. 139.

67 A. J. Cook, *The Privileged Playgoers of Shakespeare's London, 1576–1642* (Princeton: Princeton University Press, 1981), p. 266.

Between idolatry and astrology: modes of temporal repetition in *Romeo and Juliet*

In her study of Shakespeare's histories, Phyllis Rackin observes that 'the practice of historiography has become a subject of intense controversy and radical transformation' within the academy, and certainly it seems that the thorny question of the relationship between text and history still haunts literary studies of the Renaissance.[1] Although implicitly problematized by new historicism, in fact this issue has seldom been directly addressed by new historicist critics, who, as Steven Mullaney points out, have 'primarily focussed on discrete historical moments and [been] silent about processes of historical change'. In its use of the historical fragment or anecdote, new historicism has elegantly introduced a postmodern awareness of temporal relativism or 'randomization' into the field of Renaissance studies; however, new speculations about the relationship between textuality and temporality have recently begun to emerge in Shakespeare studies.[2] What may be a new intellectual trend is less indebted to quasi-Foucauldian considerations of history as a conflict-ridden site of subversion and containment than to a postmodern suspicion of history – that is, of time conceived of as linear and teleological or end-driven. In this respect the emergent set of concerns affords some interesting parallels to the speculations on time of postmodern thinkers such as Nietzsche, Heidegger, Kristeva and above all Derrida, and is sometimes explicitly influenced by this intellectual tradition.

Two important texts in this connection are Patricia Parker's *Shakespeare from the Margins* (1996) and Ned Lukacher's *Time Fetishes: The Secret History of Eternal Recurrence* (1998).[3] Both these authors – albeit in very different ways – identify a textual differing of the diachronic ordering of time and history as a recurring effect within the Shakespearean corpus. Parker's book reads the Shakespearean reconfiguring of temporality primarily as a literary device, in a brilliant analysis of Shakespeare's fondness for the rhetorical trope of the preposterous; she defines this trope as performing 'a reversal of priority, precedence and ordered sequence which also disrupts the linear orders of succession and following'.[4] Lukacher's book, on the other hand, offers an explicitly deconstructive reading of Shakespearean and other texts which stresses Shakespeare's philosophical indebt-edness to classical models of cyclical time, which he argues resemble what Nietzsche called eternal recurrence. These two studies serve to remind us of the fundamental ambivalence at the heart of Renaissance ideas of tem-porality, whereby its Christian view of time (as linear history versus unmov-ing eternity) was entwined or crossed with a circular, repetitive timing which had agricultural and astrological as well as philosophical dimensions. Similar themes have been explored in works by Renaissance critics such as Francis Barker and Michel Jeanneret, while historians such as D. R. Woolf and Nicholas Campion have re-emphasized the extent to which many Renaissance thinkers rediscovered the ancients' cyclical and repetitive version of time in works by classical writers such as Plato and Polybius.[5]

What I want to suggest in this chapter is some of the ways in which *Romeo and Juliet* puts the putative singularity and linearity of time and history into question. In its combination of frantic temporal acceleration with what might be described as a turning backwards of time (in the form of the repetitive and cyclical timing of calendrical and festive modes of memorialization) this play's imagery encapsulates the perceived multi-faceted character of time in the late sixteenth century. For as both histori-cal allusion and temporality in general are 'textualized' within the 'short time' of the tragedy, so these elements are also differed, doubled and extended, in a way which requires us to expand both our critical and our temporal perceptions.

I read Shakespeare's Juliet as the textual site through which this late Renaissance inconsistency about time – which is also an awareness of an inconsistency or rift within time itself – becomes manifest. I owe a debt, in this formulation, to Julia Kristeva's important but controversial essay 'Women's Time', in which she allies female subjectivity, and a feminine *jouis-sance* in particular, with two modes of time – repetitive or cyclical, and mon-umental (or eternal) – in opposition to the linearity of historical time. Kristeva notes that: 'female subjectivity as it gives itself up to intuition becomes a problem with respect to a certain conception of time: time as project, teleology, linear and prospective unfolding: time as departure, pro-gression and arrival – in other words, the time of history'.[6] What I shall suggest here, however, is that not only does Juliet peculiarly encompass or attract to herself the 'feminine' aspects of temporality identified by Kristeva; she also has an important connection with two apaprently contrasting aspects of time that have a historical or teleological as well as a cyclical or repetitive significance. These different timings briefly cohere in the play's focus upon a particular calendrical moment that, while it is highly specific, is also embedded in an ambivalent festive tradition encompassing both cel-ebration and destruction. Yet as the play ends we are implicitly reminded that these contrasting temporalities also cross or converge, equally briefly, in all acts of remembrance, whether these assume religious or aesthetic form.

Juliet's multi-faceted significance in respect of time is adumbrated on her first appearance, in Act 1 scene 3, when the Nurse's tedious narrative of her weaning splits her name into two suggestive syllables – as the 'Jule' who is also, since she always responds thus, 'ay', or continuous: ' "Yea", quoth my husband, "fall'st upon thy face? / Thou wilt fall backward when thou comest to age, / Wilt thou not Jule?" It stinted, and said "Ay" ' (1.3.47–8).[7] While this nominal splitting appears to equate Juliet, on the one hand, with the devouring mouth as *gula* or *gueule* (in Latin and French) – a conventional figure for forward-moving time – it implies that she also has a mysterious affinity with time's mysterious non-linear existence, as eternity, or 'ay'. Yet if we recombine them, these two syllables metamorphose Juliet into 'July', configuring her as a feminine personification of her birth month, and hence as a figure whose highly individual fate is peculiarly embedded in a calendrical cycle of temporal repetition. We are told by the Nurse and her mother, of course, that Juliet's birthday will be on the night of 31 July or Lammas Eve, a 'fortnight and odd days' after the Capulet ball.

The July setting of Shakespeare's play contrasts strikingly with that of his main source, Arthur Brooke's *Romeus and Juliet*, where the lovers first meet at a Christmas feast, and their tragedy does not escalate until Easter. One effect of the late summer dating of the tragedy is to reinvest late July with a carnival significance comparable to that which it seems to have formerly enjoyed, in pre-Reformation culture. This time of the year was still distinguished by some important forms of popular festivity, most notably pageants and fairs; before the Reformation, however, it had been full of important holy or saints' days. And at the same time, it also had enormous importance in the astrological time-reckonings of antiquity – an importance still recognized not only in the popular Elizabethan almanac but even in the almanac or liturgical calendar used by the Church of England in the Book of Common Prayer. In the calendar which prefaces Cranmer's 1559 prayer book, in fact, while the only saint's day which has been retained for veneration in the month of July is that of the apostle St James (on 25 July), the calendar notes the passage of the Sun into the astrological sign of Leo (it gives no details about the Moon) and also records the date of the beginning of the dog days – a detail to which I will return. These astrological details are retained in late sixteenth-century editions of the Prayer Book, where several saints' days are also restored.[8]

Shakespeare is thought by a number of critics to have written *Romeo and Juliet* around the same time as *A Midsummer Night's Dream*, possibly in late 1595 or 1596, and certainly it seems that the 'finding out' or consultation of an almanac is just as relevant to the concerns of this play as it is to the rehearsals of the mechanicals in *A Dream*, where Bottom calls for 'A calender, a calender – look in the almanac, find out moonshine, find our moonshine' (3.1.45–6). But while, in the comedy, the mechanicals need an almanac in order to know whether the moon will shine during their production of Pyramus and Thisbe (as indeed it does, in the form of the new moon which has been awaited so eagerly by Theseus and Hippolyta as the signal for their wedding), in the tragedy, the play's implicit concern is rather with plotting the sun's passage in late July – together with the peculiar effects of the doubling of its heat at this time, which was termed the 'canicular' or dog days. In the late sixteenth century, the dog days were calculated as extending from mid-July to mid-August, since this was the time of the heliacal rising of the brightest star in the sky, when it was once more visible on the horizon just before dawn. The star in question was Sirius, the dog-star, chief star of the constellation Canis Major, and regarded by the ancients as the near double of the sun. In the Prayer Book of 1559 the dog days are listed as beginning on 7 July and ending on 17 August, but the dates progressed forwards owing to the phenomenon of equinoctial procession.

This astrological context has a particular relevance to the lovers' definition, in the play's opening chorus, as 'star-crossed', as I will show. But while its several references to the 'fateful' influences of the stars emphasize a pagan alternative – if also a partial analogue – to the Calvinist doctrine of predestination, like the Elizabethan almanac, *Romeo and Juliet* interweaves this remnant of pagan astrological lore with traces of another model of temporal repetition, in the form of a pre-Reformation (and possibly also a recusant) calendrical piety. My contention, however, is that none of these temporal allusions has a simple or singular meaning, but serves rather to illuminate the tragedy's significance through a complex process of semiotic differentiation and even negation, as the combination of piety and festivity associated with major saints' days *before* the Reformation is replaced by the paradoxical piety of the lovers' extreme passion, whereby sexual desire is troped both as pilgrimage and as image-worship. One implication seems to be that, far from being either careful readers of almanacs or observant Catholics, the lovers fail to observe a range of different calendrical signals which might conceivably have altered their fates. Another, however, is that their tragedy cannot be made sense of according to a singular time scheme, but instead requires us to combine different versions of time, and, specifically, different types of information about late July – calendrical and religious as well as astrological and folkloric – in order to account for it.

In accounts of the Christian liturgical calendar, the month of July is sometimes characterized as marking the beginning of the half-year of 'secular time'; however, Eamon Duffy has re-emphasized the importance of this month in the context of pre-Reformation popular piety in England:

> A major feast of England's most important saint, Thomas Becket, the translation of his relics, fell on 7 July ... In the same month there were ... the feasts of St Mary Magdalene [22], St Margaret [20], St James the Apostle [25], and St Anne [26] ... all were immensely popular and very widely kept.[9]

Duffy observes also that before the Reformation the great civic festivities of the year (which had a strong religious dimension usually expressed in pageant or play) were often held at the end of July or on the first day of August (Lammas):

> At Lincoln the greatest convergence of civic and sacred ceremonial came on Saint Anne's day, at the end of July, when the city gilds organized an elaborate series of pageants. Even at York, where the most famous Corpus Christi cycle in England was normally played on the feast day itself, the Creed play and the Paternoster plays which sometimes replaced the Corpus Christi plays were performed in Lammastide.[10]

Many of the most popular saints' days of this period had been excised from the liturgical calendar in 1536 at the Reformation, partly to increase the time available for agricultural labour; all feast days falling in harvest, from 1 July to 29 September, were abolished, excepting only feasts of the Apostles, the Blessed Virgin and St George. In July, therefore, only the feast day of St James the Apostle, the patron saint of pilgrims, which was on 25 July, was initially retained, in quite splendid isolation. (Before the Reformation even this date had enjoyed an additional significance, because it was then shared by St James with the gigantic Christ-bearer – or light-bearer – St Christopher.) Yet what is often overlooked in accounts of the reformers' attacks on the cults of the saints is that it was not until 1547–48 that the images of saints were ordered to be removed from churches, or defaced.[11] Indeed, both the slowness and the uncertainty of the process of iconoclastic reform was attested to on the accession of Elizabeth I in 1559: on the one hand, there was another wave of image destruction; on the other, many saints' days were reintroduced into the Prayer Book, although not as red letter or full holy days. (This process of partial reintroduction continued through Elizabeth's reign and into that of James I.) A 1563 Convocation voiced the dissatisfaction of many clergy at the continued existence of saints' days; but it seems that purging the calendar was easier to proclaim than enforce. David Cressy points out that law terms were still marked by the ancient religious festival days, as were the legal calendars of all courts operating by civil rather than common law, while popular almanacs (which listed far more saints' days than the Prayer Book calender) likewise kept in mind memories of holy days that the reformers wanted to be forgotten.[12] Amidst this uneven process of cultic extirpation, the end of July and the beginning of August seems to have retained a symbolic significance, primarily as marking the official end of summer, the first fruits of the harvest and (specifically on 1 August, or Lammas), the time of a quarterly payment of rents and the opening of common lands for pastures. A catalogue of fairs in 1661 showed that fifty-eight towns had fairs on St James's Day, 28 on Lammas; it was probably no coincidence, also, that James I and his queen, Anna, were crowned on 25 July, the date of St James's Day and the eve of St Anne's Day.[13]

Thus, although officially abolished by Protestantism, it seems clear that the pre-Reformation calender of holy days (with its attendent connotations of idolatry or image-worship) must have continued to exert a strong imaginative and memorial influence on middle-of-the-road Protestants. And in areas with a developed culture of recusancy, such as Lancashire and Warwickshire, this memorial survival would presumably have been far more complete. As a young man growing up in Warwickshire (where there were two churches of St James the Great in his immediate vicinity: one in Stratford-upon-Avon itself, and another in his grandfather's village of Snitterfield), Shakespeare would have been especially aware of this festive calendar. The memorial importance of the abolished holy days would naturally have been augmented for the son of a (belatedly) recusant father, most of whose mother's family, the Ardens, also retained their Catholic faith. Yet (as we know from both Hamlet and Jacques Derrida) remembrance is never a simple act of repetition, since the memory which remains will always differ from the remembered object, name or event, typically expanding its significance through diverse metonymic or metaphoric associations. Before the Reformation, this process of memorial accretion had already built complex imaginative and aesthetic structures around the cults of individual saints which reformers would see as a dangerous supplement to their original religious function. And in Shakespeare's post-Reformation play, while the traces of these cults, where discernible, may have reminded some theatregoers of Catholic piety, the dramatic and secular context of these signs suggests that their emblematic function once again exceeds any dogmatic system of interpretation.

A saint's holy day equates his or her presumed date of death with a *dies natalis* or birthday in heaven, as a saint. And in *Romeo and Juliet,* the close temporal connection between Juliet's birthdate and her death configures the lovers' double death (which occurs, on the evidence of the play, some ten days before the anniversary of her birth) as the site or occasion for another quasi-festive memorialization. So we are told at the end of the play: 'That whiles Verona by that name is known, / There shall no figure at such rate be set / As that of true and faithful Juliet' (5.3.299–301). This conclusion gives material (albeit secular) form to Romeo's inaugural perception of Juliet, at the Capulet ball, as a 'dear saint' to whose (bodily) shrine he must make pilgrimage as a *romero* or pilgrim; in John Florio's *A New World of Words* (1598) he notes 'Romeo, as Romitaggio, *a roamer, a wanderer, a Palmer for devotion sake*'.[14] But in their two families' choice of the striking memorial device of two golden statues, the play's conclusion is also acutely problematic from a Reformation perspective. Indeed, it can be interpreted in several different ways. Is it a mistaken act of idolatry paralleling and reminding us of the lovers' own transference of the language of worship from divine to mutable objects of adoration? *The Second Tome of Homelyes*, published in 1563, condemns 'the glorious gylte images and ydolles [of the saints], all shynynge and glytterying with metall and stone, and covered with precious vestures', reminding us that it was just such *rich* images of the saints – presumably the gifts of wealthy donors who also signalled their social status through such acts – that were especially reviled by the reformers.[15] Or alternatively, the families' decision could serve as an oblique reminder to those in the audience who, like and yet unlike Juliet, were 'true and faithful' in their veneration of forgotten saints, and perhaps especially the those of late July and early August: saints whom Claude Gaignebet, for reasons which will become apparent below, describes as the 'canicular saints'.[16]

Only Saints Francis and Peter are specifically mentioned (as saints) in this play. Yet the names of two Capulet servants evoke those of saints who were directly connected with this period. The name of St Peter, with its Roman connotations, is both repeated and diminished in that of the Capulet serving man, Peter. This saint, to whose church Juliet is to be dragged by Capulet in order to marry Paris, 'on a hurdle', like a condemned traitor or recusant priest going to his death, formerly had 1 August or Lammas as one of his (now excised) feast days, when his miraculous liberation from prison was commemorated by the feast of St Peter-in-Chains. And the name of another Capulet servant, Samson, may echo as well as differ from not only the memory of the biblical Samson, but also that of another saint associated with this calendrical period: St Samson, whose feast was formerly held on 28 July.[17] (The name of Verona's 'holy' Friar Lawrence also evokes the feast day of Romeo's most famous post-apostolic martyr, St Lawrence, held a few days later on 10 August.) Yet it is the name of the other Capulet servant which begins Act 1 scene 1 of the play: 'Gregory'. This too was a familiar saint's name, including St Gregory the Great (sometimes called the apostle of the English), who had famously affirmed the legitimate use of icons. But it may also allude to Pope Gregory XIII, references to whose reformation of the calendar, in 1582, Steve Sohmer has recently deciphered in *Julius Caesar*.[18] Friar Lawrence comments to Paris on the abbreviated temporal perspective of the play: 'the time is very short'. In a manner both like and unlike the hasty lovers and their equally hasty families, Gregory had shortened time; in his case, because he had to jump over or omit ten days – a figurative bank of time – in order to correct the faulty Julian calendar. This faulty calendar had been created, of course, by Julius Caesar, the man who gave his name to the month of July.

The events of *Romeo and Juliet* appear to unfold in the third week of July. Yet, as pointed out by Sohmer, because of the ten-day gap between the old Julian calendar (still observed in England in the late sixteenth century) and the newly corrected Gregorian calendar, any spectator who recognized the validity of the new calendar might well have mentally adjusted the play's date-scheme: that is, moved it forward by ten days. And, given the imagery used by the lovers, a Catholic member of Shakespeare's audience might well have inferred that Capulet's 'old accustomed feast', held 'a fortnight and odd days' before Juliet's anticipated fourteenth birth-day (which according to the Julian calendar seems therefore to be some time around 14 or 15 July) is being held on what in the newly corrected Gregorian calendar was in fact the eve or feast day of Sts James and Christopher, 24 or 25 July. Certainly this was the only feast day in the latter part of July that was still observed by reformed as well as Catholic countries. It is as a 'pilgrim' and 'palmer' that Romeo presents himself at Juliet's 'shrine' – and finally, by implication, at her tomb, while the con-summation of his marriage to this earthly saint is assisted by the use of another attribute of St James – cords or ropes; the saint's traditional ability to untie the bonds of souls extended to a patronage of ropemakers. But James also has a biblical association with the motif of fire from heaven, since he shared with his brother John, Christ's most beloved disciple, the title of 'Boanerges', son of thunder; in the Gospel of St Luke, the brothers ask Jesus whether they should command fire to come down from heaven and consume the Samaritans who have refused to receive him (Luke 9, 51–6). And within the play, the motif of an uncanny fire with a specific temporality has an important resonance. But in the decision of Romeo, on his way to the Capulet ball, to be a light-bearer there seems also to be an oblique allusion to James's companion saint, St Christopher, who shared the same feast day: 'Give me a torch, I am not for this ambling; / Being but heavy, I will bear the light' (1.4.11–12). This saint, traditionally held to have been a giant from Canaan, owed his name to the story of his car-rying the Christ-child (the light of the world) over a river or sea. In the medieval hagiographic imagination, this evidently fictional narrative con-cerning the giant's assistance of a holy traveller allied him, like St James, with pilgrimage to the shrines of saints. Although St Christopher's legend and cult were singled out for attack by both Erasmus and Luther, his asso-ciation with the protection of travellers and pilgrims ensured him an espe-cial veneration which survives to this day.[19]

If there is also an allusion to St Christopher in the play's references to bearing a light, it seems in one sense extremely ironic, since one of this saint's additional but very important functions was to protect his devotees against a sudden death or *mors improvisa*. None the less, the motif of car-rying or bearing an uncanny light or fire that is also a burden is a central figurative element in *Romeo and Juliet*'s representation of death's strange duality, as the site of a mysterious chiasmus or reversal of meanings and perceptions which also appears to involve a disordering or crossing over of conventional temporality. In a multi-faceted and encrypted trope, Macbeth would image his own tragic transgression both as crossing a river and as leaping over time, as he appears to reject a linear model of time encom-passing both history (the present) and eternal judgement (the life to come): 'here, upon this bank and shoal of time / We'd jump the life to come'

(I.7.6–7). In *Romeo and Juliet*, however, this act has a calendrical specificity that is not only festive but also astrological.

For while the festive calendar of late July may plausibly have elicited
'rites of memory' on the part of Elizabethan Catholics as well as half-
hearted Protestants, it does not fully explain why that particular month was
chosen as the setting for what Friar Lawrence calls the lovers' 'violent
delights'. And here it is the residual trace, within Elizabethan calendrical
culture, of classical astrological lore and timing that accounts for their conversion of orderly festivity – in the form of Capulet's 'old accustomed feast'
– into an extremity of sexual heat or mutually devouring *jouissance*: a *jouis-
sance* of which *Ju*liet is, unconventionally, the most passionate advocate.
'Star-crossed' by a 'consequence yet hanging in the stars', the lovers seem
to have fallen under the ambivalent influence of another, stellar mode of
timing, and specifically that of the dog days, which the imagery of the play
implies to have recently commenced. So the nurse tells Romeo that the letter
which begins his name is 'the dog's name, "R" is for the –' (2.4.205), as
she inadvertently connects the growling 'ar' of the dog with the arse, while
Benvolio observes 'Now these hot days is the mad blood stirring' (3.1.4).
Associated visually with the 'enormous gaping jaws' of Leo, the chief
star of the greater dog constellation, Sirius, was described by classical
astronomers and astrologers as positioned in its mouth, like a fiery torch:
'The tip of his [Canis Major's] terrible jaw is marked by a star that keenest
of all blazes with a searing flame and him men call Serius.'[20] Traditionally,
the dog days were a time of dramatic climactic extremes, which the ancients
often figured by the fiery devouring mouth of the 'thirsty' greater dog. As
the burning heat of the sun was 'doubled' in this period, it was sometimes
compared to the phenomenon of *ekpyrosis*: this was the final conflagration
in which, according to the Stoics, both linear time and the world were to
end – only to be renewed, in a repeating cycle of fiery death and rebirth.
Manilius observes that:

> When the lion of Nemea [the constellation of Leo] lifts into view his enor-
> mous gaping jaws, the brilliant constellation of the Dog appears: it barks forth
> flame, raves with its fire, and doubles the burning heat of the sun. When it
> puts its torch to the earth and discharges its rays, the earth foresees its con-
> flagration, and tastes its ultimate fate . . . the world looks for another world
> to repair it.[21]

This ancient association of Sirius with a seasonal extreme that could be
fatal to crops extended both to humans and animals; in *The Gardens of
Adonis*, his discussion of the agricultural associations of this period in antiquity, Marcel Detienne concludes that the appearance of the dog-star was
believed to inaugurate a period of exaggerated imbalance in humans,
animals and plants, involving a switching between opposite extremes that
included a kind of sexual role reversal.[22] It was thought to be then that dogs

were most prone to rabies, yet the dangers of the period reputedly came from women as much as from dogs. The ancients had bizarrely opined that the menstrual blood of virgins, which they believed was incompletely purged because of their unbroken hymens, could become a dangerous poison in this period; Pliny even went so far as to posit a sympathetic affinity between the two 'poisons' (of the rabid dog, and unpurged menstrual blood).[23] But Hesiod had famously described women in general as having 'a doglike spirit', and as 'a flaming fire' that burns a man alive by consuming his sexual strength.[24] It is in the dog days, according to Hesiod, that 'women are most wanton, but men are feeblest, because Sirius parches head and knees, and the skin is dry through heat'.[25] Versions of these ancient superstitions survived in Europe, in popular contexts such as the almanac, until the seventeenth century; incredibly, it seems to have been quite widely believed that to have sexual intercourse or to take medicine during the dog days was dangerous.[26]

Something of the peculiar intensity of the dog days is communicated in the play's comical yet also enigmatic first scene, where the quibbles of Sampson and his fellow-servant Gregory on *coal–collar–choler* and *maidenhead* anticipate some of the play's recurring motifs, as they figuratively elide darkness with light/heat and mouths/necks/throats with the genitals:

Sampson   Gregory, on my word, we'll not carry coals.
Gregory   No, for then we should be colliers.
Samp.   I mean, and we be in choler, we'll draw.
Greg.   Ay, while you live, draw your neck out of collar . . .
Samp.   I will show myself a tyrant, when I have fought with the men, I will be civil with the maids; I will cut off their heads.
Greg.   The heads of the maids?
Samp.   Ay, the heads of the maids, or their maidenheads, take it in what sense thou wilt.
Greg.   They must take it in sense that feel it.   (1.1.1–26)

To 'carry coals' was a colloquialism for accepting an insult; however, the additional sense here is of an inert matter suddenly becoming inflamed, producing a 'choler' or rage (the hottest humour) that may lead either to literal death (the 'collar' of the hangman's noose) or to a sexual dying (the lost maidenheads).[27] The seasonal, or canicular, character of this rage is implied not just through Sampson's implied and clearly ironical association with the valour of his biblical namesake Samson, himself a famous riddle-teller, who had wrestled with the solar beast the lion, and was compared by St Jerome to the sun (whose astrological sign was Leo); but also in his attribution of choler to 'a dog of the house of Montague'.[28] At the same time, the servants' riddling exchanges introduce the crucial question of what 'sense' to make of such jests; the physical sense is clear enough, and may encompass an unspoken play on 'coal' and *cul*, French for the backside or arse. Yet given the biblical and religious associations of their names, the servants' quibbling may hint at another level of meaning, fusing their imagery of a seasonal – canicular – choler and desire with allusions to an iconoclastic repetition of martyrdom, in order to extirpate the cults of the saints (from the Latin *colere*, to venerate). Much iconoclasm, of course, simply involved cutting off the heads of saints' statues, and Huston Diehl has recently drawn attention to the way in which Protestant iconoclasts tended to trope saints' images as both sexualized and feminized.[29]

Later in the first act, the ambivalent throat/mouth imagery which seems to evoke the fiery mouth of the dog-star as well as a fiery sexuality is associated with Juliet herself. In fact, the Nurse remembers Juliet's weaning 'eleven years' ago through its metonymic association with an earthquake, in a troubling anticipation of that subterranean opening or 'maw' of the tomb in which the lovers will literally die. The devouring as well as the nurturing associations of the mouth are likewise implied in the lovers' first meetings; at the feast, Romeo tropes Juliet's mouth as 'saint's lips', while in Act 5 he reports a dream in which, as he imagines himself to be dead, she 'breath'd such life with kisses in my lips / That I reviv'd, and was an emperor' (5.1.8–9). But in the balcony scene their love is figuratively allied with the predatory mouths of hawks (the 'tassel-gentle' and the 'niesse'), and on her wedding-night, Juliet asks Night to 'Hood my unmanned blood, bating in my cheeks, / With thy black mantle' (3.2.14–15).[30] Through these avian tropes, the familiar trope of a sexual dying is expanded to encompass physical death as a mutual feasting, in which an important part of the erotic pleasure seems to be that time is itself consumed as it consumes the lovers; as Mercutio comments to Romeo on their way to the Capulet ball: 'we burn daylight' (1.4.43).

Yet the ancient astrologers had also agreed that, while the canicular days brought to most of the world a doubling of solar heat which could have *disastrous* consequences (connoting injuries resulting from the stars), it could none the less confer exceptional blessings. It was because of the extreme heat of this time, Detienne points out, that the most precious spices – frankincense, myrrh and balsam – could be harvested, and in Egyptian antiquity the heliacal rising of Sirius had marked a time of renewed fertility by heralding the annual flooding of the Nile, which simultaneously inaugurated the Egyptian new year. Roman astrologers consequently stressed the perplexing duality of Sirius' effects. So Aratus observed:

> No star comes on mankind more violently or causes more trouble when it departs. Now it rises shivering with cold, now it leaves a radiant world open to the heat of the Sun: thus it moves the world to either extreme and brings opposite effects. Those who . . . observe it ascending when it returns at its first rising learn of the various outcomes of harvest and seasons, what state of health lies in store, and what measure of harmony. It stirs up war and restores peace, and returning in different guise affects the world with the glance it

gives it and governs with its mien. Sure proof that the star has this power are its colour and the quivering of the fire that sparkles in its face. Hardly is it inferior to the Sun . . . In splendour it surpasses all other constellations.[31]

Certainly this play is full of ambivalent feasts – feasts whose festive or memorial function is always disturbingly altered. And it concludes with 'the feasting presence' of Juliet's body in the tomb, as that 'dearest morsel of the earth' upon which death's 'detestable maw' has 'gorg'd' itself. The imagery is consistent with Juliet's natal association with the Lammas festival of the first fruits of the harvest, yet her status as food seems also to have a sacrificial, quasi-eucharistic dimension.

In conclusion, then, my argument is that the calendrical subtext of this play invites us to reconsider late July – together with its momentary presiding deity or 'saint', Juliet – through several different temporal lenses, as it draws both on the perceived duality of Sirius' effects during the dog days and on the divided attitude of late Elizabethan society towards idolatry and the cults of the saints. The play seems to foreground both the disastrous and the benefic aspects of this month, which in a neglected crux from the last scene of the play is described by Escalus as 'the moneth of out-rage'; in Quarto 4, he asks that Verona 'Seal up the moneth of outrage for a while', although all later texts of the play replace 'moneth' with 'mouth' (5.3.215).

By interweaving images of festivity and death with a calendrical specificity, the play identifies this fiery devouring mouth-like month with a familiar aspect of time – as devouring time – but it also suggests that, in the moment of heightened festive as well as erotic intensity, time briefly devours itself. The 'candle-holder' or torch-bearer Romeo declares on first seeing Juliet that 'she doth teach the torches to burn bright' (1.5.43), and the subsequent intensity of the lovers' torch-like passion is seemingly so great that it can briefly illuminate the Capulet funeral vault – as well as interrupting the hostility which has formerly characterized Veronese society.

But what Romeo's torch finally and most specifically illuminates, in a suggestive elision of the astrological motif of the dog days (the devouring mouth represented by Sirius) with the religious theme of the saints' conversion of human suffering into sacred festivity, is Juliet as an uncanny feast. It seems, however, that this feast which is not a feast – just as Juliet is and is not a corpse – requires a final garnish, in the form of Romeo's death on the body of his beloved. The Nurse has previously compared Romeo to rosemary – the herb that, as Ophelia reminds us, is 'for remembrance' – and it is indeed the same herb which has already been 'stuck' on Juliet's 'fair corse' by her mourning relatives. Strewn at both weddings and funerals, rosemary's most common culinary usage was as an aid to taste and digestion, when it was 'stuck' in an incision made by a knife in a joint of meat. This emblematic aspect of the tragic catastrophe appears to problematize the desire which informs all attempts at memory or remembrance, as it reminds us of memory's eventual consumption or death along with the temporal event – or feast – upon which it briefly 'sticks'.

Thus even as the plot interpellates the lovers and their fate in a calendrical cycle of seasonal repetition and cultural memorialization, their sudden deaths (*mortes improvisi*) appear to reveal a momentary rift, not simply in the calendar but also in our very natural desire to shape and order temporality, through memory, into coherent historical forms. Derrida has described the instantaneous decision to make a gift of death:

> irreducible to presence or to presentation, it demands a temporality of the instant without ever constituting a present . . . it belongs to an atemporal temporality, to a duration that cannot be grasped: something one can neither stabilize, establish, grasp, apprehend, comprehend. Understanding, common sense, and reason cannot seize, conceive, understand, or mediate it.[32]

The *jouissance* which distinguishes the deaths of Romeo and Juliet resembles Derrida's description of an 'atemporal temporality'. Yet an important aspect of this quasi-sacrificial ecstasy is its suggestive transfiguration of remembrance. Like Romeo, remembrance is consumed along with the intensity of the moment or event – Juliet as feast – which it has both venerated and desired; none the less, it seems that, like a festive torch, this state of consciousness can briefly illuminate a momentary temporal fusion, as tragedy's historical singularity is interfused with the strangely recurrent patterns of a different timing.

Notes

1 Phyllis Rackin, *Stages of History: Shakespeare's English Chronicles* (London: Routledge, 1990), p. ix. For several historians' views of this debate, see *A New Philosophy of History*, eds Frank Ankersmit and Hans Kellner (London: Reaktion, 1995), where the 'historical' is accepted as a rhetorical practice, a form of discourse, which can consequently produce 'congeries of incompatible historical worlds' (introduction, p. 18). See also recent issues of the journal *History and Theory*.

2 The term is Perry Anderson's, who reads post-structuralism as 'the randomization of history'. See Geoff Bennington, Derek Attridge and Robert Young, *Post-structuralism and the Question of History* (Cambridge: Cambridge University Press, 1987), p. 4.

3 Patricia Parker, *Shakespeare from the Margins: Language, Culture, Context* (Chicago: University of Chicago Press, 1987); Ned Lukacher, *Time Fetishes: The Secret History of Eternal Recurrence* (Durham: Duke University Press, 1998).

4 Parker, *Shakespeare from the Margins*, p. 21.

5 See for example Michel Jeanneret, *Perpetuum Mobile: métamophoses des corps et des œuvres de Vinci à Montaigne* (Paris: Macula, 1998), chapter 7; Francis Barker, *The Culture of Violence: Tragedy and History* (Manchester: Manchester University Press, 1993); Jean Howard, 'Towards a Postmodern, Politically Committed, Historical Practice', in *The Uses of History: Marxism, Postmodernisn*

and the Renaissance, eds F. Barker *et al.* (Manchester: Manchester University Press, 1991), pp. 101–22; Jonathan Baldo, 'The Politics of Aloofness in *Macbeth*', *English Literary Renaissance* 26, iii (Autumn 1996), 531–60; Philippa Berry, *Shakespeare's Feminine Endings: Disfiguring Death in the Tragedies* (London: Routledge: 1999), chapter 5.

5 D. R. Woolf, *The Idea of History in Early Stuart England* (Toronto: University of Toronto Press, 1990); Nicholas Campion, *The Great Year: Astrology, Millenarianism and History in the Western Tradition* (Harmondsworth: Penguin, 1994).

6 'Women's Time', in *The Kristeva Reader*, ed. Toril Moi (Oxford: Basil Blackwell, 1986), pp. 187–213 (p. 192).

7 In 'Philosophy and the Fairy, Madness and *The Method*', forthcoming in *Textures of Renaissance Knowledge*, eds Philippa Berry and Margaret Tudeau-Clayton, Marie-Dominique Garnier observes that 'Juliet's solar name shifts throughout the play in a mobile, paronomastic fashion, from associations to *July* to *Jewel* and *Jule, Ay*, a configuration which displaces her towards another mobile character in the canon, Julius Caesar. Julius's own patronym is derived, according to Littré, from the Greek *youlos*, "curly" – a loop-line, a loop-hole, a figure of deviance.' Citations from *Romeo and Juliet* are from the Arden edition, ed. Brian Gibbons (London: Routledge, 1988); all others from Shakespearean texts are from *The Norton Shakespeare*, eds S. Greenblatt *et al.* (New York: W. W. Norton and Co, 1997).

8 See *The Book of Common Prayer 1559*, ed. John E. Booty (Charlottesville: University of Virginia Press, 1976). Booty comments: 'The book is a product of the sixteenth century . . . Nothing is more striking in this regard than the appearance in the Almanac of the signs of the zodiac . . . It would be quite surprising to find these signs included in the Prayer Book, particularly in such a book as that prepared by Thomas Cranmer, a person who along with many other Reformers condemned the use of astrology, if we did not remember that Elizabeth not only had an Archbishop but also had her Dr Dee, and that John Jewel, Bishop of Salisbury, while arguing against soothsayers and the like, admitted their power. The presence of the signs in the Prayer Book should be understood against the background of the times and in relation to other writings, such as the *Preces privatae* (1564), wherein the zodiac is included in the calendar, presented in special tables, and explained for the common reader' (pp. 381–2).

9 Eamon Duffy, *The Stripping of the Altars: Traditional Religion in England 1400–1580* (New Haven: Yale University Press, 1992), p. 47.

10 *Ibid.*, p. 48.

11 *Ibid.*, p. 394.

12 David Cressy, *Bonfires and Bells: National Memory and the Protestant Calendar in Elizabethan and Stuart England* (London: Weidenfeld and Nicolson, 1989).

13 *Ibid.*

14 See Thomas McAlindon, *Shakespeare's Tragic Cosmos* (Cambridge: Cambridge University Press, 1991), on Romeo as *romero*, a pilgrim. I am also indebted to Katherine Duncan-Jones for sharing with me her unpublished essay on *Romeo and Juliet*, 'Star-crossed and Double-crossed', where she mentions this passage in Florio.

15 *The Second Tome of Homelyes* (London: 1563), 2, 'Agaynste parell of Idolatry and superfluous decking of churches', sigs Dd4ff.

16 Claude Gaignebet, *Au plus hault sens: l'esoterisme spirituel et charnel de Rabelais*, 2 vols (Paris: Maissoneuve et Larose, 1986), passim. I am grateful to François Laroque for directing me to this encyclopaedic work.

17 The biblical Samson, taming the lion which was his most notable solar attribute, is carved over the gateway of Hoghton Tower in Lancashire, where Shakespeare is thought by some scholars to have spent part of his lost years in the service of a recusant Catholic household.

18 Steve Sohmer, *Shakespeare's Mystery Play: The Opening of the Globe Theatre, 1599* (Manchester: Manchester University Press, 1999).

19 Embedded in these oblique and partially ironic allusions to this 'canicular' saint (as Claude Gaignebet has described him) there may also be references to a holy traveller who was a much more immediate object of recusant piety and regret, and whose impetuous Counter-Reformation zeal seems similarly to have lacked the protection of St Christopher: this is the Jesuit priest and martyr Edmund Campion. It may not be wholly coincidental, in this connection, that the 'fearful date' of the lovers' first meeting, and the beginning of their tragedy, appears to be the eve or day of 16 July. For this was the date of an event which had sent shock waves through the entire recusant community in the Midlands and north of England. On that day in 1581, some *fourteen years* before Shakespeare's presumed composition of his play, Campion was finally arrested, while saying Mass at a house outside Oxford. (An additional coincidence is that the date chosen by Shakespeare for Juliet's anticipated fourteenth birthday, 'a fortnight and odd days' later, 31 July, was the day on which Campion was first put to the rack. 31 July was also the date of death in 1556 of the founder of the Jesuits, Ignatius Loyola; when Loyola was canonized in the seventeenth century, it became his feast day.)

20 Aratus, *Phaenomena*, trans. G. R. Mair (London: Heinemann, 1969), pp. 326–36.

21 Manilius, *Astronomica*, trans. G. P. Gould (London: Heinemann, 1977), V, pp. 206–14.

22 Marcel Detienne, *The Gardens of Adonis: Spices in Greek Mythology*, trans. Janet Lloyd (Atlantic Highlands: Humanities Press, 1977), pp. 120–2.

23 For summaries of these arguments see Gaignebet, *Au plus hault sens*, pp. 271–3, and Jean-Pierre Vernant, 'At Man's Table: Hesiod's Foundation Myth of Sacrifice', in Marcel Detienne and J.-P. Vernant, *The Cuisine of Sacrifice among the Greeks*, trans. Paula Wissy (Chicago: University of Chicago Press, 1989), pp. 21–86.

24 Hesiod, 'Works and Days', ll. 67, 185, in *The Homeric Hymns and Homerica*, trans. Hugh G. Evelyn White (London: Heinemann, 1967).

25 *Ibid.*, 586–8.

26 See Bernard Capp, *English Almanacs 1500–1800: Astrology and the Popular Press* (Ithaca: Cornell University Press 1979).

27 François Laroque notes that there is a possible (second meaning) Latin pun in this exchange, on head/*caput*, 'that refers us directly to the name Capulet, so that the word "maidenhead" could already be an indirect allusion to the play's heroine – Juliet Capulet' ('Tradition and Subversion in *Romeo and Juliet*', in

Shakspeare's 'Romeo and Juliet': Texts, Contexts and Interpretations*, ed. Jay L. Halio (Newark: University of Delaware Press, 1995), pp. 18–36.

28 St Jerome thought that the name Samson was etymologically derived from *shemesh*, the Hebrew word for sun. See Gaignebet, *Au plus hault sens*, I, pp. 343–6.

29 Huston Diehl, *Staging Reform, Reforming the Stage: Protestantism and Popular Theater in Early Modern England* (Ithaca: Cornell University Press, 1998), pp. 170–1.

30 The solar association of these birds in Egyptian antiquity is noted in *The Hieroglyphics of Horapollo*, trans. George Boas (Princeton: Princeton University Press, 1993), I, pp. 6–7.

31 Manilius, *Astronomica*, trans. G. P. Gould (London: Heinemann, 1977), I, pp. 396–417.

32 Jacques Derrida, *The Gift of Death*, trans. David Wills (Chicago: University of Chicago Press, 1995), p. 65.

Country house, Catholicity and the crypt(ic) in *Twelfth Night*

bringing out what they would keep hidden   (C. L. Barber of Twelfth Night festivities)

i siciliani, che hanno fama di non parlare, in realtà parlano, a mezza voce, cifrati, ma parlano, basta saperli interpretare

(Sicilians, who have the reputation of not talking, in reality do talk, sotto voce, in crypted language, but they talk, all one needs is to know how to interpret them)   (Andrea Camilleri, *Il Corso delle Cose*)[1]

Twelfth Night is characterized by a constellation of contextualizing characteristics that one does not come across in such close or dense association elsewhere in Shakespeare's plays. The twin 'nebuli' at the centre of this constellation are, on the one hand, the Elizabethan country house, complete with domains and dependences and, on the other, an unusually rich array of what, at this early stage, may perhaps best be referred to as the insignia and paraphernalia of Catholicism. This constellation, I want to argue, conditions the way an early modern audience, or at least a certain section of that audience, might have interpreted not only the action engendered by Shakespeare's text but the actual textuality generated by that action: this is the text-within-a-text, a feature which the play shares with the contemporaneous *Hamlet*. Composed by one of the characters in *Twelfth Night*, this text, like the famous 'cheveril glove' evoked in the course of the dialogue (3.1.12),[2] has an underside to it which reverses itself, like a Moebius band or Bacon's famous 'Tartar's bow' – or like the ingenious double architecture of the great recusant country houses in Elizabeth's England – so as to implicate, to envelop within its folds, the author, Shakespeare himself.

In her essay on *Twelfth Night*, Stevie Davies evokes 'the art world of the Renaissance country house which *Twelfth Night* reflects': the play, she writes, introduces the audience to the home-world of Tudor great houses and estates, a world of domestic interiors with bedrooms, buttery bars, gardens with box-trees and knot gardens, in a vernacular that was totally familiar, where Englishness . . . is the solid, rooted medium in which the action flourishes. To Viola's dazed question, 'What country, friends, is this?', the Captain might well be giving a coded answer . . . 'This is England (if you like), lady' [. . . hence] this sense of home-and-garden familiarity . . . – a leisured, tapestried, mirrored world of interiors, contained within panelled rooms behind leaded panes and surrounded by hedged gardens and ancestral walls.[3]

As early as 1967, in *Shakespeare Our Contemporary*, Jan Kott had not only suggested an identity for *Twelfth Night*'s ancestral halls and garden walls but given the picture a religious colouring. With his customary critical verve, and considerably darkening the atmosphere in the process, Kott categorized the setting of Shakespeare's 'festive' comedy as that of a recusant household seen through the spectacles of an Elizabethan Fellini; he even puts a name to the lord of this particular manor, that of Shakespeare's patron disgraced in 1601 – the probable year of the play's composition – for his part in the Essex rebellion. 'With all its appearances of gaiety', writes Kott, 'it is a very bitter comedy about the Elizabethan *dolce vita*, or at any rate about the *dolce vita* at every level and in every wing of the Southampton residence'.[4] The picture he paints – something along the lines of Holbein's portrait of the pious family of Sir Thomas More *chez soi*, complete with monkey, shortly before the fall from grace – is certainly seductive. Alas, however, the days when a literary text could be treated as a reflection of the world or, conversely, as a window on to the world unbefogged by the wayward wilfulness of the signifier belong to a bygone age of literary research. This is especially true in the case of a play as flamboyantly multi-layered and mutable as *Twelfth Night* which, in the emblem of the cheveril glove, wags less a finger than a gauntleted fist at those who take outsides for insides and in the process make 'idols' of images.

Cloisters and clusters

One of the contextualizing representations foregrounded from the outset is that of claustration, and it is formulated in classic Catholic mode. When, in the opening scene of *A Midsummer Night's Dream*, the irate *senex* of a father thunders at his daughter, and Duke Theseus plays Solomon, what the latter proposes to Hermia is 'the livery of a nun, / For aye to be in shady cloister mew'd' (1.1.70–1).[5] The cloister in *Twelfth Night*'s first scene is not a half-way house between penitentiary and patriarchy but the *modus vivendi* freely espoused by the heroine in the wake of her bereavement ('The element itself till seven years' heat / Shall not behold her face at ample view, / But like a cloistress she will veiled walk', 1.1.25–7). The difference

between the two is that, where Hermia is of unspecified social status, Olivia
is a countess, and for the countess, in default of father and brother, both
deceased, the cloister will be the privy portions of the country house which,
in spite of all, she will perforce continue to govern (in an age when power
was dynastic, the responsibility of an ancestral domain was not something
lightly to be shrugged off). This responsibility, in default of males to assume
it, was of course a situation where such an Elizabethan woman as Bess
of Hardwick thrived. But the Protestant Bess was a widow, and several
times over at that. If the 'Illyrian' domain closely resembles an Elizabethan
country estate, the situation of Olivia who, in the course of the play, moves,
in terms of dramatic 'stations', from cloister to chantry as she passes from
bereavement to betrothal, is closer to that of those 'adult unmarried
women', the celibate or widowed women such as those of the Arundel or
the Vaux family, scattered across the land, who are such a feature of
Elizabethan and Jacobean recusancy in the years leading up to 1605 and
the Gunpowder Plot.[6] In Olivia's case, the private version of taking the veil
within the confines of her domestic microcosm is accompanied by a further
act which Shakespeare endows with all the qualities suggestive of a secondary ritual – *a fortiori* in the case of a woman soon to be apostrophized
as 'Madonna', this comedy being Shakespeare's only play in which the word
is found. The impression of a secondary ritual is conveyed when the picture
of the intra-mural perambulations of the 'cloistress' is fleshed out by the
information that this particular novice has in her make-up more than a little
of the *Madonna lacrimosa* – 'she will veiled walk / Watering once a day her
chamber round / With eye-offending brine' (1.1.27–9). There being nothing
resembling Keats's pot of basil to 'water' in Shakespeare's scenario, the
incongruous 'once a day' transforms the pious tears of remembrance into
a ritual sprinkling of holy water: as we shall have occasion to note in the
case of father Abercromby, whom we have yet to meet, the incongruous in
such domains was wont to signal the surreptitious showing through – the
underside of the transvestite, festive 'cheveril glove'.

Cloisters, coistrels and 'Castiliano vulgo'

In *Twelfth Night* Olivia is not the only one who is haunted by the image
of the cloister. It can also be seen to haunt the creative imagination of the
author himself, where it is given to metamorphic resurgence in the most
improbable circumstances. It haunts him notably through the personage of
Sir Toby Belch, not this time as image or referent but as signifier – and as
signifier subject to the same regime of the cheveril glove as the visual order
of representation in the play where boy turns out to be girl and manser-
vant masquerades as master. This is how I interpret the terms of the
inebriated idiolect – baptized for the nonce 'Castiliano vulgo' by its prac-
titioner – in which Sir Toby's fulsome celebration of his niece the 'cloistress'
is couched. This celebration is voiced, or rather vented, when first Sir Toby

appears on stage at the beginning of the play's third scene 'drinking healths to my niece. I'll drink to her as long as there is a passage in my throat . . . He's a coward and a coistrel that will not drink to my niece till his brains turn o' th' toe, like a parish top' (1.3.35–9). This top-to-toeing of language which Toby, in a phrase for which critics have yet to find a satisfactory explanation, peremptorily proclaims to be Spanish of the purest – 'Castiliano vulgo' – works on a paradigm which is linguistic in mode and catholic in reference. In Toby's eulogy of his niece the stylistically resonant word is less the banal 'coward' than the much rarer term which rhetorically and alliteratively buttresses it: 'coistrel'. The point here is the following: what is 'coistrel' if not 'cloister', or indeed 'cloistress', writ as other? The cloister and its occupant are the top, the coistrel the toe. For in the phrase 'till his brains turn o' th' toe, like a parish top', the 'top' is not only the diminutive 'whipping-top provided for exercise and entertainment', as the Oxford edition glosses the term. In explicit conjunction here with 'toe' – like Old Hamlet's armour 'cap-à-pié' evoked at almost the same moment in the contemporaneous tragedy – *Twelfth Night*'s top acquires a supplementary definition as the top of a scale of values which in the context is at once martial and marial: the receiver of the speech is 'Maria' and the referent of the signifier 'niece' is a 'Madonna' in the making. In Toby's fulsome, festive panegyric this 'top' just happens to coincide with the top of the church ('the parish top').

This may be 'Castiliano vulgo', but what it can be identified as with certainty is what Renaissance practitioners of the carnavalesque such as François Rabelais would have identified as '*grammaire joyeuse*', the tongue of *gai savoir*. Interestingly, moreover, the word itself is eloquent also in its own right, and would no doubt have been more so in the sixteenth and seventeenth centuries than it is now, for the term hails from a medieval French word '*coustille*' which is to the world of war what Feste's cheveril glove is to the world of peace: a sword of (and for) the vulgar sort, but a sword – a (s)word – that cuts both ways because it is double-edged. Thus apropos 'coistrel' the *Oxford English Dictionary (Shorter)*: from 'a *coustillier*, soldier armed with a *coustille*, double-edged sword'.[7]

Thus, if the 'other scene' of *Hamlet*'s *incipit* is purgatory, the 'other scene' of *Twelfth Night*'s opening is the cloister, both notable vestiges of the recent Catholic past. In the tragedy we behold a – male – ghost who has just come from the confines of purgatorial fire, while in the comedy what is portrayed is a woman, who, if not a ghost, is in deep mourning, on her way to the confines of a well-watered closet which in its sterility announces her tomb. What marks the logic of Shakespeare's imagination here is a reversal into the contrary, and as we know from Freud, the most powerful motor in triggering such reversals is that of interdiction, all the more so if keenly felt. Here the reversal is all along the line: the elements (fire/water), gender (male/female), direction (from/to), location (on this or the other side of the great divide), and, as we know, both cloister and purgatory were not only now under interdict but had for centuries been pillars of popular piety, and complementary ones at that.

The upshot of all this is that it enables us to suggest a reading of one of the notable unsolved cruxes of *Twelfth Night*: in the light of the elements just evoked and the Catholic ethos to which they appertain, the riddle of the 'Castiliano vulgo' that concludes Toby's eulogy of his niece can be decrypted as a minimally transposed inscription of the object of that eulogy (Olivia): 'casta still'/'still chaste', with a feminine ending (a feminine ending cut off and stuck on later as the boy actor beneath the female persona was at one remove from femininity on the Elizabethan stage: 'call me cut', says Toby a little later). Since the riddle is prefaced by 'What wench, Castiliano . . .', the feminine ending (cast-a) is entirely proper. 'Castiliano'[8] then proceeds, however, to inflect this nucleus by adding the two final letters, '-no'. Thus, if in the first instance the riddle asks whether the wench is chaste still, the answer eventually given by the play, when cloister and bereavement have been replaced by chantry and betrothal, is 'no'. The '-no' spells out the triumph of the festive over the funereal, of comedy over tragedy. The reversal it operates works along the lines of the inversion of cloister into coistrel. This is language as 'cheveril glove' with a vengeance, and the cloth it is made of is the backcloth of religion.

This reading is confirmed by what happens elsewhere in Shakespeare. The representation transcribed by this verbal anamorphosis (cloister/coistrel) in which the top of the church is at the same time, if not exactly a crypt, at least crypted in 'Castiliano vulgo' – the purest form of the tongue used by the most powerful Catholic power on earth at the time, but here, thanks to the accompanying 'vulgo', under the erasure of another Freudian deformation, *Verleugnung*, disavowal – turns out to be a powerful one which the poet seems to have carried with him down the years and produced in very different circumstances. 'Coistrel' is an extremely rare word in Shakespeare and occurs again only in *Pericles* (c.1608?). If one has analysed the earlier occurrence in context, as we have just done, one is immediately struck by a singular air of *déjà vu*: for the word emerges in the text of *Pericles* precisely at a moment when the heroine is being depicted as having renounced the ways of the flesh and displayed the chastity – and stalwart defence of that chastity – of a nun, in spite of the fact that the scene takes place in a brothel: 'Thou art the damned door-keeper to every / Coistrel that comes inquiring for his Tib' (4.6.164–5). The brothel, of course, foots the list, is the 'toe', of cloistered establishments. Toby Belch's 'coistrel' was vented upon a character whose name, bawdy notwithstanding, is 'Maria'; in the later brothel scene, *mutatis mutandis*, the same invective is voiced by a virtual *Doppelgänger*. For the virgin 'as cold as a snowball' (139–40) who 'will not go the way of woman-kind' (149–50) but converts rakes in the Mytilene whorehouse and sends them to their orisons is the paronomastically named 'Marina'. In *Pericles* not only is the passage both framed and liberally sprinkled with oblique invocations of the Virgin, by way of the repeated oath 'Marry' (4.6.136, 148, 150), the last of these oaths goes one better in that it is relayed by the signifier encrypted within it, namely 'Mary': 'Marry, come up, my dish of chastity with rosemary and bays' (150–1). And as we know from the little lesson Ophelia delivers, not in vulgar Castilian but the choice English of Denmark, on the symbolism of flowers, rosemary stands precisely for the sentiment which makes of Olivia a nun at the beginning of *Twelfth Night*, namely remembrance: 'there's rosemary, that's for remembrance' (4.5.173). Indeed, the rose itself, of course, was one of the commonest symbols of the Virgin in Renaissance iconography thanks to its unique juxtaposition of sweetness (*odor Paradisi*) and the blood-letting, pain-giving thorns (one of the most striking examples of the genre in the form of a remarkably be-rosed and be-strawberried Virgin, dated 1425, by the so-called 'Master of the Little Garden of Paradise' (Meister des Paradiesgärtlein) is to be seen in the Fine Arts Museum in Solothurn, Switzerland). Back in Shakespeare's brothel, our impression goes beyond a mere impression of *déjà vu* when the text accompanies 'coistrel' with the very names of the pair of characters who produced this rare signifier when it first appeared in Shakespeare's work, namely 'Feste' and 'Belch', for after 'every / Coistrel that comes inquiring for his Tib', the passage continues, 'To the choleric fisting of every rogue / Thy ear is liable; thy food is such / As hath been belch'd on by infected lungs'. Certainly these names are crypted, but, crypt or no crypt, there they are in spite of all.

It is not just that, as Feste or anyone who has spent time poring over Shakespeare's texts has necessarily realized, words have a way and a life of their own: there are certain nuclei of representation particularly prone to furnishing and fostering this 'wantonness'. In *Twelfth Night* it is the sign system inherited from the Catholic religion, now under interdict and erasure, that impulses such weirdly wayward 'life' in the creative activity of the author in or round about the year 1601.

From cloister to chantry

As England's 'Virgin Queen' had ritually 'progressed' about the domains of which she was governor, so too Olivia, as earlier suggested, progresses along a path which, I would like to suggest, Shakespeare conceives in terms of 'stations'. This is not the drama of stations of the *via crucis* which had characterized medieval religious drama (and, in *The Road to Damascus*, was to inspire Strindberg and German Expressionist *Stationendrama*) but what I would like to call a *via desiderii*. Shakespeare's would-be virgin queen of Illyria is explicitly related by Shakespeare, at various moments punctuating the unfolding of the intrigue, to certain *loci* or *topoi*. If, as we have seen, her own dramatic trajectory begins in the 'cloister', it ends – specifically and insistently – in a chantry. There is an additional half-way house at approximately the middle of the play's playing time which is the garden and will be explored later.

Accordingly, it is in a 'chantry' somewhere in the demesnes of Olivia's Elizabethan country house that Shakespeare locates the beginning of the end of her trials and tribulations along the road to conjugal contentment. One has perforce to remark that this term was in no way imposed by external considerations either of prosody or of cultural context: the English 'chapel' is no less of a bisyllable, and an oxytone to boot, than the text's 'chantry'; moreover, both culturally and linguistically, 'chapel' corresponds to the Italian '*cappella*' and would thus have conveniently bridged the cultural gap. But 'chantry' is what Shakespeare chooses to write and that is where the nuptial process is indeed engaged by a priest who is identified or apostrophized as 'Father' on both the occasions when he is required to intervene. Such a degree of internal coherence in the evocation of the chantry of betrothal can hardly, one feels, be the product of mere chance, especially when, or rather because, it is structurally and symbolically symmetrical to the liminary cloistress.

The point is, of course – and it is complementary to Old Hamlet's rising from the fires of what is patently a Catholic purgatory in *Hamlet* – that the chantry was not any kind of chapel but one, if not directly abutting on to, at least in privileged communication with, what was happening in a compartment of the early modern afterlife that was specific to the Catholic vision of that particular phase of one's existence. The chantry was dedicated to the recitation or 'chanting' of prayers to alleviate the suffering of the souls of the dear departed, and if it offended the Protestant way of thinking on such matters it was for a very good reason. The chantry was a place where money changed hands in a way that subtracted the sums employed there for financing prayer from the human economy of the community at large, and, it was believed, ultimately diverted funds from the economy of England's green and pleasant land across the seas into the foreign coffers of the 'whore of Babylon'. Chantries were, so to speak, local branch offices of a worldwide insurance company – something along the lines of the Italian giant *Generali* today – where the Catholic member of the community's 'post-mortem fire-insurance', in Eamon Duffy's apt phrase, was put in competent hands and administered on behalf of the dear departed on a day-to-day basis in the form of individual masses or whole rafts of prayers like the so-called Trental of Pope Gregory (or 'Pope Trental').[9] In England, by the beginning of the fifteenth century, this latter, rather than a vulgar insurance, would seem to have turned into something of a gold-edged bond, being referred to more often as the 'Golden Trental'; as such, indeed, it had come in for discussion at some length in a Tudor play with a likely title for such a discussion: *Dives and Pauper*.[10]

Pleasantry apart, however, there is an important point to be made here which lies in the nature of the ritual that was performed in these edifices. If money was spent within their four walls it was not to earn praise but in remembrance of the souls of the dead. In this respect, therefore, the chantry scene in *Twelfth Night* is related to a scene we have already had occasion to evoke: the distribution of branches of rosemary in Shakespeare's contemporaneous tragedy of *Hamlet*. The flower ritual in the tragedy takes place at the beginning of Act 4 scene 5: the chantry scene in the comedy in Act 4 scene 3, while in *Pericles* the rose-mary of the virginal Rose-Marina appears in the text in Act 4 scene 6. There can, of course, be no question of any over-zealous totting up of figures in such matters as scene divisions in Shakespeare, but the impression is reinforced that there is certainly a common, albeit metamorphic, representational nucleus at work here, and that it involves on the one hand remembrance and on the other an insistently Catholic set of signs, symbols and sense-systems imbued with nostalgia.

This impression is reinforced even further if, before coming to the most important 'station' of all, the garden, we look briefly at the only other evocation of a chantry in the canon, to be found in a play dating from shortly before *Twelfth Night*, *Henry V* (1599). If there were any need of confirmation either of the constellation just identified or of the tone of reverence which can be detected with regard to these images even in the most grotesque or carnivalesque of attendant circumstances, then the evocation of the chantry in the last of the histories should do much to dispel it. Someone for whom the institution of the chantry was fraught with archaic, mercantile or 'papistical' associations could hardly have written Henry V's great soliloquy on the eve of Agincourt – the most moving speech in the entire play – where this particular religious institution is of the essence. A historically conscientious author could certainly have made allowances for the passing of time and traditions, but Shakespeare hardly gives the impression of working with such criteria in the forefront of his mind elsewhere. The alliterative and assonantal relays inject an incantatory elegiac emotion into the poetry that is far in excess of mere nomination – all the more so since chantries and the rituals performed therein, here evoked in stark, and for Protestants shocking, detail, were one of the prime butts of Reformed indignation and sarcasm:

Not to-day, O Lord!
O not to-day, think not upon the fault
My father made in compassing the crown!
I Richard's body have interred new,
And on it have bestow'd more contrite tears
Than from it issued forced drops of blood.
Five hundred poor I have in yearly pay,
Who twice a day their wither'd hands hold up

> Toward heaven, to pardon blood; and I have built
> Two chantries, where sad and solemn priests
> Still sing for Richard's soul. More will I do;
> Though all that I can do is nothing worth,
> Since that my penitence comes after all,
> Imploring pardon.   (5.1.298–311; emphasis added)[11]

If it is fraught with anything, this passage and the evocations of the chantry and its 'holy father' in Illyria are filled with nostalgia for a mode of piety since outlawed if not defunct, but the memory of which is green.

Rhythms of recusancy?

With its corantos, complots and various cavorting, not to mention the looming large of the occasional buccaneer, *Twelfth Night*'s characteristic turbulence tends to obscure the basic articulation between time and space. To begin with, the comedies of mistaken identity generally identified as constituting the primary intertexts involved in this comedy, the aptly named *Gl'Ingannati* (the hoodwinked) foremost amongst them, belong to the Plautine mode and are essentially town comedies (*Gl'Ingannati*, for instance, moves between Rome and Modena). Not so Shakespeare's comedy. Nor, on the other hand, was the notorious rusticity then characterizing the communities along the Illyrian coast, piratical rather than simply pastoral in nature, such as to preclude the siting of the action in an urban setting, albeit on a necessarily more modest scale than that of the Italian capital or the towns of the great Lombard plain. What is of greater consequence is the interface of this specific setting – the country house – with the calendrical cycle: the fact that the country house is the location for a celebration of (an) Epiphany – a feast day designated by Eamon Duffy, in *The Stripping of the Altars*, as having constituted 'one of the ten major feasts of Christ and Mary'.[12] The pertinence of this feast is generally glossed in terms of psychological or moral self-awareness, as when, in the study he devotes to *Twelfth Night* in *Shakespeare's Festive Comedies*, C. L. Barber begins by remarking that this comedy has to do with 'People . . . caught up by delusions or misapprehensions which take them out of themselves'. But the 'revelation' or 'manifestation' heralded in the term 'epiphany' – in the first instance a religious term to the ordinary Elizabethan – may with equal plausibility have religious connotations and hint, in the manner of a *clin d'oeil*, at a problematic, under cover of Carnival, of a more religious nature: 'bringing out', as Barber aptly puts it, 'what [otherwise] they would keep hidden'.[13]

  To begin with, in this comedy, for all the rumbustiousness that reigns within its Illyrian purlieu, for all the festive throwing down of barriers, bounds and confines of every type ('Confines? I'll confine myself no finer than I am,' proclaims Sir Toby Belch with the very first breath he draws on stage, 1.3.9), the country house setting in actual fact rhymes far less with Renaissance magnificence and 'finery' than with their negation, with a shutting out and shuttering up which is programmed from the start so that withdrawing into one's innermost world, on the one hand, and, on the contrary, overstepping the utmost limits of that world are the reverse sides of the same coin . . . or cheveril glove. These two inverse and complementary movements are like the diastole and systole at the heart of the rhythm of the action. This double regime within the narrow confines of the same royal and aristocratic purlieu, this rhythm of precipitate alternation between the centripetal and the centrifugal, was a mode of existence that had a historical correlate under Elizabeth and James. Witness, to name but one, the case – a kind of paradoxically institutionalized schizophrenia – of the confessor of James 1's Danish-born Queen, Anna, who, in the year of *Twelfth Night*'s composition, turned her back on her Calvinistic upbringing and clove to the bosom of the Roman Catholic Church. For such a one as the pious Father Abercromby, her confessor, Twelfth Night was not one day of the year but virtually every day, though (presumably) only part of every day. For him and his likes the transgressive mode of outrageous travesty had perforce become norm not exception. In 1601 'Catholic priests like Father Abercromby were permitted at court if suitably disguised as a keeper of hawks or something incongruous'.[14]

From the outset *Twelfth Night* installs just such an alternative rhythm of sombre claustration and outrageous exhibition in the system of the play's structural parameters to become one of the specificities of the 'twelfth night vision' that flow from Shakespeare's pen. Nor is this given once and for all, but shifts as the intrigue develops. It is most immediately perceptible when, having throwing off the veil of mourning, and with it propriety, Olivia is relayed in claustration by Malvolio. He it is who, in the play's second half, offers the spectacle of one close pent up in darkness, but a darkness which is dire where Olivia's was merely dreary. Ironically it is precisely for having considered himself the alter ego of the heroine – which, from the structural point of view just outlined, he indeed is – that he finds himself 'mewed up'. This may be reflected in the play's title: for the European Renaissance was an age acutely sensitive to, or obsessed with, the significance of numbers. The twelve in the play's title is amenable not only to the arithmetic of calendars, almanacs or *horae,* the Books of Hours that were still popular objects in the exercise of one's religion. For such a *mentalité,* the numbers of the title, the '1' accompanied by the number '2', is capable of yielding not only '12', one followed by two, but equally one *as* two. 'Night' presented as one in two or two in one points to the 'cheveril glove' mode of tailoring in the play's make-up and rhythmic modulation. But in the context of an Elizabethan country house where the veiled mistress is a Madonna, it had both a temporal and a spatial dimension: what one might perhaps call a rhythm of recusancy, on the one hand, and on the other a double architecture, as at Hindlip House or Huddington Court, the work of 'Little John' (Nicholas Owen), the only one of the Powder treason conspirators to be beatified by the Catholic Church (in 1970) for creating and secreting such virtuoso feats of double architecture in otherwise unremarkable noble piles.[15] For his double architectures, Shakespeare had to be content with bardolatry.

Half-way house: the modes of messengering

Between these two extremities of the play's trajectory and the religious topography that defines it is sited one of the most recurrently pored-over *loci* in Western civilization, most notably in European painting. This is the theatre of the Annunciation, along the lines of which is framed Olivia's walled garden – a notable instance of the Elizabethan, the exotic and the esoteric coming together in a multi-layered representation of great pregnancy. This has been persuasively argued by Maurice Hunt in an article entitled simply '*Twelfth Night* and the Annunciation' dating from 1989, and it is my intention not to rehearse the same argument but to supplement it.[16]

The Annunciation had not been erased from popular consciousness by the Reformation except in so far as it had been one of the favourite images which iconoclasts in their zeal had whitewashed over on the walls of the parish churches where the populace was required to gather every Sunday for holy worship – or be fined. There are, however, features of this key moment in the story of Christ that had come in for particular attention under the Catholic dispensation, some of which have a relatively high profile in the comedy of 1601. Again, these are couched in the letter rather than what appears to be the spirit of the text. The first is the use by Shakespeare of the word 'nuncio' in the play: it occurs but once when Orsino defines the function of his new retainer, 'Cesario': 'nuncio' is the word which caps the definition and encapsulates the function: 'O then unfold the passion of my love, / Surprise her with discourse of my dear faith. / It shall become thee well to act my woes. / She will attend it better in thy youth / Than in a nuncio's of more grave aspect' (1.4.28). The Arden edition glosses this with a paraphrase, '[a] permanent representative of the Roman See at a foreign court' (*OED*), a usage that dates from the rise of diplomacy in the course of the sixteenth century. In the sense of 'messenger', as here, the *Oxford English Dictionary* cites this appearance of the term in Shakespeare's comedy as the first attested occurrence. But if it is the first attested case in English, it is far from being the first occurrence in England. The word would have been familiarized by the prayers to the Virgin Mary that found their way into the Books of Hours or *Horae*, mostly in Latin. One of the pillars of Marian piety – stemming precisely from the scenario of the Annunciation – was the 'Gaude Virgo', as in the refrain of this macaronic version collected by the London grocer Richard Hill:

Gaude Maria, Cristis Moder!
Mary myld, of the I mene ;
Thou bare my Lord, thou bare my broder;
Thou bare a louly child and clene.
Thou stodyst full still withoxt blyn,
Whan in thy ere that arand was done so;
Tho gracius God the light with-yn
Gabrielis nuncio . . .[17]

In *Twelfth Night* the heroine 'above stairs' not only comes to be addressed as 'Madonna', an apostrophe reiterated a dozen or so times, one of them in association with a joke about a *pia mater* (1.5.110) as if to signal to the spectator's ear, which does not see the text, that this is no mere Italian local colour (*ma donna*: 'my lady'); at the same time, as we know, the heroine 'below stairs' is Maria, a name implanted in the spectator's consciousness right from the start by virtue of the definition and redefinition of her identity that is enacted (1.3.40–75) notably for the benefit of Sir Andrew Aguecheek, who is slow on the uptake. Against this backcloth, the word 'nuncio' itself comes into the orbit, so to speak, of that maverick meteor, the cheveril glove. It is thus both a term of the Renaissance, of courtly diplomacy, and a term of medieval – Marial – celebration. What lends added credence to this suggestion is the fact that this rare term ('nuncio') is immediately preceded by accents of especial piety in the ambivalent phrase 'my dear faith' ('Surprise her with discourse of my dear faith', 1.4.25). One feels that there is something more here than mere festive sniggering at the obsolescence or solipsism of Orsino's Petrarchist posturing, now sadly *passé*. It is as if the unexpected emergence of the word 'nuncio' *a posteriori* casts a new light, and an old aura, on the evocation of 'my dear faith'

It so happens, moreover, that as its plot unfolds *Twelfth Night* invokes not only the Virgin Mary but both of the women who were the object of angelic messengering in the Bible, both the *Annunziatae* of 'Gabrielis nuncio'. If Feste insistently apostrophizes Olivia as 'Madonna', when he is with Maria, who is about to hatch the Malvolio plot, it is not the Virgin but the Virgin's mother who appears on his lips (2.3.109). It was only in 1478 that the doctrine of the Immaculate Conception of the Virgin Mary by St Anne, intended to reinforce the holiness of the Virgin, had been admitted by the Pope; the Sorbonne sanctioned it twelve years later, and it was officially proclaimed only in the nineteenth century (1854).[18] The reason for this belatedness is that, unlike her daughter, St Anne is not mentioned in the Bible; very popular in England as elsewhere during the Middle Ages, her cult came in for particularly virulent attack from Protestant theologians. *Twelfth Night*'s is one of only two references to St Anne in Shakespeare.

What is interesting is that both this one and the other, at the beginning of
The Taming of the Shrew, in the lines that conclude the 'induction', strongly
suggest that Shakespeare associated the mother of the Virgin with the hatch-
ing of a theatrical scenario. This is patently the case with the 'Malvolio plot'
in the 1601 comedy, and it is equally true in the earlier comedy where what
is at issue is the play itself:

> *First Servant*:   My lord, you nod, an do not mind the play.
> *Sly*:   'Yes, by Saint Anne, do I. A good matter.'   (1.1.249–50)[19]

There is very probably an additional pun in this couplet on matter and the
Latin *mater*, a good mother, or in this case, for the pious Catholic, the
mother of the Mother of God, *Twelfth Night*'s *pia mater*. Thus, at the end
of the induction to the *Shrew*, it is 'Saint Anne' who presides over the birth
of the play as such. In *Twelfth Night* it is the Madonna that is Olivia's *alter
ego*.

Conclusion

The feasibility of such a reading rests not only upon a familiarity with
Renaissance hermeneutics but on taking seriously, as working hypothesis,
the theory advanced originally by Ernst Honigmann concerning Shakespeare's
'lost years', recently returned to by Richard Wilson.[20] In the singularly
Catholicized world of *Twelfth Night*'s country house, not only words but
the very letters that compose them are to be seen as the readily reversible
fingers of a cheveril glove. There are two faces to these signifiers as there
were often two façades, or two depths of façade, to the recusant country
house. Working in such a terrain, on the pourtours of such shifting seman-
tic sands, cannot but have consequences on critical hermeneutics.

   In circumstances where circumspection is paramount for survival, be it
as a Catholic in 1601, or four hundred years on as critic in 2001, when it
comes to reading Shakespeare's plays, any proposition concerning the links
between the playwright and his putative Catholicism has to come to terms
with the decoys, detours and general deviousness offered by their textual
materiality, at every level, not simply in what one infers to be the sense of
the signified or 'spirit', let alone the (historical) referent: Camilleri's statement cited at the beginning of this chapter takes its title from the proposition of Merleau-Ponty in his work on sense and nonsense, namely that 'the
course of things is sinuous' – *a fortiori* in conditions of conflict or embat-
tlement.[21] This circumspection in turn requires that the critic as much as
any Malvolio, if s/he wants to avoid falling into the crypt in which the over-
weening steward lands himself, must needs think through the strategies
that make of the text a text encrypted. This is all the more necessary as
Renaissance writers, even faraway English ones, had more than a little
of Camilleri's or Pirandello's Sicilians in their view of language: to

Shakespeare's Feste as to Camilleri's characters, words are indeed wanton. In such conditions, therefore, what is called for is a hermeneutics of wantonness.

This is why, for instance, in discussing the fascinating research Richard Wilson has been doing recently on the arrival of Edmund Campion to lead his mission on English soil – a landfall made very precisely at Dover cliffs – I suggested that this *rapprochement* between this historical scene and the fantasmatic scenario etched by Edgar for his blinded father in *King Lear* could and should be anchored in the letter (as opposed to the spirit) of the signifier which surfaces half-way down the speech, which is also, of course, half-way down the famous cliff. This signifier is 'samphire', but as any literate Frenchwoman knows – and, more to the point, as a literate Elizabethan like Gerard in his 1599 *Herbal* patently knew, the term being then closer to its French origins, samphire is *l'herbe de Saint-Pierre*, the 'herb of Saint Peter'. This is why Gerard writes a chapter not on 'samphire' but 'On Sampier', a term which is a half-way house – half-way across the Channel – between the patron saint of Rome and an English condiment served with fish (notably the John Dory, in French *Saint-Pierre*, hence the name of the fishing boat used to catch it). Such is the encrypted nature of what the man half way down the cliff is culling, a herb placed under the sign of the patron saint of Rome, especially if, as R. Wilson suggests, the culler is none other than Campion himself. As I suggested in the paper I gave at the San Francisco convention of the Shakespeare Association of America in April 1999 entitled 'Herb or Verb: Seminal Punning in Shakespeare', herbs in the latter's plays are not only verbs, they can become structural cruxes, and, in the case of Richard Wilson's important research on *Lear*, the letter of the herb samphire becomes the clinching evidence shoring up the working hypothesis which he, after the pioneering work of Ernst Honigmann, was operative in reactivating and thus opening up new vistas for Shakespeare research.

Epilogue: *Twelfth Night* and the case of the Blessed Cuthbert Mayne

When Trevor Nunn set his 1996 filmed version of *Twelfth Night* in Cornwall, the appositeness of this choice did not lie only in seeing the North Cornish coast, once famous for wrecking as a full-time professional activity, as something like an English equivalent of the coast of early modern Illyria, notorious as constituting a series of safe havens for the pirates which infested the Adriatic and ultimately brought about the decline of trade with the Levant, and thus of Venice.

In the perspective we have adopted in this study, there is another side to the pertinence of this choice. This resides in the fact that the extreme southwest, and not, as is often believed, the far north-west or north, was the first theatre of Catholic martyrdom in Elizabethan history. As early as 1577, the

Blessed Cuthbert Mayne was tried, after hideous imprisonment in Launceston castle, convicted and finally subjected to the ritual dismemberment
which was to become the fate of those who followed in his footsteps, first
to Douai, then back across the Channel to succour the great recusant households that were capable of concealing them. Nunn's film version is located
principally at Lanhydrock House near Bodmin, right at the centre of Cornwall, with other, secondary, locations scattered around the peninsula. Lanhydrock is half-way between the rugged north and the much lusher south
of the county. Cuthbert Mayne's martyrdom crystallized, as never before,
and probably never since in the history of the county, not only the interface between two terrains, which Nunn's setting for *Twelfth Night* powerfully exploits, but the resulting tension between two topographies which
are not only geographical but cultural and mental.

In Cuthbert Mayne's drama, the extreme north around Bude is represented by Sir Richard Grenville, the celebrated Elizabethan sea rover and
adventurer who would have figured honourably as an Illyrian, since he was
at the same time, as Mayne's case admirably illustrates, a predator not only
at sea but also on land. The south of the county in the drama of Cuthbert
Mayne is home to the Cornish Arundels, not only at Lanherne, where the
head of the clan, Sir John Arundel, resided, but at Golden in the vicinity of
Tregony, where the Tregians harboured Mayne. One notes, however, that
the branch of the family that resided on the north coast near Newquay, in
the superb Elizabethan manor house of Trerice (now the property of the
National Trust), were Protestant. Mayne himself came from just across the
north Cornish border, from Barnstaple in north Devon. It was the Protestant Sir Richard Grenville who was the driving force behind Mayne's trial
and execution, and the subsequent confiscation of the lands of those who
had hidden him. Till the 1570s the recusant Cornish Arundels in their
remote fastnesses had been left in peace. As in *Twelfth Night*, at the beginning was a marriage, as ardently desired by one side (who in political terms
had the upper hand) as it was adamantly refused by the other. This was the
marriage urged by Sir Richard for his daughter to the son of the Catholic
Francis Tregian, Mayne's protector ('The Grenvilles, at the other end of
the county, became interested in the prospering fortunes of the Tregians.
The daughter of the Grenvilles was not thought as suitable a match for the
Tregian heir as a daughter of the Arundels').[22]

Had this taken place, the impetus which ended in Mayne's martyrdom
would in all probability not have existed, at least not in the devastating
form it was to take in 1577. It was in essence a classic instance of the old
aristocracy against the new gentry, but it had the specificity of being a
case located in a country – or rather county – where the 'Illyrian' practices
current along its wild northern pourtours, so useful to Nunn as a backdrop,
had long been a method of survival. In the late Elizabethan age, these practices had been upgraded by those with most foresight – or appetite – from

mere survival tactics to a strategy promoting upward mobility in a national context (the south-west, as is well known, furnished a notable batch of such 'gallant' courtiers, exponents of derring-do on the high seas at a time when land opportunities for the same were becoming few and far between).

The whole point was that Grenville had indeed persuaded the Privy Council to make a public drama of it. In 1577 not only was Mayne apprehended but Grenville for the nonce rounded up the main recusants in the county: the intention was to make a test case – a theatrical 'show' case – the first of its kind, complete with a punishing verdict as climax. While the stage was being set, Mayne was put in the hellhole – it is still to this day known as such – in Launceston castle, an extraordinary eleventh-century construction of a hill fortress that still towers high above the town, the gateway to the rest of England just over the border. This situation emblemized the fact that not only did such 'monsters' lurk just beyond the English 'Pale', but that England was on the brink of subversion, if not quite yet of invasion, by his like, and was to pay due attention to the 'tragedy' that was about to be played out – complete with props. In stage-managing the first of such trials in Elizabethan history, Grenville had given particular instructions to his agents to amass a maximum of concrete objects to act as what Shakespeare was memorably to term 'ocular proof' (treatises, crosses, beads, prayer books, an Agnus Dei that was destined to have an especially damaging effect for its owner, and 'other relics used in popery'). On the day of the Assizes at Launceston, 23 September 1577, people turned out to witness 'half the Cornish gentry on the wrong side of the justice hall'.[23] In judgement Sir Roger Manwoode sat with Justice Jeffreys. The central moments of the drama could hardly have been more theatrical, first in the striking contrast between Manwoode, who thundered, and Mayne, who replied quietly (unlike some of those who followed him, he was not an orator), secondly in the exhibition of his body parts which were distributed for public display at strategic points throughout the county as a dire warning for those who intended to follow his path.

Notes

1 Andrea Camilleri, *Il Corso delle Cose* (Palermo: Sellerio, 1998, 2000), p. 9. Translation mine.
2 All references to the Oxford Edition, ed. Stanley Wells and Roger Warren (1995).
3 Stevie Davies, ed., *Twelfth Night* (Harmondsworth: Penguin, Collected Critical Studies, 1993), p. 44.
4 Jan Kott, *Shakespeare Our Contemporary*, rev. edn, trans. B. Taborski (London: Methuen; 1967: 229).
5 All references to the Arden edition, ed. Harold Brooks (London: Methuen, 1984).
6 Antonia Fraser, *The Gunpowder Plot: Terror and Faith in 1605* (London: Mandarin, 1997), p. 27.

7 *Oxford English Dictionary (Shorter)* (1977), p. 477.
8 In a paper read to the Shakespeare Society of America, in San Francisco, April 1999, I suggested that among the first puns to have come down to us from Shakespeare's pen is one on a Latin word virtually indistinguishable from 'Castiliano': 'Castalia'. I am referring to the dedication to *Venus and Adonis* which begins with the declaration that 'mihi flavus Apollo / Pocula Castalia . . . ministret'. See Ann Lecercle, 'Ombres et nombres: *Venus and Adonis* et le parergon', in *William Shakespeare, Venus and Adonis, nouvelles perspectives critiques*, eds J.-M. Maguin and C. Whitworth, *Collection Astraea*, 9 (Montpellier: Université de Montpellier, 1999), pp. 57–83, more particularly pp. 79–83.
9 Eamon Duffy, *The Stripping of the Altars* (New Haven and London: Yale University Press, 1993), p. 202.
10 Duffy, *The Stripping of the Altars*, Section D9.
11 All references to the Arden edition, ed. J. H. Walter (London and New York: Methuen, 1954, 1985).
12 Duffy, *The Stripping of the Altars*, p. 370.
13 C. L. Barber, *Shakespeare's Festive Comedies: A Study of Dramatic Form and its Relation to Social Custom* (Princeton: Princeton University Press, 1959), p. 242.
14 Fraser, *The Gunpowder Plot*, p. 16.
15 *Ibid.*, p. 107.
16 Maurice, Hunt, '*Twelfth Night* and the Annunication', *Papers in Language and Literature* 25, 3 (1989), pp. 264–71.
17 Cited by Duffy, *The Stripping of the Altars*, p. 258.
18 S. Bramly, *Leonardo: The Artist and the Man* (Harmondsworth: Penguin, 1988–91), p. 439.
19 All references to the Arden edition, ed. Brian Morris (London and New York, 1981).
20 E. A. J. Honigmann, *Shakespeare: The 'Lost Years'* (Manchester: Manchester University Press, 1985, reprinted 1998), Richard Wilson, 'Shakespeare and the Jesuits', *Times Literary Supplement*, 11–19 December 1997, 11–12; British Academy Lecture, 25 April 2001.
21 Camilleri, *Il Corso delle Cose*, p. 9.
22 Helen Whelan, *Snow on the Hedges: A Life of Cuthbert Mayne* (Leominster: Fowler Wright, 1984), p. 82.
23 *Ibid.*, p. 141.

Recusancy, festivity and community: the Simpsons at Gowlthwaite Hall

As the present volume attests, the study of Roman Catholicism in early modern England has recently been revitalized, partly because revisionist accounts of the Reformation have 'achieved the status of a new orthodoxy'.[1] In the course of elaborating, complicating and challenging that revisionist account, recent work in the field has consistently demonstrated the continuing cultural relevance of Catholics and Roman Catholicism to English culture in the Elizabethan and Jacobean periods.[2] This newer work has shown that although anti-Popery was an important part of early modern religious and political discourse, neither Catholics themselves nor the ideas and rituals associated with them in every context elicited the animosity that such virulent public polemic might predict.[3] Defining more precisely the nature of Romanist religious and cultural behaviour on the one hand, and main stream attitudes toward this religious minority on the other, while remaining sensitive to the different articulations of Catholicism in the various geographical and social communities that made up early modern England, has now become the challenge for new scholarship in the field.[4]

In this context, one well-known incident of Romanist cultural activity in the Jacobean period becomes newly interesting for the insight it can provide into the nature of the English Catholic community in the north of England. In the Christmas holidays of 1609, a group of recusant players named in subsequent Court documents as the Simpsons performed a play and an interlude with Catholic literary and political overtones at Gowlthwaite Hall in Nidderdale, Yorkshire, the home of Sir John Yorke.[5] Almost two years later, in November 1611, Yorke and about twenty co-defendants were charged in Star Chamber

> pur admittinge de certeigne comon Players, viz – les Simpsons de player in son meason un interlude in q la fuit disputation per entes popish priest, et English ministers, et le priest est de convince le minister in argument al le weapon de le minister estant le bible, et le priest le crosse, et le Diable fuit counterfeit de le prendre le English minister, et un angle prist le priest – per q interlude le religion ore professe fuit grandment scandele, et plusors del

audience fuerunt recusants come le feme Sir John Yorke et son frere Richard
Yorke et 7 autres et le resiens, ses amyes, tenants et allyes quaux (mult) deride
et applaude le play.[6]

The performance of this interlude apparently became the occasion for developing more serious accusations against Yorke, who was charged in 1611
with complicity in the Gunpowder Plot and harbouring priests, including
the notorious John Gerard. In preparation for the trial, depositions were
taken both in London and Ripon from over fifty people, many of whom
were grilled specifically about their experience at Gowlthwaite Hall in 1609.
The verdict in the case was at last handed down in July 1614, four and a
half years after the initial incident.

The extensive legal regards concerning this case have long been known
to literary critics from the work of E. K. Chambers and C. J. Sisson, and
excellent work on the incident has been done by historians (especially J. H.
C. Aveling and Christopher Howard) and literary scholars (especially John
Murphy and Masahiro Takenaka).[7] But these records have yet to be examined in the light of recent reconsiderations of Roman Catholicism's place
in the cultural geography of early modern England. The Gowlthwaite Hall
case can contribute to this recent scholarship in two specific ways. Firstly,
the incident can helpfully illustrate the complex nature of Jacobean toleration. The prosecutorial history of this case seems to provide richly textured
evidence supporting the traditional belief that Jacobean toleration was com-
prised, in Michael Questier's words, of 'theoretical moderation merged with
practical incompetence'. But a closer analysis suggests that the terms 'tolerance' and 'moderation' may need to be reconsidered, as Questier has
argued, for in this case at least the theoretical moderation could not allay
the practical harshness of the treatment Sir John and his co-defendants
received for a relatively minor infraction.[8] Secondly, the Gowlthwaite Hall
incident provides an important window into the gentry-based Catholic
culture of the North described in the work of J. H. A. Aveling and John
Bossy, among others.[9] Time had already eroded many of the communal celebratory patterns associated with the old religion, so it is probably inaccu-
rate to speak of 'continuity' or 'survival' when describing this Catholic
culture. But this incident suggests that social and religious leaders – Yorke
as well, perhaps, as the priests he intermittently harboured – may at this
time have been making a concerted (if vexed) effort to *re-create* the communal Catholic experience of late medieval England.[10] Though the case
cannot be considered representative, then, it does offer both an intriguing
snapshot of an elusive and poorly documented world, and caveats to larger
claims about the nature of English Catholicism's relationship with mainstream culture.

The major facts about the 1609 performance and its subsequent prosecution are clearly documented in the Star Chamber records, though

witnesses disagree on important details. Sometime during the twelve days of Christmas that year, the Simpsons arrived at Gowlthwaite Hall, apparently a regular stop on their regional tours of the area. That particular season the players numbered nine: Cuthbert, Christopher, Richard, John and Robert Simpson, William Harrison, Edward Whitfield, Robert Lawndes and the Simpsons' young apprentice, Thomas Pant, all from near Egton and Whitby.[11] On the Yorke side, hosting holiday plays was obviously a tradition at Gowlthwaite Hall; deponents testified that they had seen the Simpsons perform at Yorke's house on other holidays, including May Day, Easter and Ascension Day.[12] From isolated incidents of their arrest for vagrancy throughout the region, it is clear that by 1609 the Simpsons had been touring the area for at least ten years, presenting plays in gentry homes that were mostly, though not entirely, Catholic. After the trouble over the Nidderdale performance had passed, members of the company continued to perform until at least 1616.[13]

At this particular Christmas season, the Simpsons had four plays in their repertoire: *The Travels of Three English Brothers*, *Pericles*, *King Lear* and the one chosen by Sir John for the evening's entertainment, *Saint Christopher*.[14] There were 'forescore or a hundreth persons' in attendance, including the Yorkes, their servants and several friends and relatives from the surrounding area.[15] The audience was almost exclusively Catholic, as later testimony would reveal. In order to ensure religious uniformity, Sir John's habit on these occasions was to stake a servant at the door to screen out potentially hostile observers; several on this day were turned away. But Yorke's security system failed, this time, to keep out Marmaduke Darnebrook, associate of Pately Bridge's minister, William Stubbes. Sir Stephen Proctor, who would play a central role in the Yorke case, had brought Stubbes and other 'grave and learned preachers' to the area himself after learning 'that there had not been a sermon preached at Patley Bridge in Notherdale for twenty yeeres before'.[16] Both Stubbes and the Church of England were locally unpopular; another minister complained to Proctor that he 'said service sometymes to two persones, sometymes to three or fower, and sometymes there came none at all', despite the official presence of four or five hundred in his chapelry.[17] On the night the Simpsons performed at Gowthwaite Hall, Darnebrooke 'by private meanes gott into the house', perhaps with the help of his wife, a former Yorke servant. The next day he told Stubbes that the performance 'plaide & acted at Sir John Yorkes said house [had been] to the great scandall of true religion', hence beginning the series of events that would lead to Yorke's prosecution.[18]

The most scandalous part of the evening was the interlude described in the Star Chamber notice. According to Margaret Gill, then a young servant to an Anthonie Wuthon of Wormdale, 'there was in the said play disputation betweene two of the players . . . thone of them was an English minister & thother a popishe priest'. The disputation was 'of the olde Law'.[19]

The end result of the disputation was, according to another witness, that 'the foole did clapp the englishe minister on the shoulder & mocked or flowted him, & said well thou wilt away anon, and . . . in theend the Minister was overcome, & afterwards the Divells came & fetcht him away, one of them tackeinge him by the arme, & carried him away on his shoulder'.[20]

After Stubbes told Sir Stephen Proctor about the performance Proctor took action immediately, as he described in his deposition: 'he this deponent did allso send fourth his sevrall warrants & laid waite for the apprehension both of the said Simpsons & for searching for and bringinge before this Deponent all such play bookes as could or might be founde in their possessions'.[21] The Simpsons eluded capture – unfortunately, the 'play bookes' were never collected – and the case floundered for almost two years. In Trinity Term 12 Jac., however, charges were made in Star Chamber against a total of twenty-three defendants, including Sir John Yorke, his wife Julyan Yorke, his brothers Richard, Thomas and William, his nephew John Yorke, and eleven of the Yorke family servants. Sir John and his wife, along with many of the other co-defendants, were imprisoned in London.[22] Over the next two and a half years, depositions were taken from these defendants and other witnesses both in London and in Ripon, by members of the Council of the North. The case was finally heard in court on 1 July 1614; by this time, allegations of complicity in the Gunpowder Plot and priest-harbouring had been dropped, and Sir John and his co-defendants were tried solely on the charge of hosting a seditious interlude. 'The mere bringing of religion on stage being held to be libel', Sir John, his wife, his brothers, and the servants charged in the case were assessed fines totalling over £4000.[23] A few years later Sir John and his wife were imprisoned in the Fleet for failure to pay their fines; both were released in February 1617, at which time the total penalty was reduced to £1200, which Sir John paid in instalments ending in 1631.[24]

This sketch of the Gowlthwaite performance and its juridical afterlife can easily be seen to support revisionist characterizations of a practical policy of increased tolerance for Catholicism in the Jacobean period. In its opening stages, the case was brought to trial not as the result of any official zero-tolerance policy toward Catholics, but rather through the machinations of Proctor, Yorke's eccentric, highly litigious and virulently anti-papist neighbour. Without Proctor's interference, it is doubtful that any charges would have been brought against the Yorkes, their servants and their relatives. In addition, Proctor's motives for pursuing Yorke were not exclusively ideological. Since 1598 Proctor had been involved in an often violent property dispute with Sir John's neighbours and relations, Sir William Ingleby and Sir John Mallory. Yorke was named as co-defendant in one of the bills exhibited in Star Chamber on the property dispute; Ingleby's nephew and solicitor, Sir Thomas Ingleby, was initially named as a defendant in the Gowlthwaite Hall incident. The seditious interlude must have been seen by Proctor as an opportunity to harass further those aligned with Ingleby and Mallory; Yorke's Catholicism (like that of his neighbours) simply made him legally vulnerable to such harassment.[25]

Further evidence that Proctor's actions were not representative is that he was widely seen, by Protestants as well as Catholics, as a dangerous extremist. The main reason for the two-year delay in the Gowlthwaite case was that Proctor's own legal tactics had led him into a series of legal and political difficulties in London. In 1610 Proctor's over-zealous pursuit of a commission to collect outstanding fines assessed since 1588 led to the charge at the bar of the House of Commons that he had been 'receiving bribes [and] seizing the persons of thousands of people and then illegally despoiling them of money and goods'.[26] During Proctor's Commons' trial in May 1610 Sir John Mallory, Proctor's old adversary and a Member for Thirsk, charged that he had been libelled by Proctor's claim that Mallory planned to murder him. For this libel Proctor was committed to the Tower. Further evidence of widespread hostility to Proctor can be found during the Yorke trial, when Proctor became the subject of a different Star Chamber case for allegedly libelling Thomas Howard and Lord Wotton, two Catholic members of the council, as part of an elaborate scheme to plant evidence in the Yorke affair.[27]

The series of legal actions against Proctor indicate that most reasonable men in positions of authority in London in 1609–14 did not support Proctor's harassment of otherwise law-abiding Catholics. In the proceedings in the House of Commons, for example, only one member stood up in defence of Proctor – his old priest-hunting associate Sir Timothy Whittingham.[28] This moderate attitude is further illustrated by the case's judicial history. Though the exact details of the process cannot now be reconstructed, it seemed that Star Chamber moved forward with the case against Yorke only after the charges of priest-harbouring and complicity in the Gunpowder Plot had been added to the initial charge of hosting a seditious interlude; in a letter from Archbishop Abbot to James I that focuses on the charges of harbouring Gerard and of complicity in Gunpowder, 'the interlude is mentioned almost as an afterthought'.[29] The authorities' lukewarm response to Proctor's charges further suggests a reluctance to make engaging in Catholic cultural activity a treasonous offence.[30]

Proctor's eccentricities make him easily dismissable, then, as the exception that proves the rule of Jacobean tolerance. But the Yorke case also reveals a real and consequential variation in attitudes to recusancy, a disjunction that meant that, practically speaking, for many Yorkshire Catholics the 'official' position *was* persecution. If, instead of dismissing Proctor as a fanatic, we ask 'what exactly [Proctor and his allies] thought they were doing' (as Michael Questier has profitably asked about the Earl of Huntingdon and his associates), we discover in Proctor's rhetoric the belief that Catholicism challenged not religious truth but civil order.[31]

Proctor's defined goal was not to delve into the consciences of his neighbours but to ensure that they upheld the laws of the land. The Yorke case may be understandable as Proctor's opportunistic attempt to punish men in pursuit of his own economic gain, but it was also one component of a co-ordinated campaign undertaken by Proctor and two fellow anti-papists on the North Riding bench, Sir Posthumous Hoby and Sir Timothy Whittingham, to eradicate recusancy and what they saw as its associated 'treasons' from Yorkshire. In the years 1598 until 1616, these three brought cases in Star Chamber, imposed and enforced recusancy fines, arranged for arrests on recusancy statutes, co-ordinated priest-hunting activities and chased the Simpsons in a 'furious legal battle' against local Catholics.[32] The most common treason charges brought against Catholic gentry were priest-harbouring and complicity in the Essex and Gunpowder Plots.[33]

Were such claims the wild imaginings of a paranoid and essentially ineffective trio? Yorke himself was almost certainly involved in priest-harbouring; by most accounts Gowlthwaite Hall was filled with secret rooms, staircases and fireplaces, and strangers who seemed to have been priests were seen there often. One priest, James Harrison, was apprehended at the house of one of Sir John's servants; another was caught at the home of York's brother-in-law Sir William Ingleby.[34] The Gunpowder charges are more fantastic, but hardly outside the realm of possibility. Sir John was first cousin to the Wintours, and one deponent claimed that Robert Wintour had lodged with Yorke in the weeks before the plot. Fanatical and self-serving as his activities may have been, then, Sir Stephen clearly saw himself as the keeper of the peace, and not, perhaps, without some justification. Throughout his depositions he consistently reiterates the dangers posed to civic and religious order by Sir John's activities, and there was rational basis for such a position.[35] It would also be an exaggeration to call Proctor and his allies ineffectual. Though local officials 'regarded . . . with embarrassment' the anti-Catholic activities of Proctor, Hoby and Whittingham, they also by and large 'stood aloof from the fray', and therefore allowed significant financial and personal hardships to be incurred.[36] In the Yorke case alone, Sir John was imprisoned for over two years in the Fleet, and, even though his initial fines were reduced, the remaining penalty was onerous enough for him to be paying it off for sixteen years.[37] Despite a lack of enthusiasm for their activities on the part of local authorities and the centralized Jacobean government, anti-Catholic mavericks had enough law on their side to have a devastating effect on Yorkshire Catholic households.[38]

So, given the power and influence of men such as Proctor, Hoby and Whittingham, it is unlikely that Sir John Yorke and his associates had the luxury of perceiving their Catholicism as the focus of benevolent tolerance, particularly in the charged decade following the Gunpowder Plot. As the fall-out from the Gowlthwaite entertainments shows, financial and physical risks were run not only in harbouring priests and refusing to attend church but also in more prosaic activities such as hosting Catholic-tainted holiday revels. On the other hand, the long-term survival of the Simpson recusant touring company, despite repeated imprisonment and fines for recusancy and vagrancy, suggests that such entertainments were important enough to contemporary Catholics for those risks to be run by both players and hosts. Such an established pattern of defiance suggests that these activities yielded positive cultural benefits sufficient to outweigh clear and obvious risks.

The specific nature of those benefits, as well as further insight into the nature of Jacobean toleration, can be gained from an analysis of detailed descriptions of the Simpson's performance at Gowlthwaite Hall. Of particular relevance here is the longer play within which (most witnesses agree) the interlude was inserted as an entr'acte. That play is described in professional detail by Thomas Pant, then the Simpsons' apprentice, who played, magnificently, 'the parte of the Angell & one of the Devilles':

> there was one Raphabus a wilde man apparalled all in greene, with a greene hy Garland about his head that neither feared God nor the Divell, nor was of any religion, but would serve the mightiest man upon the earth, & having served two kinges and an Emperour, & hearing the Divell was of mo might than they wee, lefte them, and betooke himself to the devill his service. And afterwardes the said Raphabus beinge alone, a hermitt came in, and entered into conference with him, to drawe him from the said Divell . . . whom Raphabus answered and saith the devill was the mightiest man upon earth & him would he serve . . . [Where]upon the hermitt lefte him for that time, and the Divells came to him again to accompnie him . . . and immediately thereupon the hermit entered attyred with a . . . Cornered cappe on his head, & a Crosse of wood on his shoulder, & sett down the crosse just . . . where the Divells & Raphabus were to come, and the Divell named Lucifer & Raphabus comm[ing] & espyinge the Crosse the Divell started & shrunke backe, & willed Raphabus to take the lo[wer] path, whereupon Raphabus askinge him what he feared, Lucifer answered he feared not the wood Crosse, but the Adored Jew thereupon executed which was his enemie: whereupon Raphabus left [the Divell] saying there was a mightier man than he was, and went to the crosse, and soe the devils went all away casting fire about them. And then came the hermitt, in and Conferred with him again, and enjoyned him a Pennance for his former sinns.[39]

Obviously this play is Catholic in genre and topic. It is a saint's play, named *Saint Christopher* by a number of deponents, and based on the account of that saint in *The Golden Legend* of Jacobus de Voragine.[40] Clearly this play is unrelated to the Protestant saints' plays written by Henrician and Edwardian reformers, recently analysed by Paul Whitfield White, for this play wears its Romanist credentials brazenly.[41] Not only is the central action the conversion of a future saint, but the play dramatizes the Roman Catholic sacrament most roundly attacked by the reformers, the sacrament of penance. It also demonstrates the power of a crucifix, for the devils in the play shrink away from the cross on which is an image of 'the Adored Jew'.[42]

The play's subject, the positive representation of the sacrament of penance and the emphasis on conversion all identify the play with the saint or miracle play tradition of late medieval Europe.[43] Pant's description can be used to link *Saint Christopher* generically with the only three surviving English saints' plays, *The Conversion of Saint Paul, Mary Magdalene* and the *Play of the Sacrament*. Most of the minor revisions or embellishments made to the story of *Saint Christopher* from the narrative in *The Golden Legend* align it with these three plays.[44] The dramatic focal point of all four is the conversion of the sinner; *Saint Christopher* apparently ends at the saint's conversion, even though the account in *The Golden Legend* continues through his martyrdom and sanctification.[45] The play's focus identifies it even more directly with the late medieval English saints' play tradition; as Bevington says of the genre, 'the ritual enactment of penance and public confession characteristically protracts the action . . . after the dramatic moment of the conversion'.[46] All four of these plays end, to varying degrees, with 'heavily liturgical' action in which 'the spectators become a congregation'.[47] Minor theatrical details identify *Saint Christopher* with the medieval religious drama more generally, including the prominence of fire-bearing devils, and the interruption of serious business with comic interludes (Pant tells us that 'the fool mentioned in this Interrog: was the servant to Raphabus who in jestinge manner made sporte to the people').[48]

Saint Christopher is clearly associated with the saints' play or miracle play genre, but this association does not necessarily mean that it was an old play in 1609. Though its origins are unknown, there is no reason to challenge Aveling's suggestion that the play was written under the guidance of priests, possibly those 'brought up to the performance of plays at Douai'.[49] The writer of *Saint Christopher* could also have been influenced by contemporary Jesuit drama, if he was not a Jesuit himself, for penance and conversion were also popular elements in that tradition.[50] Even if the play was adapted, as Sisson proposed, from a sixteenth-century French or Italian play about Saint Christopher, it is entirely possible that this adaptation was done with clerical assistance.[51] Though all claims for the provenance of *Saint Christopher* are speculative, the play's existence suggests the possibility that some contemporary, educated Catholics, lay or clerical, were making a concerted effort to recreate late medieval dramatic culture. This conjecture is supported by the survival of the Stonyhurst Pageants, a series of plays based on biblical texts in a format recalling the medieval mysteries. These were written, as their editor Carlton Brown showed many years ago, by a Lancashireman during the reign of James I, probably in the years 1609–25 – roughly the same years that the Simpsons were performing in nothern England.[52] Though not conclusive, the survival of *Saint Christopher* and the Stonyhurst Pageants suggests the possible existence of a concerted effort to replicate medieval theatrical culture in early Stuart England.[53]

Whatever its origins, one of the benefits of *Saint Christopher* must have been that it provided for those attached to the Yorke household a way of connecting with 'the olde lawe' that was contingent not on individual spiritual growth and heroism but rather on a sense of communal belonging. Given both this function and the play's obvious Romanist elements, the surprisingly mild response to *Saint Christopher* by Protestant officials seems significant for larger characterizations of Jacobean 'moderation'. As Tessa Watt has rightly noted, *Saint Christopher* 'was apparently considered harmless by the authorities', a reaction that seems somewhat remarkable given that the play depicts a Catholic sacrament, administered by a priest carrying a crucifix to a nascent Catholic saint.[54] Though *Saint Christopher* was never the topic of investigation, the players themselves seemed anxious that it *could* have been. In their depositions, all of them except for Pant avoided discussing it in detail. Richard Simpson gives no description of the play except to say 'that that booke by which this depon, and the other players, did act the said play as Aforesaid was a printed book'.[55] Here Simpson seems to elide this play with others in the troupe's repertoire, for *Saint Christopher* was almost certainly not licensed for printing. Simpson's equivocating strategies are repeated by another player, William Harrison, who admits that the company performed 'two playes or Interludes' at Gowlthwaite Hall but claims 'that one of the foresaid plays . . . was Pericles Prince of Tire, and the other was King Leare', a statement uncorroborated by any other witness.[56] Harrison's claim allows him to repeat the apparently agreed-upon story of the company's repertoire, that all their plays were printed, 'usual playes . . . [s]uch as were acted in common and public places and stages'.[57] In fact the only player who refers to *Saint Christopher* is Pant, and he has an ulterior motive for being helpful with the authorities. Apparently weary with 'wandering in the country and playing of Interludes', longing for the life of the shoemaker he thought was gaining by apprenticing himself to the Simpsons, Pant had complained in October 1610 to the Justices of the Assize court at Topcliffe 'that he ha[d] not been employed in his occupation . . . but hath been trayned up for these three yeres in wandering in the country and playing of Interludes'. By the time of his deposition in August 1613, he had been released from his indenture for almost three years.[58] Pant's detailed description of *Saint Christopher*, as well as his reluctant admission of the existence of the interlude at his second interrogation, must be related to the fact that he was no longer a player and was indeed indebted to the authorities for having freed him from his unorthodox apprenticeship.[59]

All the players still active in the company at the time of their depositions, then, were skittish about the potential offensiveness of *Saint Christopher*. But our understanding of the cultural attitude toward this obviously

Catholic play must be complicated by the very different position taken to the play by both Catholic and Protestant members of the audience. The players' reluctance to discuss the play is offset by those witnesses (for both the prosecution and the defence) who find it absolutely unremarkable.[60] Even Proctor does not object to the play. Admittedly his account of the evening's entertainment is hearsay, but it nevertheless seems significant that he mentions *Saint Christopher* only to suggest that without the seditious 'interlude' it is unobjectionable: he has heard it 'credibly reported' that

> the said players upon they plaide the said play at any Protestants house they could play the said play, and would have out all that parte of the said Acte which concerned the counterfeiting of the said disputation [between the] popishe priest & englishe minister. And would & could neverthelesse when they played the said play before any popishe people where the Owners of the house were popishelie affected, play & acte the same with the said Popishe Priests and English Minister as aforesaid.[61]

Difficult as it is to believe that the Simpsons would ever perform at a Protestant house, Sir Stephen's claim is mischievously supported by William Beste, a servant to the Catholic Vavasour family, who says he heard 'by report that play of Saint Christopher was also played at Sir Stephen Proctors and other houses in the country that yeare', information repeated by Hugh Leigh.[62] The players, who had been fined for recusancy many times in the past decade, might have had a clear motive for avoiding mention of so obviously Catholic a play, but the unconcern with which everyone else (even Yorke's defendants) refer to it suggests its essential inoffensiveness.

What does this range of attitudes toward the *Saint Christopher* play suggest about the tolerance of Catholic culture as it appears in the Yorke case? To begin with, it suggests that representing saints and Catholic practices may be more upsetting to modern scholars who have internalized a model of Protestant iconoclasm than it was to most Jacobean Protestants.[63] True, the general tolerance displayed toward the Yorke theatrics might reflect the case's judicial venue: attitudes could have been different in the Court of High Commission. But since a saint's play that climaxes with a hermit administering penance to a Catholic saint fails to raise the hackles even of an anti-Papist such as Proctor, perhaps such apparently obvious markers of Romanist sympathies had become as unremarkable in the early seventeenth century as the tombs, ruined abbeys, cathedrals and parish churches that still indexed a religious past. These Catholic artefacts were readable as part of England's cultural heritage – not necessarily, or at least not always, as dangerous indications of the contemporary Papist threat.

At the same time, owning as Catholic such forms of theatricality, in this case by providing a context that insisted on a specifically Catholic meaning, seems to have been one way that this recusant community maintained a sense of cultural and religious identity. Descriptions of the evening attest to the homogenous community created at this and, one can surmise, other performances by the Simpsons. Almost everyone present was Catholic, a uniformity ensured by the screening of attendees at the door, here described by someone who was excluded from an earlier performance:

> he this Examt hearing that there was a play then to be played at the said Sir. John Yorkes said house, this Examt went thither to see it. And he this Examt. being put back once or twice by one Habbgdon the said Sir John Yorke comming to the doore, asked this Examt where he dwelt, and this Examt answering he was Sir Stephen Procters man, the said Sir. John said that there were some friends then to come to see the play, And upon they were come if there were Roome he should come in. But afterwards beinge stayed by the said Habbegdon who kept the doores, this Examt. went his weies.[64]

Within the house, the audience's response to the interlude suggests the sense of freedom created by such careful screening. William Browne claims that 'upon the Englishe Minister was taken away, the people went after, makinge a Merryment & a sporte at it'. Proctor recounts, though admittedly from hearsay, that 'when the person that played the devil's part took the English Minister on his back & carried him away there [were] great rejoicings made of such the overcoming of the English minister'.[65] Such a large gathering of Catholics can perhaps be read as a secular replacement for forbidden communal religious rituals – especially in this particular case, where the entertainment represents the administration of a sacrament. Rarely could 'fourscore or a hundred people' gather for a Mass in Jacobean England (though accounts survive of such large congregations in Lancashire), but assembling so many people together for a play would have seemed (though it does not prove) safe.[66] The festivities not only license Catholic cultural responses but in the process create the kind of communal recusant experience difficult to attain in Jacobean England.

If the interlude at Gowlthwaite hall creates a sense of Catholic identity through festivity, could it be seen as part of a range of festive practices with this social function? Proctor himself makes this argument. He sees the interlude as one of several forms of festivity associated with recusants; the other one most often named both in the Yorke case and elsewhere is piping during divine service. Proctor claims that 'divers of the said Sir John Yorkes servants and tenants wolde sometymes on the Saboath day have a piper with theme, near to the church yarde. And there with theire piping and revelling wolde make such a noyse in time of praier, as the mynyster colde not well be harde'.[67] On one specific occasion several of the defendants in the Yorke case

> to the number of three score persons or thereabouts on a Saboath day came again nere to the church Screen with a piper. And mayde the like noyse and revellings in praier tyme. And that [the minister] sending forth the church warden to require them to come into praier, answer was brought, that some

of that unruly company made answer – that it wolde hinder the Ayle wiffe.
And that thereupon those, which were towards or affected the said Sir John
Yorke and poperie, went all into the Ayle house with the piper, And those
which were better affected went into the church.[68]

Of course neither piping nor playing hooky on Sundays was an exclusively
Catholic practice in early modern England, but they could, apparently,
sometimes function as an expression of Catholic cultural identity. Records
from the Lancastrian Sabbatarian campaign of 1587–88 that identify
Sunday piping with recusancy similarly attack the practice. 'The course of
religion is exceedingly hindered', William Harrison claims in a sermon, 'the
Lords Sabbath impiously profaned, by public piping, by open and lascivi-
ous dancing on that day'; Harrison lays primary responsibility for this
'impiety' to 'our recusants and new communicants'. John White, another
Lancastrian minister, makes broader claims for the association between traditional festivity and Catholicism: 'Papists have been the ringleaders in
riotous companies, in drunken meetings, in seditious assemblies and practices, in profaning the Sabbath, in quarrels and brawls, in stage-plays,
greens, ales, and all heathenish customs.'[69] Though Proctor, Harrison and
White all attack Catholics with these descriptions, it is possible to see such
Sunday festivities as positive assertions of Catholic culture against the
dominant orthodoxy.[70]

Continuing or re-creating medieval festive practices can, then, be seen as
one way in which Catholic communities were able to perpetuate a sense of
Catholic community. At the same time, the dramatic and political aspects
of this evening mark it as a nostalgic rather than vital cultural expression
– a form of seventeenth-century medievalism. Though free expression is
allowed inside the (imperfectly) guarded and fleeting world of Gowlthwaite
Hall, these proceedings themselves are characterized by the atmosphere of
secrecy and danger that defines early modern recusant life. The prevarica-
tion that excludes non-Catholics at the door, for example, replicates a motif
repeated in countless memoirs of missionary priests: the unwelcome knock
at the door, followed by the attempt to delay intruders as priests, vestments,
altars, rosaries and books are hidden.[71] The screened audience may then
confirm their communal experience by watching a Catholic ritual in *Saint
Christopher*, but this ritual is a substitute for, and not simply a reminder
of, their own access to the sacrament of penance. Though the audience is
watching a play generically identifiable as part of Catholic festive tradition,
there is no liturgical link between the play's subject and the time of year;
St Christopher's Day is in July.

And in one sense at least the entertainments are neither medieval nor
Catholic, for the seditious interlude of the Yorke case is a satirical libel, a
form of personal attack increasingly popular in Jacobean England that
found its expression in songs and ballads, letters, pictures, personal allega-

tions and various kinds of dramatic entertainment.[72] It is of a piece with libels prosecuted, for example, in Colchester in 1623, when during Twelfth Night celebrations a libel 'showing the devil taking tobacco with various of the town's clergymen' was circulated;[73] in Worcestershire, when John Penne wrote a ballad attacking the local clergyman which began, 'If the parson were in hell / and another in his house to dwell / then it would doe well'; in Stratford-upon-Avon, where a man was 'singing profane and filthy songs, scoffing and deriding on ministers and the professions of religion'.[74] Libels aside from the Gowlthwaite Hall incident also existed in dramatic form, as Star Chamber records attest; examples include the 'jig' of Michael and Frances, written by a Yorkshire man to attack and ridicule his neighbour, and probably performed by the Simpsons themselves.[75]

It was, in fact, on the charge of libel that Yorke and his co-defendants were eventually convicted.[76] What does this verdict say about contemporary attitudes towards Catholic culture as they were expressed in the Yorke case? Sir John and his co-defendants were accused, prosecuted, imprisoned and suffer all attendant financial and practical hardships because they were Catholics. But the offence for which they were finally convicted was only tangentially related to their religion; had they been conformists making fun of a local 'godly' minister the verdict might have been the same. In this sense the judicial outcome of the trial can be read as a more temperate expression of Proctor's main concern with recusancy: that it contributed to a culture of law-breaking, incivility and disrespect for authority. Certainly we can call the opposition to Catholicism reflected in this verdict ideological, and it seems illogical, if not callous, to say that these Catholics were not suffering for their religion, since they would never have been so thoroughly harassed were it not for the legal vulnerability created by their nonconformity. But given that the continuation of a medieval Catholic cultural artefact (in the form of a saint's play) bothers hardly any one, and a clearly anti-government interlude raises the hackles of very few, recusancy in a legal sense is offensive not as a threat to religious truth but as a more general challenge to law and order.

The Yorke case can be useful, then, in considering certain aspects of early Jacobean recusant culture. It can illustrate the complicated and at times contradictory nature of 'moderation'. It confirms that moderate views toward Catholic activity were indeed the norm, but that practically speaking this moderation did not protect devoted nonconformists, even nonradicals. It shows how even in the Jacobean period attempts were being made to recreate the sense of the late medieval Catholic community described by Eamon Duffy in *The Stripping of the Altars*.[77] If Gowlthwaite is a guide, those communities were simultaneously persistent and precarious. Imprisoned (for the second time) directly following the July 1614 verdict, Sir John finally recanted his religion in 1617 and took the Oath of Allegiance, whereupon the fines levied on him by Star Chamber were substantially reduced.[78]

During the trial, holiday revels at Gowlthwaite ceased, according to several deponents, but they did not stop for ever: Yorke had apparently recovered enough by 1628 to host an interlude in which an actor playing a devil carried King James on his back to hell.[79] Sir John's persistence in hosting such theatrical events despite his experience with Star Chamber suggests that festive practices – congenial with mainstream English culture, but still coded as Catholic within certain situations – were a particularly important way for this community to assert its Catholic identity.

Notes

1 Muriel C. McClendon, 'A Moveable Feast: Saint George's Day Celebrations and Religious Change in Early Modern England', *Journal of British Studies* 38:1 (1999), 1–27, at p. 2. See also Christopher Haigh, *Reformation and Resistance in Tudor Lancashire* (Cambridge: Cambridge University Press, 1975) and *English Reformations* (Oxford: Oxford University Press (1993), Eamon Duffy, *The Stripping of the Altars* (New Haven and London: Yale University Press, 1993), and J. J. Scarisbrick, *The Reformation and the English People* (Oxford: Oxford University Press, 1984). On the history of Catholic studies of the period, especially on the hagiographic orientation of most work from the seventeenth to the early nineteenth century, see Michael Mullet, *Catholics in Britain and Ireland 1558–1829* (New York: St Martins, 1998), pp. 1–6, and Martin J. Havran, 'The British Isles', in *Catholicism in Early Modern History: A Research Guide*, ed. John O'Malley, SJ (Ann Arbor: University of Michigan Press, 1988), pp. 69–82.
2 Recent book-length work from both ecclesiastical and literary historians that suggests the continuing influence of the old religion into the Elizabeth and Jacobean periods includes Alexandra Walsham, *Church Papists: Catholicism, Conformity, and Confessional Polemic in Early Modern England* (Rochester: Boydell, 1993); Anthony Milton, *Catholic and Reformed* (Cambridge: Cambridge University Press, 1995); Michael Questier, *Conversion, Politics and Religion in England, 1580–1624* (Cambridge: Cambridge University Press, 1996); Thomas McCoog, MSJ, ed., *The Reckoned Expense: Edmund Campion and the Early English Jesuits* (Rochester: Boydell, 1996); Arthur Marotti, ed., *Catholicism and Anti-Catholicism in Early Modern English Texts* (New York: St Martins, 1999); Alison Shell, *Catholicism, Controversy and the English Literary Imagination, 1558–1660* (Cambridge: Cambridge University Press, 1999) and Frances Dolan, *Whores of Babylon: Catholicism, Gender and Seventeenth-century Print Culture* (Ithaca and London: Cornell University Press, 1999).
3 Milton, *Catholic and Reformed*, p. 86. On anti-popery see Peter Lake, 'Anti-popery: the Structure of a Prejudice', in *Conflict in Early Stuart England*, eds Richard Cust and Ann Hughes (New York: Longman, 1989), pp. 72–106, and C. Z. Weiner, 'The Beleaguered Isle: a Study of Elizabethan and Early Jacobean Anti-Catholicism', *Past & Present*, 51 (1971), 23–55.
4 Haigh, *Reformation and Resistance*, both anticipated and laid methodological groundwork for much of this recent scholarship.
5 The players are sometimes called the Cholmely Players, for in 1616 Richard Cholmely of Whitby (a member of the Essex Rebellion) was charged with har-

bouring a later incarnation of the company; see J. C. H Aveling, *Northern Catholics: The Catholic Recusants in the North Riding of Yorkshire, 1558–1790* (London: Chapman, 1966), p. 298.

6 John Southerden Burn, ed., *The Star Chamber: Notices of the Court and its Proceedings* (London: J. R. Smith, 1870), p. 78. As this notice implies, Yorke was probably not himself a recusant. Like many 'popishly inclined' heads of household, Yorke strategically attended church often enough to avoid recusant fines.

7 E. K. Chambers, *The Elizabethan Stage* (Oxford: Clarendon, 1951, rev. edn) 1, p. 304n and 2, pp. 328–9; C. J. Sisson, 'Shakespeare's Quartos as Prompt Copies', *Review of English Studies* 18:1 (1942), 135–43, and the briefer description of the Simpsons in C. J. Sisson, *Lost Plays of Shakespeare's Age* (Cambridge: Cambridge University Press, 1936), pp. 129–30; Christopher Howard, *Sir John Yorke of Nidderdale* (London: Sheed & Ward, 1939), and John Murphy, *Darkness and Devils: Exorcism and King Lear* (Athens: Ohio University Press, 1984), the most detailed investigations of the records; and Aveling, *Northern Catholics*, pp. 288–91. Professor Masahiro Takenaka has kindly shared a copy of his unpublished essay on this topic. Briefer discussions of the Simpsons and the Yorke case are in Adam Fox, 'Religious Satire in English Towns', in *The Reformation in English Towns, 1500–1640*, eds Patrick Collinson and John Craig (London: Macmillan, 1998), pp. 221–40; Tessa Watt, *Cheap Press and Popular Piety in Early Modern England* (Cambridge: Cambridge University Press, 1991), pp. 30–1, and Peter Womack, 'Shakespeare and the Sea of Stories', *Journal of Medieval and Early Modern Studies* 29:1 (1999), 168–87.

8 Michael Questier, 'Loyalty, Religion and State Power in Early Modern England: English Romanism and the Jacobean Oath of Allegiance', *Historical Journal* 40:2 (1997), 311–29, at p. 312.

9 See, for example, John Bossy, *The English Catholic Community, 1570–1800* (London: Darton, Longman and Todd, 1975), pp. 149–81; Aveling, *Northern Catholics*, pp. 199–297.

10 The case provides an example of how, as Mullet has written, 'Catholic country squires attracted, encouraged, and made religious and priestly provisions for Catholic tenants and servants', Mullett, *Catholics in Britain and Ireland*, p. 8. The dispute on 'survival' versus 'revival' between Patrick McGrath and Christopher Haigh is mostly concerned with Elizabethan Catholicism. See Patrick McGrath, 'Elizabethan Catholicism: a Reconsideration', *Journal of Ecclesiastical History* 35:3 (1984), 414–28, at pp. 414–17; Haigh's response: Christopher Haigh, 'Revisionism, the Reformation, and the History of English Catholicism', *Journal of Ecclesiastical History* 36:3 (1985), 394–406, and the overview of this controversy in Mullet, *Catholics in Britain and Ireland*, pp. 2–11.

11 Testimony of William Harrison: Public Records Office STAC 8/19/10: 31; also Robert Simpson (PRO STAC 8/19/10: 29); Robert Lawnde (PRO STAC 8/19/10: 44) and Richard Simpson (PRO: STAC 8/19/10: 29). The Simpsons were cordwainers; later members of the company included Richard Hudson of Hutton Bushell and Edward Lister of Allerston, both weavers. See The Rev. J. C. Atkinson, ed., *Quarter Sessions Records* (London: The North Riding Record Society, 1884–92), vols 1–2, at 1, p. 260.

12 For example, William Beste, servant to the Lady Vavasour, claimed he had seen the Simpsons perform at Yorke House 'about May Day' several years previously

(PRO STAC 8/19/10: 47); another deponent, George Newbalde of Pately Bridge, claimed to have been turned away from another such performance during Easter (PRO STAC 8/19/10: 15).

13 The Simpsons' activities can be reconstructed from the series of minor skirmishes with local authorities, usually for violating vagrancy statutes, especially 39 Eliz c.3 and 4, and 1 James c.7. See Atkinson, *Quarter Sessions Records*, 1, pp. 154, 204, 206, 260; 2, pp. 110, 119, 197.

14 Thomas Pant says that they offered Sir John Yorke 'the three shirleys, & Saint Christopher' (PRO STAC 8/19/10: 6); William Harrison is the player who reveals that *Pericles* and *King Lear* were also in the Simpsons' repertoire that season (PRO STAC 8/19/10: 30). All four of these plays have obvious or arguable appeals to a Catholic audience; see Murphy, *Darkness and Devils*, pp. 111–16. '[T]he three shirleys', or *Travels with Three English Brothers*, dramatizes the patriotism of the Catholic Shirley family on their recent foreign travels, and includes a positive representation of the Pope. See, on the possible contemporary appeals of *Pericles* to a Catholic audience, Womack, 'Shakespeare and the Sea of Stories', pp. 168–87; see also Bamford's recent discussion of the links between Marina and the saints' play tradition, in Karen Bamford, *Sexual Violence on the Jacobean Stage* (New York: St Martins, 2000), pp. 33–40. On *Lear* see Murphy, *Darkness and Devils*; Masahiro Takenaka, unpublished conference paper, 'The Cholmely Players and the Performance of *King Lear* in Yorkshire', and Stephen Greenblatt, *Shakespearean Negotiations* (Berkeley: University of California Press, 1988), pp. 94–128.

15 Testimony of Thomas Pant (PRO STAC 8/19/10: 6), corroborated by other witnesses.

16 Testimony of Sir Stephen Proctor (PRO STAC 8/19/10: 22). For arguments about Shakespeare's possible personal relationship to Catholicism see E. A. J. Honigmann *Shakespeare: The 'Lost Years'* (Manchester: Manchester University Press, 1985), and Richard Wilson, 'Shakespeare and the Jesuits', *Times Literary Supplement*, 11–19 December 1997, 11–13.

17 Testimony of Sir Stephen Proctor (PRO STAC 8/19/10: 41), recounting the words of George Manson, minister of Middlesmore, Sir John's parochial chapel. Howard, *Sir John Yorke*, p. 20.

18 These words are Proctor's, PRO STAC 8/19/10: 19.

19 PRO STAC 8/19/10: 10.

20 Testimony of William Browne of Golthouse in Netherdale (PRO STAC 8/10/19: 11).

21 PRO STAC 8/19/10: 19.

22 For the complete list of defendants see PRO STAC 8/19/10: 132. According to Howard, although 'Christopher and Robert Simpson were named as defendants . . . it is unlikely that writs were issued out against them'. Howard, *Sir John Yorke*, p. 66n. None of the defendants was imprisoned for the entire period of November 1611 to July 1614: 'the lesser defendants were released on bail in the summer of 1613, and Sir John on October 31st', *ibid.*, pp. 27–8. Charges against Thomas Ingleby, nephew of Sir William Ingleby, were apparently dropped much earlier.

23 Howard, *Sir John Yorke*, p. 45.

24 *Ibid.*, pp. 41, 56; Murphy, *Darkness and Devils*, pp. 93–4.

25 Murphy, *Darkness and Devils*, pp. 49, 54.

26 *Ibid.*, p. 56.

27 The bill against Proctor passed the Commons in June, though the matter apparently was subsequently dropped in the House of Lords; Howard, *Sir John Yorke*, pp. 41, 56.

28 Howard, *Sir John Yorke*, p. 41.

29 *Ibid.*, p. 64n.

30 Proctor tries to characterize the performance of the interlude as a treasonous act by claiming that it encouraged conversion: he says that "the popishe people, who said they had seene the said play acted at the said Sir. John Yorkes house in Netherdale, affirmed to some other of their neighbours who had not seene the same, that if they had seene the said play as it was plaid at Gowlthwaite they would never care for the newe lawe or for goinge to the Church more or wordes to that effecte" (PRO STAC 8/19/10: 18).

31 Michael Questier, 'Practical Antipapistry during the Reign of Elizabeth I', *Journal of British Studies* 36:4 (1997), 371–96, at p. 372.

32 Aveling, *Northern Catholics*, p. 205.

33 *Ibid.*, pp. 204–7.

34 Proctor, acting in concert with Whittingham and Hoby, was responsible for the arrest of these priests (both of whom were subsequently hanged), as well as the 1609 capture of John Mush and Matthew Flathers; the former escaped from York castle, and the latter was executed; see Howard, *Sir John Yorke*, p. 14. For descriptions of priests at Gowlthwaite Hall see, especially, the testimony of Robert Joye, STAC 8/19/10: 7–8.

35 Proctor's sense of the civic misrule caused by recusancy can be found throughout his testimony, especially PRO STAC 8/19/10: 18–22 and 40–4.

36 Aveling, *Northern Catholics*, p. 207.

37 Howard, *Sir John Yorke*, pp. 45–6.

38 See Aveling (*Northern Catholics*, pp. 199–202) on the effect of the anti-papist campaign waged by Lord Sheffield, the Lord President of the Council of the North from 1603 to 1619; also on the fate of recusant households from 1603 to 1642 during a 'period of financial stress' (*ibid.*, 257–88). On the financial burdens of recusancy in the period see Michael Questier, 'Sir Henry Spiller, Recusancy and the Efficiency of the Jacobean Exchequer', *Historical Research* 66:161 (1993), 251–66.

39 PRO STAC 8/19/10: 6. Raphebus is Christopher's pre-conversion name: 'after the conversion of the said Raphabus, the Angell came unto him, & called him by the name of Christopher' (6). The elisions and emendations in this passage are made necessary by a large tear in the manuscript.

40 On the late saints' or miracle play see Howard C. Gardiner SJ, *Mysteries' End* (New Haven: Yale University Press, 1946), pp. 53–4; Hardin Craig, *English Religious Drama of the Middle Ages* (Oxford: Clarendon, 1955), pp. 310–34; and David Bevington, *Medieval Drama* (Boston: Houghton Mifflin, 1975), pp. 661–3.

41 See White, especially the discussion of *The Life and Repentance of Mary Magdalene*: Paul Whitfield White, *Theatre and Reformation* (Cambridge: Cambridge University Press, 1993), pp. 80–7, and Peter Happé, 'The Protestant Adaptation

of the Saint Play', in *The Saint Play in Medieval Europe*, ed. Clifford Davidson (Kalamazoo: Medieval Institute Publications, 1986), pp. 205–40.

42 I am grateful to Paul Whitfield White for alerting me to the fact that this cross was apparently a crucifix, a point confirmed by other deponents.

43 On the French saint's play, see Lynette R. Muir, 'The Saint Play in Medieval France', in Davidson, ed., *The Saint Play*, pp. 123–80; on the Italian tradition, see Kathleen C. Falvey, 'The Italian Saint Play: the Example of Pengia', in *ibid.*, pp. 181–204. On the significance of the use of the cross in both *Saint Christopher* and the interlude see Murphy, *Darkness and Devils*, pp. 114–15.

44 Bevington, *Medieval Drama*, p. 662; see also Craig, who argues that 'the only complete and typical miracle play preserved in English is the Play of the Sacrament' (*English Religions Drama*, p. 324). Although so few English saints' plays are extant, evidence suggests that they were just as popular in England as on the Continent; see Clifford Davidson, 'The Middle English Saint Play and Its Iconography', in Davidson, ed., *The Saint Play*, pp. 31–122, especially the catalog of references to saints' plays throughout the period. In addition, see Gardiner, *Mysteries' End*, pp. 54–7, for speculations on what might account for the dearth of surviving English saints' plays. Gardiner suggests that these plays may have been both encouraged by, and indeed housed in, medieval monasteries, whose library catalogues note with 'regular frequency . . . "Miracula beate marie" and . . . "vitae et miracula Sanctorum" ', p. 56. The efficient destruction of these libraries might explain the absence of plays which seem to have been an important part of the general fabric of saint worship in later medieval England.

45 See, for example, the last English edition printed before the Reformation, Jacobus de Voragine, trans. W. Caxton, *The Golden Legend* (London: W. de Worde, 1527); 'The Life of Saint Christopher' is on pages 176r–8r. It is also possible that Pant describes only part of the play; see STAC 8/19/10: 1.

46 Bevington, *Medieval Drama*, p. 662.

47 *Ibid.*, p. 755.

48 PRO STAC 8/19/10: 6.

49 Aveling, *Northern Catholics*, p. 288.

50 Robert Miola first alerted me to the possible relevance of Jesuit drama to *Saint Christopher* in a paper for the 'Shakespeare and Catholicism' session of the 1999 Shakespeare Association of America conference – now published in our companion volume: Robert Miola, 'Jesuit Drama and Early Modern Drama', in Richard Dutton, Alison Findlay and Richard Wilson, eds, *Theatre and religion: Lancastrian Shakespeare* (Manchester: Manchester University Press, forthcoming) – and particularly to the central importance of penance and conversion in Campion's *Ambrosia*. See, on *Ambrosia*, the last scenes of Act 5, where Theodosius publicly repents and is absolved, in J. Simons, ed. and trans. *Ambrosia, a Neo-Latin Drama by Edmund Campion S. J.* (Assen: Van Gorcum, 1970), pp. 68–77. See also the description of the genre in Henry Schnitzler, 'The Jesuit Contribution to the Theatre', *Educational Theatre Journal* 4, 283–92 (1952), at pp. 285–6, and Wilson's characterization of the north of England as a ' "little academe" ' for Jesuit activity in the 1580s ('Shakespeare and the Jesuits', pp. 12–13). More work remains to be done both on Jesuit drama and its relation-

ship to early modern English culture; excellent recent scholarship is by Alison Shell, ' "We are made a spectacle": Campion's Dramas', in McCoog, *The Reckoned Expense*, pp. 103–18; and Shell, *Catholicism, Controversy*, pp. 188–93 and pp. 194–223.

51 Sisson, 'Shakespeare's Quartos', pp. 138–9n.

52 Carlton Brown, ed., *The Stonyhurst Pageants* (Baltimore: Johns Hopkins, 1920), pp. 12–21.

53 See Shell's description of the 'imaginative potency of nostalgia to the English Catholics'; as she points out, 'medieval patterns of life were sustained on the Continent by English, Scots, Irish and Welsh men, women and children, long after the Reformation . . . [and] there was a constant interchange of individuals between the mainland and these religious colonies', Shell, *Catholicism, Controversy*, p. 194. See also Bossy, *English Catholic Community*, pp. 110–21, for a discussion of the gentry role in sustaining festive Catholic practices.

54 Watt, *Cheap Press and Popular Piety*, p. 31.

55 PRO STAC 8/19/10: 29.

56 PRO STAC 8/19/10: 30. No other witness suggests that *Lear* and *Pericles* were performed at Gowlthwaite Hall, and such a long programme seems unlikely. However, there is no reason to doubt that these plays were part of the Simpsons' regular repertoire.

57 STAC 8/19/10: 30.

58 Atkinson, *Quarter Sessions Records*, vols 1–2, 204.

59 See, on Pant, Howard, *Sir John Yorke*, p. 24 and Murphy, *Darkness and Devils*, pp. 108–11, especially Murphy's transcription of the testimony of William Symonds, who reported that Pant acknowledged the existence of the interlude after previously denying it. *Ibid.*, pp. 108–11.

60 These include Thomas Burton and Christopher Johnson, both servants to Sir John, and Johnson, a co-defendant imprisoned at Newgate at the time of his deposition; also Hugh Leigh, William Beste, and William Brown.

61 PRO STAC 8/19/10: 18.

62 PRO STAC 8/19/10: 48–9.

63 See, on the survival of Catholic dramatic practices into the Elizabethan reign, Paul Whitfield White, 'Theater and Religious Culture', in *A New History of Early English Drama*, eds, David Scott Kastan and John D. Cox (New York: Columbia University Press, 1997), pp. 133–52, at pp. 134–5.

64 PRO STAC 8/19/10: 15.

65 PRO STAC 8/19/10: 18 and 12.

66 Haigh, *Reformation and Resistance*, pp. 292–3.

67 PRO STAC 8/19/10: 40.

68 PRO STAC 8/19/10: 40.

69 David George, ed. *Records of Early English Drama: Lancashire* (Toronto: University of Toronto Press, 1991), pp. 19, 28.

70 This understanding of the social role of traditional festivity is informed by Ronald Hutton, *The Rise and Fall of Merry England: The Ritual Year, 1400–1700* (Oxford: Oxford University Press, 1994), and David Underdown, *Revel, Riot and Rebellion: Popular Politics and Culture in England, 1603–1660* (Oxford: Oxford University Press, 1987); both suggest possible ideological meanings for festive practices in certain contexts. For a different perspective see

David Cressy, *Bonfires and Bells: National Memory and the Protestant Calendar in Elizabethan and Jacobean England* (Berkeley: University of California Press, 1989), and McClendon's analysis of the changing ideological meaning of the St George Pageants: McClendon, 'A Moveable Feast', 1–27.

71 See, for example, the account by William Weston, in *William Weston: Autobiography of an Elizabethan*, ed. and trans. Philip Caraman (London: Longman, 1995), 5, pp. 33–4.

72 See Adam Fox, 'Ballads, Libels and Popular Riddles in Jacobean England', *Past & Present* 145 (1994), 47–83, especially p. 48; and Fox, 'Religious Satire', 240. See also Appendix 8, 'Satirical poems from the Trevelyn Papers', in *Records of Early English Drama: Somerset*, ed. Robert J. Alexander (Toronto: University of Toronto Press, (1996), 2, pp. 732–43.

73 J. A. Sharpe, *Defamation and Sexual Slander in Early Modern England: The Church Courts at York* (York: Borthwick Institute, 1980), p. 5.

74 Fox, 'Religious Satire', pp. 225–6.

75 Sisson, *Lost Plays of Shakespeare's Age*, pp. 125–56.

76 Howard, *Sir John Yorke*, p. 44.

77 Duffy, *The Stripping of the Altars*.

78 Howard, *Sir John Yorke*, pp. 45–6.

79 Chambers, *The Elizabethan Stage*, 1, p. 328n.

Suicide at the Elephant and Castle, or did the lady vanish? Alternative endings for early modern women writers

In the summer of 1623 Dame Gertrude More and six other English gentlewomen, including her cousins Grace and Anne, set sail to found a missionary congregation abroad, the aim of which was to restore the Catholic faith in England. They were given an old ruined hospice in Cambrai and from these beginnings the Abbey of Our Lady of Consolation was built up both spiritually and materially, as the numbers of nuns increased and the redbrick walls rose steadily around them. Six years later, in the summer of 1629, a fourth cousin, Bridget More, arrived at Cambrai.[1] The daughters of other English Catholic families followed, so that the Mores were joined by Gascoignes, Ropers, De Hoghtons and Carys. For these young women the choice of a spiritual vocation combined personal dedication with a broader commitment by themselves and their families to the Catholic faith. Given the persistence of Catholicism in England it is readily understandable why so many of the country's families chose to send their daughters to Cambrai and similar religious houses on the Continent. Moreover, once settled in these communities, the scholarly activities and textual productivity of these young women was considerable. Their works, however, have not been fully investigated, and, as the title of this chapter suggests, their authors have often disappeared into 'unmarked graves', not unlike Virginia Woolf's fictional early modern woman 'writer', Judith Shakespeare.[2] This chapter begins by recognizing that effacement of identity, but also acknowledges the need to reclaim the textual material. Indeed, even positing the possible career of 'Judith Shakespeare' uncovers the dynamics of literary production. For, given the accumulating evidence of Shakespearean Catholicity, it makes it likely that, if William had a female relative with literary inclinations, she would have ended up in the Benedictine Abbey at Cambrai and not buried at the Elephant and Castle. Indeed, William Shakespeare might also have recalled his family's connections to the pre-Reformation Benedictine abbey at Wroxall, fifteen miles north of Stratford-upon-Avon, where Isabella Shakespeare had been prioress and Joan Shakespeare a sub-prioress. Or, as the Hoghton Tower years begin to look increasingly probable, Shakespeare might have recollected the relatives of Thomas De Hoghton who founded a seminary at Douai, where one of the Cary brothers (Patrick) was later to reside. Thus, multiple significations of gender and faith, of authoresses and nuns, converge about the fictional figure of Judith Shakespeare and her historically authentic counterparts, the women at Cambrai.

Nevertheless, the shadow of closure and erased identity cloaks the discourses invoked both by the fictional Judith's 'unmarked grave' and by the nuns' relinquishing of the material world. The ultimate desire for death and/or the loss of name posit an ending for the early modern woman writer which can only be expressed as it is silenced, made public only as it is contained within the silent walls of tomb and cloister alike. Elisabeth Bronfen in *Over Her Dead Body* uses Woolf's construction of an imagined woman writer to focus upon this 'triangulation of femininity, death and textuality' and concludes that

> Hers [the woman writer's] is a position of non-coherence, of the void or an empty space between signifiers precisely because she is constructed as [a] vanishing point . . . [and] the dilemma is that women, meaning the real historical beings, cannot as yet be defined outside these discursive formations, even though their material existence is certain.[3]

And this is precisely why we are often constrained to invoke the overused figure of Judith Shakespeare, a blatantly fictional character with an over-romanticized, stereotypical ending, alongside the 'real historical beings', such as Gertrude More, who have not, even now, been fully defined outside the 'discursive formations' which construct them as a lack, as a void, as simply vanishing – which brings me to the alternative title of this chapter.

The 1938 movie *The Lady Vanishes*, directed by Hitchcock, is a comedy-thriller, based on the novel of a woman writer (Ethel Lina White) and features the amazing Margaret Lockwood.[4] The film is deservedly the focus of scholarly research itself, but here I simply wish to invoke its basic function as a trope, as positing one of the dominant narratives of research, that of a literary mystery, where uncertain authorial identity and missing materials lend the scholar a detective-like demeanour. In this sense, the 'lady', or early modern female author, is particularly prone to 'vanishing', and the likelihood is increased still further if the woman in question came from a Catholic family and entered a convent on the Continent. Certainly the fifty-nine boxes of manuscript material from Cambrai which are now located in the public archive at Lille are packed with unidentified material – poetry, histories, devotional treatises, geographical descriptions, letters, diaries, medical texts, genealogical tables, saints' lives, biographies, account books, records of admissions and deaths, legal documents and stack upon stack of collection books. Author's names or signatures appear rarely and yet these papers represent the only material legacy of two generations of young

English women who left their families and homes in order to pursue and sustain their faith.

At first, it might seem understandable that the English Catholics would forsake a hostile homeland for the secure environment of the abbey in France. In addition, the inheritance of scholarly pursuits that characterized families such as the Mores, Gascoignes and Carys should have led seamlessly into the profession of faith and the closeted existence of the cloister walls. But these assumptions fail to tally with the material circumstances both of the abbey's foundation and the commitment of the female members to its perpetuation. To begin with, the acute persecution of the Catholics promulgated under the Protestant Tudors had become distinctly blunted by the 1620s. For example, while the Protestant Sidney/Herbert faction still exerted considerable power at Court, James's overall policy of appeasement and the possibility of a Catholic bride being chosen for Prince Charles had made life more bearable for the English Catholic families. This is not to say that persecution did not exist, but that the compelling reasons for the exiles of the English Catholics during the mid-sixteenth century were no longer in place. Indeed, the marriage of Charles to the Catholic Henrietta Maria in 1625 brought about a further curtailment of the worst form of anti-Catholic purges. Yet it was partly because of the incursion of Continental Catholicism that the English Catholics developed a need to anchor their faith more securely in the native traditions. In the More family alone the 1620s saw the publication of two Thomas More biographies, those of Cresacre and William Roper (previously circulated in manuscript form), and the establishment of the convent at Cambrai.[5] In addition, although the new abbey was located on the Continent, it was completely under the jurisdiction of the English Congregation of Monks of the Order of St Benedict. The English Catholics thus perceived the newly established religious houses as a way of reinforcing their beleaguered community's sense of itself in both spiritual and national terms.

But if the English Catholics were increasingly immersed within a discourse of idealized alienation, the individual members of the Cambrai community proved less than enthusiastic in their support of their families' endeavours. Let us begin with a manuscript account of Dame Gertrude More's early years at Cambrai that relates how at first she was

> of an excellent Judgement for her age (being but 18 year old) and of a piercing Wit, of a Very Good Nature, Gentle and Affable, of a Harmlesse Carriage, when she came first; yet withall, of a Lively Extroverted Disposition, Curious, and of a Working Imagination, prone to Solicitudes and Recreations, & Violent in her affections. She Knowing her Own Talents, and Wanting Instructions . . . decayed much in her Naturall Virtuousnesse. Her Simplicity became Turned into Craftinesses, her Tractablenesse into stoutnesse of stomach, & By wch her Guilt of Conscience Daily increased.[6]

It is not difficult to imagine the lively and witty young woman – and for a More wit was an essential characteristic – who was used to the cultured comforts or 'solicitudes' of her father's home and to the excitements of the Court's 'Recreations', being cast down by the austere life to which she found herself committed. Nor it appears had Dame Gertrude felt a missionary zeal while at home in England. On the contrary she seems to have been carried along by the displaced commitment of her father (Cresacre More), moved to fulfil a narrative in her spiritual inheritance, although this of course was in itself a perfectly More-like role.

However, the account of Dame Gertrude's struggles and final acquiescence to the Benedictine rule has since come to be perceived not as a perpetuation of her links to the English Catholic community but rather as an example of the powerful spiritual influence of Father Augustine Baker. The history of Father Baker's efforts to be accepted by the English Congregation and the changes within the Congregation itself are important for the understanding of Dame Gertrude's writing, and therefore will be dealt with briefly here.[7] When Cresacre More had helped found the abbey in Cambrai in the early 1620s he had been responding to a general trend initiated by the Council of Trent (1545–63) that called for the enclosed orders to return to their essential purpose of prayer and a perpetuation of the dialogue with God. For the English Catholics this need was particularly acute since with the suppression of religious houses there had been no formal, methodical and accepted participation in prayer. Rather, the primary activity in England had been the mission spearheaded by the Jesuits. However, by the 1620s there had been a marked shift in the direction taken by the English Catholics and the establishment at Cambrai embodied such a change.

Nevertheless, the establishment of the Continental houses proved more problematic for the English Catholics than had at first been envisaged. The form of prayer decided upon was the combination of daily meditation and frequent examination of the conscience that had helped the Jesuits on their mission. In addition, Jesuits were often chosen to act as confessors and directors in the new houses. But this Jesuitical combination of form and authority often led to a somewhat narrow and over-prescribed methodizing. While such a structure had a place within the mission, it failed to take into account the individual needs of the young women for whom the strictures of an enclosed life were strange, and who adjusted and developed into their new lives at different rates. And the new abbey at Cambrai was no exception. The postulants, including Dame Gertrude, began to be troubled in their consciences and they soon started to feel further from God than during their old secular lives in England. Realizing that these difficulties had to be quickly addressed, the Lord President of the English Congregation, Father Rudesind Barlow, appointed a new director to the abbey, Father Augustine Baker.

Father Baker had also found the methodizing of the Benedictine form of prayer too constricting, and his own experiences had caused him to develop a mode of instruction that was dedicated to guiding souls, both religious and lay, to a full dialogue with God. But although Father Baker soon proved successful with others at the abbey, at first Dame Gertrude resisted him, and it was only late in 1625 that she acquiesced to his teaching and found herself able to pray. Complete illumination finally occurred when Baker explained how those souls who were persistently beset with 'indevotions' and an alienation from God should quietly resign themselves to a state of aridity and use this negative understanding as a means of attaining divine grace.[8] To this Gertrude apparently responded, 'O, O, O, that must be my waie', and her subsequent writings attest to the manner in which barrenness, mortification and the acceptance of a negated self, actually facilitated the soul's approach to God.[9] However, although Father Baker had accomplished his mission within the walls of the abbey at Cambrai, his methods had begun to be questioned by the Chapter. It was alleged that the forms of prayer he had devised for his pupils were both too difficult and too close to the mystical meditations of the saints. Consequently, Father Baker was called to account and his papers were confiscated and examined. In the end he was vindicated, but at the very moment he stood before the ecclesiastical authorities, Dame Gertrude lay dying at Cambrai.

Before her death of smallpox in 1633 Dame Gertrude composed a number of pieces that were rescued and then arranged by Father Baker, but not published until after his death. These papers make up the body of two volumes: *The Holy Practises of a Devine Lover or the Sainctly Ideot's Devotions* (1657), which has an unsigned dedication to the Abbess Catherine Gascoigne; and *Confessiones Amantis, or A Lover's Confessions and Ideot's Devotions* (1658), which was dedicated to Bridget More by the Reverend Francis Gascoigne. There is a certain amount of overlap between the two texts, but essentially the latter work adds Dame Gertrude's *Apology* and a number of fragments that had been found in her cell at her death.[10] In both volumes, however, Gertrude continually revisits the troubled reluctance of her early days and the processes that led to her ultimate acceptance of and obedience to Benedictine authority. For example, in *The Confessions* there are several poems that directly refute those initial material yearnings,

> All things, desires, and loves are vaine,
> but only that which tends
> To God alone . . .

and she goes on to rework the courtly love metaphor of stag and hart, thereby demonstrating her own relocated discourse,

> No Stagge in chase so thirsty is,
> or greedy of sweet spring
> As is my soul of thee my God . . .
> My soul, where is thy love and lord,
> since him thou canst not find?

To him relation thou maist have,
as often as thou goes
Into the closett of thy hart,
thy griefs for to disclose.[11]

The signification of 'lord' slides from secular to spiritual, the hunt itself is transmuted from sexual pursuit to the internalized quest for Christian love, and the 'griefs' revealed within that closeted space lament life and yearn for death – 'while I live, I'll never cease, / to languish for his love'.[12] Inevitably, of course, the shadow of the secular remains imprinted upon the conversion to the spiritual, and the imagined end is couched in the terminology of courtly love, the vocabulary deliberately invoking the most sexually laden of Biblical texts, the Song of Solomon. There is certainly no rejection of 'inordinat[e] affection'. Gertrude's 'ending' therefore begins to look indistinct, almost as if the two patterns, spiritual and secular, have been superimposed but not precisely aligned. Her presentation of the self perches lightly at a point of closely related but untouching doubleness, so that, as the walls close about her, the epiphanic moment of freedom is itself veiled by the doubled tracings of her text.

These contradictions recur throughout Dame Gertrude's writings. They never overwhelm the central meditative structure of her work, but re-emerge at key moments when she self-consciously evokes opposing discourses as self-contained parallels. Overall her themes are common ones, particularly in the tradition of visionary autobiography,[13] as in the familiar mystical dialectic of spiritual and secular love described above. But the insistence upon division and separation is her own contribution to the way the English female mystical discourse was changing. Nowhere is this more apparent than in the title she chose for her treatise, *The Ideot's Devotions*. In the few criticisms that focus upon Dame Gertrude's work this phrase proved contentious from the first. The anonymous editor in the prefatory address to Catherine Gascoigne (the Abbess at Cambrai) of the first edition (1657) refers to the author, the 'Ideot' of the title, as male, perhaps in an allusion to Father Baker: 'This *Ideot*, who to others seemes ignorant, and foolish; to you is knowingly ignorant, and wisely vnlearned.'[14] This might have been an understandable error, for Marion Norman in her article 'Gertrude More and the English Mystical Tradition' (1975–76) suggests that the term 'Ideot's Devotions' was altered 'at Baker's suggestion to avoid confusion with a work of his own by that title'. Norman also points out that the word '*idiot* derives from the Greek for an uninitiated or unlearned person',[15] and this image coincides with Baker's evocation of self-negation and a sense of aridity. Of course, the 'Ideot' is all these things and more, or rather More-like. For, translated simply within the tradition of the English Catholics, the 'Ideot's Devotions' become the devotions of 'Morus', the fool, and then inevitably of Thomas More, his descendants and most especially of Gertrude *More* herself.[16] In her choice of title Dame Gertrude certainly participates in her own era's debates about the methodology of prayer and she fully supports her spiritual director within the Benedictine community, Father Baker, but she simultaneously evokes a trenchant and personalized history of English Catholicism. Of course the two are not incompatible and are easily brought together by Gertrude along the doubled lines of her other metaphorical passages. What is surprising is that subsequent critics of her work have overlooked such parallel significations. However, this omission derives mainly from the situation of Dame Gertrude's writing within a specific branch of spiritual history. Until now she has been depicted primarily as an adjunct to Father Baker in his determination to transform the English Benedictine community, rather than as a central figure within Englishwomen's Catholic discourses of the seventeenth century.

Yet, returned to her chronological and locational context, to 1625 and the redbrick walls of the Abbey of Our Lady of Consolation, Gertrude (along with her cousins, the Hoghtons, Carys and Gascoignes) emerges as the inheritor of a particularly English Catholic spirituality and not only as Father Baker's neophyte. The dominance of the familial context may be seen not only in the fact that the abbey's very existence had depended upon Cresacre More but also in the admission records to the abbey that specifically refer to the young women's genealogical associations. For example, the More family is described as:

> Entred Mrs. Helen More (in religion called De. Gertrude), of ye age of 17. Great grandchild to Sr. Thomas More . . . Mrs. Grace More (in religion D. Agnes) aged 32. Mrs. Anne More, aged 24. Both these Mores were nighly related to Mrs. Helen More, and descended from Sr. Thomas More by younger Brs. of the family . . . Entred Mrs. Brigitt More aged of 19, sister to ye aforementioned De. Gertrude More.[17]

Similarly, Catherine Gascoigne is depicted as the 'daughter to Sr John Gascoigne of Barnbow, in Yorkshire, Baronet', while her own prestigious role within the new abbey as abbess is ignored.[18] Lucy and Mary Cary are noted as 'the daughters to ye Right Honble. Harry Cary, Viscount Falkland, some time Vice Roy of Ireland', while Scholastica Hoghton is represented as 'a Lady highly distinguished in the World by her descent from an Antient and good family'.[19]

Of all the young Cambrai women, however, it was Gertrude who seems to have been persistently identified with an English Catholic inheritance through her relationship to the martyred Thomas More. For example, her *Spiritual Exercises* is prefaced with an anonymous poem that foregrounds the familial bond in begging 'Renowned *More*' to 'View heer thy Grandchilds broken Hart'; and her death notice makes the link explicit:

> In ye year 1633 ye 17 of August, died D. Gertrude more, of ye noble family of Sr Thomas ye famous Martyr of happy memory. Shee . . . lived with a great

deal of zeale, prudence & piety, as will appeare in her life writ more at large, shee left many examples worthy her blood & vocation, particularly in her last grievous sickness (being indeed very terrible) which shee embraced with much patience and conformity to ye Will of God.[20]

The phrases and vocabulary echo those used to describe Thomas More's pious life and patient acceptance of his execution as recounted in the family lives. William Roper had written that 'the loue he [Thomas More] had to god . . . conquered all his carnall affections utterly', and Cresacre noted:

So remained this unconquerable conqueror of the flesh, the world, and the devil some sevennight after his judgement in the Tower, arming himself with prayer, meditation and many holy mortifications, for the day of his martyrdom.[21]

As the contemporary accounts affirm, for her cousins, for the sisters in the abbey and probably for Father Baker himself, Gertrude More was as much the true heir of Thomas More as Margaret Roper had been a century before.

It is hardly surprising therefore that themes common to Sir Thomas More are repeated in Gertrude's writing. There are the familiar allusions to the instability of fortune as in her reworking of 1 John 2, 17:

Courted by the world, and all prosperitie.
    What then?
Let fortunes wheele aduance thee aboue the skies.
    What then? . . .
The world passes away, and the concupiscence thereof.[22]

Similarly, material things are rejected since the perfect soul must be 'cleansed from inordinate loues towards her owne selfe' and must 'aime at . . . our finall end'.[23] Humility and self-abnegation are evidenced throughout Dame Gertrude's writings, from the formal discourse in *The Holy Practices* to the '*Deuotions written by her in her Breuiary within the yeare before she dyed*'.[24] And as her own death from smallpox approached she turned increasingly to the topic of mortality. In her *Breuiary* she drew an '*image of* death' and added the words, '*O how little* to be esteemed, or desired is all that passeth away with time'.[25] Simultaneously, however, she acknowledged the 'fears and terrors that ordinarily accompany that dreadful hower [of mortality]'.[26] Unsurprisingly and with a remarkable, self-aware honesty, Gertrude More was able to summon her family's conventional rejection of worldly pleasures, to re-articulate the potency of that spiritual faith, while at the same time representing, in picture and text, the very real 'terror' aroused by the inevitability of death. In this doubled awareness Gertrude reworks the secular and spiritual tracings of her earlier work, but she also summons up the image of Thomas More in his cell awaiting his execution with both bravery and fear. Indeed, after her own death Gertrude seems to slide inexorably towards the full More discourse. She became the subject of Father Baker's saint-like vita, *The Life and Death of D. Gertrude More*, in which the trials of her soul, final sufferings and last words are described. Although only fragments of this life are extant today, it was copied by Father Leander Pritchard in his capacity as chaplain to the nuns at Cambrai (1661–69), and was subsequently scribally published with various extracts and abridgements.[27] In death, therefore, the More discourse, so precious to the English Catholic community, enclosed Dame Gertrude within the same winding metaphors of piety, humility and a saint-like endurance that had enshrined her great-great-grandfather before her.

Gertrude More's premature death at the age of twenty-seven made her a particularly appropriate subject for the romantic and saint-like descriptions subsequently produced within the English Catholic tradition. But the three remaining cousins – Bridget, Agnes and Anne – while not as prolific or lauded as Gertrude, did in their turn contribute to this inheritance. Agnes and Anne More remained in Cambrai until their respective deaths in 1655–56 and 1662, but Bridget (Gertrude's sister) left the Abbey of Our Lady of Consolation in 1651, and travelled with two other sisters to Paris where they founded the Abbey of Our Lady of Good Hope.[28] The circumstances that impelled the exiled community to undertake this unusual step were those that had similarly disrupted their homeland: the English Civil War. By 1645 funding from England for the Abbey at Cambrai had virtually ceased. At home, properties were being sequestered by Parliament, and royalist supporters were hardly able to finance their own exiles, let alone support a group of nuns. The English Congregation was in similar difficulties and could only advise that some sisters should be placed in French convents, but the Cambrai community was understandably reluctant to countenance such a separation. The solution seemed to be in founding a daughter house in Paris under the auspices of the exiled Queen Henrietta Maria, and, although they were initially discouraged from this enterprise, by 1651 their poverty had become so acute that there was no alternative. Consequently, Dames Bridget More and Clementia Cary, with the lay sister Scholastica Hodson, set out for Paris, a city already overcrowded with English exiles and itself suffering from internal conflict.

Triumphing over numerous financial, property-related and spiritual obstacles, the three nuns succeeded in establishing a daughter house by 1652, and Dame Bridget More was elected as its first Prioress. A number of moves ensued until they finally found a permanent house in 1664 at Lark's field. Meanwhile, the community had come under the authority of Cardinal de Retz, the Archbishop of Paris, and they formally left the English Benedictine Congregation in 1657. One year later Dame Gertrude's writings were published with a fulsome dedication to the Rd. Mother Bridget More,

Reverend Mother,
This deuout Book comes to you of right being your natural sisters excellent Goods, and there is no other heire left to it but your deserving self [,] *besids*

*I know few or none do any way pretend to it, but you and your Religious
flock who exactly trace by true practice (Ô Practice, divine practice the only
means) the same holy paths this booke treats of.*[29]

The direct link between Bridget and Gertrude is described in terms of their
being 'natural sisters', and Bridget is described as the sole heir to both
the More spiritual and textual inheritance.[30] Indeed, the Reverend Mother
Bridget More and the nuns at Our Lady of Good Hope are depicted as
alone in their interest in the writings of Dame Gertrude. Further, the dedication implies that the esteem in which the Mores were held had been
irredeemably erased by the changes that had already occurred in the outside
world. The religious schisms of the sixteenth century were by the mid
seventeenth century deeply imbedded in widespread political upheavals,
and the printed book had resolutely overtaken scribal publication. Consequently, although resources were summoned to reproduce the life, text and
image of Gertrude More, the result was sadly limited. Any comparison with
the equivalent mustering of support to sustain the memory of Gertrude's
great-great-grandfather Thomas More merely affirms the differences
between a young cloistered nun exiled from her home in the seventeenth
century and a powerful man whose martyrdom shook the Catholic world
of his day. Gender, wealth, immediate political and religious impact, the difference between public martyrdom and spiritual retreat, the amount and
quality of textual productivity all combined to ensure the perpetuation of
Thomas More's memory and the relative neglect of Dame Gertrude. If it is
possible to see Thomas More's image enlarged and projected as 'The Man
for All Seasons', it is equally possible to see the representation of Gertrude
'vanish' within the turmoils of exile and war.[31] This huge disparity cannot
be ignored. But at the same time the efforts of Gertrude More's 'sisters' –
those of blood and faith – to sustain an awareness of her spiritual and
textual legacy must be acknowledged.[32]

   In reading the works of Bridget, Anne and Agnes More, therefore, it is
important to recognize that the influences upon them are multiple and, to
a certain extent, divided. The sense of their national and familial identity
was still strong, with the demands of ancestry (Thomas More), fatherly
affection (Cresacre More) and sisterly loyalty (to one another) all playing
a full part in their writing. But the demands of their family of faith, of
the other women in their communities at Cambrai and Paris, of their
spiritual director Father Baker, and of the exiled English Congregation
of Benedictines, inevitably drew their hearts and souls. The influence of
Father Baker on Dame Gertrude's writings has already been discussed, and
a similar effect may be detected in Dame Agnes More's choice of work
for translation, Jeanne de Cambry's *The Ruin of Proper Love and the
Building of Divine Love*.[33] In 1625 Jeanne de Cambry had become a
recluse in the church of St André at Lille and the nuns at nearby Cambrai

would certainly have known about her intellectual and spiritual accomplishments. Indeed, Jeanne's interest in developing a system of meditative prayer with the characteristics of early seventeenth-century mysticism would have ensured that her writings were welcome within Father Baker's circle. Dame Agnes's translation was made from the 1627 second edition of Jeanne de Cambry's French original.[34] It is impossible to know at what point Agnes finished the translation, although it must have been complete by her death in 1655–56, since the single extant manuscript (now at Lille) informs us only of the translator's identity and the date the text was prepared for publication, 1691. Although she omits the first book, Agnes otherwise follows the original quite closely and her work is therefore not as distinctive within the familial discourse as her cousin's *Confessiones Amantis* is. Nevertheless, there are a number of similarities between the phraseology of Dames Agnes and Gertrude that display traces of their mutual inheritance.

The overall argument of *The Building of Divine Love* demands that the individual soul denies its material self, 'mortify[ing] all her exteriour senses . . . because [they] are the windows by which death enters the soul', and rejects the world as 'a dark and obscure desart . . . [in which] she cannot find any contentment'.[35] The soul, however, sometimes feels itself full of 'dryness, aridity, desolation [and] want of sensible devotion' and Agnes writes, following Gertrude, that such aridity 'is more acceptable to God than all that she [the soul] can do' since it demonstrates true humility.[36] The themes of mortification and martyrdom run throughout the work: the need for 'watchings, fastings, haircloth, disciplines, and other austerities' is accepted, while persecution and 'external torments' are perceived as inevitable.[37] And Agnes concludes in terms that almost replicate the phrases of the More biographers and the beliefs of the English Catholics at home:

> There are many souls and spiritual persons – both married persons and Religious persons – who are touched in so lively a way with this arrow of love that their lives are more angelical than human. But they are hidden from the wise of this world and persecuted by them.[38]

True to her inherited discourse, Agnes's translation shifts easily from the lives of 'married' and 'Religious' persons (as in Thomas and Gertrude More), through the experiences of Jeanne de Cambry and Father Augustine Baker, to the vitae of the saints and ultimately to the crucifixion of Christ. It is indicative that Dame Agnes is never described as having the fraught divisions of the soul experienced by her cousin Gertrude, and her translation through its genre, content and allusion falls completely within the multiple circumferences of the 'father's spirit'.

Unlike her cousins at Cambrai, Dame Anne More does not seem to have been called to produce spiritual texts, although it is possible that some of the manuscript works extant at Lille may yet be attributed to her. At present only a single letter is known that describes the death of Dame Gertrude, but it is supremely redolent of the English Catholic discourse:

> It was my good fortune to be with her for the time of her sickness, and by her when her happy soul departed. I beseech Jesus to grant me grace to imitate her innocent life, that I may have so happy a death. Truly she hath left so great edification to us, which are behind her, that my poor pen is not able to express . . . Verily I have seen in her Job upon the dunghill, Lazarus with his sores, an angel in paradise, so resigned to the will of God, so willing to die, so ready to suffer more if it pleased God, so firm in confidence with humility in almighty God, always praying, still calling on the sweet name of Jesus.[39]

Dame Gertrude's approach to death is presented as a spiritual example, while her innocence, resignation, suffering and humility suggest the image of 'an angel in paradise'. The terms by now are familiar, recalling that vita-like tradition which was already established in the More family and which found a ready response in the English Catholic community at Cambrai. But thirty years later a combination of extended exile, self-determined enclosure, the inevitable lack of progeny, the upheavals of the English civil war, the shifts in the English Catholic Church itself, had all militated against a continuance of such an idealized discourse.

The fragmentation had begun in the early days at Cambrai, but the final disintegration was to occur in Paris sixty years later, and as such the 1692 death notice of Bridget More almost seems to draw a line beneath the perpetuation of the spiritual and familial houses:

> The Rd. Mother Dame Brigit More the First Priouresse of this Our Monastery was profess'd of the house of Cambray, in the Year 1630, Sept. 24th: departed this life October the 12th 1692, being the last of the Venerable stock of those Religious, who coming from Cambray had liv'd and dyed so holily among Us.[40]

Of course, Bridget was the only nun remaining of those who had first come to Paris in 1651, but she was also the last of the 'Venerable stock' of the Mores who had journeyed to Cambrai, since Gertrude, Agnes and Anne were all dead. And as the century drew to a close, with Bridget's death the More Family's literary inheritance finally 'dyed . . . holily among Us'.[41]

This fragmentation would certainly not have been overtly apparent back in 1652, however, for Bridget More had just been elected prioress of the new abbey and at forty-three was the height of her organizational and compositional powers. Certainly, these skills were much in demand since in 1656–57 the community was forced to relocate to a house in Paris, on the unfortunately named rue d'Enfer. As a result of this move Bridget had to oversee the transference of the community from the authority of the English Benedictines to that of the Archbishop of Paris. A number of letters and petitions had to be written, and these were co-signed by several sisters:

Bridget More, Elizabeth Brent, Clementia Cary, Mary Cary and Justina Gascoigne. Although the originals are no longer extant, copies were made and are recounted verbatim in the manuscript house history of the Abbey of Our Lady of Good Hope, extant at St Mary's Abbey, Colwich.[42] The tone of these missives is authoritative and lucid, arguing finally that 'We have no thought, but the Glory of God, the Conversion of our Countrey, & the Good of our Community, & Congregation'. Unsurprisingly, the English Congregation and the Archbishop of Paris granted the nuns' requests. It is impossible to allocate the sole authorship of these letters to Bridget More, although she is the first signatory and in her role as prioress she would have made a significant contribution to their content. But that is precisely the point. The most important signification of the co-signed letters for the thesis discussed here is that the source of mutual literary productivity had shifted its site from the old English Catholic families to the closeted world of the convent. The genealogical relationships that generated the dialogic lines of the last century and a half had, by the mid seventeenth century, been replaced with spiritual ties in which faith replaced blood.

The moment of co-signature with its allied sense of multiple authorship erases almost to nothingness the very basis of the Cambrai convent thirty years earlier. For, in some ways, the political substance of the genealogy and the humanist agenda of the image with their patriarchal shadows are rendered redundant by these letters with their sisterly authorship. The Mores, Gascoignes and Carys at the point of mutual production breech the divisions between different inherited identities, simultaneously isolating themselves from their original ties, and forging a new relationship based upon religious community. Thus, the Abbey of Our Lady of Good Hope is through the literary activities of its members transformed into a 'family', although such a transformation adopts the forms that had long since been imbedded in the monastic tradition; for example, in the titles of brother, father, mother and sister. At first this consanguinity must have appeared particularly felicitous for the Mores, Carys and Gascoignes, since the divide between genealogy and faith had always been fine within their own familial traditions. But as the lines of descent extended over 150 years, and the removal to Cambrai was stretched in the further displacement to Paris, the old familial discourses proved increasingly difficult to sustain. As the early modern period drew to a close this fragmentation was echoed by other groups, as the identity and constituency of authorial communities changed, thereby necessitating the development of new 'familial' patterns and their ensuing discourses.

For Bridget More, however, the overriding concern would have been to settle her new community safely and solidly; and when in 1664 they settled in the house at Lark's field she felt secure enough to step down as prioress and was succeeded by the Reverend Mother Justina Gascoigne. The subsequent laudation of Dame Bridget in the history of the house depicts her as 'the pious offspring of that Renowned & Glorious Martyr, Sr. Thomas More', and as possessing 'a great deal of Patience . . . Piety, [and] Vertue'. Immediately after a link to Gertrude More is made: 'She hath ever since our Beginning bin the Model & Example of Vertue to all the Religious among us [in Paris]: As her Sister Dame Gertrude More was to our Mother-house of Cambray.'[43] Even here the shift of identity is apparent, as the great-great-grandfather, 'Sr. Thomas More', changes to the 'Sister[s]' of blood and faith, and finally to the 'Mother-house' with its assertion of spiritual community over genealogical ties. But if this seems to overthrow the patriarchal authority enshrined in the 'father's spirit', then a brief review of the men and women of the English Catholics – of their critical standing, of their biographical accounts, of the very form and location of their writings – will quickly return the gender balance to its traditional alignment. The material excavated and explored here cannot be said to provide evidence of a gender revolution. Yet the persistence of the women's literary productivity, from Gertrude More through to Clementia Cary, demands an acknowledgement of the way in which gendered authorship was being transformed.

Unlike the Mores, the Cary sisters entered Cambrai not with the patriarchal inheritance of the father, 'ye Right Honble. Harry Cary', but under the powerful influence of their mother, Elizabeth Cary. Over the last decade Elizabeth Cary's life, including her conversion to Catholicism, and her extant canon have been the focus of a number of fascinating accounts and analyses.[44] She was the sole initiator of her daughters' escape from England to the abbey at Cambrai, and certainly influential in their subsequent decisions to profess. The record book at Lille shows us that four of the Cary sisters entered the community over an eight-month period during 1638 and 1639: on 31 August 1638 Lucy Cary (Dame Magdalena) aged nineteen and Mary Cary (Dame Maria) aged seventeen came to Cambrai, and they were joined in October of that year by Elizabeth Cary (Dame Augustina) aged twenty-one and in March 1639 by Anne Cary (Dame Clementia) aged twenty-four. Subsequently, in the same book, but beginning on the other side, Lucy/Magdalena's death on 1 November 1650 is recorded with a short biography. This profile recalls that of Gertrude More, since Lucy/Magdalena is described 'an obstinate, haughty, disdainful, sneering lady' before her conversion, after which she led 'an obedient, humble life, all ye time shee had been in religion without any regard to what she had been or what might have been in the world'. This change is credited directly to Elizabeth Cary, 'a woman of an extraordinary piety as will appear in ye relation of her life written by a person who knew her very well'. This passage is important in that it substantiates the recurring narrative of near-miraculous conversion from material sin to spiritual ideal amongst the nuns' own self-definitions, clearly paralleling the description of Getrude More quoted at the beginning of this chapter.

However, this passage has also been used as evidence to identify which Cary sister wrote the hagiographic biography of their mother, Elizabeth Cary, 'The Lady Falkland, Her Life'.[45] In their edition of *The Lady Falkland: Her Life* suggest Barry Weller and Margaret Ferguson that 'the phrase [quoted above] could well be read as a coy reference to Lucy/Magdalena, in an era when women authors publicly concealed their identity but often revealed it, through coded allusions, to coterie audiences'.[46] But the manuscript life of Elizabeth Cary was written for a 'coterie audience' for whom 'coded allusions' would have had little meaning, since the sisters at Cambrai would have been able to recognize a text's author or transcriber simply by her handwriting. They were used to copying texts as a group, rather than individually, one nun taking over as another became weary, or as their tasks rotated. Whichever Cary sister wrote the account, her sisters, both in faith and blood, would have immediately recognized the author by looking at the script. Moreover, the catalogues the nuns maintained of their manuscript works, both at Cambrai and in the convent at Paris, freely recognize authorship and even comment upon handwriting, if it is deemed necessary or of interest. The 'Catalogue of the Manuscript Books Belonging to the Library of the English Benedictine Nunnes of our Blessed Lady of Good Hope in Paris' lists 'Eight Collection Bookes of the Verie Rvd Mo: Maother Clementia Cary who was the beginere or Foundrisse of our Monistarie . . . Fower and parte of the fift are in her owne handes writting'; also 'The spirituall songs of our verie Rd Deare Mothere Clementia Carys in three parts' and finally, 'Little books of colections . . . the Fift is Colections of R. Dame Madelene Carys'.[47] No other Cary is listed in the Paris catalogue. A similar list exists in the Mediathèque in Cambrai, which notes 'The writings of the most religious dame D. Magdalena Carie de St. Cruce professed religious of the most holy order of St Benedict'.[48] What is made clear by these contemporary manuscript listings is that 'coy allusions' were inappropriate for the language of the convent, and that of the four Cary sisters at least two were recognized as authors by their community – Anne/Clementia and Lucy/Magdalena. This does not mean that Elizabeth/Augustina and Mary/Maria did not write, but that they might initially appear to have 'vanished' more effectively than did their sisters.

This still leaves us with the question of which sister wrote *The Life*, but we can now categorically rule out Anne/Clementia; here I am verifying Weller and Ferguson's assumptions and fully concurring with Heather Wolfe's well-researched arguments.[49] There are two extant letters signed by Anne/Clementia and a page of transcribed quotations noted as in her writing that clearly define her handwriting.[50] It is manifest therefore that *The Life* is simply not composed by Anne/Clementia, although she does contribute some of the marginal annotation. In fact *The Lady Falkland: Her Life* reveals four distinct hands: the main text and three separate marginal annotators, whose additions may be found throughout the manuscript. Two of these annotators are easy to recognize: the squared-off notes belong to Clementia and the rougher notes made by Patrick Cary, one of Elizabeth Cary's sons.[51] Patrick's contribution to the text helps us to date the manuscript between 1643 (the death of Lucius Cary, another brother, in this year is referred to) and 1650 when Patrick left the monastery at Douai and so would have had no subsequent access to the manuscript. Sometimes his notes have been cropped during the binding of the pages and have been copied out in the inner margin by Anne/Clementia, in order to preserve them. Since, as has already been described, Anne/Clementia left for Paris in November 1651, we can assume that her emendations occur before that date. This, I believe, gives us a composition date somewhere between the late 1640s, when the text was originally prepared by one of the Cary sisters, probably Lucy/Magdalena, and 1650, when Patrick Cary, residing at nearby Douai, and certainly in touch with his sisters, made his annotations. Subsequently, before her departure for Paris, Anne/Clementia added her own elucidating comments and tidied up the text before it was cropped for binding. This dating affirms Lucy/Magdalena's authorship since her death in November 1650, two months after the departure of her brother Patrick, would have allowed Anne/Clementia to organize the material so that it could be preserved for posterity. However, the manuscript contains evidence of a third annotator, and the personalized knowledge of the marginal notes, as in 'She was acquainted with Mr Clayton sooner', suggests that another of the Cary sisters read and commented upon the life of their mother. These notes could either, therefore, be made by Augustina or Maria. While there are no manuscripts that are fully verifiable as Maria's, Dame Augustina wrote a letter to Colonel Grace in 1659, and since her handwriting does not appear on the *Life* it is possible to eliminate her, thereby revealing the final annotator to be Dame Maria.[52] But while these investigations are a fascinating decoding of authorial identity, at the same time the manuscript invokes more potent and often conflicting discourses. For the familial inheritance of the Carys and their mother's important role within the conversion narratives of the English Catholic community are set against a mutuality of authorship in which individual identity is submerged for the benefit of a single spiritual purpose. Just as Clementia's name appears alongside Briget More's in their Paris correspondance, so the Cary sisters began to redefine their 'family' in spiritual terms as the More cousins had relocated theirs within the confines of the abbey.

But the Cary sisters do not quite 'vanish', for by investigating the authorship of *The Lady Falkland: Her Life*, the identification of various scripts uncovers the fact that Anne/Clementia was just as prolific an author as was her mother. Works by Anne/Clementia are extant in the public archives at Lille and Arras, in the archives at Downside, Stanbrook and Colwich Abbeys and in the Bodleian Library. Form and content are varied, but all contribute to the further dissemination and consolidation of the Catholic faith in English. Translations and copies therefore predominate, although even these demonstrate a marked authorial independence. Perhaps the clearest example of Anne/Clementia's style and interests occur within her translations of the psalms. For example, her loose translation of Psalm 122 runs,

> Twas ye best news I wish to heare,
> My very soul stood ravisht at my Eare;
> Lets go, they said; Come lets away!
> Already we have tarry'd long enough,
> Now let our speed declare our Love;
> Why should we thus from Sion stay,
> And only be unhappy by our owne delay?
>
> Let's goe; see at ye City Gates
> How God himself to greet our coming waites;
> We come O God, nor will we rest
> Till we ye place have in Jeruslame found,
> Till we have trod ye holy Ground,
> Wch thou of all ye world lov'st best,
> Wch thou of all ye world hast wth thy Presence blest. –
>
> Wch in thy Borders Warr shall cease,
> For He, who is thy Gardian, is ye God of Peace.[53]

What is immediately apparent is the Donne-like direct colloquial address of the first line, 'Twas ye best news I wish to heare', and it is no coincidence that Donne himself was related to the More family and so, through the intricate but tightly mapped world of English seventeenth-century Catholicism, to discourse of the Benedictine community at Cambrai. Secondly, the text shows that Anne/Clementia was translating within a mid-seventeenth-century context, so that the political concerns of her period emerge jaggedly into the dominant spiritual discourse. Cary's reference to 'warr', which is replicated throughout her translations of the later psalms and some of the original poems, her writing participates in the overwhelming discourse of civil bloodshed which had engulfed English authors on the Continent as well as at home. Indeed, her brother Lucius Cary, whose death has already been noted in *The Life*, rode to his death at the battle of Newbury on 20 September 1643. He was said to have exposed himself willingly to danger as he had grown disillusioned with life and 'longed to be out of it ere night'.[54] And Anne/Clementia's translation echoes this wish, for while the psalm relates the hopes of the exiles in Egypt as they are led by Moses to the promised land, it simultaneously calls for death, 'Come lets away!' and the final journey to the new Jerusalem where 'God himself to greet our coming, waites'. Thus, as with the spiritual verses of the other women at Cambrai, the discourses of the material, of family and of civil war, reside alongside the spiritual rejection of life or, as Gertrude More has it, the 'languishing' for death.

Even as the detective work of scholarship uncovers the 'real historical women' who wrote, their very texts construct a doubled signification which precipitates them into the void between the divided discourses. Thus, we have Gertrude's denial of the world's 'solicitudes' and 'recreations' coupled with her own overtly romanticized annihilation of the self; Lucy/Magdalena's rejection of 'what she had been or might have been in the world' set alongside her noble inheritance and her role as family biographer; and finally Anne/Clementia's celebration of death riven through with her sharply voiced fears for the fate of her brothers and country. The Benedictine nuns at Cambrai were neither of this world nor out of it, and as such their writings exist at the interstice between the material and the spiritual, the families of blood and of faith, of open political awareness or personal exclusion, and between overt textual production and closeted authorial anonymity. Yet these separate discourses are beginning to converge. The indistinct tracings are gradually being clarified, and as the 'real historical women' – the More, Cary and De Hoghton nuns at Cambrai – replace the fictional corpse of Judith Shakespeare, so 'the lady' will cease to 'vanish', allowing the early modern woman writer to emerge into the light of a critical canon with, as it were, her textual body intact.

Notes

1 Helen More (Dame Gertrude) and Bridget More (Dame Bridget) were the daughters of Cresacre More. Anne More (Dame Anne) was the daughter of Edward More and sister to Thomas More (V) and Henry More. The final cousin, Grace More (Dame Agnes), was the daughter of Mary More who was Cresacre's sister. Dames Gertrude, Bridget and Agnes were therefore all first cousins whose grandfather was Thomas More (II), while Dame Anne was a second cousin whose father, Edward was Thomas More (II)'s brother. The Cambrai convent was active in promoting Catholicism at home. There is evidence of several examples of significant political involvement: support for Jesuit priests and help to prepare for their secret missions in England; a safe house for those recusant women who defied their families; and copying and disseminating key Catholic tracts to the remaining faithful at home. Moreover, the community was considered so dangerous to the new French Republic that in the summer of 1793 the convent was destroyed by the people of Cambrai and the nuns were taken to Compiegne, where they were stripped of their possessions, starved, interrogated and finally encouraged to prepare themselves for the guillotine. They finally escaped and ended up in Liverpool.

2 Virginia Woolf, *A Room of One's Own* (London: Hogarth Press, 1929), pp. 69–75.

3 Elisabeth Bronfen, *Over Her Dead Body* (Manchester: Manchester University Press, 1992), p. 403.

4 *The Lady Vanishes* (1938), dir. Alfred Hitchcock.

5 William Roper, *The Life of Sir Thomas Moore Knighte*, ed. Elsie Vaughan Hitchcock (London: Oxford University Press, 1935), and Cresacre More, *The Life and Death of Sir Thomas Moore* (Douay: Balthasar Ballère, 1631).

6 Dame Gertrude More (formerly Helen More), Ms 1755 Bibliothèque Mazzarine, Paris, ff. 179–80.

7 The history of Father Baker's role in developing the methodologies of prayer in the Benedictine church is summarized, along with his remarkable biography, in, for example, Peter Salvin and Serenus Cressy, *The Life of Father Augustine Baker, 1575–1641* (London: Burns, Oates and Washbourne, 1933) and Justine McCann and Hugh Connolly (eds), *Memorials of Father Augustine Baker, Publications of the Catholic Record Society*, 33 (1933). For a discussion of the role of the Council of Trent on the establishment of English religious houses on the continent see Alison Shell, *Catholicism, Controversy and the English Literary Imagination, 1558–1660* (Cambridge: Cambridge University Press, 1999), pp. 169–223.

8 Father Baker was reading and translating into English the Latin text of Barbanson's, *De semitis occultis divini amoris*, for Gertrude and another novice, and it is in the preface to this book that the theory of the aridity of the soul is discussed. See also Marion Norman, 'Dame Gertrude More and the English Mystical Tradition', *Recusant History* 13 (1975–1976), pp. 196–211, and Dame Frideswide Sandeman, *Dame Gertrude More* (Leominster: Gracewing, 1997).

9 The quotation is taken from Father Augustine's manuscript life of Dame Gertrude, *The Life and Death of D. Gertrude More*, Stanbrook Abbey MS III, p. 26.

10 Gertrude More, *The Holy Practises of a Divine Lover, or the Sainctly Ideot's Devotions* (Paris: Lewis de la Fosse, 1657) and *The Spiritual Exercises . . . Confessiones Amantis, or A Lover's Confessions and Ideot's Devotions* (Paris: Lewis de la Fosse, 1658).

11 Gertrude More, *The Spiritual Exercises*, pp. 46–7.

12 *Ibid.*, p. 46.

13 Dame Gertrude's writing echoes the mystical and visionary writing of a number of women in the medieval and early modern periods; this is discussed by Marion Norman in 'Dame Gertrude More'. A more general account of this tradition may be found in Emilie Zum Brunn and Georgette Epiney-Burgard, *Women Mystics in Medieval Europe*, trans. Sheila Hughes (New York: Paragon House, 1989); and Rosalynn Voaden, *God's Words, Women's Voices: The Discernment of Spirits in the Writing of Late-medieval Women Visionaries* (Rochester: York Medieval Press, 1999).

14 Gertrude More, *The Holy Practises* (1657), p. 2.

15 Marion Norman, 'Dame Gertrude More', pp. 203 and 211.

16 This interpretation is further affirmed by a similar usage of 'fool' adopted by Gertrude's cousin, Mother Margaret Clement, who had also become a nun. Sister Elizabeth Shirley in her contemporary manuscript life of Margaret Clement recounts that she was often called 'God Almighty's fool', and C. S. Durrant in an analysis of this biography notes that 'The expression "fool" is, of course, an allusion to the custom then in vogue of keeping a jester in great

families; the Clements will have remembered affectionately Sir Thomas More's faithful fool, Pattenson' (C. S. Durrant, *A Link Between Flemish Mystics and English Martyrs* (London: Burns Oates and Washbourne, 1925), p. 188).

17 Ms Lille 20 h. 7, transcribed in *Catholic Record Society* XIII, *Miscellanea* VIII, pp. 39–43. The notice refers to Gertrude as the 'great grandchild' of Thomas More when she was in fact his great-great-granddaughter; such looseness in naming the exact place in a line of direct descent is common to the period. Other postulants with More connections are also listed as such, for example Mary Lusher, while the list also includes a number of surnames associated with the More genealogy such as Roper.

18 *Catholic Record Society*, p. 40.

19 *Ibid.*, pp. 44 and 81.

20 The dedicatory poem may be found at the beginning of Gertrude More's *The Spiritual Exercises* (no pagination). Marion Norman assumes that the poem is written by Gertrude herself but I think this unlikely since stylistically her poetry is different and the verse itself refers to her as dead (see Marion Norman, 'Dame Gertrude More', p. 203). I believe that it was composed at the time of the work's publication along with the other prefatory material, perhaps by Father Francis Gascoigne, who arranged the material for publication. Gascoigne was the brother of Dame Catherine Gascoigne, the Abbess of the daughter house of Our Lady of Good Hope in Paris; he was also known to support Father Baker's teachings.

21 William Roper, *The Life of Sir Thomas Moore, Knighte*, p. 73. Cresacre More, *The Life of Sir Thomas More*, p. 279.

22 Gertrude More, *The Holy Practises*, p. 38.

23 *Ibid.*, p. 7.

24 Gertrude More, *The Holy Practises* and *The Spiritual Exercises*, p. 276.

25 Gertrude More, *The Spiritual Exercises*, p. 276. The image was probably a skull, as this recurs as one of the common pen and ink symbols used by the nuns at Cambrai in their commonplace books, still extant in the Public Archive at Lille. Unfortunately most of these commonplace books are anonymous, although with an investigation into handwriting it would be possible to make specific attributions for almost all.

26 Gertrude More, *The Spiritual Exercises*, pp. 276 and 278.

27 See Dom Justin McCann, 'Father Baker's Dame Gertrude', *Downside Review* 47 (1929), pp. 157–67. McCann includes a detailed list of manuscript copies of the life. The presence of versions in Ampleforth, Stanbrook, Downside, Colwich (that is, those Benedictine houses of the English Congregation that were forced to return to the United Kingdom during the French Revolution) demonstrate the importance of the life to the continuing tradition of a saintly More-like identity for Dame Gertrude.

28 Details of the founding of the daughter house in Paris may be gleaned from the house history at St Mary's Abbey, Colwich (Ms. R1 ms. 41). I am grateful to Sr Benedict of St Mary's Abbey, Colwich, for showing me the manuscript copy of the house history together with other materials relating to the English Benedictine nuns at the Abbey of Our Lady of Consolation at Paris. I am also indebted to her advice and assistance in tracing the roles of R. Mother Bridget More and Mother Clementia Cary in the establishing of the community. Several booklets about the history of the Colwich community have been produced by Sr Benedict

and are available from Colwich (St Mary's Abbey, Colwich, Stafford, ST18 OUF; please address all letters initially to the Mother Abbess).

29 Gertrude More, *The Spiritual Exercises*, p. 3.

30 This was, of course, not true since Anne More was alive and well at Cambrai; she died in 1662. In another way, the dedication was particularly prescient, for Agnes More, the only other More to contribute substantially to the literary traditions of the family, was already dead (1655–56).

31 *A Man for All Seasons* (1966), dir. Fred Zinnemann. The screenplay, by Robert Bolt, told the story of Thomas More's relationship with the King.

32 One of the enterprises of this essay is the reclamation of women's writing that has, for various reasons, become lost over the centuries. This active purpose means that the material here participates in the ongoing dialogue of feminist literary criticism (a late twentieth-century 'family'), just as much as it reworks the writings of the women at Cambrai.

33 The manuscript version of the translation is at Lille Public Archive Ms 20 H 19. An accurate edition of this manuscript was produced by Dorothy Latz, *The Building of Divine Love, as Translated by Dame Agnes More* (Lewiston: Edwin Mellen Press, 1992). In her introduction Dorothy Latz writes that 'there is a translation into English of one of Francis de Sales' works in the British Library, London, attributed to her efforts' (p. x), but I have not been able to locate it.

34 See Agnes More, *The Building of Divine Love*, ed. Dorothy Latz, p. xxii.

35 *Ibid.*, pp. 16 and 37.

36 *Ibid.*, pp. 100–1.

37 *Ibid.*, pp. 11 and 77.

38 *Ibid.*, p. 207.

39 Anne More's letter is quoted in Sandeman, *Dame Gertrude More*, p. 26.

40 Colwich, Ms. R1 ms 41, p. 256.

41 This is not to say that the More family themselves died out, and there are detailed family trees to prove such a continuity of inheritance; but the particular elements that constituted the More discourse of the early modern period do fragment and disintegrate at the end of the seventeenth century. Ironically, they are taken up, not by members of the blood family but by future More biographers.

42 Colwich, Ms R1 ms 41.

43 The description of Dame Bridget More occurs in Colwich Ms R1 ms 41, ff. 225–7.

44 Elizabeth Cary's biography was edited in Barry Weller and Margaret W. Ferguson, *Elizabeth Cary, Lady Falkland. The Tragedy of Mariam. The Fair Queen of Jewry. With The Lady Falkland: Her Life by One of Her Daughters* (Berkeley: University of California Press, 1994). Cary was one of the first early modern women writers to be 'reclaimed' as in Elaine V. Beilin, *Redeeming Eve: Women Writers of the English Renaissance* (Princeton: Princeton University Press, 1987).

45 Weller and Ferguson, *Elizabeth Cary*.

46 *Ibid.*, p. 52.

47 *Catalogue of the Manuscript Books Belonging to the Library of the English Benedictine Nunnes of our Blessed Lady of Good Hope in Paris*, Bibliothèque Mazzarine, Paris, Ms 4058.

48 *French Revolution Catalogue*, Mediathèque, Cambrai, Ms B 1004, p. 533.
49 I am particularly grateful to Heather Wolfe for her help in writing this essay and look forward to the publication of two works on Elizabeth Cary, a monograph and a collection of essays (forthcoming from Ashgate).
50 Two letters to 'The Right Honourable Sr Edward Hide', Bodleian Library Ms. Clarendon 247 and 327.
51 For Patrick Cary's handwriting see several letters to Lord Hyde, as in Bodleian Library, Ms Clarendon, 256.
52 Elizabeth Augustina, letter to Col. Grace in Bodleian Library, Ms Clarendon 63.
53 Anne/Celementia Cary, Lille MS 20.h.50.
54 *Dictionary of National Biography*, entry on 'Patrick Cary'.

Shakespeare and Lancaster

Warwick: Be Duke of Lancaster, let him be King.
Westmerland: He is both King and Duke of Lancaster,
      And that the Lord of Westmerland shall maintain.   (*3 Henry VI*
      1.1.86–8[1])

Lancaster resonates through both the first and second tetralogies of Shakespeare's English history plays. As the name of one of the two royal houses that contested the throne from the deposition of Richard II (1399) to the defeat of Richard III by Henry Tudor at Bosworth Field (1485), including 'York and Lancaster's long jars', it could hardly do otherwise.[2] Yet the precise resonance of 'Lancaster' – what associations it might have had for Shakespeare and his contemporaries, two centuries after the beginning of that historical sequence – has not been examined in detail. The possibility that Shakespeare spent some of his early 'lost years' in Lancashire (the county of which Lancaster is county town) is a starting-point for this chapter, though it is not my theme.[3] 'Lancaster', as we shall see, has a national significance, not merely a local one, and in that respect its status in the texts he wrote reveals nothing unequivocally biographical. But an investigation of 'Lancaster' and its resonances does eventually associate Shakespeare with Roman Catholicism, however indirectly: and one of the likeliest inferences of his being the 'William Shakeshafte' mentioned in the 1581 will of Alexander Hoghton of Lea in Lancashire is that he was himself, at least at that time, a Catholic recusant.[4] This enquiry also suggests new ways in which the second tetralogy, the sequence from *Richard II* to *Henry V*, may be seen as succession plays, obliquely addressing the tensions surrounding an ageing Queen with no acknowledged successor.[5]

The Duchy of Lancaster and its origins

It will be necessary first to conduct a detailed archaeology of Lancaster and its associations in this period, bearing in mind that much of what we discuss will of necessity be speculative. In Elizabethan England 'Lancaster's' primary association was with what was, and indeed still is, a unique constitutional anomaly, the Duchy of Lancaster. To this day a member of the British Cabinet is Chancellor of the Duchy of Lancaster, marking 'the historic importance of the Office . . . in the Royal Household'.[6] By the same token, Her Majesty the Queen 'is by long custom toasted as "The Queen, Duke of Lancaster"' within Lancashire and at gatherings of the Duchy – Duke, not Duchess, because uniquely the rights, titles and inheritance of this dukedom are not affected by the vagaries of gender (or indeed by minorities).[7] Since the time of Henry V the title – and much more than the title – has always been held by the English monarch, in a way that distinguishes it from all other duchies and titles in the possession of the Crown. If all this today is something of a quaint anachronism, in Shakespeare's day it still represented significant political and constitutional issues.

To understand why this should be so we may start with that crucial moment represented in *Richard II* when Richard determines to 'seize to us / The plate, coin, revenues, and movables / Whereof our uncle Gaunt did stand possessed' (2.1.160–2). The King, preoccupied with the need to finance his Irish wars, sees the death of Gaunt and the absence of his banished son purely as a convenient cash windfall. His last surviving uncle, York, sees it entirely otherwise:

> If you do wrongfully seize Herford's rights,
> Call in the letters-patents that he hath
> By his attorneys-general to sue
> His livery, and deny his off'red homage,
> You pluck a thousand dangers on your head.   (201–5)

That is, York recognizes that what Richard is doing fundamentally disrupts the principles and process of inheritance by which Henry, Duke of Hereford, seeks royal and legal acknowledgement of his succession to the rights and title of his father as Duke of Lancaster; and in denying as much the King also denies the reciprocal 'off'red homage' whereby Henry would submit himself as Richard's loyal subject even as he assumes the senior title. Richard sees nothing of this: 'Think what you will, we seize into our hands / His plate, his goods, his money, and his lands' (209–10).

So it is that, when Henry returns from exile and Lord Berkeley salutes him as 'my Lord of Herford', he replies:

> My lord, my answer is to Lancaster,
> And I come to seek that name in England,
> And I must find that title in your tongue,
> Before I make reply to aught you say.   (2.3.70–3)

This flusters Berkeley, who fails to see the point of principle and offers to address him as 'what lord you will' (76). Yet this is the cause Henry claims has brought him out of exile. In fact and in the play (2.1.277–88) he had put to sea before the death of his father. But he makes no other public claims, whatever private ambitions he might harbour, until Richard effectively deposes himself. That is also the cause for which so many nobles publicly attach themselves to Henry, whatever private motives they may be pursuing. As Northumberland puts it:

> The noble Duke hath sworn his coming is
> But for his own; and for the right of that
> We all have strongly sworn to give him aid.   (148–50)

The perception of his peers that Henry has an inalienable right to be 'Lancaster' – an issue to which Richard gives no apparent thought – is what loses the King his throne. Later, of course, Henry's claim that he had returned only for his 'new-fall'n right, / The seat of Gaunt, dukedom of Lancaster' (Worcester: *I Henry IV* 5.1.44–5) comes back to haunt him.

Yet the plays give no real indication of how much was meant by that title. It is clear that Gaunt was a wealthy man, and in the late sixteenth century 'duke' signified immense power and prestige – so much so that Elizabeth never created one, and pointedly put an end to the last of the medieval dukedoms when Norfolk was executed in 1572. There were thus no living dukes when Shakespeare's English history plays were staged: except that Elizabeth, like her modern namesake, was Duke of Lancaster as well as Queen. That the title survived as it did, and was not simply merged with the over-arching dignity of the Crown, was due as we shall see to a constitutional arrangement instituted by Henry IV.

But to understand why he should be minded to make this arrangement, we need to appreciate what exactly Henry was being denied when his right to be 'Lancaster' was called into question, since it went far beyond the status of even other royal dukes of the day (such as York). John of Gaunt, Earl of Richmond and a son of Edward III, came to be Duke of Lancaster in 1362, after marrying his first wife, Blanche, daughter of Henry, first Duke of Lancaster. Blanche's forebears (dating back to Edmund, first Earl of Lancaster, a son of Henry III) had built up estates throughout England and Wales, and eventually all of these – with others granted by Richard II, and some associated with two subsequent marriages – accrued to Gaunt. These lands were so extensive, and their associated powers and privileges so complex, that it was necessary to administer them via a quasi-royal Chancellor and Council and to appoint separate Chief Stewards for the North and South Parts, setting up a comprehensive and effective system of management that the Crown itself was to emulate under Richard III and Henry VII. (Some sense of their extent will emerge later, when I point out how many Duchy properties figure in Shakespeare's histories; suffice it for now to say that, after the dissolution of the monasteries, they formed the largest single estate after that of the Crown itself, with property in every county.)[8]

Furthermore, Gaunt was granted the franchise of a County Palatine in Lancashire; in 1390, it was vested in his heirs male (Somerville, *Duchy*, pp. 56–61, 64). This was in effect the devolution of the Crown's legal powers to an individual within a specific jurisdiction, an unusual dilution of royal sovereignty for which the only precedents were the Earldom of Chester, historic bulwark against the Welsh, and the Prince-Bishopric of Durham, which had a similar defensive role in relation to Scotland. While the Duke of Lancaster still clearly owed allegiance to the Crown, he ruled a kingdom within the kingdom, enforcing law in his own County Court (in addition to a separate Court which had jurisdiction over matters relating to the lands of the Duchy itself, throughout the country: Somerville, *Duchy*, p. 318, and below).[9]

It is hardly surprising that, once Gaunt was dead, the historical Richard should want to dismantle this private kingdom; or that Henry should demand 'Lancaster', to enjoy what his 'time-honoured' father had in his will dubbed the 'heritage of Lancaster' (Somerville, *Duchy*, Preface, p. vii). Yet Shakespeare is not at all specific in *Richard II* about the unique privileges of the Duchy of Lancaster being denied to Henry: it is perhaps sufficient, in the context of the play, that the normal rights of aristocratic inheritance are seen to be flouted by Richard. But it is also possible that Shakespeare felt less need to be so specific simply because the situation would still have been quite apparent in his own day. 'The Duchy reached the height of its influence in the 16th Century. If anyone spoke of "the Duchy" there was no doubt that they were referring to the Duchy of Lancaster.'[10] It held vast holdings in its own right – substantially more, in fact, than Henry actually inherited – including large parts of London, where its offices and court were quite separate from their Crown equivalents.

The Duchy in the sixteenth century

Ordinary Londoners in Shakespeare's day would certainly have known the Savoy manor, the area adjoining the site of the old Palace of Savoy, site of the Duchy's administration during the fourteenth century, but destroyed during Wat Tyler's rebellion because Gaunt had stirred up much public resentment in acquiring his private empire – a side of the man not reflected in Shakespeare.[11] (Indeed, Shakespeare heavily distorts history in making Gaunt a venerable figure, the voice of an England dishonoured by Richard's misgovernment.) Henry VIII endowed a splendid Hospital of the Savoy on the manor site, and the administration of the Duchy returned there, taking over a house in the hospital precincts. This became known as Duchy House (adjacent to Somerset House, on the Strand), and Elizabeth's Chancellors of the Duchy usually used it as their London lodgings.[12] Also on the Savoy site was a prison, used on occasion by the Duchy Council and Court, and at least one alehouse (Somerville, *Duchy*, pp. 328–30). The Duchy Chamber, where that Council and Court usually convened, was in the Palace of Westminster, and members of the Council had at their disposal a sermon house near Paul's Cross where, on holy days, they could go to hear the sermons preached. 'At the beginning of Elizabeth's reign a board was hung up at the outer part of the house bearing the arms and crests of the Duchy in gilt and colours' (Somerville, *Duchy*, pp. 330–1). The arms of the Duchy were familiar enough, though subtly unusual: 'The arms are those of England with a label of France, or more correctly gules three leopards or, a label of three points azure floretty or' (Somerville, *Duchy*, p. 154 note) – what most of us would call the lions of England, overlaid with a 'label' of French blue, decorated with golden fleurs-de-lis.

Apart from its formal and administrative presence, the Duchy was a significant London landowner, as John Stow recognized in his *Survey of London* (1598), where he describes the 'Liberties of the Duchie' (pp. 365–69); in the following passage he relates the property to its Duchy administration:

> This said middle row of houses stretching west to a stone crosse now head-less, by or against the Strand including the said parish church of St Clement, is wholy of the libertie of Dutchie of Lancaster which libertie is governed by the Chancelor of the said Dutchie, now at present, Sir Robert Cecill knight principal Secretarie to her Majestie, and one of her Majesties most honorable privie Councellors, there is under him a stewarde that keepeth court and leete for the Queene, giveth the charge and taketh the othes of every under officer, then is there four Burgesses, and 4 Assistantes to take up Controversies, a Bayliffe which hath two or three under Bayliffes that make Arrests within that libertie, 4 constables, four Wardens that keepe the Lands and Stocke for the Poore, four Wardens for high wayes, a Jury or Inquest of foureteene or sixteene to present defaultes, four Alecunners [= aleconners] which loke to assisse of weights and measures, &c foure scavengers and a beadle, and their Common Prison in Newgate. (p. 369)

Although the precise offices varied, every estate in the Duchy (of which there were dozens) had a similar hierarchy of officers – notably stewards, constables, feodaries and bailiffs – all ultimately answerable to the Chancellor and Council, and via them to the Duke/Queen. There was, in effect, a massive structure of patronage, parallel to that which operated for Crown lands. The structures were kept quite distinct, though of course the personnel overlapped – as the mention of Robert Cecil here indicates.

For most of Elizabeth's reign she awarded the Chancellorship to proven Crown servants, especially to men who were staunch Protestants, since Lancashire in general was such a hot bed of recusancy (the Hoghtons being to that extent quite typical). As Robert Somerville points out, four Elizabethan Chancellors in succession died in office – Sir Ambrose Cave (Chancellor 1559–68), Sir Ralph Sadler (1568–87), Sir Francis

Walsingham (1587–90), Sir Thomas Heneage (1590–95) – all men who 'were given this office towards the close of successful careers as statesmen' (Stow, *Survey*, p. 336). The office was a great focus of power and patronage (including Parliamentary patronage) and a potential source of considerable wealth, especially in its position as head of a Court of Equity. Sir Thomas Smith described the Duchy Court in *The Common-Welth of England* (1589):

> The Duchie Court of Lancaster is also the Queens Court of Recorde. In it are holden all pleas real & personall which concerne any of the Duchy landes, now in her Majesties handes and parcel of her crowne: but severed in Court and jurisdiction.
>
> The Judge in this Court is the Chauncelor assisted by the Attorney of the Duchie for the Queene, the Clarke of the Court, divers Surveyors, two Common Attornies, divers auditors, two assistantes, the Serjeant of her Majestie.
>
> The Chauncelor is a judge of the Court to see justice administered betweene her majestie and hir subjectes, and betweene partie and partie.
>
> The Attorney is to maintaine the Queenes right, and is assistant to the Chauncelor, and showeth him what the law is.   (pp. 127–8)

Smith goes on to discuss the office of Vice-Chancellor, at which point he confuses the Duchy Court with that of the County Palatine – an entirely understandable mistake, which underlines the breadth and complexity of the 'heritage of Lancaster'.

In general, however, his description of the Court reinforces our sense of the Duchy as a kingdom within the kingdom, and once more indicates the scope of its potential for patronage, especially in the hands of the Chancellor. It is probably for these reasons that Elizabeth did not fill the post of Chancellor for most of the years between 1595 and 1603, leaving its functions in commission: it had become a bone of contention between the Cecil and Essex factions at Court. Robert Cecil did obtain the post briefly (1597–99), at the time Stow was writing, but was required to vacate it when he achieved the even more lucrative position of Master of the Wards. All of this would have been well known to those who 'Talk of court news ... Who loses and who wins, who's in, who's out' (*King Lear* 5.3.14–15). But we have to recognize that, at a less conspicuous level, the disposition of myriad more minor offices throughout the country was central to the careful reciprocities of patronage on which the power structures of early modern England depended. The Crown and the Church were the great fountainheads of that patronage, but the Duchy was a significant third national strand, and so always of potential interest to the gentry and yeomanry (and their unprovided sons) who were looking for office or status. In that sense the Duchy was always potentially a matter of concern for those 'privileged playgoers' whom Ann Jennalie Cook has argued were the preponderant element in Elizabethan audiences.[13]

Perhaps the most striking single example of the potential patronage at Elizabeth's disposal from the Duchy was her creation of Robert Dudley as Earl of Leicester in 1564. The choice of title was itself significant, since it was in many ways the starting-point of the 'heritage of Lancaster' – Edmund, first Earl of Lancaster, was granted the lands and possessions of Simon De Montfort after his defeat in 1265, and these included the county and honour of Leicester. It was, therefore, a mark of especial honour, and remarked upon as such at the time, that Elizabeth alienated this particular title from royal and Lancastrian possession for the first time in three hundred years.[14] But titles required estates to sustain them, and to this end the Queen granted Dudley many parcels of land, several of them from the Duchy, the most memorable of which was the castle and manor of Kenilworth. Unlike her successors, Elizabeth was extremely reluctant to dispose of Duchy lands, so these were marks of especial favour. It was much more usual to reward people with offices of profit, and here again Dudley's association with the Duchy is instructive; he was Steward and Receiver of Pickering from 1564, and also Steward of Tickhill from 1577, in both instances for life – small threads in the mesh of patronage and profit which sustained the Elizabethan aristocracy, and within which the Duchy played its distinctive role.

Occasionally there were splendid ceremonials to remind Londoners of the prestige of the Duchy and its officers. In December 1594 Elizabeth honoured Sir Thomas Heneage by visiting him at his lodgings in Duchy House – like all such visitations an expensive honour, since it cost the Duchy £360 to widen the stairs and extend some of the rooms, before she even set foot in the place (Somerville, *Duchy*, p. 335 and note). But perhaps the most significant reminder of the importance of the Duchy came with the entertainments to greet James I on his ceremonial entry into London, delayed by the plague until March 1604. Most of the 'monuments' or arches around which the entertainments were staged were commissioned by the great livery companies of the City, expressions of their own magnificence as much as of humble loyalty; two were mounted by foreign communities resident in London, the Italians and the Dutch; but the last, 'In the Strand' – the great highway linking London and Westminster, adjacent to the Duchy liberties – specifically marked the King's exit from his capital. As Thomas Dekker put it, in his account of *The Magnificent Entertainment*:

> The City of Westminster and Duchy of Lancaster, perceiving what preparation their neighbour city made to entertain her Sovereign; though in greatness they could not match her, yet in greatness of love and duty, they gave testimony that both were equal. And in token they were so, hands and hearts went together: and in the Strand erected up a monument of their affection.[15]

So James as Duke of Lancaster greeted himself as King of England. It was especially fitting that Westminster, the administrative nub of the Crown, and the Duchy, the Crown's other self, should collaborate in this way.

The constitutional anomaly and Shakespeare's histories

The obvious questions are how this constitutional anomaly arose in the first place, and why it should have been allowed to persist so long. These were questions that the Elizabethans themselves asked. Early in Elizabeth's reign her first Chancellor of the Duchy, Sir Ambrose Cave, was required to conduct a thorough review of its affairs and responsibilities, and in June 1564 there was a conference in Star Chamber, with all the major officers of state, to determine how Cave's findings should be prosecuted. Parallel to these enquiries, Edmund Plowden, regarded as the leading and least corruptible lawyer of his day, compiled an authoritative report on the legal status of the Duchy and its court, later published in his *Cases* or *Commentaries* (1571, expanded in 1578 and 1599). Of the distinction between the Crown and the Duchy, Plowden suggested it was a

> politic scheme of King Henry IV who well knew that he had the Duchy of Lancaster upon a good and indefeasible title, and that his title to the crown was not so good, and therefore having some distrust that in time to come the crown might be taken from him or his heirs, and being desirous nevertheless that the Duchy should continue to him and his heirs, and knowing at the same time that if the possessions of the Duchy should be mixed with the possessions of the crown, and not be notoriously cut and dissevered from the possessions of the crown, it might be a means of causing the Duchy the sooner to be taken away from him or his heirs.[16]

William Camden examined the precise nature of Henry IV's settlement in *Britannia*:

> After him, Henrie of Bollingbroke, his sonne, succeeded in the Dukedome of Lancaster, who when he had dispossessed Richard the second and obtained the Kingdom of England. He considering that being now King he could not beare the title of Duke of Lancaster, and unwilling that the said title should be discontinued, ordained by assent of Parliament that Henrie his eldest sonne should enjoy the same, and be stilid Prince of Wales, Duke of Aquitaine, Lancaster, and Cornwall; and earl of Chester: and also that the liberties and franchesies of the Dutchy of Lancaster, should remain to his said sonne severed from the Crowne of England.[17]

Camden may be forgiven for confusing here the Duchy (in the sense of what Gaunt's will called the 'heritage of Lancaster', the estates and all their attendant privileges) with the dukedom, that is the title Duke of Lancaster. Because what Henry IV actually did (and carefully obtained Parliamentary approval for doing) was to retain the Duchy for himself, though separate from the Crown estates, and to confer the title Duke of Lancaster on his son, later Henry V (Somerville, *Duchy*, p. 144 and note 4).[18] The latter was thus already Duke when he inherited both the Crown and the Duchy. But this was the only time the dukedom and the Duchy were severed – Henry

VI inherited both simultaneously with the Crown, as in effect have all his successors. The Yorkist kings, Edward IV and Richard III, seem to have been relatively indifferent to the title of Duke of Lancaster, but both laid firm claim to the Duchy as a perquisite of the Crown (albeit still separate from it), even though this was contrary to the intentions of Henry IV, which were to keep the Duchy in his own family inheritance, whatever happened to the Crown; nobody challenged their right to do this. Henry VII was, in factional terms, a 'Lancastrian' king and had a stronger claim to the Duchy than either of his Yorkist predecessors. But his blood ties to the House of Lancaster were tenuous, compared with those of Henry IV, V and VI,[19] and neither his claim to the throne nor his right to the Duchy was (as we shall see) indisputable.

The fundamental issue here, I would suggest, for Shakespeare writing his histories in the late sixteenth century, is that the Duchy of Lancaster was a living, tangible and inescapable reminder of the fact that the monarchy after Richard II was compromised. If Richard's deposition does indeed represent 'a second fall of cursed man' (*Richard II* 3.4.76), then the Duchy is a permanent expression of the expulsion from Eden, its constitutional separation from the Crown the careful expedient of a monarch with a less than perfect claim to the throne. And none of Henry IV's successors, including the Tudors, could be entirely free of this taint, however much lawyers, historians and rhetoricians might seek to gloss over the fact. Their motives for preserving the Duchy as a constitutional anomaly seem on the whole to have been pragmatic rather than (as in Henry IV's case) prudential: as a source of considerable income (not all of it pre-committed to regular royal expenditure, though much of it in practice was), and as an alternative line of patronage, it gave successive monarchs down to Elizabeth a freedom of manoeuvre they would not otherwise have enjoyed.[20] But the price they paid for this was to be inescapably the heirs of Henry IV and his usurpation. I suggest that this is very much part of the resonance of 'Lancaster' in Shakespeare's English histories, with which this chapter began. The living constitutional anomaly of the 'heritage of Lancaster' is one of the factors that helps to bridge two hundred years of history, one of the triggers which prompted Shakespeare's contemporaries to see themselves in representations of the past.

This is the kind of suggestion that can hardly be sustained without recourse to unprovable assertions about what 'every Elizabethan' knew or thought. But I have already established that the Duchy was a living, working presence for Londoners, and have given some grounds for supposing that the patronage at its disposal was likely to be a matter of interest to 'privileged playgoers' – and that is the key audience here. The least controvertible evidence that Shakespeare himself understood something of the constitutional position of the Crown and the Duchy is the passage from *3 Henry VI* which stands at the head of this chapter. This occurs in the aftermath of what the play constructs as a major reverse for the forces of Henry VI, the first battle of St Albans, where (with some fictionalization and historical compression) a number of leading Lancastrian supporters are killed, including the Second Earl of Northumberland, the elder Lord Clifford and the Duke of Somerset.[21] Buoyed by this success, Richard, Duke of York has claimed the throne, backed by 'kingmaker' Warwick – who proposes to King Henry that the Crown and the Duchy be separated, in a reversion to the situation before the death of Gaunt. Westmerland, however, refuses to accept that such a separation is possible: 'He [Henry] is both king and Duke of Lancaster.'

The play could hardly be said to endorse the view of either Warwick or Westmerland. Indeed, the further this scene proceeds with its recitation of the conflicting claims to the throne, the less tenable they all seem. The younger Lord Clifford sums up the extremities of the situation by asking at one moment 'Whom should he [Exeter] follow but his natural king' (meaning Henry) and at another declaring 'King Henry, be thy title right or wrong, / Lord Clifford vows to fight in thy defence' (1.1.82, 160–1). Any pretence that there might be such a position as a 'natural king' dissolves into naked factional allegiances, where legitimacy is a matter of indifference. The immediate impasse is resolved by an agreement that Henry shall remain king for the rest of his life, while assuring York 'I here entail / The crown to thee and to thine heirs for ever' (194–5). This would involve a deferred version of Warwick's proposal: Henry's son, Edward, would become Duke of Lancaster, while York or his heir would become king. In fact, this never materializes, because it is overtaken by events on the battlefield. But discussion of the relationship between the Crown and the Duchy hangs in the air, complicating all definitions of royal legitimacy.

Another moment in the first tetralogy when the legacy of the Duchy focuses the dramatic issues is during 2 _Henry VI_ when Jack Cade unaccountably orders, 'So, sirs. Now go some and pull down the Savoy; others to th' Inns of Court; down with them all' (4.7.1–2). The order is unaccountable because in fact the Savoy had been destroyed during Wat Tyler's rebellion in 1381, seventy-nine years before Cade, and never rebuilt. All modern commentators on the play note that Shakespeare here conflates Holinshed's accounts of the two rebellions (which are widely separated in the original, so it can hardly be accidental), though they differ markedly in their views of what he was trying to achieve by this. For E. M. W. Tillyard it produced an 'impious spectacle of the proper order reversed', and for Philip Brockbank a 'timeless impression of the chaos that occurs whenever the irrational phantoms of desire walk unchecked'.[22] More recently, in the work of Annabel Patterson, Richard Wilson and Michael Hattaway, there has been a consensus that the issue is less one of universal order than of local forms of 1590s urban unrest which Shakespeare is here mirroring, though they disagree about Shakespeare's attitude to what he depicts.[23] The

Savoy and its associations are relevant to both perceptions. Gaunt's great palace, part of which still remained in a ruinous state, must have been a universal reminder of chaos unchecked, of the potential revenge of the oppressed on their oppressors; at the same time, its Tudor re-adoption specifically as a site for the Duchy of Lancaster offices was emblematic of the precariousness of the Elizabethan political settlement, with no peaceful succession to either Crown or Duchy assured. However we look at it, this anachronistic evocation of the Savoy offered educated Elizabethans a particular bridge between history and contemporary concerns.

The idea that the Savoy reference points to the uncertainties of Elizabethan politics is reinforced by the one glimpse we have of King Henry at the height of the Cade rebellion, which he does not confront himself (as Richard II had done the Peasants' Revolt) but leaves to his followers. He accepts Buckingham's advice to 'retire to Killingworth', urging Lord Saye also to come 'away with us to Killingworth' because he is so unpopular with the mob (4.4.39, 44). Killingworth was Kenilworth, of which all educated Elizabethans would have known something because of its famous associations with the Earl of Leicester. Henry was doing something that members of his family did on numerous occasions – taking refuge in one of his strongest and most loyal bastions, which was not a Crown property but a Duchy estate. He thus underlines the fact that, in the last resort, the King is only one factional leader among several possible claimants, dependent less on divine right than on political consensus.

The sense of the Duchy as a kingdom within a kingdom is never more pronounced in Shakespeare than in what we might call the verbal geography of its estates – though few of these were as famous as Kenilworth, and so we cannot know how much of this would have registered with individual members of the audience, or indeed what they would have made of what did register. In that sense, much of what follows is highly speculative, though I suggest that the evidence is cumulatively suggestive. A degree of telling 'verbal geography' occurs in the first tetralogy, but it is much more pronounced in the second, where the first two Lancastrian kings are consistently identified with their places of birth – Bolingbroke (or Bullingbrook, as the early texts have it) and Monmouth – which were both Duchy strongholds. It was quite normal for an aristocrat to be known by such a style as 'Henry Bullingbrook', which is how the man has himself announced to King Richard on his return from exile (*Richard II* 3.3.35). But the same man had a raft of other titles, including Duke of Hereford – by which style he is consistently known in Holinshed, for example, until he takes the throne. When he formally challenges Mowbray, he is repeatedly 'Harry/Henry of Herford, Lancaster, and Derby' (1.3.35, 100, 113) – Duke of Hereford in his own right, with the family courtesy titles of Earl of Lancaster and Earl of Derby. We never entirely lose touch with 'Herford' – it is, pointedly, the only title the Bishop of Carlisle allows him when he tries to prevent Henry's assumption of the throne: 'My Lord of Herford here, whom you call king, / Is a foul traitor to proud Herford's king' (4.1.134–5). Yet, as the play progresses, Bolingbroke becomes the most insistent style by which he is known – 'proud Bullingbrook', 'mounting Bullingbrook' (Richard, 5.1.4, 56), 'great Bullingbrook' (York, 5.2.7) – and for those reading the play it is how he is known in all the speech headings and stage directions (though the latter also accord him his dukedoms) until he becomes king.

It would be a lengthy process to unravel all the nuances and inflections here. Some usages, like those of Richard, are clearly scornful; York's 'great' seems unironic, underlining how he has acquiesced to the realities of a change of power. But what do we make of Northumberland, announcing to Richard, 'My lord, the mind of Bullingbrook is chang'd' (5.1.51)? Is this simple brusqueness, or does it betray Northumberland's ominous lack of respect for the man whose message he carries? However we construe specific inflections, the cumulative effect of this style is to demystify the man who becomes king – he is always a scion of Lancaster and can never carry the absolute authority Shakespeare ascribes to his predecessor. It is hardly accidental that, in *1 Henry IV*, when he is well established on the throne, the first person to use this style of him ('this ingrate and cank'red Bullingbrook', 1.3.137) is the disaffected Hotspur.[24]

What we may describe as the factional associations of 'Bolingbroke' are reinforced in *1 Henry IV* by the elevation to prominence there of Sir Walter Blunt, a man with only a sketchy existence in the principal sources, Holinshed, Daniel and Stow. As Arthur Humphreys puts it: 'Holinshed mentions Blunt merely as the King's standard-bearer at Shrewsbury; Shakespeare makes him the King's adviser and emissary throughout',[25] and Henry addresses him with particular warmth: 'Here is [a] dear, a true industrious friend, / Sir Walter Blunt' (1.1.62–63). Did Shakespeare know – from some source not yet identified – that Blunt was one of the key figures in John of Gaunt's household, his Chamberlain, instructed at one point to prosecute Gaunt's claim to the kingdom of Castile?[26] He had other notable positions in the Duchy, including those of Constable of Tutbury Castle and Master Forester of Needwood Forest, and it was from this long-standing position as a Lancaster man that he emerged as Henry IV's banner-bearer. This could explain the origins of the supposed disguisings at the battle of Shrewsbury where (in Shakespeare's version) Douglas kills Blunt, thinking he is the King; Blunt might very properly have been wearing the Lancaster arms which, as we have observed, were very similar to the royal arms themselves. In the play, these disguisings underline the extent to which Henry IV is an actor king, one of a number who might play the role; the Lancastrian Blunt dies for 'Bolingbroke' rather than an unequivocal 'deputy elected by the Lord'[27] – his 'grinning honour' (5.3.59), as Falstaff ghoulishly describes it, achieved in defence of faction as much as of the country.[28]

A similar derogation to that of 'Bolingbroke' attaches to the familiar naming of Henry V as 'Henry [of] Monmouth'. This sometimes hints at the human fallibility in a prince who wants to be, or seem, infallible – an inflection picked up in 2 *Henry IV* by Rumour when he announces that his office is 'To noise abroad that Harry Monmouth fell / Under the wrath of noble Hotspur's sword' (Induction, 29–30). But unlike 'Bolingbroke', 'Henry of Monmouth' is commonly a term of affection, a mark of Henry's common humanity which emerges so strongly (or, more cynically, is so shrewdly deployed) in the 'band of brothers' speech at Agincourt. Yet ironically it comes most fully under scrutiny in the words of his most fervent admirer and fellow Welshman, Fluellen, when he defends Henry for the order to cut the French prisoners' throats (*Henry V* 4.7) – one of the actions which even those who accept the Chorus's estimate of Henry as 'the mirror of all Christian kings' (Chorus to Act 2, 6) find most difficult to swallow.

Fluellen's defence takes the form of an entirely inconsequential comparison of Henry with 'Alexander the Pig' (13), mainly centring on the fact that one was born in Macedon and the other in Monmouth, and that there are rivers in both these places. This somehow becomes a justification of the fact that both of them could lose their tempers under extreme provocation, though it is to Henry's advantage that unlike Alexander he did not kill any of his friends in such a rage – which is true, though a marginal boast in the light of his treatment of Falstaff (whose rejection is pointedly remembered here, 47–8) and Bardolph. As with Henry's own attempts to justify his actions to Bates and Williams on the night before the battle, this is an uncomfortable scene, one which seems to offer to celebrate 'Harry Monmouth' (46) but succeeds in doing the opposite, as Shakespeare must have appreciated. If Henry does bear comparison with Alexander – something Fluellen never really establishes – one wonders what the likeness says about either of them. 'Monmouth', then, the Lancastrian stronghold on the Welsh marches, mentioned six times in this short scene, is a constant reminder of Henry V's human fallibility; it is also a reminder of the inherited illegitimacy of his crown – indeed, crowns, since his claim to the French Crown is just as suspect as that to the English one. The play acknowledges this openly in his prayer before Agincourt – but, like all the other histories, it also does so implicitly and more pervasively whenever he is styled 'Henry of Monmouth' (twice in *1 Henry IV*, five times in *2 Henry IV*, twice in *1 Henry VI*).

Bolingbroke and Monmouth were still very much part of the Duchy of Lancaster in Elizabethan times, the key office-holders in the 1590s major political figures. The Steward of Bolingbroke was the indispensable Lord Burghley, succeeded on his death in 1598 by his elder son, Thomas; this position consolidated their local standing in Lincolnshire, complementing their major holdings in Northamptonshire. The Steward of Monmouth (as also of Hungerford Manor) was the immensely rich and powerful Henry, Earl of Pembroke, who dominated the West Country and Wales (Somerville,

Duchy, pp. 577, 628, 649). Other Duchy properties similarly straddled the years between Henry IV and Elizabeth. The great northern strongholds remained firmly in Elizabeth's hands, for example, their Stewards being loyal and powerful servants, Burghley (Dunstanburgh), the Earl of Cumberland (Knaresborough) and the Earl of Huntingdon (Pickering). It is unlikely that members of Shakespeare's audience would have had an encyclopaedic knowledge of these posts and their histories; but past and present overlapped so pervasively in this context that there is every likelihood they appreciated the general phenomenon.

No property straddled the years more strikingly than Pontefract or Pomfret Castle; its Steward in the 1590s was the Earl of Shrewsbury. When Northumberland comes to tell Richard that Bolingbroke has changed his mind, it is about where to keep him in prison – not in the Tower of London, as everyone expects (Queen: 'This way the King will come, this is the way / To Julius Caesar's ill-erected Tower', 5.1.1–2) but in Pontefract: 'You must to Pomfret, not unto the Tower' (52). So Henry decides against the Tower, immemorially associated with the Crown, in favour of the strongest of his Duchy castles, where a loyal Lancastrian garrison would make rescue unlikely – and politic murder all too possible.[29] We are reminded of this in *2 Henry IV* (1.1.205) and in *2 Henry VI* (2.2.26) but it is in *Richard III* that the castle's ominous reputation becomes most resonantly an issue. Lords Rivers and Gray are taken there to be murdered, and Rivers curses the place: 'O Pomfret, Pomfret! O thou bloody prison! / Fatal and ominous to noble peers!' (3.3.9–10), its name echoing throughout the text (2.4.42; 3.1.183; 3.2.50, 83, 114; 3.4.90; 5.3.140) in a way that suggests it still had resonance for Shakespeare's audience.[30]

The succession question

Yet I see no pattern or underlying agenda to the way the Duchy repeatedly surfaces in the plays.[31] It was in large measure inevitable that, as Shakespeare depicted the history that brought it into being and preserved it, the Duchy would figure. That its continuing place in Elizabethan political life might thereby come under scrutiny could hardly be construed as more than an accidental consequence. Nevertheless, the situation in the later 1590s did conspire to give this history a renewed significance. Once it became plain that Elizabeth would die with no heir of her own body, and that Henry VIII's line would therefore die with her, the rights and wrongs of the succession became a legal and genealogical minefield that clearly preoccupied everyone who thought about such matters – though Elizabeth's refusal either to name a successor or to allow Parliament to discuss the issue meant that there was almost no public discussion of it.

Into this fraught vacuum fell *A Conference About the Next Succession to the Crown of Ingland* (1594–95), ascribed to one R. Doleman but probably written (or at least edited) by the indefatigable Jesuit polemicist Robert Persons.[32] Although it claimed on the title-page to be 'Imprinted at N. with licence' it was actually printed on the Continent and smuggled into England; Parliament made it high treason to possess a copy, but it still achieved a fair circulation, as we see in the number of attempts to repudiate it.[33] The book is a masterpiece of mischief, ostensibly a dispassionate survey of all possible claims to the throne, but implicitly supporting certain Catholic and Spanish ones, and bent on destroying the credibility of some of those in England who would have sought to steer the actual succession. These start with the Earl of Essex, to whom the book is fulsomely dedicated,[34] but also include such as Burghley, who is hooked with a knowing aside about Lady Arbella Stuart, 'whom the Lord Treasurer is sayd especially to favour at this present'.[35] It is at the beginning of the second part of the book that Persons introduces the issue of the Duchy of Lancaster, citing a 1571 document by one Robert Highington, a secretary to the Earl of Northumberland:

> this man (I meane Highington) maketh the king of Spayne to be the next and most rightful pretender by the house of Lancaster, for proofe whereof he holdeth first that king Henry the 7. had no title in deede to the crowne by Lancaster, but only by the house of Yorke, that is to saye, by his marriage of Queene Elizabeth eldest daughter to king Edward the fourth, for that albeit himselfe were discended by his mother from John of Gaunt duke of Lancaster, yet this was but by his third wife Catherin Swynford, and that the true heyres of Blanch his first wife duches and heyre of Lancaster (to whom sayth he apperteyned only the succession after the death of king Henry the sixth, and his sonne, with whom ended the line male of that house), remayned only in Portugal by the marriage of Lady Phillip, daughter of the foresaid Blanch, to kinge Jhon the first of Portugal, & that for as much as king Phillip of Spaine saith this man, hath now succeeded to al the righte of the kings of Portugal, to him appertayneth also, the only right succession of the house of Lancaster, and that al the other discendents of king Henry the 7. are to pretend only by the title of Yorke, I meane aswel the line of Scotland as also of Suffolk and Huntington, for that in the house of Lancaster king Phillip was evidently before them al. Thus holdeth Heghington . . . (II, p. 6–7)

Persons's own agenda here is less immediately relevant than that he should openly voice the possibility that none of the Tudors (and so implicitly none of the current possible English and Scottish claimants) had a right to the throne by virtue of their descent from the house of Lancaster. He goes on to point out that that there is a separate debate to be conducted 'as wel touching the succession to the dukedom of Lancaster alone, as also to the crowne joyntly' (II, p. 9) – the very issue which had kept the Duchy distinct from the crown to begin with. Elsewhere he goes on to deny the Yorkist claim to the throne, and to affirm that of Lancaster – but only through the Portuguese/Spanish line, by the 1590s essentially vested in the

Spanish Infanta, daughter of Philip II. Part of that affirmation depends on the legality of the deposition of Richard II, which he strongly defends:

> First for that it was done by the choice and innitiation of al the realme or greater and better parte thereof as hath bin said. Secondly for that it was done without slaughter, and thirdly for that the king was deposed by act of parlament, and himself convinced of his unworthy government.   (II, p. 67)

As in Camden's account of Henry IV's arrangements for the Duchy, Parliamentary sanction of the deposition becomes of paramount importance.

We do not know whether Shakespeare knew *A Conference About the Next Succession*, which may not have been available in England when he began the second tetralogy with *Richard II*. Strikingly, however, one contemporary appears to have associated him and these plays directly with Persons. In his *History of Great Britain* (1611) John Speed declared

> That N.D. . . . hath made Oldcastle a ruffian, a robber, and a rebel, and his authority, taken from the stage-players, is more befitting the pen of his slanderous report, than the credit of the judicious, being only grounded from this papist and his poet, of like conscience for lies, the one ever feigning, and the other ever falsifying the truth . . . I am not ignorant.

N.D[olman] is another of Persons's pseudonyms, and Speed is specifically referring to his *Examen of the Calender or Catalogue of Protestant Saints* (1604), in which he refers to 'Sir John Oldcastle, a ruffian-knight as all England knoweth, and commonly brought in by comedians on their stages'.[36] Oldcastle, of course, was the name Shakespeare originally gave to Falstaff.[37] It is commonly argued that Shakespeare made an inadvertent mistake in so traducing the Lollard martyr, following his source in *The Famous Victories of Henry Fifth*. But Speed certainly construed it as deliberate papist propaganda, later recycled by Persons.[38] Moreover, he links Persons and Shakespeare in ways that suggest rather more than a one-off borrowing: 'this papist and his poet . . . the one ever feigning, and the other ever falsifying the truth'. Is he suggesting that Shakespeare was regularly engaged in Persons-style Catholic propaganda, of which Oldcastle/Falstaff slanders were only the most marked examples?

What seems indisputable is that the issues that Persons's *Conference* raised openly were privately part of the political climate within which those plays were received, the climate that required the Cobhams to respond to the Oldcastle/Falstaff slurs and prompted the performance of *Richard II* on the eve of the Essex rebellion, instances which show beyond dispute that Elizabethans sometimes read the historical tensions of the second tetralogy in the light of their own circumstances.[39] It also seems inescapable that the tensions surrounding the succession question had a bearing on some of the censorship to which plays at the time were subject, including that of the deposition scene in the 1597 *Richard II* and the references to Richard himself in the 1600 *2 Henry IV.*[40] In that climate some of the Lancaster references I have been tracing here may have been – or perhaps became – more particularly charged.

I have rehearsed elsewhere the difficulties surrounding the question of whether *Richard II* was censored in 1597, and if so by whom.[41] The key difficulty about assuming that censorship accounts for the absence of the deposition scene in the 1597 versions of the play is that, *prima facie*, it makes little sense to cut a scene depicting the deposition of a king while leaving one that showed his murder. Professor Cyndia Clegg's recent suggestion, that it may have been the issue of Parliamentary legitimation of the deposition which caused alarm is the most compelling argument I have seen for why this particular cut may have been made at this time.[42] In the 1597 text a stage direction says 'Enter Bullingbrooke with the Lords to parliament', but in what follows there is no clear indication of Parliamentary procedure; in the fuller 1608 text the stage direction is amended to 'Enter Bullingbrooke, Aumerle, and others' (and Parliament as such is not mentioned) but Northumberland's direction of the action clearly shows he is following Parliamentary process – in effect showing Parliament as separate from, and sovereign to, the monarch. As Persons well knew, this was far from being the accepted constitutional position in Elizabethan England. But it had indeed been a marked feature of Henry IV's entire 'Lancastrian' settlement (part of which we have seen in Camden's account) that it was conducted with the open assent of Parliament, in the absence of other forms of legitimation. Reminders of this in 1597 might well simply have seemed tactless, more so even (because Persons had made it so central an issue) than when the play was written two years earlier. In this context it makes no difference whether the cut in *Richard II* was made by a censor (either for performance or for print) or by the actors hoping to avoid trouble – any prudential cut here reflects a very tense political climate, to which the entire 'heritage of Lancaster', and definitions of its legitimacy, was highly material.

There is one further instance, though far from clear cut, where Shakespeare might be suspected of *deliberately* foregrounding the questionable legitimacy of parts of the Lancastrian inheritance. That is in *2 Henry IV*, where Shakespeare takes some interesting liberties with the figure of Prince John of Lancaster. In particular he makes the Prince (in reality only fifteen at the time) more prominent in the action against the Northern Rebellion than the records warrant; in reality, and in the sources, the Earl of Westmorland was responsible for the trickery by which the rebels were undone, and they were taken to the King (as it happens, in his Lancaster stronghold of Pontefract) for judgement. But Shakespeare's account makes 'Lancaster' central to this treacherous act of 'chivalry'.[43]

We cannot really divorce this passage from Shakespeare's accentuation of Prince John's role throughout the *Henry IV* plays. He has him fighting

gallantly at the battle of Shrewsbury, for example, when none of the chroniclers mentions him there and he was in fact only thirteen years old. Shakespeare seems in essence to have promoted him as a foil to Prince Hal; just
as it is well known that he ignored the sources to the extent of making
Hotspur and Hal coevals (when the former was older than Hal's father),
so John is made to seem next in line to Hal, the loyal son who supports
his father while the Prince of Wales fritters his time away in Eastcheap. In
reality Thomas of Clarence was the second-eldest son. One clear consequence of this enhancement of his role is that it keeps 'Lancaster' to the
forefront of our attention, since he is repeatedly addressed or referred to as
Prince/Lord John of Lancaster.

Like Bolingbroke or Monmouth, this is not a title but denotes his place
of birth, the county town where John of Gaunt as palatinate duke had
begun building a castle worthy of his dignity. Holinshed understood this,
but Stow (in his *Annals*, 1592) did not, and in 2 *Henry IV* Shakespeare
followed the latter in making him 'The Prince, Lord John, and Duke of
Lancaster' (4.1.28; see also 1.3.82). As we observed in Camden, Henry IV
actually bestowed the title of Duke of Lancaster on Hal, the Prince of Wales.
It is normal, of course, to recognize that Shakespeare was a dramatist, not
a historian, and that anyway the array of names and titles he encountered
in his chronicle sources was truly baffling. But in this instance Shakespeare
had less excuse than usual for making the mistake, since the same man had
figured prominently (and under his correct title, Duke of Bedford, Regent
of France) in an earlier play, *I Henry VI*.

Whatever the reason for it, Shakespeare's mistake keeps Lancaster and
its Duchy firmly in the minds of his audiences in the *Henry IV* plays, and
never more so than in the deception by which Prince John overcomes the
rebels in Gaultree Forest, which is thereby associated with the whole
dynasty as much as it is with the individual. This makes the even more
fictitious following scene all the more intriguing. In it, Prince John berates
Falstaff for arriving too late to fight but departs promising to speak better
of him than he deserves; Falstaff, left on his own, insultingly says:

> I would you had the wit, 'twere better than your dukedom. Good faith, this
> same young sober-blooded boy doth not love me, nor a man cannot make
> him laugh, but that's no marvel, he drinks no wine. There's never none of
> these demure boys come to any proof, for thin drink doth so over-cool their
> blood, and making many fish-meals, that they fall into a kind of male green-
> sickness, and then when they marry, they get wenches.   (4.3.86–94)

Firstly, this suggests that Shakespeare *did* know how young Prince John
actually was, and may even imply that he was played on stage by one of
the boy actors (which would give an added dimension to the gibe about 'a
kind of male green-sickness', alluding to the female roles such boys would
commonly perform). More generally the passage serves as an elaborate

introduction to a soliloquy by Falstaff on the virtues of sherry-sack, which he equates with virility – an attribute he specifically denies Prince John. Jürgen Schäfer observes, in a very detailed explication of this passage:

> It is interesting to note that John of Lancaster, Duke of Bedford (1389–1435), actually did not have any legitimate male children. He married twice after his royal brother's death, in each case for political reasons. He left no children by either of his wives, though he had a natural son, Richard (cf. *Dictionary of National Biography*, s.v. John of Lancaster). It is idle to speculate whether Shakespeare meant Falstaff's words to be prophetic since there are no further allusions to the Duke of Bedford's family state either in *Henry V*, where he plays a minor role, or in *I Henry VI*, where he is regent of France.[44]

It is indeed idle to speculate about Prince John as an individual, but may be less so if we consider his fictitious status as Duke of Lancaster grounds for applying this to the dynasty as a whole, which Falstaff almost invites us to do when he begins the speech with a reference to the 'dukedom'. There are further grounds for thinking in this way when we consider how drink elsewhere in the play is related to questions of virility and kingship (Hal himself considers 'Doth it not show vildly in me to desire small beer?' 2.2.5–6), and Falstaff repeatedly opens up questions of legitimacy, as when he identifies Hal as 'a bastard son of the King's' (2.4.283). John of Gaunt's principal male line ran unbroken through Henry IV, V and VI, but none of Henry V's brothers – the Dukes of Clarence, Bedford and Gloucester – was survived by any legitimate children. A belatedly legitimized second male line ran from Gaunt's marriage to Katherine Swinford, the Beauforts. It is one of the marks of Henry V's kingship that the potential rivalry between these two lines does not materialize: his Beaufort uncle, the Duke of Exeter, is an honoured comrade alongside the King's brothers.

But after Henry's death that rivalry breaks out in earnest in the feud between Humphrey, Duke of Gloucester, and Henry Beaufort, Bishop of Winchester, which features in *I Henry VI* as the main domestic counterpart to the disasters overtaking England in France. Gloucester challenges 'the bastard of my grandfather' and is accused in turn by Winchester of being 'one imperious in another's throne' (3.1.42, 44). The one alludes openly to the taint of bastardy on the whole Beaufort line; the other accuses Gloucester of abusing his position as Protector of England during Henry VI's minority, but thereby opens up the issue of whose throne it ought to be in the first place – the whole Lancastrian succession being called into question yet again. The contestation between the two Lancastrian male lines was overtaken by the Wars of the Roses, in which the Beauforts in fact loyally supported Henry VI, but both lines actually came to an end in the same year, 1471, when Henry himself and his son, Prince Edward, were murdered (shown in *3 Henry VI*, 5.5, 6), and the last male Beaufort heir died with the execution of the Fourth Duke of Somerset.

Hence the situation which Persons astutely spelled out in *A Conference to the Next Succession*: by the end of the fifteenth century the 'heritage of Lancaster' rightly fell to one of two female lines – either that of the Tudors, in the right of Margaret Beaufort, mother of Henry VII, or that of the royal house of Portugal, in the right of Gaunt's daughter, Philippa, who was a full sister of Henry IV and married John I of Portugal. Persons sought to discredit the former line altogether, and give precedence to the latter, but (even if we leave Persons out of the equation) it was clear that the Tudors had reached the end of another female line with Elizabeth, while all the Scottish claims derived from yet another female line, stemming from Margaret, daughter of Henry VII. In short, Falstaff's gibe, 'they fall into a kind of male green-sickness, and then when they marry they get wenches', ostensibly directed at John of Lancaster, had a wider resonance in relation to the house of Lancaster as a whole, speaking to the uncertainties of the succession in the late 1590s, after more than forty years with childless women on the English throne – and with another 'Lancastrian' woman, the Spanish Infanta, possibly waiting in the wings.

It would be a hypercritical censor, however, who saw anything subversive in this, whatever John Speed may have made of it. Shakespeare is really betraying the tensions of the time, not (like Persons) generating an alternative agenda. This seems to me true of 'Lancaster' and its resonances throughout these plays, even if we accept that those resonances are more pervasive than we might at first have thought and that they became more charged in the years after Persons's book, which are, of course, the years of the second tetralogy. 'Lancaster' helps us to recognize that in these plays (as in early modern England itself), whatever they have to say about the divine right or sacred institution of kingship, the business of government was a pragmatic matter of implicating as many people as possible within the structures of power, prestige and profit – and of over-awing those who could not thus be accommodated. It was the failure of Henry IV and Henry VI (or those who acted on his behalf) to achieve these aims that led to the chronic instability of their reigns, just as – on a much smaller scale – Elizabeth's final inability to accommodate both the Cecils' and Essex's followers fuelled the tensions at the end of her reign.

Henry V's ability to redirect the factional feuding of his aristocracy, including the tensions inherent in his own Lancastrian heritage, towards a united national enterprise must have spoken very forcefully to audiences in 1599. But so must the Epilogue, reminding how short-lived that achievement was, and evoking Henry VI

> whose state so many had the managing
> That they lost France, and made this England bleed;
> Which oft our stage hath shown. (ll. 11–13)

In the long run, the simple fact of having an acknowledged heir does not guarantee that a country or its monarchy will flourish. The metaphysics of the king's – or queen's – two bodies certainly exercised constitutional lawyers and informed such debate about the succession as there was.[45] But the tangible reality of Elizabeth's two bodies – as Queen and as Duke of Lancaster – was a constant reminder of the political jostling and factional accommodations that were bound to attend on even a peaceful succession: which, until it was accomplished, hardly anyone dared believe was possible, given the precedents which her twin fiefdoms embodied.[46]

Notes

1 Unless otherwise stated, quotations from Shakespeare are taken from *The Riverside Shakespeare*, textual ed. G. Blakemore Evans (Boston: Houghton Mifflin Company, 1974).

2 The quotation is from Ben Jonson, Prologue to the 1616 Folio *Every Man In His Humour*, line 11.

3 The idea that Shakespeare might be the 'William Shakeshafte' mentioned in the 1581 will of Alexander Hoghton of Lea in Lancashire was advanced by Oliver Baker in his *In Shakespeare's Warwickshire* (1937) and by E. K. Chambers in an article reprinted in *Shakespearean Gleanings* (Oxford: Oxford University Press, 1944), but has been most forcefully re-asserted in recent times by E. A. J. Honigmann in his *Shakespeare: The 'Lost Years'* (Manchester: Manchester University Press, 1985).

4 S. Schoenbaum reviews the possibility of Shakespeare's Roman Catholicism, with his usual even-handed scepticism, in *William Shakespeare: A Compact Documentary Life*, revised edition (New York: Oxford University Press, 1987), pp. 112–15, 45–62. For a much less sceptical view see Gary Taylor, 'Forms of Opposition: Shakespeare and Middleton', *ELR* 24 (1994), 283–314.

5 The major study of Elizabethan drama and the succession question is Marie Axton, *The Queen's Two Bodies: Drama and the Elizabethan Succession* (London: Royal Historical Society, 1977); but, among Shakespeare's plays, Axton considers only *King John* in this regard.

6 I am quoting from private correspondence with the present Clerk of the Council of the Duchy of Lancaster, M. K. Ridley Esq. He points out that 'the appointment of Chancellor is frequently of a Minister who does not have extensive departmental responsibilities but whom the Prime Minister wishes to have in the Cabinet'. Among the Chancellor's Duchy duties is the appointment of magistrates in the old County Palatine of Lancashire, comprising the modern counties of Lancashire, Merseyside and Greater Manchester – a function performed throughout the rest of England and Wales by the Lord Chancellor as head of the national judiciary. This is a legacy of the special courts operating in the Duchy and the County Palatine, which I describe below. I am very grateful to Mr Ridley for his help.

7 *Duchy of Lancaster*, p. 21. (This is a Duchy pamphlet, dated 1996, though with no other publishing details.)

8 I am relying, for most of the historical information about the Duchy, on Robert Somerville's authoritative *History of the Duchy of Lancaster, vol. 1, 1265–1603* (London: Chancellor and Council of the Duchy of Lancaster, 1953): hereafter cited as Somerville, *Duchy*. Perhaps the easiest way of getting an impression of

how substantial the Duchy's holdings were is to glance through the 'List of Officers', pp. 363–654. On the Duchy as a model for Crown practices see pp. 257, 282ff.

9 At the meeting of the Theater History seminar at the SAA in Washington (April 1997), where a version of this article was presented as a paper, David Harris Sacks challenged the phrase 'a kingdom within the kingdom' as implying a level of independence of the Crown that was never intended or presumed. I merely wish to indicate that a County Palatine gave Gaunt *quasi*-royal legal powers, and a degree of authority enjoyed by no other subject of Richard II – though clearly he did remain a subject. I am grateful to Professor Sacks and other members of the seminar for their comments.

10 Somerville, *Duchy*, p. 10.

11 Shakespeare mentions the destruction of the Savoy Palace in 2 *Henry VI*; I discuss this below.

12 The only visible remains of the hospital are incorporated today in the walls of the Queen's Chapel of the Savoy. Between the Strand and the Victoria Embankment numerous road names keep alive the Savoy and Lancaster connections.

13 Ann Jennalie Cook, *The Privileged Playgoers of Shakespeare's London, 1576–1642* (Princeton: Princeton University Press, 1981). It is impossible to tell at this remove how widely known were the affairs of particular estates and the disposition of their offices. But modern academic experience suggests, by analogy, that such knowledge may have been extensive, simply because the demand for posts always outstripped supply. Academics reading this might reflect on how much they actually know (without really trying) about vacant posts in their own fields, about the varied nature of the institutions in which they occur, about the pressures of patronage and of ideology that will be exerted before those post are filled. I doubt if advancement in Tudor England was essentially different.

14 See Simon Adams, ' "Because I am of that countrye & mynde to plant myself there": Robert Dudley, Earl of Leicester and the West Midlands', *Midlands History* 20 (1995), 21–74, esp. 30–2.

15 See *Jacobean Civic Pageants*, ed. Richard Dutton (Keele: Keele University Press, 1995), p. 113; Ben Jonson, not Dekker, actually wrote the speech delivered at the monument in the Strand: see pp. 107–12.

16 Edmund Plowden, *Commentaries*, pp. 215b–216a: the pagination is the same in 1571, 1578 and 1599 editions. Translated from the legal Norman French by Robert Somerville, *Duchy*, p. 139. Strikingly, this determination to keep the Duchy inheritance separate from other Crown lands has persisted to this day; even in 1760, when George III negotiated what is still essentially the modern financial arrangement of the royal family, trading the income from Crown lands for a civil list voted by Parliament, the Duchy was excluded.

17 William Camden, *Britannia*, 1586 (in Latin); 6th revised edition 1607, translated by Philemon Holland, 1610, from which this quotation is taken (p. 757).

18 The issue of Parliamentary assent was, as we shall see, paramount; the passage in Camden continues: 'and to make better assurances to himselfe his heires and successours in these inheritances, by authority of Parliament he ordained in these words: *Wee, not willing that our said inheritance or the liberties of the same, by occasion of this present assumption upon us of our regall state and dignitie,*

should be in any thing changed, transferred, diminished, or impaired; will that the same our inheritance with the forisaid rights and liberties thereof, be kept, continued, and held fully and wholly; to us and our said heires in the said Charters specified, in the same maner and forme, condition and state, as they descended and came unto us; and also with all and every such liberties and francheses, and other priviledges, commodities and profits whatsoever, in which our Lord and father whiles' he lived had and held it for terme of his owne life, by the grant of Richard late King. And by the tenour of these presents, of our owne certaine knowledge, with the consent of this our present Parliament, we graunte, declare, decree, and ordaine for us and our heires, that as well our Dutchy of Lancaster, as all other things and every one, Counties, Honours, Castles, Manours, Fees or Inheritances, Advocations, possessions, Annuities and Seigniories whatsoever, descended unto us, before the obtaining of our regal dignity, howsoever and wheresoever, by right of inheritance in service, or in reversion, or any way whatsoever, remaine for ever to us and our said heires, specified in the Charters abovesaid, in forme afore said.'

19 Henry VII's claim to the crown, like that to the Duchy, derived mainly in the descent of his mother (Margaret Beaufort, daughter of the first Duke of Somerset) from John of Gaunt by his third wife, Katherine Swinford. The Beaufort children of that marriage were born out of wedlock and legitimized only after the marriage in 1396, and the line never entirely lost the taint of bastardy. Henry's paternal grandfather (Owen Tudor) had married Henry V's widow – or at least entered a liaison with her that was later recognized as legitimate – and Henry VI created their son, Edmund Tudor, Earl of Richmond, Gaunt's title before becoming Duke of Lancaster. It was part of Henry VII's propaganda after seizing the throne to play down his specifically Lancastrian derivations; in marrying Elizabeth of York – blending the red and white roses – he wanted to put the Tudor hold on the crown above dynastic squabbling. Nevertheless, he retained the separate constitution of the Duchy.

20 See Somerville, *Duchy*, pp. 317–18, for an account of the money available to Elizabeth from the Duchy.

21 Throughout the first tetralogy Shakespeare conflates Henry and Edmund Beaufort, who were brothers and successively Third and Fourth Dukes of Somerset, and neither of them actually died at the first battle of St Albans; since both of them were grandsons of John of Gaunt by his third wife, their lineage was crucial: see note 20.

22 E. M. W. Tillyard, *Shakespeare's History Plays* (London: Chatto and Windus, 1944), p. 183; J. P. Brockbank, 'The Frame of Disorder: *Henry VI*', in *Early Shakespeare*, ed. J. R. Brown and B. Harris, Stratford-upon-Avon Studies 3 (London: Edward Arnold, 1961), pp. 73–99, p. 88.

23 Annabel Patterson, *Shakespeare and the Popular Voice* (London: Blackwell, 1989); Michael Hattaway (ed.), *The Second Part of Henry VI* (Cambridge: Cambridge University Press, 1991), pp. 21–34; Richard Wilson, *Will Power* (Hemel Hempstead: Harvester Press, 1993), pp. 22–44.

24 The name of the conjuror who is condemned with Eleanor Cobham in 2 *Henry VI* (1.4, 2.3) – Roger Bolingbrook – came to Shakespeare from his sources, such as Hall's Chronicles: see *Narrative and Dramatic Sources of Shakespeare*, ed Geoffrey Bullough, 8 vols (London: Routledge and Kegan Paul, 1962), III, 102.

It is never actually voiced in the play, though in the written text 'Roger Bolingbrook' can hardly do otherwise than demean Henry of that name.

25 *I Henry IV*, edited by Arthur Humphreys, Arden edition (London: Methuen,
1960), p. xxv.

26 If Shakespeare was indeed employed by the Hoghtons (see note 3), these are
matters he could have heard from the family, who were key Duchy and
Lancashire figures in the time of Henry Bolingbroke. Henry Hoghton accompanied Bolingbroke on his expedition to join the Teutonic knights in Lithuania
during the exile imposed by Richard II, while his elder brother, Sir Richard, was
sheriff of the county from 1399. Both brothers held significant Duchy posts.
See George C. Miller, *Hoghton Tower* (Preston: The Guardian Press, 1948),
pp. 143ff.

27 *Richard II*, 3.2.57.

28 Falstaff makes as much of Blunt's dead body as he later does of Hotspur's,
though the latter is much more remarked upon, both fuelling his cynicism about
honour. It seems that Shakespeare wanted to balance the death of the 'rebel'
Hotspur with that of the 'loyal' Blunt in order to emphasize how meaningless
– at some level – these distinctions were.

29 Henry had himself returned from exile by landing at Ravenspur in Yorkshire
(cf. *Richard II*, 2.1.296), 'where the Lancastrian interests (outside Lancashire)
were strongest' (Somerville, *Duchy*, p. 137), in order to draw support from his
Duchy estates of Dunstanburgh, Knaresborough, Pontefract and Pickering,
before moving south and west *via* Kenilworth and other Lancastrian strongholds – travelling as much as possible on territory where his private interests
were strongest.

30 The Yorkist kings did not, in fact, significantly alter the status of Duchy, which
they found as valuable as their Lancastrian predecessors and Tudor successors.
Before he became king, for example, Richard III had himself been chief steward
of the Duchy in the North Parts, then surveyor general of the whole Duchy (a
new post) as well as a beneficiary of Duchy lands – it was a key element in his
power-base, and its offices helped to tie in allies (while it suited him) such as
Hastings, Buckingham and Sir William Catesby (Somerville, *Duchy*, pp. 256–68,
and see index on Richard's supporters).

   Pontefract was still a key Duchy property under Elizabeth. Shrewsbury was
also Steward of the great West Midlands Duchy holdings at Tutbury in Staffordshire, succeeding to both posts on the death of his father. Tutbury under the
elder Shrewsbury had served as a royal prison, like Pontefract centuries earlier:
Mary, Queen of Scots, was taken there in 1569, removed from its 'gloom', but
brought back at the height of the Norfolk rising, and she was to return there
briefly in 1585. When Shrewsbury was suspected of criminal intercourse with
the Queen he was replaced as her keeper by Sir Ralph Sadler, Chancellor of the
Duchy of Lancaster and an ardent Protestant.

   In Elizabethan politics more widely it may be that the Duchy still had a role
of special trust, though it is very difficult to generalize. Many key figures, as
we have seen, were Duchy officers – the Cecils, Leicester, Walsingham, and we
could add others, such as Sir Christopher Hatton. But we also have to observe
that many others were never associated with it, and if these include some we
might regard as 'unreliable' – Essex and Ralegh, for example – they also include

some bulwarks of the regime, such as Lord Hunsdon, Howard of Effingham and the Sidneys. The Duchy was an important part of the Elizabethan political fabric, but never in the sense of fostering an exclusive coterie or elite of royal support.

31 I have examined references to the Duchy in *The First Part of the Contention* (1594) and *The True Tragedy* (1595), the early versions of 2 and 3 *Henry VI* respectively, but this is not an issue on which earlier and later versions differ significantly.

32 The authorship has been disputed, but it is certainly the case that Elizabethans *thought* Persons was responsible.

33 On responses to the *Conference* see Axton, *The Queen's Two Bodies*, pp. 92–7. James VI of Scotland took it very seriously and wrote *The Trew Law of Free Monarchies* (1598) at least partly in repudiation of it. See Maurice Lee, Jr, *Great Britain's Solomon: James VI and I in his Three Kingdoms* (Urbana and Chicago: University of Illinois Press, 1990), pp. 82–3, 101; and D. H. Willson, *King James VI and I* (London: Cape, 1956), p. 140.

34 On this, and Essex's belief that his position as earl marshal gave him a special role in a disputed succession, see Richard C. McCoy, *The Rites of Knighthood: The Literature and Politics of Elizabethan Chivalry* (Berkeley, Los Angeles and London: University of California Press, 1989), pp. 90–5.

35 II, p. 241. Quotations are from the copy of the *Conference* in the Bodleian Library.

36 The Speed and Persons quotations here are both taken from Schoenbaum, *Shakespeare: Compact Documentary Life*, p. 193.

37 For relevant general discussion of the Oldcastle–Falstaff question see Alice-Lyle Scoufos, *Shakespeare's Topological Satire: A Study of the Falstaff–Oldcastle Problem* (Athens: Ohio University Press, 1979), and Gary Taylor, 'The Fortunes of Oldcastle', *Shakespeare Survey* 33 (1985), 85–100, and 'William Shakespeare, Richard James and the House of Cobham', *Review of English Studies* n.s. 38 (1987), 334–54.

38 Speed never names Shakespeare directly, and it is not impossible that the 'poet' referred to is the anonymous author of *The Famous Victories*. But the enormous popularity of Shakespeare's Oldcastle/Falstaff makes it far more likely that the 'commonly brought in by comedians on their stages' refers to his plays.

39 On the political climate surrounding the succession question in general see Axton, *The Queen's Two Bodies*. On *Richard II* and the Essex rebellion see Leeds Barroll, 'A New History for Shakespeare and His Time', *Shakespeare Quarterly* 39 (1988), 441–64, esp. 442–54.

40 On the elision of the references to Richard II in 2 *Henry IV* see Arthur Humphreys's Arden edition of the play (London: Methuen, 1966), pp. lxx–lxxii.

41 See Richard Dutton, *Mastering The Revels: The Regulation and Censorship of English Renaissance Drama* (Houndmills and London: Macmillan, 1991), pp. 124–7.

42 See Cyndia Susan Clegg, ' "By the choice and inuitation of al the realme": *Richard II* and Elizabethan Press Censorship', *Shakespeare Quarterly* 48 (1997), pp. 432–48. I saw a version of this article as paper (from which the observations on the different states of the 1597 and 1608 versions of the play also derive) at the World Shakespeare Congress in Los Angeles, April 1996. I am

grateful to the Research Committee of Lancaster University, and to the British Academy, for funding that made it possible for me to attend the Congress.

43 See Paul A. Jorgensen, 'The "Dastardly Treachery" of Prince John of Lancaster', *PMLA* 76 (1961), 488–92.

44 Jürgen Schäfer, '"When They Marry, They Get Wenches"', *Shakespeare Quarterly* 22 (1971), 203–11.

45 See Ernst H. Kantorowicz, *The King's Two Bodies: A Study in Medieval Political Theology* (Princeton: Princeton University Press, 1957); and Axton, *The Queen's Two Bodies*.

46 An early version of parts of this chapter was delivered at a seminar at the University of York in October 1996; I am grateful to Michael Cordner for the invitation and to members of the seminar for their comments. I am also particularly grateful to my colleagues Alison Findlay and Richard Wilson for suggestions which have been incorporated in the final version.

The Shireburnes of Stonyhurst: memory and survival in a Lancashire Catholic recusant family

The story of the Catholic recusant gentry family of Shireburne of Stonyhurst forms a paradigm of the experience of those of their rank and faith in 'Catholic Lancashire' between the onset of acute persecution under Elizabeth and the cessation of penal conditions from the later eighteenth century onwards. Although our longer-range study of their rise and demise departs somewhat from the normal chronological limits of the present book, we feel that such a departure is in fact warranted by the centrality to the classic Lancashire Catholic gentry experience of the family whose history we have studied. Acquiring and retaining considerable landed wealth in Lancashire's Ribble valley, the Shireburnes were eventually to embark on an ambitious programme of munificent philanthropy but were also to commemorate their own history in a programme of legendary iconography and monument-building of magnificent nostalgia. For generations in the late medieval and Tudor period this family consistently followed a strategy of dynastic advancement through land acquisition, Crown service and sheer relentless and ruthless collective assertiveness against rivals. To this combination they added a carefully cultivated piety focused on a lovely medieval church within their sphere of influence and power, All Hallows at Great Mitton, which they both expensively embellished and came to regard as a family chapel and mausoleum. Their Catholic piety eventually issued in an overt recusancy whose effect was that of severing in two their hereditary dual stance of catholicity combined with an opportunistic but none the less committed royalism and Crown service. Their wealth – despite the penal laws – became legendary, their philanthropy ardent, and their eventual Jacobite political alienation complete. All Hallows church was to become a temple to their mythos.

The Shireburne family was anciently placed on its Lancashire estates, traceable there back to 1246. In medieval Lancashire they strove and throve, schemed and litigated and gradually rose up the regional hierarchy of power. An early founder of the family's fortunes, Robert Shireburne, occupied regional office under Edward I and is believed to have been offered a knighthood in 1294. As well as being deeply occupied with the real-estate deals typical of the late medieval English gentry, Robert was chiefly responsible for first establishing his family's prominence in politics and the law. As a major figure in the Honor of Clitheroe, he was a natural ally of Thomas Earl of Lancaster in the successful conspiracy that magnate led in 1312 to destroy Edward II's favourite, Piers Gaveston. However, Robert Shireburne may have been the pioneer of his descendants' remarkable capacity for adaptation and survival. Having conspired in the execution of the King's protégé, he was included in the pardon for the deed and in fact proceeded to improve further upon his official public career: in 1318 Shireburne was made conservator of the peace for Lancashire, by 1320 was Vice-Justice of the county and Vice-Justice of Cheshire in 1327. The murder of his patron Edward II in 1327 and the subsequent accession of Edward III (of whose council he had been a member before the accession) did his career no harm: by 1332 he was chosen to recruit troops to accompany Edward III on a Scottish military expedition and in the following year was a collector of royal taxation in Lancashire. He remained on the new king's council, and his career in public life established his family's prestige and influence in Lancashire life.[1]

Military as well as political and parliamentary distinction characterized the career of the John Shireburne who represented Lancashire in Parliament in 1336, who fought at Crécy in 1346, who represented York in Parliament later in the same year and who in the following year took part in the siege of Calais, being knighted in 1344 by Edward III.[2] A knighthood also accrued to Richard de Shireburne whose grandson, Richard (1381–1441), renewed the family's traditions of steady service to the Crown, albeit transferring allegiance almost immediately to the Lancastrians after their seizure of power in 1399 and, seemingly, serving against the Scots in 1400. He was called to represent his county in the defence of the realm against the French in 1419 and he served in the King's council at Westminster, as well as representing Lancashire in Parliament in 1420 and 1421.[3] Sir Richard should also be seen as making an early contribution to the gentry-sponsored Catholic revival in pre-Reformation Lancashire which, Haigh argues, formed the background to the exceptional prevalence of recusancy in the county from the reign of Elizabeth onwards.[4]

Shireburne's piety was of the ostentatious aristocratic style of the fifteenth century, gorgeous and public, winning a papal licence to have a portable altar. He was also a land-grabber with appetite who, by the end of his life, was in possession of Lancashire estates in Chorley, Clitheroe, Bolton and elsewhere in the county. In effect selling a son into marriage (the large fee of over £86 being demanded in regular instalments), he epitomized the tough, assertive belligerence of the country gentry in the competitive world of Lancastrian England, and in 1429 he had to be bound over to keep the peace in a quarrel over property with a rival local gentry family. Yet the demonstrative religiosity was undeniable, and most fully encapsulated in his will, dated 1436. This was redolent of ardent devotion to the saints and generosity to the mendicant orders in a group of northern towns, love of dramatic liturgy, especially in his own carefully pre-arranged obsequies, a serious attitude to purgatory, and detailed attention to his own obituary Masses:

> First and forthermoste I bewitt my saule to Gode Almighty and to oure Lady Seyntt Mary and to all ye Haloes, and my body for to be berede in ye paryshe kirke of Mitton before ye auter of Seynt Nicholas. Also I be wytt to ye auter before sayde a vestiment of blewe velewett, four auter clothes, thre towels, a missal, a chales, a corporax, a pax brede, a feriell vestment, and a kyste for to kepe all yis gere in. . . . Also I be wytt to a preste for to syng a yere aut ye sayde auter of Seynt Nicholas for my sauel and for all Chrysten saules six marc and a half of sterlinges, and he sall fynde hymselfe brede and wyne and wax . . . Also I will yat fife sergez be sett upon my hers and be offerd up ye day of my beriall, ilk serge contenand two ponds of wax. Also I gif and I be wyte to ye freers of Loncastre xx s. of silver. And to ye Freers of Preston xiii s. iiii d. of silver . . .[5]

The most salient in all these provisions for piety, purgatory and property are the specifications for Great Mitton parish church, in which Sir Richard took such a strong proprietory interest, including, probably, building its main aisle, the 'little chapel of St Nicholas', which was to become the dynasty's mausoleum, and providing a screen, which contained a request for obituary prayers, to fence in the altar of the beloved St Nicholas. His lordly attitude to the parish church was even reflected in his settling one of those endemic medieval congregational quarrels about precedence of place within the church building. This bellicose, acquisitive, politically active Richard Shireburne can be seen also as the instigator of a family tradition of Catholic piety, closely involved with worship in their neighbourhood church, that was to surface in the dangerous recusancy of a descendant and namesake under Elizabeth. His widow Agnes was subsequently to follow in the grooves of his devout bequests, with friars of northern towns again benefiting handsomely, and a gift 'to ye vicar of Mitton a pare of get bedds [rosary beads] for to myn my saule and mynde me in his prayers'. The much-favoured parish church was further embellished in the 'hornments' of its high altar. These pre-Reformation Shireburnes were, then, the founders of their later family's devout and inescapably Catholic styles and traditions, evident, for example, in the possession by Nicholas, son of Richard and Agnes, of the lovely book of hours of the Blessed Virgin Mary now in the library of Stonyhurst College.[6]

Robert Shireburne (1431/2–92) maintained the family tradition of landed wealth, with fourteen estates around Lancashire, along with piety: the family made donations to the dominant abbey of the area, Whalley, went to Great Mitton parish church for christenings, weddings and funerals, but also kept at Stonyhurst a household chapel at which Mass was celebrated four times every week.[7] Another head of the clan, Richard (d. 1513), was a Yorkist client, securing both office and a knighthood from Edward IV but surviving and prospering past the accession of the Tudors, to serve as an important local magistrate and in a county position similar to that of the later deputy-lieutenant, though also having to contend with at least a threat of force with a rival for power in the county, Sir Peter Legh of Lyme. He also added twelve estates to the family's already extensive holdings and honoured the family tradition of favouring Great Mitton church by being buried in its choir.[8] His heir, Hugh (d. 1528), also showed his attachment to a traditional religiosity soon to come under official attack by donating handsomely to Whalley Abbey and piously re-endowing the family chantry in Great Mitton church.[9] Hugh's son, Thomas (d. 1536), strengthened the family relationship with a clan who were to emerge, like the Shireburnes themselves, as classic Lancashire gentry recusants, the Towneleys of Towneley, but also extended not only the family's land-holding, but also its pattern of service to the Crown by acting as Henry VIII's governor of the Isle of Man in 1530 and in 1535 as high sheriff of Lancashire.[10] The life of the next heir, Sir Richard, however, witnessed the bifurcation of the Shireburnes' once undivided political and religious identity and ideology and would, indeed, see the start of a progression, through religious alienation, from a position that once upheld royal allegiance and service into disaffection and treason.

As far as public, civilian and military service was concerned, this Richard (1526–94) was the most active and famous of his distinguished house. Although he took up his dynasty's trait of often violent assertiveness, put up two men to burn down the house of a priest who stood in the way of his self-enrichment and was, at one stage, and along with a family ally, Sir Richard Towneley, accused of illegal retaining of the sovereign's own tenants, he served the throne well and was rewarded for it.[11] His earlier offices, appointments and honours included: knighthood in 1544, at the age of only twenty-one, for his courage shown in the Scottish war; royal commissioner under Edward VI in 1547 to examine coal and lead deposits and forest enclosures in Lancashire; knight of the shire for Lancashire in Mary's Parliament in 1553, going on to represent Preston in 1554, Liverpool in 1555 and Preston once more in 1558. Mary also made him a commissioner to investigate the possessions of dissolved chantries and appointed him Master Forester of the royal Forest of Bowland. Though his prominence under the Catholic Queen, and especially his sitting in her Parliaments, in which she aimed at a membership made up entirely of her co-religionists, was no doubt a reflection of his holding to his family's traditional faith, he had no difficulty in adapting – for adaptation was an inherited Shireburne trait – to Elizabeth's Protestant regime. The new queen confirmed him as Steward of Radholme and in 1561 he was assisting the Earl of Derby as a lieutenant of the Isle of Man. Derby even named him to serve in a special embassy to France, though ill-health prevented his going. He emerges as an effective, sagacious, careful, practical man, trustworthy and trusted in examining complex cases and as an arbitrator. In 1574 Shireburne was required to provide extensive military equipment and in 1587, as Deputy Lieutenant, received his notification of war alert in view of 'the report that the King of Spain is about to invade this realm'; the previous year, he was driving a very Protestant-sounding offensive to suppress 'enormities of the Sabbothe'. In 1589 Shireburne was raising troops for the English campaign in Ireland and in the same year was involved as a Justice enquiring into a riot, while in 1590 he summoned his fellow justices to a militia muster for the county. In 1591 Shireburne was accused of excessive zeal in levying royal taxes and even of threatening laggards with hanging under martial law. Almost from start to finish, then, Shireburne served all the Tudors who reigned during his lifetime, apparently irrespective of their faith or his. Not surprisingly, an earlier historian, quoted by the family chronicler, saw him as the perfect type of the Vicar of Bray: 'Always clinging to the Roman obedience, he was not a man of the strongest religious convictions, or he could scarcely have retained the goodwill of Henry VIII, Edward VI, Mary, and Elizabeth'.[12]

Yet in point of fact Shireburne sought for decades to continue to hold together his family's traditional synthesis of Catholicism, loyalism, royalism and patriotism, until in the end his failure to keep the texture integrated became unmistakable, so that as an administrator he could be accused of an excess of loyalty and as a Catholic of a deficit of allegiance. From early in the reign his religious dissidence was apparent: in 1564 he was one of twenty-six Lancashire Justices listed as being unfavourable to the government's Protestant religious policies and he may also have been one of a group of recusant gentry whom the Catholic agent William Allen encouraged in his itinerary of Lancashire to remain 'steadfast in the Faith'. Even so, duplicity and even betrayal were the condition of his holding in tension two essentially conflicting allegiances. In 1568 he actually made up one of the Ecclesiastical Commission charged with confronting eight Lancashire gentlemen accused of recusancy: he might equally have been accuser or accused. Yet, as J. Stanley Leatherbarow writes, 'Evidently Shireburne, though suspected as an unsatisfactory magistrate, was not yet indicted as a notorious recusant. There must have been easy exchanges of allegiance in those years, a man sometimes figuring on the government's side after some act of conformity, sometimes on the recusant side after a gesture of disobedience.' In 1584 came a classic 'act of conformity' and one that was entirely in line with Shireburne's political conscience both as a loyal subject and also a member of a family for whom considerations both of advantage and of political ideology made fealty instinctive: along with eight known recusant squires, he signed the patriotic Protestant Association in defence of Elizabeth against all her enemies. Yet just five years later suspicion was once more aroused over his position on the religious spectrum – or rather not his but that of his family and its female members, for the recusancy of the Catholic gentry was conserved more actively by the women than by the men of that class, who often conformed, at least externally, in order to stay in office or avoid crippling fines, or both. Shireburne retained his position of justice *and* ecclesiastical commissioner and would try to explain his failure to act against priests on grounds of belief in the principles of religious toleration. However, his wife, children and servants were in breach of the recusancy laws, 'seldom come to church and never communicate, and some of his daughters married, and not known by whom, but suspected by Mass priests'. In fact, Shireburne himself was said to be 'an intelligencer to the papists of Lancashire'. Fresh allegations were made in 1595 accusing the family of blatant church papistry – attending church but blocking their ears to avoid hearing the Prayer Book services. It was further alleged that Shireburne had had a priest attend his sick wife, and was part of a network that led through various Jesuits up to Cardinal William Allen.[13]

In the course of the seventeenth century Sir Richard Shireburne's ambiguities were to be resolved by his descendants into a positive and overt catholicity. The political correlate of that religious stance was royalism. In turn, that ideology came to be transmuted into a defiant Jacobite stance as if, through a second Stuart restoration, the family might resume the alignment of religious and political allegiances that had been their hallmark until the Elizabethan Sir Richard had to face up to fatal choices of one casket or another. Following Sir Richard's death his immediate heirs adopted safer courses. His son Richard (1546/7–1629), who inherited all of Sir Richard's litigious quarrelsomeness, dutifully continued his father's ambitious building programme, completing the Stonyhurst fabric, and, a passionate purchaser of land, brought the family's estates to their broadest extent. Richard, in the family tradition, served the Crown, as Sheriff of Lancashire in 1612–13, and seemingly as 'captain' of the Isle of Man. Overt recusancy was recorded only in the case of his (third) wife rather than his: she was buried in the 'new quire' of Great Mitton church, over which this Richard extended the family's tightening hold by acquiring the advowson in 1603.[14] The building was to emerge as the anomaly of a parish church of the Church of England in the proprietory grip of a proud, wealthy and increasingly open Catholic family who came to treat it, and ornament it, as the mausoleum of their history and of their defiance.

Another Richard Shireburne (1586–1667) married, firstly into the Lancashire Catholic noble family of the Molyneux of Sefton and, secondly Elizabeth, *née* Walmesley, presented for recusancy in 1633, on whose behalf Richard paid a fine of £10 in 1638. In fact, he and his wife were co-religionists and he, whether or not he was cavalier in arms in the civil war, was forced at the time of the battle of Preston in 1648 to act as host to

Cromwell and his officers at 'Stanyares Hall, a Papists' house, one Sherburne's'. Richard Shireburne henceforward paid a steady drain of fines (including those for sending his children abroad for a Catholic education) and compounding fees, his royalism incriminating his recusancy, and vice versa.[15] Richard compounded his estates in 1649 and, with his health failing, adopted the persona of the 'Eminent Sufferer', who had sacrificed everything that was dear to him, in order to be of service to his cause. This image of the devout patriarch, a gentleman brought low and reduced to the status of an invalid through the adherence to his religious principles, was a potent one which was consistently perpetuated by his descendants and was to be afforded the fullest expression in the funerary monument raised to him, by his daughter-in-law and grandson, a quarter of a century after his death.[16] Indeed, even though the Restoration brought about the rapid resurgence of the family's fortunes, the concept of their willing sacrifice for the conjoined causes of the Stuart monarchy and the Roman Catholic Church in England was continually appealed to and successfully reactivated at times of grave crisis – whether in 1678, 1688–89, 1694 or 1715 – up until their eventual eschewal of active involvement in Jacobite politics during the 1740s.

Oates's Popish Plot found a strong echo in east Lancashire and the West Riding of Yorkshire in the winter of 1678–79, when the hall at Stonyhurst was searched, though its windowless chapel went undetected and its altar remained hidden behind thick curtains.[17] Although the family's Jesuit chaplains either fled or took refuge in one of the many priest holes that honeycombed the house, the damage done to the Catholic operation in the north was considerable. Furthermore, the justices of the peace were now required to enforce the recusancy laws. As a result, on 28 November 1678, the entire Shireburne clan – comprising Squire Richard (1636–89); his wife, Isabella; and their two sons, Richard of Wigglesworth (1652–90) and Nicholas (1658–1717) – were indicted and subsequently fined before the magistrates at Blackburn. Worse still, the younger Richard was implicated in allegations of a popish conspiracy and in December 1680 went into hiding; while his father underwent a brief spell of imprisonment.[18]

The reign of James II promised to and, indeed, did deliver much to the family. There is evidence to suggest that the Shireburnes enjoyed cordial relations with the Duke of York before his accession, and Nicholas Shireburne appears to have come swiftly to James's attention and to have been quickly recognized, and rewarded, for his loyalty and potential ability. Despite his position as a younger son, it was he – rather than his shadowy elder brother, Richard, of Wigglesworth – who appears to have been active in promoting the profile of the family at Court.[19] In the period from 1685 to 1688 Nicholas enjoyed the trust and friendship of the King, and based himself in London and at Cartington in Northumberland, while his brother took over the running of the Shireburne manor and estates at Wigglesworth, in North Yorkshire. Having co-ordinated the efforts of James II's land agents in Ireland, having liaised with Talbot about the future scheme of government for that kingdom and having established cordial relations with Irish Catholic gentry, Nicholas was created a baronet – during the lifetime of his father – on 4 February 1686, by a grateful sovereign.[20] Other official appointments followed, which restored the Shireburnes to a prominence within the administration of northern England that they had not enjoyed since the Reformation. On 25 June 1688 Sir Nicholas was one of a number of ultra-loyalist gentlemen, including his kinsmen, the Widdringtons, and the future Jacobite agent and plotter, Sir John Fenwick, who were appointed to serve as Deputy Lieutenants of Northumberland; on 17 September 1688 his father was authorized to serve as a deputy lieutenant in the West Riding of Yorkshire.[21] The elder Richard was not slow in asserting his family's renewed authority and self-confidence. In November 1685 he employed the Catholic teacher John Cottam, who may conceivably have been of the same extended family as Shakespeare's schoolmaster, John Cottom of Tarnacre, son of Lawrence Cottom of Dilworth and Tarnacre, Lancashire, to instruct his tenants' children in religion and grammar, and proceeded to endow a 'free' school at Hurst Green early in the following year. Cottam's long tenure as master, and the Shireburnes' insistence that the 'said School-mas[te]r . . . [should] be nominated placed and displaced at the will and pleasure of Richard Scireburne and his Heires male . . . for ever hereafter' reinforce the picture of a family who intended to reward good service to them, while keeping a tight control over the running of their estates, and providing tangible evidence of the resurgence of their Catholic faith.[22] This sense of a strict and highly devout paternalism was given further expression in Richard's charitable bequests to the poor and his covert establishment of an almshouse on Longridge, a branch of which was possibly also situated at Hurst Green. There is good evidence that he intended to formalize these arrangements and to build a permanent hostel, circumventing the normal operation of the Poor Law entirely and rendering the Shireburnes the most generous local dispensers of charity and outdoor relief.[23]

However the collapse of James II's government in the winter of 1688–89 brought a dramatic halt to all of these schemes and to the family's bid for regional predominance. The Shireburnes were marked out as a dangerous and malicious clan under the Whigs; Richard was arrested in June 1689, and died under the watch of the militiamen, on 8 August 1689.[24] In a double blow to the dynasty, he was followed to the grave only a few months later by his heir apparent, leaving his widow and younger son to attempt to rebuild the family's shattered local influence.[25] A recourse to active Jacobitism appeared to be a natural path for Sir Nicholas, offering him the prospect of a return to power and influence in the event of a second Stuart restoration. Unsurprisingly, by May 1693 Sir Nicholas was once more in trouble with the authorities, for advancing money to the exiled Court at St

Germain and maintaining a regular correspondence with their absent sovereign and his servants. The ignominious collapse of the Manchester Jacobite treason trials in the following year may have caused the local and national authorities to relent in their pursuit of Sir Nicholas.[26] During the 1690s and early 1700s he was afforded remarkable scope for expressing his family's enduring political allegiance.

Sir Nicholas's wife, Katherine, shuttled between the port of Harwich and the Dutch coast, with apparent impunity, in 1693 and again in 1695, on what appear to have been part of a regular pattern of annual visits to the Jacobite Court.[27] In 1698 his ailing daughter Mary was sent to St Germain and touched for the king's evil by James II in a carefully scripted liturgical ceremony which was used both to emphasize her father's continued refusal to acknowledge the legitimacy of the post-Revolution government and to proclaim his faith in the quasi-divine properties of the exiled monarch.[28] Far more durable monuments were also explicitly designed to underline the links between the Shireburnes, their religion and the Stuart cause by Sir Nicholas's mother, the widowed Isabella Shireburne. Upon the death of her husband, she projected the remodelling of the Shireburne chapel at Great Mitton to accommodate her own future tomb, together with those of her spouse, her eldest son and her father-in-law. Sculpted from a common basic design, by William Stanton, a London mason, these figures represent the last examples of cross-legged, recumbent effigies to be commissioned as part of important funerary art in England and Wales. Even though the choice of carved figures reflects a conscious medievalism, and a direct appeal to chivalric values, Isabella also ordered that the Shireburnes should be depicted in the dress of their day. This attempt to update a monumental tradition that had already gone into steep decline before the onset of the Reformation was no less strange and anachronistic to observers at the close of the seventeenth century than it is today. Despite the passage of more than twenty years that separated the deaths of the three male figures, all are shown in the dress of gentlemen of the mid- to late 1690s, complete with square-toed court shoes, curled periwigs and cravats tied fashionably in the Steenkirk knot. Each of the effigies holds a small prayer book, or breviary, and Isabella, as the only woman in the group, is shown as being shrouded in a simple smock, her head turned to regard her husband. There is evidence that these figures were originally railed in, and that lighted tapers or candles were suspended from the sides of each tomb, to provide not only light in order to illuminate them but also the tangible proof that prayers for the dead were being recited, regularly, and in strict accordance with their wishes.[29]

Thus the Shireburne family's honoured and Catholic bloodline could be traced in the mannered medievalism of the Great Mitton tombs, with the highly detailed accompanying dedicatory inscriptions which carefully set out the genealogies of each of the deceased and traced complex patterns of intermarriage with other, predominantly local, noble and gentry families. It is no surprise to discover that during this period Sir Nicholas was endeavouring to clarify and chart his own pedigree, and the evolution of his family's coat of arms.[30] The Shireburne chapel was intended to promote the ongoing cult of family and to link them directly with their northern fiefdom. Their epitaphs also offered a lasting testimony of their services in the Stuart cause and a direct challenge to the authority of the Anglican state church that now held formal possession of the fabric of All Hallows. It was readily apparent to the worshippers at Great Mitton that the piety and loyalty celebrated upon the text of their lordships' tombs was neither to the Established Church nor to the spirit of the Revolution Settlement.

Having finally taken possession of the Shireburne estates at Michaelmas 1695, Sir Nicholas combined the, by now, traditional pursuits of his house – Jacobitism, ambitious building projects and the provision of welfare, based upon Catholic religious models of 'good works' of charity – and pursued them with renewed vigour.[31] He completed the refashioning of the mortuary chapel in All Hallows church, and redeveloped the old Elizabethan hall at Stonyhurst into a grand palladian mansion. By the late 1690s, with hopes of a swift return by the Stuarts fading, Sir Nicholas dedicated himself to the perpetuation of an influential Catholic dynasty. The lavish education of his son and heir, Richard Francis, 'a Child very Extraordinary in all Respects, both beautiful and forward', seems to have been part of this wider project.[32] Such youthful promise was, however, to be cut tragically short when the little boy suddenly sickened and died on 8 June 1702, aged eight and a half years. In the wake of the disaster, Sir Nicholas gave expression to his grief in the form of raising an enormous and, indeed, to our taste macabre tomb for his son, while local popular tradition began to elaborate upon the tragic story of his getting lost in the new maze at Stonyhurst and stopping to eat some poisonous berries.[33] Richard Francis's death suddenly transformed the social standing and dynastic importance of his sister, Mary. Her wealth, religion and politics made her extremely eligible for marriage into the declining circle of great Jacobite and Roman Catholic families in England. In successfully negotiating a marriage between Mary and Thomas Howard, Eighth Duke of Norfolk, in May 1709, Sir Nicholas brought off a major political and dynastic coup, which served to propel his family into the first flight of the English aristocracy.

In staking the future of his house upon both a high-profile marriage and the implicit assumption that an heir would in time be born in order to unite the Shireburne and Howard patrimonies, Sir Nicholas had placed his own finances under considerable strain. As a result, the cost of projecting his family's power was borne primarily by the tenant farmers who rented the Shireburne lands. Both Sir Nicholas and, subsequently, his daughter oversaw the running of their estates with a ruthless and clinical efficiency, and, as if genetically imprinted, proved themselves to be notoriously litigious. In particular, Shireburne came to rely heavily on the skills in land conveyancing of a co-religionist, Nathaniel Piggott of the Inner Temple. In addition to negotiating Mary's marriage contract, and expanding upon the family's property rights, Piggott was also employed in a less secular function: to circumvent the operation of the penal laws in regard to the provision of private charity.[34]

The Shireburnes had always endowed charitable concerns, linked directly to the propagation of their faith and family name. However, this drive reached new levels upon the succession to the lordship of Sir Nicholas and was, under him, formalized and injected with a new impetus. The need to maximize profits in order to sustain the displays of conspicuous consumption of the late 1690s and early 1700s had effectively pauperized or driven out many of the Shireburnes' tenants and labourers. Consequently, an interest in charity was based upon an entirely practical rationale and enabled the family to exercise a sense of paternalism in regard to their favoured servants, while weeding out of their estates those whose religious or political views did not conform to their own. Despite the grand claims of his parents to have firmly endowed charitable bequests and almshouses, little had been achieved by the mid-1690s that was either durable or securely financed. Many of the promises for endowments remained simply that.[35] It fell to Sir Nicholas to confirm and provide for these grants, and to initiate a comprehensive programme of building which would further stamp the landscape with physical evidence of the Shireburne presence.

While his wife, Katherine, established an apothecary shop for 'the distres'd sick and poor lame' inside the coach-house at Stonyhurst, he himself attempted both to generate fresh wealth and to stimulate new patterns of employment through investment in the spinning of Jersey wools.[36] A more traditional response to poverty was provided by the regular doles paid to the old and the destitute, through the almshouses or directly by the Lady Katherine on All Souls' Day.[37] Sir Nicholas had been quick to convert his father's limited bequests into perpetual endowments, and by 1713 had extended the reach of his charitable concerns to encompass the poor of Wigglesworth and Guysley (each place receiving £6 per annum), Carleton and Hambleton (which were allotted £7 per annum between them) and Burnley and Chorley, which received £9 10s and £2 respectively.[38] Dependent upon these payments was the clause that these disbursements should be made – by churchwardens of the Church of England – every year, upon 16 August. This date was rich in symbolism for the Shireburnes, for Squire Richard died a prisoner on that date in 1689. Those doles, then, may be seen as obituary gifts for the honoured ancestor – the kind of vicarious good works that sped a soul out of purgatory – and it was, no doubt with a cold sensation of revenge that Sir Nicholas also saw his father's Jacobite 'martyrdom' honoured by the Established Church, while the handouts were – in all likelihood – dispensed with a similar, grudging, ill grace.[39] Money was also to be allocated to already ensconced Jesuit chaplains at the Hall, and concern with souls of the departed family members in purgatory was expressed in the specification that the Fathers should pray three times a week for sixteen named members of the Shireburne clan, both alive and dead, and that they would regularly travel around the family estates in order to minister to the needs of their tenants.[40]

The earlier, smaller almshouse at Hurst Green was supplanted in 1706 by a much larger building at the nearby site of Kemple End.[41] On the pediment Sir Nicholas's lead coat of arms proudly announced his continuing patronage and enduring presence as benefactor. A similar pattern for the building and endowing of almshouses would be followed by the family's subsequent dedication of almshouses at Stydd, near Ribchester, confirming its role as the leading charitable benefactors in the entire locality.[42]

Even though they had systematically extended their control over their northern strongholds, and flaunted portraits of popes and the exiled Stuarts upon their walls, the Shireburnes were by no means invulnerable.[43] The bags of Jacobite gold, shuttled to and from St Germain, did not go entirely unnoticed by the authorities. In 1710 a government informer testified that Sir Nicholas was one of those gentlemen in Lancashire who were regularly collecting revenues and soliciting loans for the Old Pretender's cause. The attitudes of the Queen's Tory administration, influential friends within the legal profession and memories of the debacle caused by the trials of 1694 all combined once again to secure the dropping of all charges, but Sir Nicholas's recusancy ensured that he fell prey to sporadic fines throughout this period.[44] This willingness to prosecute half-heartedly, or not at all, on the grounds of religious dissent, and outright failure to prosecute for political activism and insurgency, were to show themselves even more clearly as the Jacobite army pushed on towards Preston in the winter of 1715.

Though, as a man approaching sixty and in poor health, Sir Nicholas had declined to join the rebels, he allowed local Jacobites to feast at his house, in expectation of victory, and supplied them with horses and arms. From his absence from the supper party it can be concluded that Sir Nicholas was unsure as to both the wisdom and the outcome of the rebellion and that he had little wish to be personally associated with it until the Pretender was already installed in Whitehall. His caution was well founded, for as local government slowly regained its footing in the north-west, following the surrender of the Jacobites at Preston, he was called to account. His political sympathies were only too well known, and his kinsmen the Widdringtons were captured at the battle and were facing the possibility of a trial for high treason. On the evening of 27 December 1715 the Constable of Aighton, Bayley and Chaidgley, accompanied by twenty followers, presented a search warrant at the gates of Stonyhurst and demanded in the King's name that the steward of the house open up. Sir Nicholas refused to submit, and escaped prosecution, the authorities apparently feeling that a fresh treason trial would be counterproductive, unsure of success and liable only to present the Jacobite movement with another popular martyr.[45] Sir Nicholas's little victory had served in effect to place a shot across the bows of county government in Lancashire, limiting its further recourse to action against himself and his family and marking the switch in policy of the Shireburnes: from one of active assistance of the Stuart cause to the adoption only of 'gesture politics' in support of the ends. Yet the exterior threat to the family from magistrates and mayors was as nothing when compared to the internal pitfalls created by genetic imperfections and strained marital relations. Ironically, it was Sir Nicholas's crowning achievement, the Norfolk marriage, that led to the final eclipse of his line.

Whatever the scale of the expenditure on feasting and hunting with the Howards and their dependents, nothing could disguise the failure of the Duchess Mary to provide an heir, or hide from public view the gradual, though total, disintegration of her marriage. There is little evidence to suggest that the couple were ever particularly close, and Mary, following the death of her father in 1717, maintained a peripatetic existence, continually in motion between her Shireburne estates in the north and the manors owned by the Howards in the Midlands.[46] It is possible that an outright breach had occurred between husband and wife in 1715–16 over the Duke of Norfolk's willingness to acknowledge the legitimacy of the Hanoverian succession after the failure of the Jacobite rising. Worse still, the Duke's attempts in 1719 to negotiate a triple concordat between the Pope, the Hanoverian government and the Catholic community in England provoked Mary's open and vociferous opposition. Her influence did much to erode support for the concordat scheme within the ducal household and hardened the resolve of many English Catholics to resist calls for the abjuration of the Stuarts and for the recognition of the legitimacy of King George I and his heirs. Narrowly escaping charges of complicity in a Jacobite plot of 1722, Thomas Howard had little further desire to bring himself to the attention of the authorities and waged a bitter, protracted battle with his wife over the choice of priests appointed to their household.[47] Though Mary was eventually successful in the removal of Franciscans, and the appointment of Jesuits to important posts within the Norfolk establishment, she and the Duke chose to live increasingly separate lives.

At some point after the Duke's premature death, on 23 December 1732, Mary embarked upon a sexual relationship with her kinsman Peregrine Widdrington, whom she had known since early childhood. This irregular partnership, conducted discreetly, effectively removed her, as the last of the Shireburne dynasty, from the arena of national and regional politics. The failure of the couple to acknowledge, or to deny, their affair caused a serious breach with their erstwhile supporters within the Society of Jesus. Fr Thomas Lawson SJ, the Duchess's personal chaplain and spiritual director, attempted to reach a compromise with them whereby they would have publicly acknowledged a morganatic marriage. However, both declined and the priest suddenly fell into disfavour, being dismissed from the Duchess's service, on 1 January 1734. This breach also served to distance the Duchess from the Society and damaged the traditional image, fostered by generations of Shireburnes, which explicitly associated the activities of the family with high moral sensibilities, and identified them as close adherents of the Church of Rome in general, and of the Society of Jesus in particular.[48] Though her subsequent attachments to both Catholicism and Jacobitism remained undiminished, after 1734 these were henceforth manifested only in terms of display, through the raising of memorials, and through limited financial support, via charitable endowments and gifts to the supporters of the Old Pretender – rather than in terms of forceful or concrete political action. The potentially scandalous nature of her 'marriage' to Widdrington nullified any advantages that the support of Duchess could have brought to the rebellion of 1745–46, and there is an abiding sense, implicit in the text of the tablets which she crowded on to the walls of Great Mitton church, that her drama was already played out. As a fresh Jacobite army headed south, on the road to Derby, the ageing couple had no involvement at all in the momentous proceedings, remaining in safe, secluded retirement. The symbols of Jacobite and Catholic allegiance remained, but the form and substance of Shireburne power had already been lost, long before the deaths of Widdrington in 1748 and of the Duchess in 1754. The continual reiteration of the family's claims to prominence, respect and grandeur, through the granting of charity and the willingness of sacrifice, already outdated, even in the 1690s, could no longer be squared with the reality of an elderly, childless dowager, whose political activity was effectively nullified on account of her unconventional, extramarital sex life. While there was nothing pre-ordained in this collapse of Shireburne power – the Duchess's gender and religion should not be considered as being fatal handicaps when compared with her failure to give birth to an heir – the period from 1732 to 1754 can be seen as marking a watershed in local politics. The extinction of the Shireburnes and the passing of their patrimony to their kinsmen, the Welds of Lulworth, was taken for granted years before the Duchess's servants and retainers turned out to bear her coffin, on its last journey, across the fell tops towards its resting place in Mitton. Sheer bad luck and personal tragedy, in terms of a barren marriage bed and the accidental death of a beloved child, had achieved far more than the enforcement of the penal laws, the accomplishment of the Glorious Revolution and the sustained hostility of the Hanoverian government ever could have. In this light the most fitting relic to the end of the dynasty remains the grim *memento mori* to young Richard Francis. Flanked by carvings of weeping cherubim, overturned hourglasses and trampled bounty, the monument to the little boy, already vandalized by 1878, today makes for an odd and uncomfortable companion to the Sunday School playmates whose chairs, tables and boxes of crayons are today regularly pushed up around its base.[49] The grief of a devoted father could not be more forcefully expressed, in the idealized depiction of the blameless infant called, prematurely, to celestial rather than earthly honours. However, the monument is equally eloquent in its testimony to the transience of power of a clan that came so close, in the 1680s and again in the early 1700s, to breaking free from the shackles imposed upon it by the recusancy statutes and to charting a daring, and remarkable, course in the governance of the locality and of the realm alike.

The later Shireburnes of Stonyhurst, 1586–1754

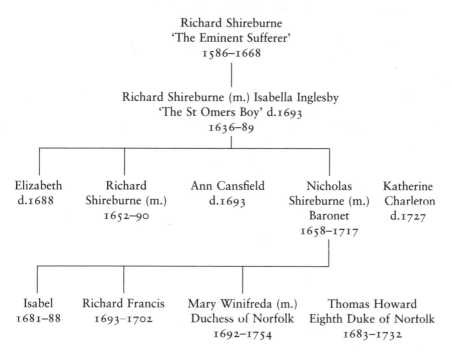

Richard Shireburne
'The Eminent Sufferer'
1586–1668

Richard Shireburne (m.) Isabella Inglesby
'The St Omers Boy' d.1693
1636–89

| Elizabeth d.1688 | Richard Shireburne (m.) 1652–90 | Ann Cansfield d.1693 | Nicholas Shireburne (m.) Baronet 1658–1717 | Katherine Charleton d.1727 |

| Isabel 1681–88 | Richard Francis 1693–1702 | Mary Winifreda (m.) Duchess of Norfolk 1692–1754 | Thomas Howard Eighth Duke of Norfolk 1683–1732 |

Notes

1 Charles Davies Sherborn, *A History of the Family of Sherborn* (London: Mitchell and Hughes, 1901), pp. 2, 5–9: we have standardized the many variants of the family surname to 'Shireburne'; Robert Somerville, *History of the Duchy of Lancaster, volume 1 1265–1603* (London, Chancellor and Council of the Duchy of Lancaster, 1953), p. 350.
2 Sherborn, *History of the Family of Sherborn*, pp. 10–17.
3 J. S. Roskell, Linda Clark and Carole Rawcliffe (eds), *The History of Parliament: The House of Commons, 1386–1421*, IV: *Members P–Z* (Stroud: 1992), pp. 363–4.

4 Christopher Haigh, *Reformation and Resistance in Tudor Lancashire* (Cambridge: Cambridge University Press, 1975), Chapter 2.
5 Sherborn, *History of the Family of Sherborn*, pp. 13–14.
6 *Ibid.*, pp. 15, 17.
7 *Ibid.*, p. 17.
8 *Ibid.*, pp. 19–21.
9 *Ibid.*, p. 23.
10 *Ibid.*, p. 26.
11 Haigh, *Reformation and Resistance*, pp. 60, 96.
12 Sherborn, *History of the Family of Sherborn*, pp. 28–30, 32–3.
13 J. Stanley Leatherbarow, *The Lancashire Elizabethan Recusants*, Chetham Society, new series 110 (1947), pp. 26, 98–9, 107, 109.
14 Sherborn, *History of the Family of Sherborn*, pp. 38–43.
15 *Ibid.*, pp. 43–5.
16 A. E. Green (ed.), *Calendar of the Proceedings of the Committee for the Advance of Money* (Nendeln/Liechtenstein: Klaus Reprints, 1967), III, p. 1362.
17 Lancashire Record Office (LRO): DDSt: 'Inventory . . . 12th day of December . . . 1705', f. 202.
18 *Historical Manuscripts Commission: The Manuscripts of Lord Kenyon* (London: HMSO, 1894), p. 109.
19 LRO: DDSt, Box 27, passim and Box 115, item 10.
20 LRO: DDSt, Box 95, item 3.
21 *Calendar of State Papers Domestic (CSPD), James II*, II, June 1687–Feb 1689 (London: HMSO, 1972), pp. 220, 277.
22 H. Chadwick, 'Richard Shireburne and his Charities', *Stonyhurst Magazine* 362 (October 1946), p. 286.
23 LRO: DDSt, Box, 94, item 2; DDSt 5: 'Mr. Kemp's Disbursements from the 1st Jan 1712–1713 to the 25th March 1713–14 . . .', ff. 1–2.
24 *HMC: The Manuscripts of Lord Kenyon*, pp. 313–14.
25 LRO: PR 3031/1/1–4: Mitton Registers, 1655–1699. The younger Richard, described as 'of Stonyhurst, Esq.', died 6 April 1690 and was buried in Great Mitton church on the 15th of the same month.
26 William Beaumont, *The Jacobite Trials at Manchester in 1694* (Manchester: Chetham Society, vol. 28, 1853), p. 7.
27 *CSPD, William III, 1693* (London: HMSO, 1903), p. 327, *CSPD, William III, 1695* (London: HMSO, 1908), p. 77.
28 J. Lofthouse, *Lancashire's Old Families* (London: Hale, 1972), p. 153; F. Skeat, 'The Eighth Duchess of Norfolk, Part I', *The Stonyhurst Magazine* 257 (June 1925), pp. 73–4.
29 The specifications and costings for the construction of the tombs are recorded in: LRO: DDSt: 'Account book of Catherine [*sic*] Shireburne', ff. 3–4, 6, 8–10, 12, 15, 18–19, 21; DDSt, 5: 'Mr Kemp's Disbursements', ff. 1–2.
30 LRO: DDSt, Box 97, item 4.
31 LRO: DDSt, Box, 94, item 1.
32 Charles Davies Sherborn, *A History of the Family of Sherborn*, 2 vols, unpublished typescript, 1901, 1918), II, p. 51.
33 LRO: PR 3031/1/1–4: Great Mitton Registers, 1700–39. The burial registers record only that on 15 June 1702 'Richard the son of Sir Nicholas Shireburne

of Stonyhurst' was buried. His tomb lies on the west wall of the Shireburne chapel. For discussion of the legends surrounding his death see J. A. Entwistle, *A Brief History of All Hallows Church, Mitton* . . . (n.p., 1979).

34 'P. G.', 'Apropos of an Account Book', *Stonyhurst Magazine* 368 (April 1948), pp. 126–7; Stonyhurst College Archives, MS E.2/4/4, no. 3.

35 LRO: DDSt, Box 1, items 9–11, 17–18; Box 94, item 2; Box 95, items 2, 4; 'Mr. Kemp's Disbursements', ff. 1, 7, 9; Stonyhurst College Archives, MS E. 2/4/4, no. 3 and b.

36 A. J. Berry, *The Story of Lancashire* (London: Pitman, 1927), pp. 240–1.

37 LRO: DDSt: 'Mr. Kemp's Disbursements', f. 1.

38 LRO: DDSt: 'Mr Kemp's Disbursements', f. 1.

39 Chadwick, 'Sir Richard Shireburne and his Charities', p. 286.

40 T. E. Muir, *Stonyhurst College, 1593–1993* (Stonyhurst: James and James, 1992), p. 51.

41 LRO: DDSt, Box 95, item 25.

42 Michael A Mullett, *Catholics in Britain and Ireland 1558–1829* (Basingstoke and London: Macmillan, 1998), p. 90.

43 LRO; DDSt, 'An Inventory . . . 12th day of December . . . 1705', ff. 196, 198.

44 Paul Kleber Monod, *Jacobitism and the English People, 1688–1788* (Cambridge: Cambridge University Press, 1993), p. 313.

45 Gerard, *Centenary Record: Stonyhurst College and Its Life Beyond the Seas 1592–1749 and on English Soil 1794–1894* (Belfast, London, New York and Sydney: M. Ward and Co., 1894), pp. 77–8.

46 Gerald Brenan and Edward Phillips Statham, *The House of Howard* (2 vols, London: Hutchinson, 1907), II, pp. 449, 616; see also John Callow, 'Mary Shireburne, Eighth Duchess of Norfolk', *New Dictionary of National Biography*, forthcoming.

47 Brenan and Statham, *The House of Howard*, 2, pp. 616–17.

48 Callow, 'Mary Shireburne'; Skeat, 'The Eighth Duchess of Norfolk', part II, pp. 119–21, part III, pp. 173–5.

49 Anthony Hewitson, *Stonyhurst College, Present and Past* (Preston: Preston Chronicle Office, 1878), p. 9.

Lancashire, Shakespeare and the construction of cultural neighbourhoods in sixteenth-century England

As citizens of the so-called global village of the late twentieth century, the international group of conference participants brought together in Hoghton in 1999 through the conveniences of e-mail, fax, air mail, plane and train travel might seem to have been a long way from the mix of audience and performers that would have graced Hoghton Tower in Shakespeare's day. With respect to mobility, networking and the common experiences that link communities within cultural neighbourhoods, however, apparent differences may ultimately be more in degree than in kind.

One of the chief obstacles to scholarly acceptance of the 'William Shakshafte' in Alexander Hoghton's will as the William Shakespeare who later became one of the King's players and the Globe Theatre playwright appears to derive from a failure to recognize important parallels between our own age and Shakespeare's. The fact that on the verge of the twenty-first century Shakespeare is enjoying larger than ever global audiences – and that he is even inspiring more than one book on such subjects as business management practices – would suggest that non-specialists may be able to recognize these parallels with less difficulty.[1] Objections to Lancashire as the site of Shakespeare's so-called lost years have frequently derived from the perception that the county is geographically remote from both Stratford and London,[2] but such objections must be qualified if we recognize that Shakespeare also lived in an age of comparative mobility where wide-ranging networks were equally important to the cultural and economic fabric. These networks may not have been electronic, but they contributed significantly to the dynamics of Tudor 'self-fashioning' in the case of not only reigning monarchs but also upwardly mobile individuals such as Shakespeare, who eventually retired to his well-appointed town house to manage his lands in the Warwickshire countryside. The extent to which this 'self-fashioning' involved the production of space, the conscious acquisition, identification, containment, redefinition and characterization of space either architecturally or geographically is clear when one notes that the Tudor expansion of incorporated boroughs was accompanied by architectural and cartographic initiatives seeking to establish or enhance civic identity and the authority of burgesses.[3] Not unrelated to this were corresponding architectural and cartographic initiatives on the part of Tudor gentry, such as the Hoghtons, and nobility, such as the Stanleys, who enhanced their country estates and sought to establish their prestige architecturally through town houses in London and city centres within their circle of influence.[4] In short, geography, place and space in Tudor England were perceived not as static givens or as fixed obstacles but rather increasingly as shifting, plastic commodities or sites of negotiated meaning.

Central to this process of spatial self-fashioning were a group of individuals akin to what Anthony Smith has categorized as 'transitional men', individuals for whom education and/or talent became the ticket to mobility – both social and spatial. Such individuals functioned as one of the vehicles for Tudor networking and the increasingly inextricable construction of person and place in Elizabethan England. Preachers, cartographers, playwrights and some performers can be seen as belonging to this group of individuals whose connection with a patron enabled them to envision and affect a transition from traditional village life to modern urban society while recognizing 'connections between . . . private dilemmas and public issues'.[5] As in our own age, education and knowledge functioned as the currency for gaining a ticket to a patron's preferment, economic advancement and mobility.

Such individuals might begin life from the perspective of a traditionally defined community such as Stratford-upon-Avon, within a geographically contiguous Warwickshire neighbourhood, but our challenge is to understand how someone like Shakespeare could make the transition from the perspective of a local community with its provincial micro-structures to the perspective of an English nation state and the social and cultural macro-structures conjured up in a work such as *Henry V*. To this end it might be wise to consider the advice of local historian Charles Phythian-Adams who has observed 'the degree of misfit between the untidiness of society on the ground and the ideal tidiness of administrative units':

> In terms of the underlying relationship between the macro-structure and the micro-structures on the ground, indeed, much more important than administrative institutions will be the manner in which 'national' power is informally distributed and supra-regional influence is filtered down to the level of 'neighbourhoods'. If, consequently these last could be spatially defined, the situation and distribution of noble and gentry estates within and amongst them might tell us much about the ways in which the tentacles of patronage and clientage at different periods reached down to local dynastic grass-roots.[6]

Focusing on supra-regional spatial definition, Phythian-Adams has identified English 'cultural provinces' which often cut across county boundaries. Such spatial analysis reduces the apparent geographical leap that Shakespeare might have taken between Warwickshire and Lancashire in that he would have simply been moving between contiguous cultural provinces – one containing Gloucestershire, Warwickshire, Worcestershire and Shropshire and identified as the 'Severn/Avon' province, and the other containing Cheshire, Lancashire and south-western parts of Westmorland and identified as the 'Irish Sea' province.[7] As a local historian Phythian-Adams has gone from a primary focus on community to a concern with identifying neighbourhhoods and provinces which

> might be seen to coalesce with the macro-structure of the national society. By macro-structure is meant the formal and informal conventions that are held to apply nationally to such matters as family and kinship, the distribution of power and the social ordering of 'classes', expectations of local 'community' at various levels, and the perception of national allegiance and identity.[8]

Ironically, in this journey from local focus to national focus, Phythian-Adams parallels the journey undertaken by Elizabethan transitionals such as cartographer Christopher Saxton and playwright William Shakespeare. It was their ultimate ability to position the particular and local within a constructed image of England as a whole that led to their preferment by like-minded patrons such as Lord Burleigh and the Lord Chamberlain.

Saxton began his apprenticeship in Yorkshire in the service of vicar John Rudd, but it is very likely that when Rudd applied for leave to undertake a survey of England Saxton travelled with him around the countryside. It is thought that the material they gathered at this time may have formed the basis of Saxton's national survey commissioned later most likely through the patronage of William Cecil and with the backing of the central government. In this light Shakespeare's proposed apprenticeship in Lancashire becomes quite reasonable and his possible transition from household entertainments to touring theatre to court entertainments and London's Globe closely parallels Saxton's pattern of mobility. Having been authorized directly by the Queen and received a licence from the Privy Council to tour the countryside, Saxton contributed to the construction of local identity through city and estate maps and plans, to regional identity through his national survey which produced county and regional maps between 1574 and 1579 and finally to national identity in 1579 with the publication of an atlas including his earlier county and regional maps as well as a general map of England and Wales.[9]

Similarly Shakespeare's proposed residency in Lancashire and apprenticeship in theatre would have led him to participate in the negotiation of a local cultural identity and eventually on tour to contribute to the construction of a broader cultural neighbourhood – geographically more widely dispersed but drawn together by a shared vocabulary of dramatic texts and current events as well as alliances and allegiances arising out of the ties of kinship, patronage, educational background, religious loyalties, business interests and politics. A prime motivation for any member of the gentry or nobility to patronize touring performers would have been the desire to participate in the construction of such neighbourhoods, to establish, promote and extend their influence. The public and social nature of theatrical performance, however, created sites of negotiated power and meaning whereby the influence of the patron was but one element in the determination of cultural identity. As currency in this network of power and allegiance, a player/playwright such as Shakespeare would have gained considerable influence. Through his experiences in the market town of Stratford, the households of the Lancashire gentry and the cultural neighbourhoods created by touring under Stanley patronage he could have gained a vision of England less tangible than the one created by Christopher Saxton, but, once he reached the London theatre, a vision dramatically more powerful in its ability to engage thousands of people in the collective, participatory construction of the English nation state. Given the potential importance to Shakespeare's later work and the Elizabethan concept of the English commonwealth, it will be useful to sketch the skeleton of the cultural neighbourhoods produced by performers associated with the Lancashire households in which Shakespeare might have served and to suggest some of the other neighbourhoods that would have intersected with them. In the end it should be clear how involvement in such neighbourhoods might have contributed to the writing of such an intensely nationalistic work as *Henry V*.

If William Shakeshaft was indeed William Shakespeare then his position in the Hoghton household would have situated him within one of the most steadfastly recusant local communities in the country. Formal charges of recusancy abound during the 1580s in the Diocese of Cheshire (which conforms quite closely to Phythian-Adams's cultural province of the Irish Sea) – particularly in south-west Lancashire where Shakespeare would have been situated and including members of the Hoghton and Hesketh families.[10] When Alexander Hoghton's will was read in 1581, for instance, Thomas Hesketh, who was to be Shakespeare's new patron, was in fact in jail for recusancy – where he would remain on and off until at least 1584. The papers of William Cecil, which offer both official and unofficial records of recusancy for the county, suggest much effort was being spent by the Queen's officials in determining who was trustworthy and who was not – largely on the basis of religious allegiances.[11] Lists submitted to Cecil in the 1590s appear to have been carefully perused and translated into annotations in Cecil's own hand on a manuscript map of Lancashire (see figure 1).[12] The extent of recusancy in Lancashire appears to have been alarming to authorities in the south, but charting that community by marking crosses on the estates of the members of the gentry perceived to be most dangerous may have been regarded as one way to begin effecting some kind of control over it. Another map in the same collection, this one a printed map

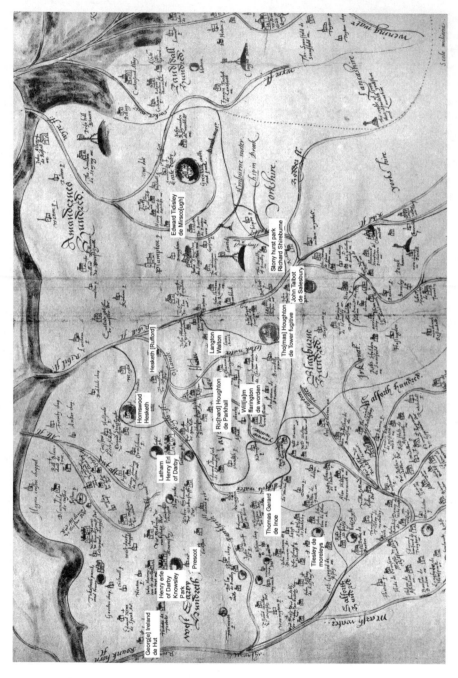

Figure 1 Lord Burghley's map of Lancashire c.1590, emendations added by editors. Royal 18 Diii, f. 81v–82

by Saxton consisting of Cheshire and parts of Lancashire, shows similarly motivated signs of annotation by Burleigh with additional markings noting lands held in the two counties by the Queen, through the Duchy of Lancaster, and by loyal members of the nobility as well as questionable members of the gentry.[13]

Cecil's charts and lists clearly identify the Hoghtons and the Heskeths as recusants,[14] and his manuscript map denotes Hoghton Tower with a reference to Alexander's exiled brother, 'Tho: Hoghton de Tower Fugitive'. Cecil, therefore, gives us some idea of the local families of recusant gentry with whom Shakespeare might have interacted under the patronage of Alexander Hoghton and possibly Thomas Hesketh, but this community also included other performers such as Elwes the Harper, other tutors and schoolmasters such as Thomas Latham of Rickstie, and of course numerous priests including two going by the names of Yestes and Thomas Hescotte.[15] As Richard Wilson has demonstrated, however, the network of recusancy extended well beyond the county boundaries through the ties of kinship which may have helped Shakespeare to come north and which connected exiled family members on the Continent with their Lancashire home base.[16] Thomas Hoghton's exile in Belgium lasted from 1569 until his death in 1580, but his brother Richard got permission to visit him in 1576.[17] A particular Lancashire connection existed with the college at Douai, which was founded by Cardinal William Allen, a Lancashireman, and endowed by the Hoghtons. Not surprisingly, Lancashire men composed a substantial portion of the college's recruitments and in 1580 it benefited from a bequest in the will of the exiled Thomas Hoghton.[18]

Graduates of these English colleges returned to England as itinerant Jesuit priests who created networks not unlike those traced by performers. Wilson argues that for six months the Hoghton household served as the centre of this network, as 'nothing less than the secret college and headquarters of the English Counter-Reformation'.[19] With the Hoghton library as his home base, Campion's travels from recusant household to recusant household, sometimes with an apparent entourage, amount to a counter-effort to reconstruct the map of England and Europe and reclaim English territory for the Pope. This clandestine community may be the best example of a widely dispersed sixteenth-century 'neighbourhood' lacking visible, contiguous geographical connections but constructed by common cultural links – in this case, through the intercession of itinerant priests – and possibly performers.

The secretive nature of the process whereby this community was forged and reinforced makes it unlikely that substantial involvement of performers will ever be confirmed in public records, but Alexander Hoghton's care in helping his players to a good Catholic patron – either his brother, the strongly recusant Thomas Hesketh, or one recommended by Hesketh – would suggest that Hoghton's players may have had a role to play in the construction of that community either within the household or on tour. The apparent availability of a library which could have contributed to a substantive commonality of belief and perspective within this cultural community further supports Shakespeare's development as a 'transitional man' in that increased literacy and wider access to printed and manuscript materials can be seen as one important development which ran parallel with increased social mobility in Tudor England and the educated background of most of the successful playwrights. It is possible, however, that the role of players within the recusant network extended beyond the stage. In the records of the Lancashire Protestant Sir Richard Shuttleworth we find references to the visits of performers patronized by his father-in-law Sir Peter Leigh. At Smithills in October 1588 Shuttleworth rewards Leigh's players apparently for performing, but a second entry suggests that players could be called upon for other duties: 'Item geven to onne of the said mene to gete a letter conveied from hornbie [Lancs] to barbone [Westm] vjd'.[20] Performers travelling from house to house within the recusant community as well must certainly have carried news orally, but here we see the possibility that they may also have doubled as couriers of written material – although there may have been good reasons for not formally recording this fact in account books.

Despite the lack of such detailed evidence, we do have two records relating to performers associated with Thomas Hesketh. One notes a payment by the executors of Robert Nowell of Read in 1569 and the other notes the appearance of his players at the Earl of Derby's seat at Knowsley in December of 1587.[21] Given the substantial number of musical instruments and music itemized in a seventeenth-century family inventory, it is possible that the 1587 players were actually musicians.[22] Certainly within recusant circles musicians familiar with liturgical music would have been capable of contributing to the Catholic discourse just as much as players so, although the politics of performance may have differed in kind for musicians, they may not have differed fundamentally in substance and the value placed on them by recusant patrons. However, the on-going tradition of players suggested by both the reference in Hoghton's will and the continuing employment of Shakespeare's colleague Fulk Gyllom by Hesketh in 1591[23] encourage a reading of the *Derby Household Book* as referring to actors, and, if Hesketh had not already helped Shakespeare to a new patron, then it is of course possible he was performing with them and/or writing for them. If so, his participation in and perspective with respect to cultural neighbourhoods may have been beginning to alter. Rather than the ideologically closed community of a recusant, gentry household such as that found at Rufford, Shakespeare would have had to make a transition to a more public and diversified audience in which religious and political allegiances were openly under negotiation.

Of course Shakespeare could have already made that transition by moving into the direct patronage of the Earl of Derby or his son Lord

Strange before this date. In 1581, the year of Alexander Hoghton's death, Hesketh was jailed for recusancy and might not have been in an especially strong position to support his own players or assist Shakespeare to another patron.[24] He could have recommended Shakespeare to the Stanleys at that time or it is possible that this hiatus motivated Shakespeare to return to Stratford and led to his marriage a year later to Anne Hathaway and the successive birth of his children. Whatever the case, by this date he would have undergone a change in family circumstances which has been known to motivate more than one individual's interest in 'getting on'. The occasion of a performance at the Stanley household would have given Shakespeare the opportunity to participate in a much broader cultural neighbourhood. Even a brief sampling of names frequently found in the family's household books suggests that the possible audience for this performance included a rather different range of religious orientations: Mr Thomas Gerrard was recognized as a recusant.[25] Although outwardly supportive of the reformed religion, William Farrington, servant to the Earl of Derby, was thought to be inwardly sympathetic to Catholicism (he is marked with an X on Burleigh's map),[26] but Mr William Fox, also a servant to the Earl of Derby, would appear to have been a clear supporter of the reformed church as of course was William Chaderton, Lord Bishop of Chester.[27] Thomas Langton, otherwise known as Baron of Walton, was identified on Burleigh's map as a recusant but graphically demonstrated the potential dissension within recusant ranks a couple of years later when he murdered Alexander Hoghton's stepbrother and heir in an affray.[28]

The most distinguished and important audience member, however, was the Earl himself who had just returned from Court where he would have been participating in both Privy Council meetings and less formal holiday festivities.[29] Thus we see that the cultural neighbourhood constructed through this performance draws in the Court and Cheshire as well as both Catholic and Protestant members of the Earl's household and gentry from the local area.

If Shakespeare had been picked up earlier by the Derby household, then extant civic and household records allow us to trace an even wider cultural neighbourhood. Unfortunately, though, only one Derby household account book survives, that for the period 1586–90, so it is not always possible to clearly connect the players of Lord Derby and Lord Strange with their Lancashire seat during the time Shakespeare could have been connected with one of their companies. It is reasonable, however, to assume the companies did visit their patrons in Lancashire – especially when we have other records from the period of their appearance in the north.[30] It is also difficult to know which if any of the Stanley companies Shakespeare might have been involved with from August of 1581. We know that he must have made his way to London before 1592 in order to engender Robert Greene's ire. If therefore he was connected with a Stanley during his early years in London, it would have had to be Lord Strange's company since the Earl's company did not establish a presence in London or at Court. However, whether Shakespeare might also have begun his involvement with the Stanleys in Lord Strange's company or first began in Lord Derby's company is impossible to determine.

If he began in Derby's company then he was becoming involved with players who had established a comparatively broad cultural neighbourhood since 1564 – including Stratford as recently as 1580. They also appeared locally in Lancashire. In 1582–83, for instance, they visited Liverpool, a town which depended on the Earl of Derby as its principal patron. In 1576 the town had lavishly entertained the Earl on his way to the Isle of Man and in 1585 it elected Ferdinando, the Earl's son and heir, as mayor. A measure of the respect accorded both Derby and his players is the 10s they were rewarded in comparison with the 3s 4d given to the Earl of Oxford's players who also visited the same year. Looking further afield – and recognizing that extant records most likely tell only part of the story – from 1581 into 1582–83 we know that Derby's Men also visited Bath, Abingdon, Winchester, Southampton, Norwich, Ipswich and Nottingham. The company had visited at least three of these locations before – Winchester, Ipswich and Nottingham – and it had visited Coventry (the company's only recorded visit for 1584) several times since the mid-1570s.[31]

If Shakespeare had been taken directly into Lord Strange's company, he would have also been joining an established company which had been touring since 1563–64. Starting in 1580–81 through to 1584–85, he would have traced a wide-ranging cultural neighbourhood incorporating Kent and Norwich in the east, Devon, Gloucestershire and Bath in the west, and Coventry, Nottingham, Liverpool and Beverley in the Midlands and the north. He might also have been involved in two Court appearances – one in 1581 and another in 1583. After 1584, however, there are no more references to touring visits by the Lord Strange's players until 1588 when they make a single appearance in Coventry. There are also no further references to Lord Derby's players until the 1590s when Shakespeare would have already been in London.[32] The timing of this hiatus in the activities of both Stanley companies is interesting in that it coincides roughly with a number of potentially related events. Those include the Earl's mission to the Continent in 1584–85 and his enhanced political profile as a Privy Councillor from at least 1585.[33] Between 1582 and 1585 as well, Shakespeare got married and started a family in Stratford. It was also at this time that the Queen's company was formed by Edmund Tilney, who raided existing companies, possibly including the more established performers in the Stanley companies.[34]

Whatever the cause for the hiatus, Lord Strange's company reappeared in 1588, no doubt at least partly owing to the death of the Earl of Leicester and the migration of some of his performers. Over the next few years

Plate I Hesketh family tree, Add.44206. ff. 7v–8, 9.
By Permission of the British Library.

Plate II Lord Burghley's map of Lancashire c. 1590. Royal 18 Diii f. 81v–82. By permission of the British Library.

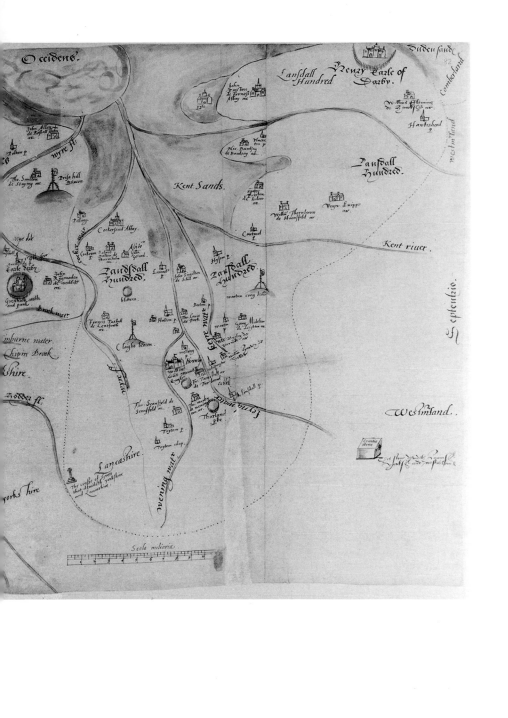

Occidens

Suden sand

Lansdall Hundred

Henry Earle of Darby

Cumberland

John Preston of Furnesse Abbay ar

Furnesse Ile

Willm Fleming of Cononhed ar

John Allein de Rossall ar

Wyre fl.

Hankeshead

westmerland

Nic Bardsey de Bardsey ar

Pansdall Hundred

The Smith de Stayning ar

Prise hill Beacon

Wyre Ile

Kent Sands

Willm Thornborow de Hamsfeld ar

Henry Knipe ar

Tullong

Cockersand Abbay

Cartmel

Ashto Gede Gerard

Kent riuer

Cockorsond

Cocksom Robert Dalton de Thornholm

Pansdall Hundred

Pansdall Hundred

Lonsdell

John Singelton de Skill ar

Hyto

Earle Derby

John Irmaden de Treddill

Bratern

watton crag ar

Greenhall castle and park

Brock water

Bolton p

Watton

Halton p

The Court de York

Middelton

Leighton ar

Tymmes Tuddall de Lentforth

Claytos Beacon

Melling

Kerre water

Sherne

Lomburne water

Lancashire

Wenning water ar

Shipm Brook

Shire

Wodscar Engsom

Tansdall de Turlend

Robert fl

lonsdall p

Wesimland

Tho. Scarsfield de Scarsfield ar

Lune fl. 16 3

Tharland Loke

Grondie stone

Sorda fl.

Toytom p

Toytom chap

Lancashire

The crosse of stones that diuideth yorkshire and Lancashire

yorkshire

Wenning water

Scala miliaria

Plate III Detail from Hesketh family tree, Add.44026. ff. 8–9.
By permission of the British Library.
Top: Sir Thomas Hesketh, 'knight, sone and here to Sir Robert, Lord of Rufford,
Holmes and Holmeswood … Martholme' (in Alexander Hoghton's will) and his
wife Dame Alice (suspected of harbouring priests as a widow at Martholme).
Below: Richard (3rd son), Thomas (2nd son), Blanche, second wife of Robert and
widow of William Stopforth, Secretary to the Earl of Derby), Robert Hesketh
(centre, 1st son), Mary Stanley d. 1586 (first wife of Robert, daughter of George
Stanley of Cross Hall, cousin to Early of Derby), Dorothy, Margaret. Robert
Hesketh's third wife, Jane (not pictured), outlived him and married Sir Richard
Hoghton of Hoghton Tower.

Strange's players proceeded to perform at London's Cross Keys and eventually mount a stunning run of Court appearances in the 1590s.[35] Although
we cannot be certain, I would suggest that a 31 December 1588 performance at Lathom House may have marked the rejuvenation of Strange's
acting company. The *Household Book* notes that 'on mondaye came mr
Stewarde, on Tvsedaye the reste of my Lords cownsell & also Sir Ihon
Savadge, at nyght a playe was had in the halle & the same nyght my Lord
strandge came home'.[36]

The *Household Book* goes on to record another performance on the following Sunday night, and in this case as well there appears to have been a
substantial audience. The list of playgoers includes many of the Justices of
the Peace for Lancashire, some important gentry in the Earl's service from
Nottinghamshire and Cheshire, as well as the Bishop of Chester, William
Chaderton. What united this audience was its loyalty to the local magnate,
the Earl of Derby, but, at least from the perspective of Lord Burleigh's maps
and lists, they would have been quite divided on matters of religion with a
clear majority favouring the old religion. If Shakespeare were at this time
associated with Lord Strange's company then he would have most likely
been there, and it is tempting to interpret the December 1588 account
of the company's visit to Coventry as a preview performance motivated
by Shakespeare's local connections. These late 1588 performances as well
as what may be another household appearance the next year could have
marked an important turning point for William Shakespeare.[37] Rather than
being concerned with the construction of cultural neighbourhoods through
wide-ranging travels in the provinces, Shakespeare was to shift to a London
base focusing on performances at Court and in the public theatres. It could
well have been his apprenticeship in Lancashire, however, and the wider
cultural neighbourhoods within which it was situated that enabled him
to appeal to the many other transitionals who were gravitating towards the
opportunities offered by urban London.

The Stanleys' patronage of performers was no doubt seen as part of the
responsibilities of local magnates of their stature, but it would also appear
to have been an expectation of loyal Privy Councillors and those ambitious
to rise on the scale of power and influence. On occasion we can see patrons
and Privy Councillors themselves travelling in the provinces clearly in the
context of negotiating their relative power bases and circles of influence.
For instance, the Earls of Derby and Lords Strange were frequent visitors
in the city of Chester, with the city often organizing performances of plays
or speeches in their honour. In 1583, though, the Earl of Leicester (then
Chamberlain of Chester) and Earl of Essex as well as the Earl of Derby
visited Chester together. This occasioned a public and inflammatory negotiation of loyalties when an oration delivered ostensibly in honour of Leicester liberally complimented Derby as the more local magnate and concluded,
'God bless the Earl of Derby'.[38] Such public, face-to-face competition for

provincial strongholds, however, was less common than the indirect competition reflected in civic accounts as clients and servants vied for rewards
appropriate to the relative importance of their patrons as perceived by local
officials. Performers figured prominently in these negotiations, and it
was not uncommon for membership on the Privy Council to coincide with
increased activity as a patron of performers. As we shall see, the Earl of
Derby's residences themselves became important sites for this negotiation
of power by performers associated with these and other patrons, but of
course chief among them all were the performers associated with the Queen.

In 1583 the Queen had signalled the importance she placed on the politics of touring performers by lending her patronage to a group of players, and
these performers proceeded to travel widely, creating one of the farthest-
reaching cultural neighbourhoods of the period.[39] Just as the Queen's
progresses were a mechanism for laying physical claim to her realm, com-
municating her policies and personal image directly to her people and seeing
for herself the state of her country and the allegiance of her people,[40] so
too her players' travels were a mechanism for extending these initiatives
beyond the reaches of her own progresses. During the politically sensitive
years of 1588–90, when we know that Cecil was personally preoccupied
with the state of recusancy in Lancashire to the point of commissioning
intelligence and annotating maps, the Queen's Men visited the Earl's residences at New Park, Lathom and Knowsley five times – an unusually high
frequency particularly in such a northerly location.[41] The extensive cultural
neighbourhood traced by the Queen's Men at this time was made possible
primarily because, by 1590–91, they split into two separate companies
the identity of which is not usually clear from extant records – including
the *Derby Household Book*. Taken together, however, between 1587 and
1590 they situated the Earl of Derby's Lancashire residences within a
wide-ranging cultural neighbourhood which included the Court, London,
Winchester, Devon, Marlborough, Bath, Oxford, Gloucestershire, Coventry,
Shropshire, Worcester, Chester, Carlisle, Nottingham, Leicester, Norwich,
Ipswich, Kent and Rye. Travels in 1586–87, 1592 and 1593 included Stratford in the itinerary, and on two occasions in 1589–90 while in Lancashire
they used the county as a springboard to places even further afield: Dublin
in the summer and Scotland at the invitation of the King during the time
of his wedding in the autumn.[42] I would argue that the company's official
and extensive touring responsibilities may have contributed to its split, its
failure to achieve a secure London playing space outside the Court and its
ultimate demise.

Closely associated with the Queen's players in the Derby household
accounts are the players of another Privy Councillor, the Earl of Essex,
aspiring heir to Leicester's position of influence on the Council. Players
under Essex's patronage visited Knowsley for at least one performance in
September of 1589 and possibly another one depending on interpretation

of the Comptroller's wording. In both cases the Queen's players would have given an initial performance to be followed by a performance by Essex's Men as happened on Sunday 7 September: 'mr Leigh preached the quenes players played in the after none & my Lord off Essix at nyght'.[43] This would have been in anyone's book a full day, the wider, full composition of which we will consider in a moment, but these joint appearances were not isolated instances. They appear to have gone on to Ireland together where they were received in Dublin, and they were also entertained together in Faversham, Kent, in 1590. Although it has been argued by some that the two companies may have joined forces for individual performances, the Knowsley record makes it clear that there were separate, successive performances and suggests a rather more political than practical motivation for their joint travels. Obviously for someone with Essex's ambitions, the spectacle of his players touring the countryside in conjunction with the Queen's players would have been a particularly desirable element in the public image he was constructing. The opportunity to intersect with the cultural neighbourhood established by the Queen's players to the extent that his players could play to the same audience immediately afterwards would clearly have enhanced his influence and extended it geographically. Although occasionally travelling to the north of Essex's seat in Staffordshire, the primary cultural neighbourhood established by Essex's players on their own between 1588 and 1590 was based in the south, in Rye, Kent, Ipswich, Norwich, Leicester, Coventry, Reading, Bath and Bristol.[44]

Understandably, the Earl of Leicester's players were the earliest troupe connected with an Elizabethan Privy Councillor to establish a wide provincial touring network. It continued until the Earl's death in 1588, and their visit to Lathom House in 1586–87, not long after Derby had assumed an active role on the Privy Council, drew the household into what was primarily a more southerly cultural neighbourhood including the Court during Christmas 1586, Devon, Abingdon, Bath, Gloucestershire, Marlborough, Reading, Oxford, Coventry, Leicester, Nottingham, York, Norwich, Ipswich, Kent, Rye and Southampton. However, at the same time another branch of the company was also travelling with their patron on the Continent, some fifteen strong.[45] Just as Leicester relied on his performers at home to reinforce a cultural neighbourhood in which his political and religious interests maintained a profile, so, too, he enlisted a troupe of performers in his efforts to secure additional territory and power in the Low Countries. The performers' travels were simply another mechanism for reconstituting spatially the political relationship between the Low Countries, England, Spain and other countries such as Denmark. It is important to keep this connection in mind when one considers the visit of Leicester's English company to Lancashire where the audience for their two performances was composed at least partially of recusants, several of whom were engaged in sending Lancashire boys to English colleges on the Continent and harbouring the Jesuit priests who returned. The appearance of Leicester's players in July was after all followed in December with the appearance of Sir Thomas Hesketh's players.[46] The parallel and opposing forces surrounding the circumstances of the players' travels, the composition of their audiences and the religious or political allegiances of the various patrons must surely have made players and playwrights mindful of their position, power and vulnerability within these dynamics. Rather than being at the margins, these dynamics of mobility and performance in the widest sense had the power to resituate the Derby household at the centre of negotiated meaning and identity.

The records of Leicester's Men on the Continent at this time also add further weight to the concept of players as 'transitional men', men of mobility in an Elizabethan network of communication. We learn from Philip Sidney, who was based in Holland in 1586, that 'Will, my lord of Lester's jesting plaier' had been charged with carrying a letter to his wife which also contained a letter for Walsingham – apparently relating intelligence of some significance to the state. Unfortunately, Kemp must have misunderstood and delivered the letters to Leicester's wife, who was no doubt puzzled and amused by turns.[47]

Thanks to the Earl of Derby's *Household Book* we are fortunate to have a substantial list of individuals who made up the local community with which any performer might have interacted while in residence and, in particular the audience members who could have attended dramatic performances. Although there are too many names to address individually within the scope of this chapter, it is possible to identify one important category of playgoer or performer regularly listed in the book. It testifies to the mobility of not only players and patrons but also preachers. The mobility of Jesuit priests in Lancashire was being matched by the mobility of Protestant preachers. For instance, not inappropriately, in July 1587 the Earl of Leicester's players were followed by a sermon preached by Thomas Sorocold, a native of Manchester who was popular in the county. Like Shakespeare and Saxton, he was a 'transitional man' who rose from comparative obscurity thanks to opportunities such as this to preach before individuals such as the solicitor general Thomas Egerton, whose patronage may have led the Queen in 1590 to present Sorocold as rector of St Mildred in the Poultry in London.[48]

Less appropriately, however, in 1587–88 the household hosted Sir Thomas Hesketh's players as well as Edward Fleetwood, rector of Wigan, one of the most energetic denouncers of local recusants and a supporter of acts to suppress entertainments on the Sabbath. He supplied Burleigh with intelligence and advice on the loyalty of potential appointees to local offices, and only three months earlier he had written to Cecil proposing a new ecclesiastical commission to deal with county recusants. Eventually Derby and other local officials were forced to act on Fleetwood's complaints, but this does not appear to have affected the frequent combination of preaching and playing in the Derby household. With apparently masochistic timing, Fleetwood was invited to preach again the day after what may have been the first performance by the newly revived Lord Strange's Men. John Caldwell, Derby's chaplain, preached just before the second performance on a Sunday and William Chaderton, Bishop of Chester, preached the following day. The preaching of William Leigh, rector of Standish and chaplain of Knowsley, was sandwiched in on a Sunday morning between Saturday and Sunday performances by the Queen's players and Essex's players. All this confirms the claims of a 1590 Protestant publication which boasted that Henry Stanley 'hath preachinge in his house Sabothly, by the best preachers in ye countie, and he giveth honorable countenaunce to all the professors of religion, and is very forwarde in the publique actions for religion'.[49] Given Shakespeare's assumed Catholic background and the apparently recusant preferences of so many members of Derby's household and council – including the majority of people usually present for these sermons – Shakespeare could have found the changeable religious climate in the Derby household to require some adjustment – adjustment that would have prepared him for his transition to London.

The foregoing sketch is ultimately only a bare skeleton of the rich cultural neighbourhood in which Shakespeare or any player might have functioned if based in Lancashire during the 1580s. It is drawn primarily from the perspective of the connections created by touring performers, but the full richness and significance of this cultural neighbourhood can be understood only through an exploration of further connections well beyond the scope of this chapter. The entire *Derby Household Book* – not just the entries associated with performers (and their immediate audiences) – can be used to define the wider neighbourhood including ties of kinship, business and official connections such as those associated with the Duchy of Lancaster, the Privy Council and patron–client relationships with individuals and urban or rural locations. Other documents might further illuminate the position of Shakespeare's possible patrons within the recusant network and connect them with activities on the Continent – such as attendance at and endowment of the English Catholic colleges, printing of tracts, networks of intelligence, presence on the Continent of the Earl of Derby and members of his family, the Earl of Leicester and his players. Parallel types of patronage on the part of Shakespeare's possible patrons and the urban centres which he might have visited as a touring player might also tell us much about the extent to which patrons and sponsors were engaged in other forms of 'spatial self-fashioning' such as the Elizabethan refurbishment of Hoghton Tower, the mapping of civic, estate and Duchy lands by individuals such as Christopher Saxton, and the patronage of itinerant priests and preachers.

However, evidence viewed from the perspective of travelling performers is sufficient to establish the possibility of Shakespeare's mobility and his progress as a 'transitional' within a network encompassing Stratford, Lancashire and London. The daily comings and goings itemized in the *Derby Household Book* illustrate especially well not only the geographical mobility of individuals in a range of social positions but also the obligations of clientage and patronage which facilitated social mobility. The wide-ranging network created by performers alone requires the reconsideration of perceptions of Elizabethan Lancashire as a remote and isolated backwater. The pattern of Shakespeare's proposed involvement in this network is also consistent with the formation of such a 'transitional man'. In exploring this network it is important to acknowledge that it may never be possible to know for certain whether the William Shakeshafte in Alexander Houghton's will was, in fact, William Shakespeare of Stratford-upon-Avon. However, such a study highlights the importance of more detailed research concerning such networks because it was through them that Shakespeare and other 'transitional men' like him were transforming English society. Rising in the chain of patronage as a result of his education and gradual refinement of his craft, Shakespeare became a 'man-in-motion' whose origins and travels in rural England ultimately led him to an urban base from which he could draw upon his knowledge of England's past and present to fashion not only a place for himself at Court but also an image of the English commonwealth which engaged both monarch and public playgoer.

This perspective, then, could help to explain to some degree the evolution of a play such as *Henry V* in the Shakespearean canon. In establishing Shakespeare's Lancashire connections most scholars have focused on the Henry VI plays and his references to the Stanley family's historic role, but such local connections are more challenging to make in *Henry V*. Whereas the Henry VI plays are concerned with disintegration and dissension, *Henry V* is concerned with the unification, construction and extension of the country. The image of England constructed as the sum of its parts is defined as a commonwealth which eventually encompasses supposedly reclaimed territory in France. This expansive vision, however, is exactly what we might expect of a 'transitional' evolving out of the cultural neighbourhood we have traced. Smith described his 'transitional man' as 'perceiving "connections between . . . private dilemmas and public issues" ', exhibiting 'the key traits of inconsistency and ambivalence over old and new values and life-styles', 'torn by the conflict between "new aspirations and old traditions" ', and moved most powerfully 'by the symbols of "nation" and "class" '.[50]

In fashioning *Henry V* as one of the most powerful symbols of the English nation state, Shakespeare was in fact highlighting parallels with transitional men such as himself. Harry's unconventional education outside the Court and universities on the highways and battlefields and in the margins of society leaves clergymen at a loss to explain this 'sudden scholar'.[51] His restless mobility exhibits itself on a large scale as he moves to extend his boundaries and on a smaller scale as he perambulates amongst his men the night before Agincourt. Only his repeated references to himself as a Christian king seem at odds with Smith's characterization of the 'transitional man' for whom 'the ritual and symbols of religion have lost their meaning'. I would argue, however, that the religious point of view of Henry V and his playwright reveal an 'ambivalence over old and new values' that we might expect of a 'transitional' fashioned by a cultural neighbourhood of charged religious polarities.[52] The play begins by characterizing Roman Catholic prelates as being motivated by greed rather than charity, but Henry V was after all a Catholic king, and he treats these prelates as having access to important knowledge of the law. He is also determined and severe in his punishment of individuals who would loot symbols of church ritual. On the other hand he has acquired a distinctly Protestant sensibility so that what is referred to as the 'reformation' of the King has led him to reject Falstaff and the shows and pastimes which served to educate him in his youth.[53]

Ultimately the religious perspective afforded by the play suggests careful craftsmanship which can embrace either a Catholic or a Protestant interpretation of Henry. By comparison with what Richard Helgerson has argued to be overtly proto-Protestant dramatic interpretations of the same material by his contemporaries,[54] Shakespeare's approach suggests ambivalence or pragmatism and possible unease with religious extremes on all sides. Ultimately this king is of a rather more 'transitional' than 'Christian' nature as he plays a role which incorporates threatened rape and murder as well as the execution of prisoners and old friends. Fundamentally, both King and playwright are concerned with the construction of a commonwealth. Any activities which are potentially destructive to that commonwealth are punished while the importance of every individual's participation in that process of construction is emphasized. When Henry remarks that he as monarch is 'subject to the breath / Of every fool',[55] he is acknowledging the monarch's dependence on his subjects in general and his players in particular for the construction of his own image and circle of influence. In performing before the Queen, London and provincial audiences, players created a space of negotiation sometimes 'crammed within the wooden O' of the Globe, sometimes 'shifting the scene'[56] further afield to the provincial sites of a cultural neighbourhood, but consistently inviting the English public to participate in the transition to and construction of an imagined commonwealth.

Notes

1 Jay M. Shafritz, *Shakespeare on Management: Wise Business Counsel for the Bard* (New York: Harper Business, 1999); Norman Augustine and Ken

Adelman, *Shakespeare in Charge: The Bard's Guide to Leading and Succeeding on the Business Stage* (New York: Hyperion-Talk-Miramax, c.1999); Frederick Talbott, *Shakespeare on Leadership: Timeless Wisdom for Daily Challenges* (Nashville: T. Nelson, c.1994); John Whitney and Tina Packer, *Power Plays: Shakespeare's Lessons in Leaderships and Management* (New York: Simon & Schuster, c.2000).

2 Peter Levi, *The Life and Times of William Shakespeare* (London: Macmillan, 1988), pp. 39–42.

3 See for example Robert Tittler, *Architecture and Power: The Town Hall and the English Urban Community c.1500–1640* (Oxford: Clarendon, 1991) and P. D. A. Harvey, *Maps in Tudor England* (London: British Library and the Public Record Office, 1993), pp. 66–77.

4 See for example Frank Singleton, *Hoghton Tower* (North Preston: Hoghton Tower Preservation Trust, 1999); Barry Coward, *The Stanleys, Lords Stanley and Earls of Derby, 1385–1672: The Origins, Wealth, and Power of a Landowning Family* (Manchester: Manchester University Press for the Chetham Society, 1983); David N. Durant, *Bess of Hardwick: Portrait of an Elizabethan Dynast* (London: Peter Owen, 1977); Alice T. Friedman, *House and Household in Elizabethan England* (Chicago: University of Chicago Press, 1988); J. J. Bagley and A. G. Hodgkiss, *Lancashire: A History of the County Palatine in Early Maps* (Manchester: Neil Richardson, 1985), pp. 22–4; Harvey, *Maps in Tudor England*, pp. 78–93; Catherine Delano-Smith and Roger J. P. Kain, *English Maps: A History*, The British Library Studies in Map History, vol. 2 (London: The British Library, 1999), pp. 122–4; J. B. Harley, 'Meaning and Ambiguity in Tudor Cartography', in *English Map Making 1500–1650*, ed. Sarah Tyacke (London: The British Library, 1983), pp. 22–45; Victor Morgan, 'The Cartographic Image of "The Country" in Early Modern England', *Transactions of the Royal Historical Society*, 5th series, 29 (1979), 129–54.

5 Anthony D. Smith, *Theories of Nationalism* (London: Duckworth, 1971), pp. 89–90.

6 Charles Phythian-Adams, *Re-thinking English Local History*, Department of English Local History Occasional Papers, 4th ser., no. 1 (Leicester: Leicester University Press, 1987), p. 46.

7 Charles Phythian-Adams, 'Introduction: an Agenda for English Local History', in *Societies, Cultures and Kinship 1580–1850: Cultural Provinces and English Local History*, ed. Phythian-Adams, Collected papers in English Local History, Department of English Local History (Leicester: Leicester University Press, 1993), pp. 1–23.

8 Phythian-Adams, *Re-thinking*, p. 45.

9 Sarah Tyacke and John Huddy, *Christopher Saxton and Tudor Map-making*, British Library Series, no. 2 (London: The British Library, 1980).

10 For example see *Calendar of State Papers, Domestic Series, of the Reigns of Edward VI, Mary, Elizabeth . . .* , eds Robert Lemon and M. A. E. Green, 12 vols (London, 1856–72), II, pp. 155, 159, 214, 220.

11 *Miscellanea: Recusant Records*, ed. Clare Talbot, *Publications of the Catholic Record Society* 53 (1961), 66–107.

12 *Miscellanea*, pp. 123–7, 189–90; British Library, Royal 18 DIII, f. 81v–82.

13 BL, Royal 18 DIII, ff. 83–4.
14 *Miscellanea*, pp. 124, 126–7, 189.
15 *Miscellanea*, pp. 124, 127, 190.
16 Richard Wilson, 'Shakespeare and the Jesuits: New Connections Supporting the Theory of the Lost Catholic Years in Lancashire', *Times Literary Supplement*, 19 December 1997, 11–13.
17 *Lancashire and Cheshire Records Preserved in the Public Record Office, London*, ed. Walford D. Selby, 2 vols, Publications of the Record Society for the Publication of Original Documents Relating to Lancashire and Cheshire, 8 (1883), 342.
18 *The Letters and Memorials of William Cardinal Allen (1532–1594)*, Fathers of the Congregation of the London Oratory, Records of the English Catholics under the Penal Laws (London, 1882), pp. 85, 87; Joseph Gillow, *The Haydock Papers: A Glimpse into English Catholic Life* . . . (London, 1888), pp. 9, 17; Joseph Gillow, *A Literary and Biographical History, or Bibliographical Dictionary of the English Catholics* . . . , 5 vols (London, 1887), III, pp. 325–8.
19 Wilson, 'Shakespeare and the Jesuits', p. 12.
20 David George, ed., Records of Early English Drama: *Lancashire* (Toronto: University of Toronto Press, 1991), p. 167.
21 *Ibid.*, pp. 160, 180.
22 *Ibid.*, p. 153.
23 *Ibid.*, pp. 156, 350; E. A. J. Honigmann, *Shakespeare: 'The Lost Years'*, 2nd edn (Manchester: Manchester University Press, 1998), pp. 31–2.
24 Honigmann, *Shakespeare*, p. 34.
25 P. W. Hasler, ed., *The House of Commons 1558–1603*, 3 vols, The History of Parliament (London: HMSO, 1981), II, pp. 185–6.
26 *Miscellanea*, p. 124.
27 A Mr John Fox, also connected with the Earl of Derby, was included in a 1592 Burleigh list of individuals whose 'fidelities and sowndnes in Religion' suited them to the Queen's service; *Miscellanea*, p. 125; James Croston, *County Families of Lancashire and Cheshire* (London, 1887), p. 60.
28 *The House of Commons*, II, p. 439.
29 Derby's last Privy Council meeting before the holidays was on December 21 1587; *Acts of the Privy Council of England*, ed. John Roche Dasent, n.s. 15 (London, 1897), p. 302.
30 Both companies were in Nottingham in 1581–82 and in Liverpool in 1583. Derby's players were in Beverley in 1584–85; Andrew Gurr, *The Shakespearian Playing Companies* (Oxford: Clarendon, 1996), pp. 274, 276.
31 Gurr, *Shakespearian Playing Companies*, pp. 275–6; George, ed., *Lancashire*, pp. xxviii–xxix, 41–7.
32 Gurr, *Shakespearian Playing Companies*, pp. 274, 276.
33 G. E. C[okayne], Vicary Gibbs *et al.*, *The Complete Peerage of England, Scotland, Ireland, Great Britain and the United Kingdom*, 13 vols; rpt 6 vols (1910–59; New York: St Martin's Press, 1984), IV, p. 211.
34 Gurr, *Shakespearian Playing Companies*, pp. 200–1.
35 *Ibid.*, p. 274.
36 George, ed., *Lancashire*, pp. 180–1.
37 *Ibid.*, pp. 181–2.

38 Lawrence M. Clopper, ed., *Chester*, Records of Early English Drama (Toronto: University of Toronto, 1979), pp. 124, 126, 136–7, 139, 152, 154; Croston, *County Families*, p. 61.
39 Gurr, *Shakespearian Playing Companies*, pp. 211–17.
40 Clifford Geertz, *Local Knowledge: Further Essays in Interpretive Anthropology* (n.p.: Basic Books, 1983), pp. 125–9.
41 George, ed., *Lancashire*, pp. 180–2.
42 Gurr, *Shakespearian Playing Companies*, pp. 204–5, 213–15; *Lancashire*, pp. 182–3.
43 George, ed., *Lancashire*, pp. 181–2.
44 Gurr, *Shakespearian Playing Companies*, p. 179.
45 George, ed., *Lancashire*, p. 180; Gurr, *Shakespearian Playing Companies*, pp. 190–1, 193, 195.
46 George, ed., *Lancashire*, p. 180.
47 Harl. MS 287, f. 1; E. K. Chambers, *The Elizabethan Stage*, 4 vols (Oxford: Clarendon, 1923), II, p. 90.
48 George, ed., *Lancashire*, p. 180; *The Stanley Papers, Pt. 2: The Derby Household Books; Comprising an Account of the Household Regulations and Expenses of Edward and Henry, Third and Fourth Earls of Derby; Together with a Diary Containing the Names of the Guests Who Visited the Latter Earl at His Houses in Lancashire: by William Ffarington, Esquire, the Comptroller,* ed. F. R. Raines, Chetham Society, 31 (Manchester, 1853), pp. 32, 142; *The Dictionary of National Biography . . . ,* eds Leslie Stephen and Sidney Lee, 22 vols (London: Oxford University Press, 1949), XVIII, p. 672.
49 George, ed., *Lancashire*, pp. xix, xxiv, xxv, xxxvi, 180–2, 219–27, 324, 355, 363–8; *The Stanley Papers*, pp. 46, 50, 56, 57, 65, 117–19, 132–3, 168–9, 188–90.
50 Smith, *Theories of Nationalism*, p. 90.
51 William Shakespeare, *King Henry V*, ed. J. H. Walter, Arden edn (London: Methuen, 1979), 1.1.32.
52 Smith, *Theories of Nationalism*, p. 90.
53 *King Henry V*, 1.1.33.
54 Richard Helgerson, *Forms of Nationhood: The Elizabethan Writing of England* (Chicago: University of Chicago Press, 1994), p. 230.
55 *King Henry V*, 4.1.240–1.
56 *King Henry V*, Prologue, 12–13; 2.Chorus.42.

A family tradition: dramatic patronage by the Earls of Derby

In the early 1580s one of the most prominent playing companies at Court and in the country was the Earl of Derby's troupe. Featured first before the Queen at Shrovetide 1579/80 and subsequently in Christmas performances in 1580/81 and 1582/83, Derby's Men had maintained a regular provincial tour on record in the Midlands, East Anglia and the south for the first decade following their patron's accession to his title in October 1572.[1] Although no notices of their London appearances have yet been discovered, it is reasonable to assume that they would have previewed their plays at one or more of the city inns and local playhouses before performing at Court, as seems to have been the custom for other troupes in the period.

The patron of this popular troupe was Henry Stanley, Fourth Earl of Derby, a member of the landed aristocracy without equal in the north-west where his vast estates found their centre in the two residences of Lathom and Knowsley in south-western Lancashire.[2] As the luck of survival dictates, we know more about the troupe's activities from sources geographically far removed from their patron's base of power. Yet renewed interest in Elizabethan acting companies presses us to ask further questions of sometimes resistant or incomplete sources: what were the basis for and terms of relationship between this patron and his players? Was there a theatrical tradition in the north-west implied by the troupe's success elsewhere?

The question of tradition is fundamental to the exploration of Derby's patronage of players. If we want to probe for the motives underlying his public support for an acting company, we may find some clues in the evolution of such patronage in previous generations of the family. The founding member, in our terms, is, in fact, the First Earl, the same Lord Stanley familiar from the final scene on Bosworth Field in *Richard III*. A cunning politician, Thomas Stanley was able to parlay his inherited position as Second Lord Stanley and lord of the Isle of Man into an earldom in 1485 from a grateful Henry VII. Although this Tudor elevation to the higher nobility brought him a windfall of lands and important offices, Stanley had managed to develop political status through two previous Yorkist reigns, serving Edward IV and Richard III as a councillor and Lord Steward of the royal household (1471–85), while accumulating numerous local appointments across the kingdom in addition to Cheshire and Lancashire offices where his family had held lands for several generations.[3] A telling indication of his ability to manoeuvre his way through the upheavals of the time is the back-to-back appointments as constable of England, first in 1483 by Richard III, followed by a renewal in 1485/86 by Henry VII. Not all his strategies were in the political forum, however. Lord Thomas first married Eleanor Nevill, sister of Warwick the Kingmaker and then, a decade after her death in 1472, took a significant partner from the other side of the conflict, Lady Margaret Beaufort, mother of Henry VII.

By 1489 Lord Thomas stood confirmed as a leading member of the new Tudor peerage and landowner of estates in no fewer than fifteen counties, stretching from the north-west through the Midlands as far south as Somerset.[4] The marriage of his eldest son, George Stanley, to the heiress of the Lestrange estates in Shropshire and the Welsh marches had brought further lands and the title Strange of Knockin into the family earlier in the same decade. Thus was established 'an extensive territorial empire that was to last virtually unchanged for over two centuries'.[5]

Numerous members of the gentry, nobility and royalty in the later fifteenth century are known to have patronized performers with varied talents, both for their own personal entertainment when in residence or as part of their travelling retinues. Such individual performers or small troupes seem to have toured on their own as well, though the extent of their circuits can be difficult to trace because of sporadic survival of records from the period. Such members of a retinue would have worn their lord's livery, thereby claiming his protection while upholding his honour, at home, at Court or on the road. This traditional bond between medieval minstrel and lord underlies the later Elizabethan links between patron and player which are of such interest in current scholarship.[6]

The accounts of medieval households are more elusive than civic records although one roll of Lord Thomas Stanley's accounts from an early stage in his career happens to be among those extant.[7] In 1459–60 Lord Stanley paid wages for a piper, Thomas, and a trumpeter, Mordoc, neatly specified in this context, but likely to be noticed in more summary fashion in Latin civic accounts of the period, perhaps as 'fistulatores', 'ministralli' or even the generic 'mimi' or 'histriones'.[8] Stanley's two musicians were therefore attached to his household based in south-west Lancashire, but they may have travelled with their busy lord when he went south to Court or elsewhere in the country on JP or other commission duties. From this early period only one external record has surfaced, for a 'minstrel' or 'minstrels' at King's Lynn in 1457–58.[9] The most consistent form of entertainment associated with Lord Stanley's name before and immediately after his acquisition of the Derby title is the itinerant bearward who was rewarded eleven

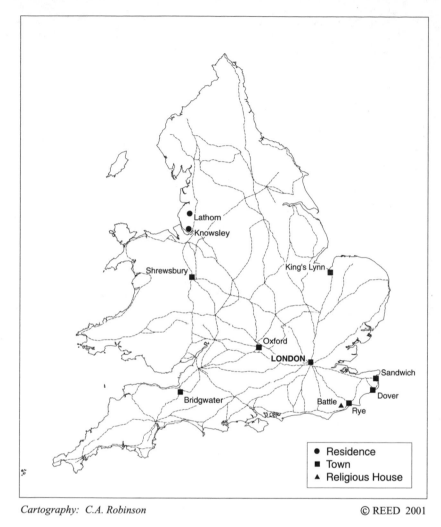

Cartography: C.A. Robinson   © REED 2001

Figure 2   Tour stops by the entertainers of Thomas Stanley, First Earl of Derby

times along the south-east coast not far from London between 1474 and 1489 (see Figure 2).[10]

Apart from what was probably a bear-baiting act, the First Earl of Derby seems not to have been an especially active patron of performers. One or more of his 'minstrels' appear on their own at Rye in 1491 and at Bridgwater in 1504, but these are isolated occurrences in a period for which civic accounts do survive in various parts of the country.[11] The only other notice of a Derby troupe, termed 'histriones', has been found at Shrewsbury in July 1495, in company with several royal troupes which were part

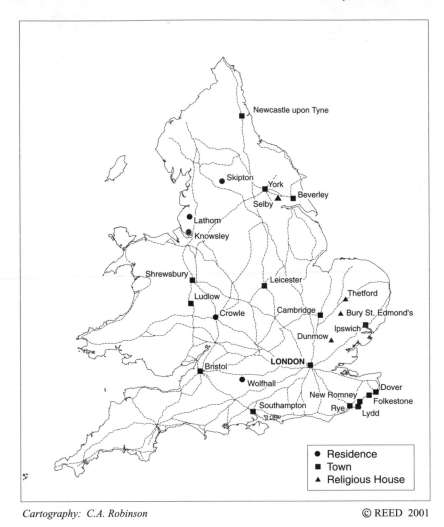

Cartography: C.A. Robinson   © REED 2001

Figure 3   Tour stops by the entertainers of Edward Stanley, Third Earl of Derby

of the royal family's entourage travelling through the West Midlands possibly on their way to or from their visit to the Derby residences of Knowsley
and Lathom the same month.[12]

Thomas Stanley's grandson, the Second Earl Thomas, inherited the title
in 1504. His offices and appointments were mostly confined to the north-
west where he principally resided. The only evidence of his patronage
of household entertainers comes from the Shrewsbury bailiffs' accounts,
1517–21. The fact that Shrewsbury is just a few miles south-west of the
residence he inherited from his mother at Knockin may explain why the

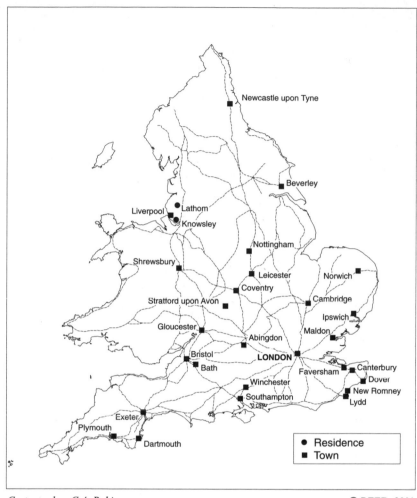

Cartography: C.A. Robinson   © REED 2001

Figure 4   Tour stops by the entertainers of Henry Stanley, Fourth Earl of Derby

Second Earl's bearward and two entertainers ('histriones') appeared there.[13] One wonders whether they may have made similar neighbourhood appearances at Liverpool, adjacent to their patron's residence at Knowsley, or at Ormskirk, near Lathom in Lancashire, but no early sixteenth-century records survive for either of those towns.

Like its dominant family, the county of Lancashire in this period may not have had the diversified cultural life that some of the southern regions enjoyed. Its parishes were large and somewhat isolated and its towns were relatively small. The terrain was difficult and underpopulated, with marsh-

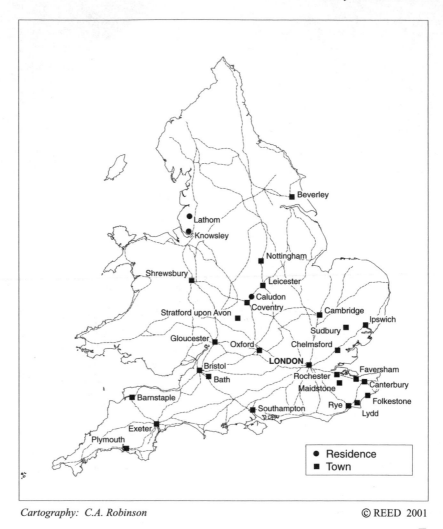

Cartography: C.A. Robinson   © REED 2001

Figure 5   Tour stops by the entertainers of Ferdinando Stanley, Fifth Earl of Derby

land near the coast and higher moorlands to the north and east. Even in the later sixteenth and early seventeenth centuries, the history of entertainment in the region centres on the private residences of the Lancashire gentry, although a vigourous popular appetite for bear-baiting can be traced in ecclesiastical court records.[14] The first two Derby earls were probably typical of other Lancashire nobility in their limited patronage of entertainers. Although relevant records are lacking in this region for the late fifteenth and early sixteenth centuries, we can trace very few small minstrel bands with Lancashire patrons on the road elsewhere in the country during this period.[15]

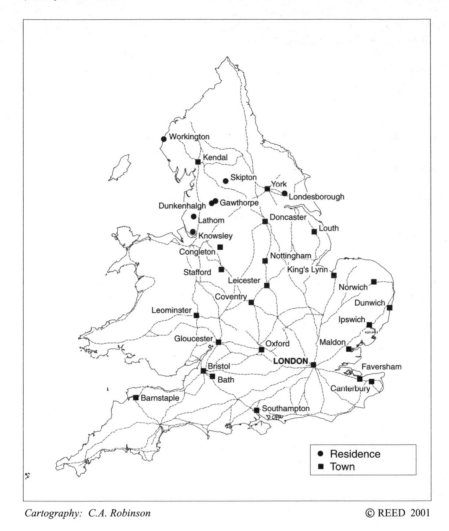

Cartography: C.A. Robinson © REED 2001

Figure 6 Tour stops by the entertainers of William Stanley, Sixth Earl of Derby

There is a notable change in attitude towards patronage discernible in the touring records for the Third Earl of Derby's entertainers. A glance at Figure 2 for the First Earl, compared with Figure 3, for Edward Stanley, the Third Earl, illustrates an expanding vision. There are eight tour stops recorded for the First Earl's troupes, whether bearwards, heraldic minstrels or other entertainers, and a single location, Shrewsbury, for his successor. Earl Edward's entertainers, on the other hand, had a wider range of travel, their payments appearing at twenty-two locations, including several in the north-east. Forty-three performances have been found so far, starting with the earliest at Shrewsbury in 1524–25, three years after he had succeeded as Earl of Derby at the age of twelve.[16]

During the early years of his long tenure of the earldom Edward seems to have maintained the modest pattern of patronage inherited from his father. The annual appearance of Stanley family 'histriones' at Shrewsbury near the estate at Knockin is embellished with some helpful details in the civic accounts. It seems likely that Edward had one 'entertainer' travelling with another patronized by his cousin Thomas, Second Lord Monteagle. The consistent references to the bailiffs listening to 'melodiam eor*um*' makes it apparent that these were musicians and in one year, 1525–26, names are supplied. Ralph Hubbard seems likely to have been touring under Derby's patronage, while Lokkett was Monteagle's man.[17] The Derby minstrels appearing in the Southampton records for 1526–27 were more modestly paid but may have been offering the same type of entertainment, and it is possible that Ralph Hubbard was one of those who made that journey south.[18]

During these formative years young Edward was a ward in the household of Cardinal Wolsey, whose opulent (if ill-advised) lifestyle may have influenced the magnificent household and style of hospitality which the Third Earl was later to establish for himself in the north-west. After Wolsey's fall in 1529 Edward was married to Dorothy Howard, daughter of the Duke of Norfolk and shortly thereafter was granted livery of his own lands in January 1530/31. He continued to be active at Court and it is, perhaps, no coincidence that the next decade, 1530 to 1540, was the most active for his touring entertainers. Although the ever-popular bearward continued to circulate wearing Derby livery, his circuit, still mostly in the southeast, differed from that of the players now patronized by the Third Earl.[19]

A troupe of players under Derby's patronage becomes distinguishable in the English records for several towns in the 1530s for the first time. Pursuing one of the most popular performance circuits in East Anglia, they were touring a region where the patron's in-laws, the Howards, held sway, not far from London and the Court. The performance locations – Ipswich, Bury St Edmunds, Cambridge, Dunmow and probably Thetford, where the Latin records use the term 'jocatores' – were all new to Derby entertainers.[20]

Also new were Bristol and the Seymour home at Wolfhall in the southwest, Leicester in the Midlands and Selby in the north-east.[21] Were the minstrels who also appeared in the north-east at Skipton in 1535 the same troupe? It is impossible to be sure, just as we cannot make secure connections with the 'minstrels' who appear a decade later in the Dover accounts or at Ludlow in 1550–51.[22]

The most active years on record for Derby's troupe of players seem to coincide with a time of strong connection with the south in their patron's life, either through a continuing need to appear at Court or through affiliation in East Anglia with his first wife's family. There is a noticeable gap in the record in the 1540s and 1550s. Although the Stanleys had extensive land-holdings across England, the centre of Derby's power was in south-west Lancashire where he spent much of his time at Lathom and Knowsley. Although he was named to the Privy Council in 1551, he almost simultaneously acquired offices that further affirmed his status as principal magnate of the north-west: Lord Lieutenant for Lancashire (from 1552) and Vice-Admiral for Chester and Lancashire (1553). As a religious conservative, he played a cautious role during the reigns of the two Protestant monarchs, coming infrequently to Privy Council meetings.[23] In the 1560s he added further northern offices to his list: Lord Lieutenant for Cheshire (from 1569) and Chamberlain of the County Palatine of Chester (from 1559).

It is clear that Derby became less interested in life at Court than in establishing a splendid household of his own. Christopher Haigh has summarized the Earl's position as follows:

> the third earl of Derby remained a powerful feudal magnate. He had his own council, consisting of a group of the most important and able men in Lancashire, which met to deal with the affairs of the county and implement royal policies. His household, with a treasurer, a receiver-general, a comptroller, secretaries, chaplains, two almoners and gentlemen-in-waiting, provided posts for members of gentry families and formed a school in which the sons of the influential learned the courtly and military arts. By the 1560s the earl had a household staff of 120, and it cost £1500 a year to feed this vast concourse and the family and its guests. The Stanley household formed the core of the earl's local power, and the patronage he provided gave him considerable influence over the county gentry.[24]

What role did entertainers play in this household? Unfortunately, this is almost impossible to document. Most of the family household records have been destroyed, probably during the siege of Lathom in the Civil War. Only one manuscript survives for the Third Earl's era, an account of his expenses in 1560–61 as well as his household regulations for 1568.[25] But the expenses are not itemized, so the summary totals for servants' livery and wages cannot be further broken down to help in the search for entertainers retained by the Earl. What the totals do indicate is that the Earl spent at least seven weeks and four days 'in progress' to and from London.[26] Most of the year his household was likely in Lancashire where he became famous for his lavish hospitality.[27]

The evidence for Derby entertainers in other extant 1550s and 1560s sources is very fragmentary. In the county records of Cheshire and Lancashire, there seems to be no trace of them, although it must be admitted that almost no household or civic accounts survive in that region to shed light on the touring players of the period.[28] Elsewhere players under Derby's patronage show up at Newcastle-upon-Tyne in the spring of 1566 and at New Romney some time during 1569–70. A bearward was circulating in 1558–59 in the north, appearing at Shrewsbury and York, and again in 1563–64 at Beverley and Leicester. An isolated payment to Derby's bearwards also occurs in the Dover accounts for 1566–67.[29] That other traditional entertainer type, the minstrel, is also known to have been affiliated still, however loosely, with Derby's retinue in this period. 'The Lament of Richard Sheale', a ballad surviving in manuscript, pays tribute to Sheale the minstrel's 'good lord and master, whom I sarve, / In my greatist povertie from me dyd never swarve / But dyd wryt for me frendly after a lovyng facion. And my lord Strang also on me dyd tak compassion.'[30] Sheale's patron and 'good lord' was Edward, the Third Earl, and Lord Strange was Henry, his eldest son and heir. Sheale's epitaph for Margaret, the Countess of Derby and Edward's second wife, is included in the same manuscript; her death in 1558 helps to date both the poem and the manuscript. Although Sheale lived in Tamworth, Staffordshire, it is apparent that he received direct payment, on occasion, from his patron and that there must have been some personal contact with the family, even though he was not a resident member of the household.[31]

Sporadic records of Derby's entertainers in the later years of his life might seem to imply that his patronage was occasional and perhaps even somewhat old-fashioned, with minstrels such as Sheale and bearwards still associated with the family in the 1560s. Was Derby's patronage of players merely a youthful enthusiasm, an early emulation of others he witnessed during time spent with Wolsey or at Court? The compassionate support of his son Henry, Lord Strange, was praised by Sheale alongside his father's, so the attitude of the younger generation of Stanleys in this hospitable noble household is worth attending to.

Henry Stanley was born in 1531, Edward's oldest son by his first wife, Dorothy Howard. He spent much of his youth at Court as companion to Edward VI and as a gentleman of the privy chamber, to both Edward and Philip I. In 1555 he was married to Margaret, daughter of Henry Clifford, Earl of Cumberland, in a lavish ceremony at Whitehall in the presence of Mary and Philip. Like his father, Henry's formative years must have been influenced by Court culture but his roots, through family, marriage and later office appointments were in the north-west. In January 1558/59 he was summoned to Parliament as Lord Strange.

In the early 1560s, at a time when other members of the nobility were adding players to their retinues, Henry seems to have done the same. His players have been detected first in the south, at Winchester and Southampton in 1563, followed by a south-western tour that included Bristol and Gloucester in 1564, and Canterbury in the south-east and Maldon in East Anglia some time in the same year.[32] From then on, Lord Strange's troupe can be found on tour almost annually in various parts of the kingdom, though never in the region where their patron's family held its greatest influence. The places on the tour are farflung but mostly unconnected with the family's widespread land-holdings – Cambridge (1565–66), Ipswich (1566–67) in East Anglia; Beverley (1566–67) in the north-east; Canterbury and Dover (1568–69), Lydd and New Romney (1569–70) in Kent; and Plymouth and Bristol (1569) in the south-west.[33] This would seem to have been touring for its own lucrative sake, probably at times when the Derby family had no personal call for household entertainment. If we can know little from extant documents about cultural life at Lathom and Knowsley during the last decade of the Third Earl's life, the regular appearances of his son's troupe elsewhere suggest that plays at home were an option, whether Earl Edward maintained a troupe himself or not.

The Stanleys were probably pioneers in their patronage of players in their home region, in fact. Evidence for other touring players originating in the north-west is meagre in the rest of the kingdom before 1600, suggesting an insular culture that may have focused on other forms of entertainment. Certainly at Chester, the centre of a county palatine, there was a fine tradition of locally sponsored play productions in the sixteenth century until the religious conflicts of the 1570s brought the Whitsun biblical play cycle to a close. This was a continuation of a medieval form of theatre, however.

The Stanleys are known to have been honoured visitors in the audience for a couple of local Chester productions – George, First Lord Strange, in 1490 for a special performance of the Assumption play, and the Fourth Earl and his son Ferdinando, Lord Strange, in 1577, for a revival of the Shepherds' Play.[34] But it seems more likely that their personal dramatic tastes were developed at Court in the south rather than in the north-west. And their players' choices for any tour may have been similarly influenced by an awareness of more sophisticated audiences in East Anglia and other parts of the south known to be favoured by other noble and royal troupes. When Henry became the Fourth Earl of Derby in 1572, it is reasonable to assume that his troupe continued under his patronage, with a change of title. And the touring in the same southern regions continued for the next decade (see Figure 4) – Ipswich (1577–78, 1581–82) and Norwich (1581–82) in East Anglia; Dover (1577–78) and Faversham (1577–78, 1579–80) in Kent; and Southampton (1578–79, 1582–83) on the road south-west to Bath (1578–79, 1582–83) and Bristol (1578–79).[35] Other stops in the south-west were made in 1579–80: Gloucester, Dartmouth and Exeter, and in 1580–81 the route south-west to and from Exeter included Abingdon, Winchester and Bath. Part of the same route was retraced in 1581–82 when Derby's Men played Winchester again. [36]

The troupe seems to have pursued new directions as well: Coventry, strategically positioned at the crossroads (1573–74, 1577–78, 1579–80), with nearby Stratford (1579–80); and a very popular eastern Midlands route that included Leicester (1579–80, 1580–81, 1582–83) and Nottingham (1577–78, 1579–80, 1580–81, 1581–82).[37] By the later 1570s Derby's troupe was one of the most prominent, and probably prosperous, of the Elizabethan acting companies. Their touring routes seem less likely to have been motivated by their patron's need to promote his political or landed interests, by contrast with others at Court, such as the Earl of Leicester.[38]

The Earl of Derby was pre-eminent in the north-west, with what amounted to an hereditary claim on the lord lieutenantship of Lancashire and a central link between the Crown and the north-west, a region under suspicion for its stubborn recusancy and potential for political disaffection.[39] For the most part his players toured along popular and lucrative routes where their patron would have been known as a powerful member of the landed aristocracy. They were evidently successful on their own terms as well, not only in the provinces but also at Court. Between 1579/80 and 1582/83 they were chosen by Tilney for three performances at Court, either at Christmas or Shrovetide, although never both.[40] Were they with their patron's family in the north-west for the other key festive date in any household calendar? We cannot know, for lack of family accounts in this period, but it is worth noting that there is a rare appearance by Derby's players in the 1582–83 Liverpool town records.[41]

Derby's commitment to the patronage of players can therefore be documented, through external sources, if not family records, for two decades. Their quality must have been high, if Court performances are any measure of excellence. But in 1583 they vanish from the records. What could be the explanation? Their patron experienced no fall from grace in this period. In the 1580s he added further appointments: Privy Councillor in 1585; ambasssador extraordinary to France, 1584/85; commissioner at the trial of Mary, Queen of Scots, 1586; Lord Steward of the Household after Leicester's death in 1588; Chamberlain of the County Palatine of Chester, 1588.

A key moment in Elizabethan theatre history occurred in 1583 that may have some bearing on the interruption in Derby's patronage. In early March 1582/83 Sir Francis Walsingham instructed the Master of the Revels to appoint twelve actors to a newly formed troupe under the patronage of the Queen.[42] These actors were plucked from the ranks of the leading troupes of the day – Robert Wilson, John Lanham and William Johnson from Leicester's Men, Tarlton and John Adams from Sussex's, and possibly John Dutton from Oxford's. But what of the remaining six? The troupes of origin for John Bentley, Toby Mills, John Towne, John Singer, Lionel Cooke and John Garland have not yet been traced, but it is probable that they were drafted from one or more of the companies featured at Court in the early 1580s. Derby's is a leading contender, therefore, and the formation of the Queen's Men in 1583 may explain why the company disappears from the records at this point.

Did the Fourth Earl lose all interest in family patronage of drama as a result? It seems that he did not re-form a new troupe, as Leicester did, within two years.[43] However, another Stanley tradition had been observed for some years past that may help to account for this apparent break in

Henry's longstanding public support of actors. His heir, Ferdinando, Lord Strange, also had a troupe of performers, not as prominent on tour as his father's perhaps, but traceable in the provinces from 1576–77 onwards when they first appeared in the south at Exeter and Southampton.[44] The Southampton payment in June 1577 is of particular interest as it provides a clue to the special character of Strange's troupe. The reward of 10s is for five 'vaulters' or 'tumblers', and when Strange's players appear several years later for performances at Court, it is for 'feats of activity,' or 'tumbling' that they are featured.[45] Such specialties are not usually detectable in provincial civic accounts, where the expression 'men' or 'players' is more typical. As such, Strange's are recorded at Faversham (1577–78); Ipswich, Nottingham, Coventry, Stratford-upon-Avon and Bath (1578–79); Canterbury, Lydd, Rye, Bath, Bristol and Gloucester (1580–81), Nottingham and Plymouth (1581–82); Barnstaple (1583–84); Beverley (1584–85); and Coventry in 1587–88.[46] Unlike Derby's Men their career was apparently not interrupted by recruitment to the Queen's Men despite their appearances at Court at Christmas or shortly thereafter in 1579/80, 1580/81, and 1582/83.[47] It is also worth noticing that Strange's performers did not appear on the same bill with Derby's during these years at Court: in 1579/80 they did their act in mid-January rather than at Shrovetide, and in 1580/81 Derby's were elsewhere.[48]

Several years later, in 1587, the career of Strange's company becomes even more intriguing, although we still have only tantalizing clues to work with. A unique Stanley household book survives to shed light on expenses for the periods when the Fourth Earl and his family were in residence at Lathom or Knowsley between May 1587 and late August 1590. A checkroll of household servants was drawn up in May 1587, but amongst the 118 persons listed there are no players, only two trumpeters, John King and George Campe, probably the same paid at King's College, Cambridge, in 1590–91.[49] The household book includes, amongst its domestic expenses, somewhat curt journal entries about the activities of family members and their numerous guests.

Although the visits by preachers far outnumber the notices of players, as becomes a good Protestant household, it is obvious that the family also enjoyed entertainments of a more secular nature. Their taste does seem to differ from that of other Lancashire gentry whose family papers survive for the late sixteenth and early seventeenth centuries, however. The numerous local bands of musicians, mummers or players sponsored by Lancashire gentry do not appear in the Derby records, as they do so frequently in those of the Shuttleworths of Smithills and Gawthorpe, or the Walmsleys of Dunkenhalgh.[50] The Stanleys seem to have had more sophisticated tastes for their personal entertainment – the companies noticed by their steward, William Farington, are mostly from the south: the Queen's Men, Leicester's and Essex's although there is an undesignated company which seems most likely to have been under the patronage of Lord Strange himself.

The timing of the appearances is worth analysis. On 29 December 1587 the Earl of Derby returned to Knowsley to join his family (including Lord Strange) during the Christmas season, and the following day 'players wente awaie'.[51] The following Christmas the family was again in residence in the north-west, this time at Lathom, where Lord Strange joined them on New Year's Day (1588/89). That same night 'a playe was had in the halle' and several days later, on Epiphany night, 'plaiers plaid'. A year later, a week or so before the other traditional festive season of Shrovetide, the Earl of Derby upon his return home to Lathom enjoyed another performance in company with Lord and Lady Strange when 'players played at nyght'.[52] For the three years when the family is known to have been in residence during the Christmas and Shrovetide seasons, we therefore have a consistent pattern of performances by players whose patron or town of origin need not be named (as was the custom in the period). At other times of the year, other troupes appeared, but we can deduce that the Stanleys were here observing an older custom in favouring entertainment by performers under their own patronage. Derby himself seems not to have had a troupe during these years, so these were likely Strange's Men, a company in the process of establishing itself in London and soon to gain ascendancy at Court in the early 1590s, with plays and 'feats of activities'.

The relationship between patron and players suggested by these records may have been closer than often assumed. We may also reflect on the elusive possibilities of the other performance records in this precious household book. There is not a lot of traffic in touring companies, in fact. Both the Fourth Earl and Lord Strange were spending significant periods of time at Court or, in the Earl's case, abroad during these years, so the household did break up while they were absent. Two of the three troupes which did make the trip to south-west Lancashire may have had personal connections with the Stanleys as patrons, either past or future. If some of Derby's Men were drafted by Tilney to join the Queen's Men in 1583, we can assume that they were familiar with the Stanleys' welcoming household. The Queen's Men visited the Stanleys four times, in October 1588, July 1589, September 1589 (apparently in company with Essex's men) and June 1590. Intriguingly, this is the period (1588–90) when notice was taken at various points along their tour route of the special tumbling act featured. John Symons, known to have been under Strange's patronage earlier in the decade, is specifically mentioned in the Nottingham civic accounts as receiving payment for the Queen's Men in the autumn of 1588, probably some time not long after the troupe played at Stanley's lodge of New Park on the grounds of Lathom House.[53] The fluidity of membership in acting companies of the period is worthy of further exploration, and Symons's varied affiliations have not yet been definitively identified. Suffice to say that he enjoyed the patronage of several in the 1580s: the Queen, Lord Strange and the Earl of Oxford.[54]

The other troupe which played Lathom for two days running in July 1587 was the re-formed Leicester's Men. The Earl of Leicester was on the Privy Council with the Fourth Earl and, according to his biographer, Simon Adams, he had worked hard in the 1580s to win Derby's loyalty and friendship.[55] Leicester's household accounts for 1584–86 include some payments for his expedition to the Low Countries, accompanied by an extravagant retinue. Twelve musicians accompanied him, as well as fifteen players, including Robert Wilson, recruited back from the Queen's Men to make the trip.[56] One payment links Leicester's retinue with Strange's: on 1 June 1586 he paid four of Lord Strange's 'musicians' 20s at Arnhem, at the same time that he dispatched five of his players (George Bryan, Thomas King, Robert Percy, Thomas Pope, Thomas Stephens) to the Danish court at Elsinore.[57] Will Kemp and his boy were to follow the players later.

When Leicester's Men returned from their Continental travels in 1587, they resumed their extensive provincial touring. A little over a year later, in 1588 when their patron died, it is generally accepted that some actors from this same company would transfer their loyalty to Lord Strange and go on to success in London and at Court. By 1589 Strange's Men are known to have been performing at the Cross Keys and then in 1590–91 at the Theatre founded by Burbage, a former Leicester's man.[58] In 1590 too, they would make the first of numerous appearances at Court between 1590 and 1593, while maintaining a vigourous touring schedule along the favoured routes in the south-east, East Anglia and south-west.[59] Whether they came north to Lancashire again is not on record, but they would presumably have had other opportunities to connect with their patron at Court.

The history of Strange's Men in the 1590s is a complex subject that has been treated elsewhere.[60] More than Derby's Men, they were transformed into a London-centred company, though their roots lay in the provinces. Their patron's tenure as Fifth Earl of Derby was a brief seven months, and, when his brother William succeeded as Sixth Earl, the family's centre of patronage returned again to the north-west. The new Derby's Men were to maintain their touring career for an extraordinary thirty years, starting in 1594 and extending at least as far as 1636–37, when they were rewarded at Doncaster (Figure 6).[61] From 1609 onwards they seem to have favoured northern circuits where the household records of nobility and gentry are a primary source of information.[62]

The Sixth Earl was perhaps the keenest of his clan in his patronage of players. Known to have been 'busy penning comedies for the common players' in 1599, William Stanley continued in his patronage even as he retreated from public life in the 1620s, gradually handing over management of his estates and official duties to his son, James, Lord Strange.[63]

The tradition of patronage which had evolved from the First Earl Thomas reached its culmination in the drama-loving sons of Henry, the Fourth Earl. But of the two, William perhaps had the strongest link with his remote ancestor. He alone continued to associate the family name with that popular northern form of entertainment, the bearward. Between 1596 and 1618, Derby's bears appeared at Coventry and Nottingham, although in the south-east, where Earl Thomas's bearwards had first made their tour, popular taste had long since shifted.[64]

Notes

1 For principal biographical details for Henry Stanley, Earl of Derby (1572–93) see the *Dictionary of National Biography* and *The Complete Peerage*.

2 See Barry Coward's detailed study, *The Stanleys, Lords Stanley and Earls of Derby 1385–1672* (Manchester: Manchester University Press, for the Chetham Society, 1983). I am following the more familiar succession numbers for this line of Derby earls from the *DNB*, rather than the *Complete Peerage*'s absolute succession numbers. According to the latter system, Henry, the Fourth Earl in the Stanley line, was the Thirteenth Earl of Derby.

3 For a brief synopsis of the family's landholdings, including the estates at Lathom and Knowsley, see William Farrer and J. Brownbill, ed., *The Victoria History of the County of Lancaster*, vol. 3 (London, 1907; rpt 1966), pp. 157–68, 251–2. For Thomas Stanley's principal biographical details see the *Complete Peerage*; the *DNB*; and Coward, *The Stanleys*, pp. 2–19.

4 Coward lists grants of five forfeited estates in Bedfordshire, Berkshire, Cheshire, Flintshire, Hertfordshire, Huntingdonshire, Lancashire, London, Rutland, Somerset, Warwickshire and Wiltshire, made by Richard III to Thomas and his son George in 1484 and a further seven estates in Cumberland, Lancashire and Westmorland granted to Thomas in 1489 by Henry VII (*The Stanleys*, pp. 12–14). The Stanleys had also owned lands in Staffordshire for several generations.

5 Coward, *The Stanleys*, p. 15.

6 See further J. M. W. Bean, *From Lord to Patron: Lordship in Late Medieval England* (Manchester: Manchester University Press, 1989), especially pp. 18–22, 145.

7 The six-sheet account roll for 1459–60 is now held at the Lancashire Record Office: DDHi, Box 23. See David George, ed., *Records of Early English Drama: Lancashire* (Toronto: University of Toronto Press, 1991), pp. lxxxix, 179.

8 For the difficulties inherent in translating such terms see Abigail Ann Young, 'Plays and Players: the Latin Terms for Performance', *REED Newsletter* 9:2 (1984), 56–62; 10:1, 9–16. These are the heraldic minstrels adopted by many noble households in the fifteenth century, described by Suzanne Westfall, *Patrons and Performance: Early Tudor Household Revels* (Oxford: Clarendon Press, 1990), pp. 64–74.

9 For the King's Lynn reward see *Collections XI*, Malone Society (Oxford, 1980), p. 50.

10 For payments at Rye and Battle Abbey see Cameron Louis, ed., *Records of Early English Drama: Sussex*, (Toronto: University of Toronto Press, 2000), pp. 55,

59, 60, 62, 184. The payments from the coastal Kentish town records are in James M. Gibson, ed., *Records of Early English Drama: Kent: Diocese of Canterbury*, vol. 2 (Toronto: University of Toronto Press, 2002), pp. 351, 353, 369, 370, 374, 829.

11 See Louis, ed., *Sussex*, p. 62, and James M. Stokes with Robert J. Alexander, eds, *Records of Early English Drama: Somerset including Bath*, 1 (Toronto: University of Toronto Press, 1996), p. 42.

12 See J. A. B. Somerset, ed., *Records of Early English Drama: Shropshire*, 1 (Toronto: University of Toronto Press, 1994), pp. 161–2, for the visit of the King, Queen and Prince of Wales to Shrewsbury. *The Complete Peerage* notes the royal visit to Knowsley in July 1495.

13 Somerset, ed., *Shropshire*, pp. 173–4, 176. In 1520–21 the accountant notes that Derby's entertainers provided music. In the same year the Countess of Derby's musical entertainers also appeared at Shrewsbury.

14 See, for example, George, ed., *Lancashire*, p. l.

15 A more extensive study of regional patronage has been published recently. See my chapter, 'A Road Less Travelled? Touring Performers in Medieval and Renaissance Lancashire', in Sarah Carpenter, Pamela King and Peter Meredith, eds, *Porci ante Margaritum: Essays in Honour of Meg Twycross* (Leeds: University of Leeds, 2001), pp. 321–43.

16 Somerset, ed., *Shropshire*, 1, p. 181.

17 *Ibid.*, pp. 182, 187.

18 A number of factors may have influenced the level of civic reward at the two locations, but it is obvious that Stanley influence was stronger in the north-west Midlands where they held substantial properties. The 12*d* given to Derby's minstrels at Southampton was an average amount for that city. By contrast, the Shrewsbury reward was consistently 6*s* 8*d*, with the additional perquisite of wine clearly indicated in 1524–25. My thanks to Peter Greenfield, *REED* co-editor for the Hampshire dramatic records, for sharing his transcripts from the Southampton Book of Fines (Southampton Record Office: SC5/3/1, f. 61v).

19 Derby's bearward was rewarded in the south-east at Lydd (22 July 1530 to 21 July 1531), Southampton (1530–32), Dover (1532–33, 1534), Rye (1533, 1534) and Folkestone (1543–44), with more than one bearward appearing in the New Romney records (1534–35, 1543–44). In addition, along the West Midlands circuit, Derby's bearward appeared at Shrewsbury several times (1532–33, 1537–38, 1542–43) and at the abbot of Worcester's house at Crowle in 1534. See Gibson, ed., *Kent: Diocese of Canterbury*, 2, pp. 429, 431, 578, 684, 771, 775; Louis, ed., *Sussex*, pp. 102–4; Somerset, ed., *Shropshire*, 1, pp. 190, 196, 199; and David N. Klausner, ed., *Records of Early English Drama: Herefordshire / Worcestershire* (Toronto: University of Toronto Press, 1990), p. 527. The Southampton record is found in Southampton Record Office: SC5/3/1, f. 67.

20 See *Collections XI*, pp. 113–14, 148, 182 for Bury St Edmunds, Ipswich and Thetford; Alan H. Nelson, ed., *Records of Early English Drama: Cambridge*, 1 (Toronto: University of Toronto Press, 1988), pp. 106, 110; and *Letters and Papers Foreign and Domestic of Henry VIII*, vol. 8 (London, 1885), p. 338 for Dunmow Priory.

21 See Mark C. Pilkinton, ed., *Records of Early English Drama: Bristol* (Toronto: University of Toronto Press, 1997), p. 43; Canon J. E. Jackson, 'Wulfhall and

the Seymours', *Wiltshire Archaeological Natural History Magazine* 15 (1875), p. 174; Leicester Chamberlains' Accounts, Leicestershire Record Office: BR III/2/11, mb 1 to be published in Alice B. Hamilton's edition of Leicestershire for the *REED* series; and Glynne Wickham, *Early English Stages 1300–1660*, 1 (London and Henley: Routledge, 1980), p. 337 for Selby Abbey.

22 See Gibson, ed., *Kent: Diocese of Canterbury*, 2, p. 446; and Somerset, ed., *Shropshire*, 1, p. 80. The Clifford Steward's Account record (Chatsworth House: Bolton Abbey MS 12, f. 31) will be published in Barbara Palmer and John M. Wasson's edition of the Yorkshire West Riding dramatic records in the *REED* series. My thanks to both editors for allowing me advance access to transcripts of the Clifford papers.

23 According to Neville Williams, *All the Queen's Men: Elizabeth I and her Courtiers* (New York: Macmillan, 1972), p. 55: 'He first became sworn a privy councillor under Somerset, on condition that he need attend meetings only when specifically summoned, and this proviso saved him from the intrigues of Edward's reign, even if his eldest son was principal witness at Somerset's trial. Derby happily identified himself with the Marian reaction, coming to council meetings much more frequently and playing an active part in persecuting heretics. Under Elizabeth he received no office at court beyond his seat on the council, which he rarely occupied.'

24 Christopher Haigh, *Reformation and Resistance in Tudor Lancashire* (Cambridge: Cambridge University Press, 1975), pp. 104–5.

25 The household expense account for July 1560 through July 1561 and the regulations have been published with Henry, the Fourth Earl's household expenses for 1587–90, in Rev. F. R. Raines, ed., *The Derby Household Books*, Chetham Society, 31 (Manchester: Manchester University Press, 1853).

26 *Ibid.*, p. 6.

27 Early chroniclers paid tribute to the Third Earl's generosity. Among others Arthur Collins cites Camden's succinct eulogy: 'with Edward Earl of Derby's death, the glory of hospitality seemed to fall asleep' (*Peerage of England*, 3rd edn, vol. 2 (London, 1756), pp. 72–3).

28 Of the known gentry households, there is only a Shireburn of Stonyhurst rental and account book covering 1567–71. Of the principal towns on established performance routes, only Liverpool and Chester have records before 1572 (the year of Earl Edward's death) and these are very limited. See further George, ed., *Lancashire*, and Lawrence M. Clopper, ed., *Records of Early English Drama: Chester* (Toronto: University of Toronto Press, 1979). The records of Cheshire are being edited for the REED series by David Mills and Elizabeth Baldwin.

29 See Gibson, ed., *Kent: Diocese of Canterbury*, 2, p. 466; J. J. Anderson, ed., *Records of Early English Drama: Newcastle upon Tyne* (Toronto: University of Toronto Press, 1982), p. 45; Somerset, ed., *Shropshire*, 1, p. 206; A. F. Johnston and Margaret Rogerson, eds, *Records of Early English Drama: York*, vol. 1 (Toronto: University of Toronto Press, 1979), p. 330. The Leicester Chamberlains' Account is in Leicestershire Record Office: BRIII/2/31, mb. 1. I am grateful to Diana Wyatt for access to her Beverley Town Accounts transcripts for REED (East Riding of Yorkshire Archive Office: BCII/6/27, mb. 3).

30 The text is taken from Thomas Wright's *Songs and Ballads, with Other Short Poems, Chiefly of the Reign of Philip and Mary* (London: Roxburghe Club, 1860) and quoted in Appendix 4 to Andrew Taylor's PhD dissertation, 'Narrative Minstrelsy in Late Medieval England' (Toronto, University of Toronto, 1988), p. 344.

31 For further analysis of Sheale's career and repertoire, as well as the Bodleian Library's MS Ashmole 48, see Andrew Taylor's dissertation cited above.

32 See Pilkinton, ed., *Bristol*, p. 71; Audrey Douglas and Peter Greenfield, eds, *Records of Early English Drama: Cumberland / Westmorland / Gloucestershire* (Toronto: University of Toronto Press, 1986), p. 300; and Gibson, ed., *Kent: Diocese of Canterbury*, 1, p. 193. The Southampton Steward's Account entry occurs in Southampton Record Office: SC5/1/45, f. [13v] and the Maldon Chamberlains' Account in the Essex Record Office: D/B3/3/252, mb. 4. The Winchester Chamberlains' Account (Hampshire Record Office: W/E1/93, mb. [5]) appears in Jane Cowling, 'An Edition of the Records of Drama, Ceremony and Secular Music in Winchester City and College 1556–1642' (PhD thesis, University of Southampton, 1993).

33 See Nelson, ed., *Cambridge*, 1, p. 249; *Collections II.3*, p. 264; Gibson, ed., *Kent: Diocese of Canterbury*, vol. 1, p. 196, vol. 2, pp. 467, 699, 799; John M. Wasson, ed., *Records of Early English Drama: Devon* (Toronto: University of Toronto Press, 1986), p. 239; Pilkinton, ed., *Bristol*, p. 77. The Beverley record comes from the Governors' Minute Book, East Riding of Yorkshire Archive Office: II/7/2, f. 86v.

34 See Clopper, ed., *Chester*, pp. 20, 124–5. A. W. Titherley, *Shakespeare's Identity: William Stanley, 6th Earl of Derby* (Winchester: Warren, 1952), p. 15, suggests, perhaps fancifully, that the Third Earl and Henry, Lord Strange, were present at a performance of 'The History of Aeneas and Queen Dido' but Clopper's edition of Chester dramatic records does not include any documentary evidence for this addition to the list.

35 See *Collections II.3*, pp. 270, 272; David Galloway, ed., *Records of Early English Drama: Norwich 1540–1642*, (Toronto: University of Toronto Press, 1984), p. 63; Gibson, ed., *Kent: Diocese of Canterbury*, 2, pp. 471, 554; Alexander, ed., *Somerset including Bath*, 1, pp. 12, 13; and Pilkinton, ed., *Bristol*, p. 117. The two Southampton payments appear in the Stewards' Accounts and Book of Fines respectively (Southampton Record Office: SC5/1/48, f. [15]; SC5/3/1, f. 184v).

36 Greenfield, ed., *Cumberland / Westmorland / Gloucestershire*, p. 306; Wasson, ed., *Devon*, pp. 68, 157, 158; and Alexander, ed., *Somerset including Bath*, p. 12. See also the Winchester Chamberlains' Accounts (Hampshire Record Office: W/E1/102, mb. 5d, W/E1/103, mb. 5); my thanks to Alexandra Johnston for access to her transcript from the Abingdon Chamberlains' Accounts (Berkshire Record Office: A/FA c/1, f. 178v), to be included in her edition of Berkshire records for REED.

37 See R. W. Ingram, ed., *Records of Early English Drama: Coventry*, (Toronto: University of Toronto Press, 1981), pp. 265, 286, 294; Stratford upon Avon Council Book A (Shakespeare Birthplace Trust: BRU 2/1, p. 95); Leicester Chamberlains' Accounts (Leicestershire Record Office: BRIII/2/47 mb. 1; BRIII/2/48, mb. 1; BRIII/2/50, mb. 1); and Nottingham Chamberlains' Accounts (Nottinghamshire Record Office: CA 1617, f. 3v; CA 1619, f. 3v; CA 1620,

f. 4; CA 1621, f. 4v). My thanks to John Coldewey for access to his Notting-ham transcripts, to be published in REED's Nottinghamshire volume.

38 See my study of Leicester's politically motivated patronage, 'Tracking Leicester's Men: the Patronage of a Performance Troupe', in *Shakespeare and Theatrical Patronage in Early Modern England*, eds Paul Whitfield White and Suzanne Westfall (Cambridge: Cambridge University Press, 2002), pp. 246–71.

39 In 1573 Derby had also been appointed vice-admiral of Lancashire and Cheshire. He regularly served on ecclesiastical commissions for the diocese of Chester.

40 For the court calendar and Tilney's particular interests in promoting the troupes of his extended family see Scott McMillin, 'The Queen's Men and the London Theatre of 1583', in *Elizabethan Theatre* X, ed. C. E. McGee (Port Credit: D. P. Meany, 1988), pp. 11–12. Two of the plays performed by Derby's Men at Court have been lost, although one of their titles is known: 'The soldan and the duke of . . .' (14 February 1579/80); the 1 January 1580/81 performance lacks a title. 'A History of Love and Fortune' (30 December 1582), likely with eight players in leading roles, was later published under the title *The Rare Triumphs of Love and Fortune*. For details and the Court calendar of plays, see John H. Astington, *English Court Theatre 1558–1642* (Cambridge, 1999), pp. 190, 230.

41 See George, ed., *Lancashire*, p. 46.

42 Further analysis of this notable event and the newly formed company of actors can be found in Scott McMillin and Sally-Beth MacLean, *The Queen's Men and their Plays* (Cambridge: Cambridge University Press, 1998).

43 See further MacLean, 'Tracking Leicester's Men', p. 262. There is an odd, iso-lated payment at Ipswich on 7 August 1592 to 'therll of Darbys players and to the Lorde admirals players' (*Collections II.3*, p. 277). It seems likely that this may have been an error, given the complete absence of evidence for a troupe patronized by the Fourth Earl over the previous decade. Furthermore, this is the year when Strange's Men are on record elsewhere with Admiral's Men, so a con-fusion as to which Stanley was patron of this troupe seems a plausible expla-nation (see, for example, Somerset, ed., *Shropshire*, p. 277).

44 See Wasson, ed., *Devon*, p. 156, and Southampton Book of Fines, Southampton Record Office: SC5/3/1, f. 165v.

45 See *Collections VI*, Malone Society (Oxford, 1962), pp. 16–21, for Court pay-ments to Derby's and Strange's troupes in this period in the declared accounts of the treasurer of the chamber. See also E. K. Chambers, *Elizabethan Stage*, 4 (Oxford: Clarendon Press, 1923), pp. 156–64, for details from the Revels Accounts and Chamber Accounts.

46 Gibson, ed., *Kent: Diocese of Canterbury*, vol. 1, p. 213, vol. 2, pp. 554, 701; *Collections II.3*, p. 271; Ingram, ed., *Coventry*, pp. 290, 321; Alexander, ed., *Somerset including Bath*, p. 12; Louis, ed., *Sussex*, p. 128; Pilkinton, ed., *Bristol*, p. 121; Greenfield, ed., *Cumberland/Westmorland/Gloucestershire*, p. 308; and Wasson, ed., *Devon*, pp. 45, 248. See also Nottingham Chamberlains' Accounts (Nottinghamshire Record Office: CA 1618, f. 3; CA 1621, f. 2); Stratford Council Book A (Shakespeare Birthplace Trust: BRU 2/1, p. 83; and Beverley Town Accounts, BCII/6/37, mb. 2).

47 See Chambers, *Elizabethan Stage*, 4, pp. 156, 158–9. Provincial payments indi-cate that Strange's continued.

48 In 1582/83, the Derby and Strange troupes appeared within two days of each other (30 December and 1 January).

49 See Nelson, ed., *Cambridge*, 1, p`. 330. There are also Derby musicians noticed at Shrewsbury in company with the Earl of Worcester's players, perhaps another appearance by the trumpeters in the same year (see Somerset, ed., *Shropshire*, 1, p. 248). For complete transcripts of the checkroll and household book see Raines, ed., *Derby Household Book*. David George has edited the dramatic records from this source in *Lancashire*, pp. 179–82. The 'Henry ffoolle' at the end of the checkroll may have been another household entertainer (see Raines, ed., *Derby Household Book*, p. 27).

50 For these dramatic records of the gentry see George, ed., *Lancashire*, pp. 166–78, 184–212.

51 Like Alvin Thaler and Raines, I interpret the cryptic (and unpunctuated) entry, 'on saturedaye Sir *Thomas* hesketh players wente awaie' as shorthand for the presence of Hesketh as a guest rather than as a unique appearance by a playing troupe under Hesketh's patronage. See also Thaler, '*Faire Em* (and Shakspere's Company?) in Lancashire', *PMLA* 46 (1931), 657, and Raines, ed., *Derby Household Book*, p. 46.

52 The performance was on Saturday 21 February 1589/90.

53 See further McMillin and MacLean, *Queen's Men*, pp. 63, 178–80.

54 The maverick Symons was rewarded as a leading member of Oxford's troupe in 1584/85, as Strange's man in 1582/83, with 'Mr Standleyes Boyes' in 1585/86, on his own in 1587 and then possibly as a Queen's Man in 1588/89 (Chambers, *Elizabethan Stage*, 4, pp. 159, 160–2).

55 Simon Adams, ed., *Household Accounts and Disbursement Books of Robert Dudley, Earl of Leicester, 1558–1561, 1584–1586*, Camden Society, 5th series, vol. 6 (Cambridges, 1995), p. 233, n. 494.

56 See further MacLean, 'Tracking Leicester's Men', p. 264.

57 Adams, ed., *Household Accounts of Robert Dudley*, pp. 352–3.

58 See further Chambers, *Elizabethan Stage*, pp. 119–20, 124. George Bryan, Thomas Pope and Will Kemp all joined Strange's troupe some time after Leicester's death.

59 See Astington, *English Court Theatre*, pp. 233–4, for their Court appearances in the 1590s and Figure 6 for provincial tour stops.

60 See, for example, Chambers, *Elizabethan Stage*, 2, pp. 118–27; John Tucker Murray, *English Dramatic Companies 1558–1642* (New York Russell and Russell, 1963), pp. 73–91, 105–8; and Andrew Gurr, *The Shakespearian Playing Companies* (Oxford: Oxford University Press, 1996), 258–77.

61 The Doncaster reference comes from Appendix II to Barbara Palmer's unpublished paper, 'Traveling Players in Derbyshire: Bess of Hardwick's Records' for the SAA theatre history seminar (April 2001).

62 See George, ed., *Lancashire*, pp. 170, 173–6, 185, 187–9, 190, 193 for Gawthorpe entries (1609–17) and Dunkenhalgh (1613–25); and Douglas, ed., *Cumberland/Westmorland/Gloucestershire*, pp. 129, 204, 212 for Workington (1628–29) and Kendal (1628–29, 1635–36). The Congleton records (1609–36) will be published in Mills and Baldwin's Cheshire collection; the 1609–10 Stafford entry in J. A. B. Somerset's Staffordshire collection for REED; and the Londesborough (1610–24), Skipton (1615, 1617) and Doncaster (1629/30–37)

records in Barbara Palmer and John M. Wasson's REED edition for Yorkshire West Riding.

63 Cited by Chambers, *Elizabethan Stage*, 2, p. 127.

64 See Ingram, ed., *Coventry*, pp. 348, 349, 353, 358, 397, and Nottingham Chamberlains' Accounts, Nottinghamshire Record Office: CA 1633B, f. 12. Only the King's bearward seems to have been rewarded in Kent during the early seventeenth century.

The playhouse at Prescot and the 1592–94 plague

Nothing in the records of Prescot, Lancashire, a town with a population of about four hundred in the late sixteenth century, explains the sudden appearance of a playhouse about 1593. Prescot was a poor place with its inhabitants engaged in the making of clay pots and coal mining. In 1586 the vicar of Prescot, Thomas Meade, wrote to the Provost of King's College, Cambridge, Dr Roger Goad, that 'Ther is in this poore towne of Prescote one hundred and five severall families, amonge which ther be scarce xx that be able to helpe themselves without begginge', and in 1591 Meade told Goad that Prescot had 'at the lest iiij hundred soules, three parts of them not able to live of themselves except they be releved by neighbours, and of this iiij hundred sixe score vnder the adge of xvj years'.[1] The playhouse's builder was Richard Harrington (born about 1552), tenant of Prescot Hall and a gentleman. He acquired a cottage and garden 150 yards from the playhouse in 1595, presumably the better to manage the property.[2] He died in February 1603; about that time Meade noted that 2 *s* 6 *d* in rent was owing to Prescot Grammar School for 'the play house bwilded vppon the wast by Mr Richard Harrington'.[3] Harrington was 'the younger brother of Percival Harrington, the Derby steward who presided over Prescot's local court, the court leet'.[4] In 1603 'both cottage and playhouse are alluded to in the roll of Prescot court leet dated 23 June'. The court noted that Harrington 'has erected one messuage in Prescotte aforesaid, at the upper end of the street leading towards Eccleston, which messuage is now in the occupation of Elizabeth Harrington, widow, late wife of the said Richard Harrington, at the will of the lord, and rendering 2s. 6d. annually'. 'Messuage' here refers to the playhouse. In 1604 Elizabeth petitioned the Duchy Court at Westminster about Alice Harrington's intransigence in the matter of Richard's will. (Richard had unfortunately made his wife and mother joint executrices.) In passing, Elizabeth mentioned that she lacked any guidance in the matter of 'repayringe of the mess[u]age aforesayde with nedfull reparation'.[5]

In 1609, however, the playhouse had fallen on evil days. The jurors of Prescot Court Leet presented one Thomas Malbon for converting the

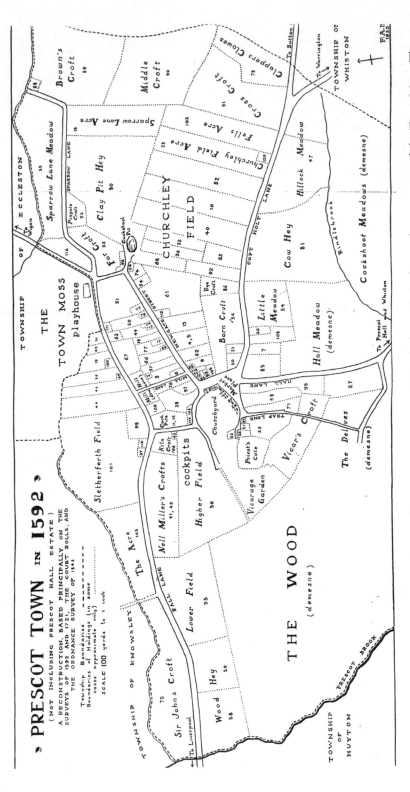

Figure 7 F. A. Bailey's 1935 conjectural map of Prescot Town in 1592. The playhouse is in the south-east corner of the Town Moss. The cockpits adjoin the north side of the grammar school lot (nos. 11, 12).

playhouse into 'a howse for habitacion' and installing an undesirable tenant named Whiteside. It seems likely that Malbon had married Elizabeth Harrington and thus come into possession of the playhouse. Malbon ignored the court's disapproval and permitted Whiteside to remain in the playhouse for another year, but he was so undesirable that the Court Leet directed in 1610 he be driven from the town. One imagines that the playhouse made a wretched 'howse for habitacion', and after Whiteside left there is no further explicit record of tenants being installed.[6]

The building may have been used again as a playhouse after its conversion into a rental. Malbon lost control of the building and site when Elizabeth Harrington died in 1614. Probably the playhouse now came under the control of the steward of the manor, Henry Stanley; Stanley may have received it in trust from Richard and Elizabeth Harrington's daughters. In 1614 Prescot Grammar School accounts were again calling it 'the play House' in a list of Christmas quarter rents collected by Philip Hare. The building could not have been much altered by Malbon if, as is likely, Hare took it over to make it pay again as a playhouse. In 1615 the land it stood on was described as 'nine yards and two feet on its eastern end', 'five yards on its western end', and 'comprising in length nineteen yards' on the north and south sides. That is, the parcel narrowed in breadth from 29 feet to 15 feet and was 57 feet long, a sort of trapezoid shape. It follows that the playhouse could not have exceeded 15 feet by 57 feet if it had any sort of rectangular plan. The picture one gets is of a long narrow room covered by a roof, the roof allowing for easy conversion into an odd-sized apartment.

When Philip Hare died in 1615, John Mercer entered into possession of the property that year:

> John Mercer of Eccleston near Knowsley . . . sought permission to enter into one parcel of land in Prescot . . . lying at the upper end of the High Street leading to Eccleston, near to Churchley Field Gate . . . [O]f and upon the aforesaid parcel of land a building has been put up, earlier used as a certain house called 'a playhouse', and for these [i.e., the building and the land] a rent of 2 s 6 d has been paid annually to the school of Prescot.

In a conveyance of a nearby barn in 1617 the clerk of the court described the barn as 'lyinge neire vnto the play howse in Prescott'.[7]

Mercer died in 1634, still in possession of the property, which was taken over by Edward Stockley. Stockley was married to Jane, a daughter of Richard Harrington, and in 1634 Jane's two daughters applied for the right to be admitted as tenants. Thereafter the property remained in Stockley hands. 'Stockley, and those who claim under him and under the estate of the late Richard Harrington, gentleman, have quietly enjoyed the aforesaid premises for the space of thirty-one years or thereabout and have received its rent, revenue, and profit.'[8] So states a Prescot Court Leet record of 1668, indicating that Malbon must have held the 'property as lifetime freehold and in reversion to the Harringtons'.[9]

What we know, then, about the Prescot playhouse is that it lasted for many years and was therefore sturdily built, stood on the 'wast', and was used as a playhouse at least from 1595 to 1603 and probably till 1609. It comes as a surprise that anyone could build on the 'wast' (waste or town moss). Probably only the Earl of Derby could have authorized such use of the common land since the town moss lay outside the town boundaries. In 1579 Dr Goad wrote to Edward Sutton, the Deputy Steward of the Prescot manor, concerning 'the wast about the towne (belonging peculierly to the lords of the soile)'. Not that Prescot was without spectacle; it had cockpits in 1592, abutting 'on the south side upon the school house'. Both these entertainment sites contributed to the maintenance of Prescot Grammar School. On 7 June 1592 'Dr. Goad attended a meeting convened by Lord Derby at Knowsley to settle the future of Prescot Grammar School', which had undergone a financial crisis in June 1587.[10] We may imagine that the playhouse and cockpits formed two sources of rental revenue. The cockpits were close to the school and church, and the playhouse was 250 yards along Fall Lane: an early provincial entertainment complex. The cockpits were sufficiently well known for Nicholas Assheton and his friends to ride over from Whalley 'to Prescod to a cocking' on 2 June 1618.[11]

Only a member of the Derby family, stewards of the manor, could have allowed the Four Men of Prescot (governors of the manor and liberty) to oversee such commercial sports and games in the centre of the tiny town. The main candidate for promoter of plays in Prescot is Henry Stanley, Fourth Earl of Derby (1531–93), whose estate at Knowsley lay only four miles from the town. He was almost an exact contemporary of Elizabeth I (1533–1603) and would have shared the Queen's enthusiasm for plays and players. This would especially have been true when he was appointed to the Privy Council in 1585 and after he became Lord High Steward of the Queen's Household in c.1589. The Earl had patronized a provincial troupe of players since at least 1573–74, and this company won the honour of appearing at the royal Court in London in early 1580.[12] In late January 1583 Derby's Men visited Liverpool, and surely went on to play privately at Knowsley House.

More important companies than Derby's were to come to Knowsley and the two other Derby houses (Lathom and New Park, near Ormskirk). The cause of their visits was probably the appointment in c.1585 of Earl Henry to the Privy Council, on which he remained until 1589. Fortunately the years 1586–90 are covered by the *Derby Household Book* of accounts with appended diary entries. The *Household Book* records five playing companies visiting Derby houses between July 1587 and February 1590: Leicester's Men (July 1587), Sir Thomas Hesketh's players (December 1587), the Queen's Men (October 1588, July and September 1589, June and September 1590), Lord Strange's Men (December 1588, January and September 1589, February 1590), and Essex's Men (September 1589). Actually, the wording for Strange's Men is oblique: 'at nyght a playe was had in the halle & the same nyght my Lord strandge came home' (31 December 1588); 'that nyght plaiers plaied' (5 January 1589); 'players played at nyght' (February 1590). Evidently these players did not arrive from or leave for anywhere, and are generally assumed to be Lord Strange's Men living at or near Knowsley. Alwin Thaler calls Strange's 'the only company known to have been under the patronage of the Stanleys in the late eighties' and notes that 'all but one of these performances came during the Christmas holiday season, exactly when the Stanleys would, presumably, have been most likely to see plays by their own company'.[13]

Major London companies, then, became familiar with the Prescot area and Earl Henry's patronage. Yet apart from appointments to play at Knowsley, Lathom House, and New Park, these companies may not have found south-west Lancashire a particularly attractive proposition. They could play in Chester and perhaps Liverpool and Manchester, but after that the dearth of important Lancashire boroughs restricted them to the homes of Lancashire gentry for playing venues. Possibly then the idea of a playhouse in Prescot was mooted. When plague struck London in 1592, the idea seems to have matured into reality.

Plague regularly visited London and sometimes other parts of England in Tudor and Stuart times. It came in 1563, 1570, 1574, 1583, 1592–94, 1603, 1606, 1609 and 1625, and it often disrupted the London playhouses. Acting companies had no remedy but to quit London and tour if the authorities deemed assemblies dangerous for the spread of infection. Typical is the Privy Council order of 3 February 1594 which 'prohibited any resort to common plays within the compass of five miles from London until there was better assurance of health'.[14] Once on the road, the companies found life precarious since they had to find money for lodging, food and horsefeed, while not being able to guarantee a daily performance as they could in London. Income must have been much reduced and the travel an additional burden to the day's acting work. Clearly, an extended stay in one place would be the closest equivalent to acting in a London playhouse, and to win such security a company would find a fixed venue essential.

The two companies most likely to have wanted a playhouse near Knowsley in the early 1590s were Derby's own men and those of his son, Ferdinando, Lord Strange. Strange was born in 1559 or 1560 and did some acting in the 1580s in London, probably at the royal household. On 28 January 1589 he was summoned to the House of Lords as Lord Strange. He patronized a company recorded as playing in the provinces from 1576–77 until 1583–84 and thereafter at Court and in London. They are called Strange's tumblers in Court records of January 1580, December 1581 and January 1583, and these boys continued to play at Court at Christmas until 1588. We have seen that Ferdinando's troupe was likely the company playing at Lathom House in December 1588, January 1589 and February 1590. They may have played seasons at the Theatre and the Rose in 1590 and 1591. In 1592 the troupe included William Kempe, Thomas Pope, John Heminges, Augustine Phillips, George Bryan and the Admiral's player Edward Alleyn. They were acting at the Rose from February till late June 1592, and again from late December 1592 till 1 February 1593, after petitioning the Privy Council to let them continue playing in London.

The plague was too mortal to allow for further stay in London, however, and so on 6 May 1593 Strange's sought and got a travelling licence from the Privy Council. They must have left soon after, and kept touring for a long time, for 'the silence as regards Strange's both of the Court records and of Henslowe's diary during the winter of 1593–4 makes it unlikely that they were in London'. Fortunately, 'thanks to Alleyn's correspondence with his wife and father-in-law, and the provincial records, we can follow the company's tour with some certainty'. From Bristol on I August 1593, Alleyn writes that the company will be visiting Shrewsbury, Chester and York, and will not be back in London till I November.[15] In the event Strange's men did not return to London – if they returned at all in 1593 – until after 2 December, when they played at Coventry. In all, then, the company was on the road around eight months, but did not plan to venture north of York. Evidently there was a lengthy stop somewhere, and the Derby houses provide the most logical, most hospitable venue.

In the middle of Strange's tour, on 25 September 1593, Earl Henry died and Ferdinando succeeded to the earldom. This would have augured well for Strange's company had not the same day a man named Richard Hesketh sounded out the new earl about making a claim to the throne as soon as the Queen died. A week later Hesketh was arrested and by November orders came from the government that he was to be executed. Hesketh's death was followed swiftly by Ferdinando's. On 16 April 1594 the new earl died suddenly at the age of thirty-four or thirty-five, suspected of being poisoned or bewitched for betraying Hesketh.[16] Lord Strange's Men may have seized this short window of opportunity – a matter of less than seven months – to press their need for a playhouse. If they were in Lancashire in late September, when their patron became the Earl of Derby and they became Derby's Men, what better opportunity to ask for a playhouse near Earl Ferdinando's estates? After all, they must have heard that London playing was going to be delayed by a month at least, and they could scarcely play night after night at Knowsley House.

Ferdinando seems the most likely factor and financial backer in the building of a playhouse at Prescot. Perhaps it was run up quickly and used in the autumn of 1593. One wishes for evidence it was built at that time. If it was not, then we must turn to Ferdinando's brother William as the factor. According to J. J. Bagley, 'it seems very likely that [Earl William] approved and encouraged, if he did not plan, the building of the playhouse at Prescot, the market town just beyond the limits of his Knowsley estate'.[17]

William Stanley, Sixth Earl of Derby, was born in 1561, and in January 1595 married Elizabeth Vere, daughter of Edward de Vere, Seventeenth Earl of Oxford. Earl William loved music and drama; for example, we hear of him 'busy penning comedies for the common players' in June 1599. About that time his wife wrote to Sir Robert Cecil on behalf of her husband, requesting that

> his man [Robert] Browne, with his companye, may not be bar[r]ed from ther accustomed plaing, in maintenance wherof they have consumde the better part of ther substance, if so vaine a matter shall not seame troublesum to you, I could desier that your furderance might be a meane to uphold them, for that my Lord taking delite in them, it will kepe him from moer prodigall courses.

Browne was the leader of Derby's Men; he had been the payee for their performances at Court in the winter seasons of 1599–1600 and 1600–1.[18]

Earl William became the new patron of Derby's Men in 1594. This company's career is so tangled up with that of Lord Strange's Men that any account of Derby's is necessarily provisional. The Third Earl of Derby had a company of that name in Henry VIII's reign, and the Fourth Earl also patronized them. They were at Coventry in 1573–74, at Gloucester in 1579–80 and at Court on 14 February 1580, 1 January 1581 and 30 December 1582. In 1582–83 they were at Bath, Norwich and Southampton. After that their story grows dim until the 1590s; 'in 1583 they vanish from the records', perhaps broken up by the recruitment of key players to the newly formed Queen's Men.[19] They may have been with the Admiral's Men at Shrewsbury on 3 February 1592, but Chambers suspects an error. They are next heard of on c.18 May (probably 1593) at Southampton, together with Lord Morley's players. They were at Leicester in October–December 1593, at Coventry on 2 December 1593 and at Ipswich, together with the Admiral's, on 7 March 1594. Given the gap in their history in the 1580s, one cannot tell whether this 1590s company is the same as the earlier one. Certainly the *Derby Household Book* of 1587–90 contains no notice of them.

On 16 May 1594 a company was paid at Winchester under the title 'the Countess of Derby's players'. Now Earl Ferdinando had died on 16 April 1594, and Murray thinks that 'for a short time after his death his company of players may have acted under the patronage of his widow'. Then he adds that the whole of Earl Ferdinando's company soon 'passed under the patronage of Henry Carey, Lord Hunsdon. As Henry Carey was at this time Lord Chamberlain, the company assumed that title.'[20] Still, the Sixth Earl of Derby continued to patronize his own players for many years. It may be the case that Ferdinando patronized two companies after he became earl, one company calling itself Lord Strange's Men and another the Earl of

Derby's Men. When William Stanley became earl, he patronized only one company, Derby's Men. Chambers thinks that Ferdinando's troupe may have split into two companies.[21] If so, those Strange's Men who did not go into Lord Hunsdon's service perhaps joined the provincial troupe Derby's Men. They played at Court on 3 and 5 February 1600, and 1 and 6 January 1601. After these Court performances, the troupe is found in Lancashire and Yorkshire until 1636–37.[22]

Earl William may have been the financial backer of the Prescot playhouse. However, his financial status was weak even at the time of his marriage in 1595. Likely, then, the Prescot playhouse was planned to meet the needs of Strange's Men in the depths of the plague years. Derby's may also have used it. If the playhouse was erected about 1593, the date is explained by the plague that struck London in 1592 becoming worse by 1593. In 'Shakespeare's own lifetime none was wholly comparable to the violence of the pestilence that struck as Shakespeare's dramatic writing career was beginning in 1593. In one year at least 15,000 persons of a London population of 123,000 died – more than 12 percent.'[23] The Privy Council banned resort to common plays within five miles of London on 3 February 1594, and by 6 February, when Sussex's Men had paid Philip Henslowe a portion of the Rose playhouse revenues, it was the last time of any playing there till after Easter (31 March).[24] Any playing in April and May was cut short by high weekly plague bills. The hiatus in London playing essentially lasted from late June 1592 to May 1594. By 1593 it would have made sense for someone in Lancashire to suggest building a playhouse for displaced London troupes to play in. The idea could have been sold to the zealous vicar Meade and the godly of Prescot only as a source of income for the grammar school. Ordinarily both would have opposed playing and cock-fighting strenuously. As it happens, there is extant a survey of Prescot manor of 1592, and no playhouse is mentioned. We can therefore put the construction date confidently between 1593 and 1595.

Lord Strange's Men had some connection with the young Shakespeare, then in his late twenties. They had in their repertory in the first half of 1592 *harey the vj*, likely enough the first part of Shakespeare's eventual *Henry VI* trilogy. This was probably acted at the Rose in London. In 1594 the name of Derby's Men appeared on the title-page of *Titus Andronicus*, hinting that they also had some connection with Shakespeare. The early – perhaps first – performances of these two plays have led to two lines of enquiry, firstly into the repertory and make-up of an obscure offshoot of the 1591 Strange's–Admiral's company called the Earl of Pembroke's Men; and secondly into Shakespeare's possible connection with Lancashire.

The Earl of Pembroke's Men appeared in the autumn of 1592 at Leicester, played at Court at Christmas, acted Marlowe's *Edward II* in London, toured in the Welsh border country in the first six months of 1593, and travelled from York to Rye in Sussex in the space of June and July that year. Edward Alleyn, leading Strange's Men, wrote asking Philip Henslowe what had become of Pembroke's. Henslowe replied in September 1593 that Pembroke's had gone bankrupt and had been home in London for five or six weeks. Pembroke's company has long been considered an overflow from the large Strange's–Admiral's London company, obliged to reduce its size when it went on tour:

> it is necessary to point out the close connection of the Strange–Chamberlain's, the Lord Admiral's, and the Earl of Pembroke's companies from 1592 to 1597–8. These companies were all, more or less, connected with the Henslowe–Alleyn theatrical ventures . . . The relationship of these companies being thus intimate, frequent transfers of players and plays from one company to the other would be very probable.[25]

Pembroke's thus has a tenuous connection with the Stanleys through Lord Strange's Men, but its patron was Henry Herbert, Earl of Pembroke.

In 1595 a version of *3 Henry VI* called *The True Tragedy of Richard, Duke of York*, with Pembroke's name on the title-page, appeared on the bookstalls; and in the first half of 1594 appeared a version of *2 Henry VI*, called *The First Part of the Contention betwixt the Two Famous Houses of York and Lancaster*, with no company named on the title-page. It probably also belonged to Pembroke's Men. These texts are shorter by a thousand lines or so than their Folio equivalents, seem altered to require fewer actors and were probably intended for provincial acting.[26]

In all, then, four early Shakespeare plays are connected with Strange's, Derby's and Pembroke's Men. To this repertory we may add *Fair Em, the Miller's Daughter of Manchester*, acted by Strange's Men in London by 1593. The play has two references to Sir Edmund Trafford of Trafford near Manchester, which suggested to Alwin Thaler that the play was intended for Lancashire performances before the Traffords and their friends the Stanleys.[27] The autumn of 1593 would have been a good occasion for Alleyn, who was leading Strange's Men, to stop at Knowsley on the company's way from Chester to York and entertain the Stanleys. *Fair Em* would have been a good choice for a Knowsley performance.

In addition an unnamed company playing at the Rose in January 1593 acted *The Jealous Comedy*; Chambers supposes that the company was Strange's and the play *The Comedy of Errors*.[28] The evidence from play ownership hints that Shakespeare was writing for Strange's and its offshoot Pembroke's in the plague years. Did he therefore belong to Strange's company and was he known at Knowsley House?

To these questions there is no ready answer, but biographers of Shakespeare are familiar with the cases made out by Alan Keen and Roger Lubbock in 1954 and by E. A. J. Honigmann in 1985. Keen and Lubbock found that Shakespeare could have gone to Lancashire to serve Alexander Hoghton at Lea Hall, near Preston:

> Shakespeare's hypothetical progress might be dated as follows: – 1578, or earlier: John Shakespeare's money or religious troubles had begun, and he sent the fourteen-year-old William to Lea. Towards the end of 1581, the ex-singing boy received an extra year's wages and returned to Stratford. 1582, marriage to Anne Hathaway. 1585, to Rufford to join the Hesketh Players.
>
> Three years after this date, Sir Thomas Hesketh died, and his players were in all likelihood absorbed into Strange's Men . . . After . . . 1592, we move among known facts and charted landmarks. Greene's sneer in *A Groatsworth of Wit* warned his fellow dramatists against a successful actor-playwright, now evidently established in London. Then the publication of *Venus and Adonis* in 1593, and *Lucrece* in 1594, both dedicated to the young and influential Earl of Southampton, showed that Shakespeare had safely reached shelter under the wing of friends at Court.[29]

The bases for this account are Alexander Hoghton's will, 1581, and the *Derby Household Book*, 1586–90. Hoghton (c.1520–81) made a bequest in his will (3 August 1581) to Sir Thomas Hesketh of his instruments and play clothes if Thomas Hoghton, Alexander's half-brother, did not want them. He also required Hesketh to be 'ffrendlye vnto ffoke gyllome & William Shakshafte now dwellynge with me & ether to take theym vnto his Servyce or, els to helpe theym to some good master'. In addition Gillom and Shakeshafte got forty shillings annually with promise of more as other servants died off and their bequests were shared out among the survivors. This is quite a lot more than 'an extra year's wages', and it implies that all of the thirty servants granted annuities by the will remained in touch with the executors, Thomas Fleetwood and Robert Talbot.[30]

Keen and Lubbock also give Shakespeare a sabbatical from the terms of the will. Shakespeare goes home to Stratford in 1581 and does not join Hesketh's household until 1585. When Shakespeare does finally get around to Rufford Hall, he joins Hesketh's players. (Perhaps it was just as well he waited, since Sir Thomas was imprisoned in 1581 for recusancy.) Hesketh's players thus appear in the *Derby Household Book* on 30 December 1587: 'on saturedaye Sir *Thomas* hesketh plaiers wente awaie', presumably having arrived on Friday in time to entertain Earl Henry, the Lord Bishop (of Chester), and others who came to Knowsley that night. 'Players', however, could mean either musicians or actors, and, in view of the musical instruments that came to Hesketh from Hoghton, the entertainment could have been music. In any case, there are no other records of Hesketh's men.[31]

Keen and Lubbock's case does not stand up well in the light of an examination of the will and the *Derby Household Book* entry. Their best point is the number of Stanleys who appear favourably in *1* and *2 Henry VI*, and in *Richard III* – Sir William Stanley, John Stanley and Sir Thomas Stanley, who crowns Henry VII in *Richard III*.

Honigmann's claims are a good deal more sophisticated than those of Keen and Lubbock. Honigmann's Shakespeare stays in school longer, and is propelled from Stratford in 1579 or 1580 by John Cottam, Stratford's Lancastrian schoolmaster. Cottam, from Dilworth near Preston, sends Shakespeare to teach for Alexander Hoghton at Lea Hall. When Shakespeare arrives, he finds central Lancashire thick with Catholic recusants, and, mindful of Protestant sensitivities in Stratford, alters his name to Shakeshafte. In this way any rumour of his having become a Catholic will be avoided. The post lasts for a year, whereupon Hoghton, dying, commends Gillom and Shakeshafte to Thomas Hoghton and Sir Thomas Hesketh. The two players spend a little time with Hoghton, but quickly move on to Hesketh, who has a real troupe of players. Hesketh's players often act at nearby Knowsley, where the eighteen-year-old Shakespeare becomes a favourite. However, in August of 1582 the handsome boy impregnates Anne Hathaway while on a visit home, and there he has to remain until 1585. Then he makes his escape and joins Lord Strange's Men at Knowsley; the company's success means that Shakespeare is in London acting and writing by 1587 or 1588. He remains with Strange's Men until 1594.[32]

Honigmann's Shakespeare writes a lot more for Strange's Men than I have suggested above: in addition to the three parts of *Henry VI* and *The Comedy of Errors*, he writes *Titus Andronicus*, *The Two Gentlemen of Verona*, *The Taming of the Shrew*, *Richard III*, *King John*, *Romeo and Juliet* and *Love's Labor's Lost*, all between 1586 and 1592. Needless to say, evidence of such early dates for these plays is almost entirely lacking.

The general effect of Keen and Lubbock's book, and of Honigmann's, is to create a feeling that, though they cannot prove that Shakespeare knew Earl Henry or Ferdinando Strange, he certainly should have visited Knowsley by any odds. Derby's and Strange's Men must often have passed through Lancashire. The problem is whether they used the Prescot playhouse on a regular basis, or whether it was used by many passing companies, or was not in use. Lancashire dramatic records are thin for the period 1593–1609, when we guess the playhouse was open. In effect they are useless for proving that acting troupes regularly passed through the Prescot area. For what they are worth, these are the only relevant nobly patronized companies:

Essex's players	Smithills, 1594
Lord Vaux's players	Castle Rushen, 1602–3
Hertford's men	Lathom, 1606
James Lord Strange's players	Gawthorpe, 1609

Cheshire records also offer a few troupes who could have made their way northwards into south Lancashire:

Queen's players	Chester, 1592
Lord Stafford's players	Congleton, 1595–96
Queen's players	Congleton, 1597–98
Queen's players	Congleton, 1599–1600
Queen's players	Congleton, 1600–1
Lord Dudley's players	Chester, 1602

Westmorland and Cumberland records reflect troupes that had come north from Lancashire since they all played there:

Derby's Men	Kendal, 1597–98
Lord Morley's players	Carlisle, 1603
Derby's Men	Kendal, 1609
Lord Stafford's players	Carlisle, 1609

The records of York and Londesborough (about twenty miles east of York) also mention nobly patronized troupes who could have come by way of Lancashire. These are considerably fuller than Lancashire records:

Queen's players	York, 1592
Queen's players	York, 1593
Earl of Sussex's players	York, 1593
Earl of Worcester's players	York, 1593
Lord Admiral's players	York, 1593
Earl of Pembroke's players	York, 1593
Lord Ogle's players	York, 1593
Lord Darcy's players	York, 1593
Lord Burrough's players	York, 1594
Lord Wharton's Men	Londesborough, 1594
Queen's players	York, 1595
Earl of Worcester's players	York, 1595
Lord Willoughby's Men	York, 1595
Lord Ogle's Men	Londesborough, 1595
Queen's players	Londesborough, 1595
Lord Vaux's players	Londesborough, 1595
Lord Willoughby's players	Londesborough, 1595
Queen's players	York, 1596
Lord Darcy's Men	York, 1596
Earl of Derby's Men	York, 1596
Lord Chandos's Men	York, 1597
Earl of Derby's Men	Londesborough, 1598
Lord Wharton's Men	Londesborough, 1599
Lord Ogle's Men	Londesborough, 1599
Earl of Pembroke's Men	Londesborough, 1600
Lord Wharton's Men	Londesborough, 1600
Queen's Men	Londesborough, 1600

Lord Evers's players	Londesborough, 1600
Lord Clinton's players	Londesborough, 1600
Lord Wharton's Men	Londesborough, 1601
Earl of Shrewsbury's Men	Londesborough, 1601
Earl of Stafford's Men	Londesborough, 1608
Lord Vaux's players	Londesborough, 1609
Children of the Revels	Skipton Castle, 1609
Queen's Men	Londesborough, 1609

The York entries probably do not relate much to companies travelling from Lancashire. As John Wasson has noted, companies who visited York sometimes came up by the more easterly route from Hardwick Hall in Derbyshire. However, the Londesborough entries could well relate to companies that came from Skipton Castle in the West Riding of Yorkshire. Both houses were Clifford family residences. A company visiting Skipton would learn that it was also welcome at Londesborough. Such companies who made their way to Skipton Castle would almost certainly have come through north Lancashire.[33]

The relative frequency of players in Clifford family records should be a hint about the frequency with which companies came to Knowsley and similar noble and gentry homes in the accessible parts of Lancashire. The Derby family accounts are simply missing for all but three years of Shakespeare's lifetime. An interesting indication of what we have lost is the case of the Queen's Men in 1618. They visited Gawthorpe Hall in east Lancashire on 10 March 1618, and were involved in a court case in Prescot on 5 June.[34] The distance between the two places is about thirty miles; how did the troupe manage to fill in almost three months? The possibility of their staying at Knowsley and playing at other noble houses in Lancashire is very strong.

To sum up, the building of the Prescot playhouse is connected with 1593, the terrible year of plague in London and elsewhere. The companies who could best have got the ear of the Stanleys of Knowsley were Derby's and Strange's, the family's own servants. They may well have played in Prescot during the autumn and winter of 1593–94. Strange's had the advantage of owning some of Shakespeare's early plays. They became Lord Hunsdon's Men in 1594 and then the Lord Chamberlain's Men in the same year, a company that included Shakespeare. Perhaps they owed their survival to Earl Ferdinand, the Fifth Earl of Derby, and the playhouse at Prescot. The site should be recognized and commemorated in some way.[35]

Notes

1 F. A. Bailey, *A Selection from the Prescot Court Leet and Other Records 1447–1600* (Liverpool: The Record Society of Lancashire and Cheshire, Vol. 89, 1937), p. 300. The Prescot rectory had been appropriated to King's College in

1448. The vicar had the lesser tithes of the parish, but in 1453 the Stanleys began to collect the tithes and pay King's College an annual rent. The Grammar School was maintained by money from six sources (rents and cattle), and, as these were ecclesiastical in origin, the rectory was responsible for the school (pp. 1–10, 315–17).

2   F. A. Bailey, 'The Elizabethan Playhouse at Prescot, Lancashire', *Transactions of the Historic Society of Lancashire and Cheshire* 103 (1951), 69–81, p. 71.

3   David George, ed., *Records of Early English Drama: Lancashire* (Toronto: University of Toronto Press, 1991), p. 77.

4   J. J. Bagley, *The Earls of Derby, 1485–1985* (London: Sidgwick & Jackson, 1985), p. 76.

5   Bailey, 'The Elizabethan Playhouse', pp. 73–4, 80–1.

6   George, ed., *Lancashire*, pp. 80–1.

7   *Ibid.*, pp. 81–3.

8   *Ibid.*, pp. 240–1.

9   The original is in Latin, printed in George, ed., *Lancashire*, pp. 240–1.

10 Bailey, *A Selection from the Prescot Court Leet*, pp. 296, 187.

11 George, ed., *Lancashire*, p. 147. This ride suggests that the audience for plays at Prescot came from all over south-west Lancashire, but principally from Liverpool, nine miles away. Liverpool had no playhouse.

12 E. K. Chambers, *The Elizabethan Stage*, 4 vols (Oxford: Clarendon Press, 1923), 2, pp. 118–19.

13 Alwin Thaler, '*Faire Em* (and Shakspere's Company?) in Lancashire', *PMLA* 46 (1931), 647–58. To Thaler, who read 'Sr Tho. Hesketh; Players wente awaie', the 'Players' were anonymous. He did not see the original wording ('Sr T hesketh plaiers wente awaie'). Hesketh almost certainly did patronize players; see E. A. J. Honigmann, *Shakespeare: 'The Lost Years'*, second edition (Manchester: Manchester University Press, 1998), p. 38.

14 F. P. Wilson, *The Plague in Shakespeare's London* (Oxford: Oxford University Press, 1927); rpt. 1963, p. 53.

15 Chambers, *The Elizabethan Stage*, 2, pp. 118–26, 131. On Alleyn see John Tucker Murray, *English Dramatic Companies 1558–1642* (New York: Russell and Russell, 1963), 1, pp. 88–9.

16 Bagley, *The Earls of Derby*, pp. 66–7.

17 *Ibid.*, p. 76.

18 Chambers, *The Elizabethan Stage*, 2, pp. 126–7.

19 Sally-Beth MacLean, Chapter 11 above.

20 Murray, *English Dramatic Companies*, 1, pp. 91, 294–6.

21 Chambers, *The Elizabethan Stage*, 2, pp. 126–7.

22 MacLean, Chapter 11 above p. 219. The patronage sequence for Derby's men is Third Earl, Fourth Earl to 1583, gap between 1583 and 1593, Sixth Earl from 1594 to 1637 and probably beyond. The sequence for Strange's boys and men is Ferdinando, Ferdinando's Countess, Hunsdon, Lord Chamberlain, King. Evidently on Ferdinando's death in 1594, Earl William quickly arranged for Strange's Men to come under Lord Hunsdon's patronage and bestowed patronage on a revived Derby's company. For a chart showing the chaos caused to the acting companies by the plague years 1592–94, see my article in *Shakespeare Quarterly* 32:3 (1981), 322. The revived Derby's company was created by the

large, combined Strange's–Admiral's company of 1591–94 dividing into three – the Earl of Derby's, the Lord Chamberlain's and the Lord Admiral's.

23 See Bagley, *The Earls of Derby*, p. 69, on Derby's finances. J. L. Barroll, *Politics, Plague, and Shakespeare's Theater* (Ithaca: Cornell University Press, 1991), p. 74.

24 Wilson, *Plague in Shakespeare's London*, p. 53; Barroll, *Politics, Plague, and Shakespeare's Theater*, p. 212.

25 Murray, *English Dramatic Companies*, 1, p. 62.

26 Madeleine Doran, *Henry VI, Parts II and III: Their Relation to the Contention and True Tragedy* (Iowa City: University of Iowa Humanities Studies 4, 1928), pp. 5–6, 75–6. Laurie E. Maguire describes *I Contention* (2,219 lines) as 'an abridged and corrupt version of Shakespeare's *Henry VI*, pt. 2'; and *True Tragedy* (2,313 lines) as 'an abridged and mangled version of Shakespeare's *Henry VI*, pt. 3'. Whether plays were abridged for provincial performance has never been proved (*Shakespeare's Suspect Texts* (Cambridge: Cambridge University Press, 1996), pp. 238, 320, 68).

27 Thaler, '*Faire Em* (and Shakspere's Company?)', pp. 647–51.

28 Chambers, *The Elizabethan Stage*, 2, p. 123.

29 Alan Keen and Roger Lubbock, *The Annotator: The Pursuit of an Elizabethan Reader of Halle's Chronicle Involving Some Surmises about the Early Life of William Shakespeare* (London: Putnam, 1954), pp. 81–2.

30 George, ed., *Lancashire*, pp. 156–8.

31 Samuel Schoenbaum writes, 'And what of Steward Farington's reference "Sir Tho[mas] Hesketh, players went away"? True, a comma has been editorially supplied but there is no possessive. More likely Farington refers not to Hesketh's players but to the fact that both Hesketh and the players left at the same time' (*William Shakespeare: A Compact Documentary Life* (New York: Oxford University Press, 1977), p. 114). Schoenbaum did not know of the common early usage of the possessive without s. The substantive 'mother' for example was frequently used without a possessive marker: the *Oxford English Dictionary* yields 'moderr wambe' (~ c.1200); 'moder body' (Hampole, 1340); 'modyre banys' (Wintoun, c.1425). *OED* notes: 'In OE. the genitive sing. normally coincided in form with the nom., and many instances of the uninflected genitive occur in ME. and early mod. E.'. See for example two Scottish writers who bracket Farington's 1587–88 entry: Lindesay (*a* 1578), 'Thair captane Monsr de Gwise our quens mother brother', and Dalrymple (1596), 'He was the kingis mother brother'. Under 'father~' *OED* notes that Old English had two possessive forms, 'faeder' and 'faederes', adding that 'the uninflected form survived in occasional use down to the 15th c'. To this I can add that 'Iames, sir Thomas heskethe Minstrell' performed at Read Hall, near Padiham, in 1569. Note the lack of a possessive 's' on 'heskethe', and also that the Nowell steward called him a 'minstrell', the common word in Lancashire for a musician (George, ed., *Lancashire*, p. 160). We can now say that Hesketh had players – 'Sir Thomas hesketh plaiers wente awaie' is a perfectly good reading of Farington's entry, bearing in mind that Lancashire speech had (and has) more in common with Scots than with southern English.

32 Honigmann, *Shakespeare: The 'Lost Years'*, pp. 5–7, 15, 19–21, 24–9, 32–9, 59–76.

33 The Lancashire entries are from *Records*. The Cheshire entries are used with the
    kind permission of David Mills, editor of the forthcoming Cheshire volume of
    Records of Early English Drama, and the General Editor of the *Records of Early
    English Drama*. The Cumbria entries are from *Records of Early English Drama:
    Cumberland / Westmorland / Gloucestershire*, eds Audrey Douglas and Peter
    Greenfield (Toronto: University of Toronto Press, 1986). The Clifford family
    and York entries are from Barbara D. Palmer and John M. Wasson, 'Profes-
    sional Players in Northern England, Parts I and II', forthcoming in *Records of
    Early English Drama: Yorkshire, West Riding*, eds Barbara Palmer and John M.
    Wasson, and are reprinted here by their kind permission. Further acknowl-
    edgement for permission to use this excellent essay here is made to the *Records
    of Early English Drama* project and the National Endowment for the Human-
    ities, which supported the research in Yorkshire.
34 George, ed., *Lancashire*, pp. 177, 83.
35 Bailey notes that the playhouse site has never been excavated. He writes, 'A plan
    of the site made in 1807, when it was sold by auction, and still owed a rent
    of 2 s. 6 d. to the Grammar School, is preserved amongst other deeds in a
    Liverpool solicitor's office. Down to 1902 the site was occupied by a very old
    cottage called, doubtless from its shape, Flatiron Cottage, but in that year the
    cottage was taken down and replaced by business premises called the Ware-
    house' (p. 77). The site should be excavated as soon as possible.

Regional performance in Shakespeare's time

Shakespeare grew up in the provinces, and received his education – in the broadest sense – from the provinces. That education included the rich and diverse native dramatic traditions, traditions which Shakespeare combined so effectively with more learned sources. If Shakespeare spent the so-called 'lost years' in Lancashire, then his provincial experience was wider and perhaps more important than if he had gone immediately to London from Stratford. Certainly he could not have been exposed to the full breadth and variety of provincial dramatic activity, but the north held on to its dramatic traditions as fiercely as it did its Roman Catholicism. By the time Shakespeare retired to Stratford, dramatic activity in the provinces had dwindled to a trickle. In the 1570s and 1580s, however, when he was an adolescent and young man, when he was learning his trade as a player and writer, the old forms still survived outside London – though they were having to struggle for that survival.

The Reformation led to the decline of provincial dramatic traditions that had existed from at least the fifteenth century, but they did not disappear overnight. In fact an important recognition of recent scholarship has been that those forms disappeared only when they were actively suppressed by ecclesiastical and civil officials. Like the dinosaurs, they did not die out in competition with superior forms in a neat evolutionary progression; it took a cataclysmic event – the meteor of Protestantism – to eliminate what had been very successful dramatic species. And like the dinosaurs, provincial dramatic traditions are worth studying in themselves, and not just as evolutionary precursors of Elizabethan drama. As literature, those forms may have been inferior to the drama of the capital, but they held a crucial place in the social fabric of the local communities that performed them, serving as expressions of piety and communal unity. They also often provided the most successful means of raising money for such communal functions as upkeep of the church fabric and poor relief.

Our tendency to separate medieval drama from Renaissance, or early modern, drama has obscured the survival of provincial traditions to the end of the sixteenth century – and, in the north, into the seventeenth. Recently, the use of the term 'early drama' to refer to any drama before 1642 has begun to break down these sharp divisions. The bulk of the evidence for what is usually considered 'medieval' drama in fact comes from texts and records produced in the second half of the sixteenth century, when traditional forms found in the provinces were being suppressed. Indeed, the texts we have of Chester's great biblical cycle present a revised version of the cycle performed only about a decade before Shakespeare's first plays saw the stage. The York cycle was last performed in 1569, Chester in 1575 and Wakefield in 1576. The Coventry cycle saw its final performance in 1579, late enough and close enough to Stratford that Hamlet's remark about actors 'out-Heroding Herod' has long been thought to have come from Shakespeare's memory of seeing the Coventry cycle as a child.

Further north this tradition held on even longer. Kendal's Corpus Christi play, involving several pageants organized by the craft guilds, was not suppressed until 1605.[1] A Shakespeare living at Hoghton Tower might have seen Herod raging at Lancaster or Preston, as both had some form of Corpus Christi play as late as the beginning of the seventeenth century. The Preston play is first mentioned in a Lancashire official's information against a Mr Hawxworthe and a Richard Wilson, accusing them of being Catholic priests. Among Hawxworthe's suspicious activities, in addition to saying Mass, was being in the audience at the Preston Corpus Christi play in 1595.[2] An especially intriguing possibility is that the Preston Corpus Christi play was taken on the road to local towns and great houses, as such plays were elsewhere. The household accounts of Sir Richard Shuttleworth at Smithills, near Bolton, record a payment of 5s to 'the plaers of prestone' at New Year 1589.[3] Unfortunately, similar records have not survived from Hoghton Tower. Given Alexander Hoghton's Catholic sympathies and interest in the theatre, it is possible to imagine that the William Shakeshafte who dwelled in Hoghton's household around 1580 might have witnessed some Prestonian Bottom endeavoring to 'out-Herod Herod'.

These civic Corpus Christi cycles sponsored by towns and their guilds were not, however, the only form of provincial dramatic activity, though they are the best known. In fact the civic cycles were relatively unusual; elsewhere in England we find quite different dramatic traditions. In the south the parish, not the town and guilds, more commonly sponsored plays. These plays were also performed at Corpus Christi or Whitsun or midsummer, and were put on to raise money for the parish. Some towns had biblical plays of less than cyclical scope. New Romney, in Kent, had a passion play, or rather four plays, that began with Christ's baptism and ministry and concluded with the Ascension. This passion play had existed since at least the early fifteenth century, and received its last performances in 1560 and 1562.[4]

Several Essex parishes performed plays with biblical subjects in the 1560s: Maldon stopped by 1564, but Chelmsford continued to 1574 and Braintree to 1579.[5] In Lincolnshire, Donnington had a play about Nebuchadnezzar and his attempt to burn the three boys as late as 1563. Spalding had a play of the battle between St Michael and the Devil that included fireworks and machines. People from Stamford, Peterborough and other towns in the region attended the Spalding play, and it may also have travelled to those towns into the 1570s.[6] The local Lancashire players that visited Sir Richard Shuttleworth in the 1590s from towns and villages near Smithills – Rochdale, Blackburn, Garstang and Downham – may have performed something similar, or perhaps they brought a folk play like those discussed below.[7]

Closer to Shakespeare's Stratford, Worcester's tradition resembled the northern ones: five pageants, which may have been plays or merely tableaux, were organized by the craft guilds and brought out at Corpus Christi until 1567. Worcester Cathedral rented out its stock of costumes to surrounding parishes until at least 1576.[8] Nearby Tewkesbury, which is as close to Stratford as Coventry is, also rented out its 'players' geare'. Tewkesbury's wardrobe was clearly intended for plays on New Testament subjects, as it included garments for Christ made of sheep skins, a mask for the Devil, and wigs and beards for the apostles. Payments for rental on these costumes continued until 1585, and as late as 1600 the parish put on three 'stage plays' at Whitsun, in order to finance a new battlement on the tower. The churchwardens paid to hire costumes and musicians, and to construct a 'a place to playe in'.[9]

While all these examples probably represent survivals or adaptations of medieval dramatic traditions, the case of Sherborne, Dorset, reveals that those traditions were still vital enough after the Reformation to start up in new places. Sherborne was dominated by its Benedictine Abbey during the Middle Ages, but in 1540 the lay parish of Sherborne took over the former abbey as its parish church. Rosalind Hays has argued that the parish 'celebrated its triumph over the abbey with the substitution of a play for the old Corpus Christi procession'. Records from the 1540s mention both playing garments and a play book, but by the 1550s the book had disappeared from the churchwardens' inventories, and the garments were rented out to other parishes, and finally sold in 1562 to the parish of Yeovil.[10] Then, in the early 1570s, the parish once again put on a play at Corpus Christi, and the wardens had to pay for costumes for Lot's wife and the inhabitants of Sodom. They even spent 6d 'for a peacke of Wheatten meal for to macke louttes Wyfe', presumably when she had been turned into a pillar of salt.[11] These expenditures suggest energetic support for the the play, but it did not last beyond 1575, when Sherborne's Corpus Christi play received its last performance.[12]

Methley, in the West Riding of Yorkshire, provides another late example of dramatic activity surviving longer in the north, but that survival may have depended on moving away from controversial religious subject matters. In 1614 parishioners of Methley performed a play called *Canimore and Lionley* in a large barn belonging to the parish over four days in Whitsun week. Richard Shann, one of the local gentry, mentions the play in his commonplace book and provides a cast list of some twenty characters, to be played by seventeen actors – six of them members of Shann's family. The title characters are a prince and princess, and the cast also included kings, nobles, two knight adventurers, 'Invention the paracite', and a ghost. John Wasson suggests that this cast list indicates a dramatic romance like *The Winter's Tale* or *Cymbeline*, a genre popular in London theatre at the time, but among parish plays Methley's is unique.[13]

While the big civic biblical cycles involved a great deal of expenditure on the part of the cities and their guilds, these smaller-scale parish plays were intended to raise money, usually for poor relief and the upkeep of the church fabric. At both Tewkesbury and Sherborne the parishes were under special pressure to raise funds, as at the Dissolution both had purchased large monastic churches from the Crown to be the parish church, resulting in significant debts and heavy maintenance costs on the large buildings. The method they chose to deal with these expenses was one that parishes had been using for at least the two previous centuries. The religious plays were offered in conjunction with an ale, the plays perhaps legitimizing the drinking. Grain provided by parishioners was brewed into ale, and the ale sold at a feast accompanied by a play. The wardens also made collections, to which the parishioners contributed, perhaps more generously than they would have without the lubricating effects of the ale on their purses. The £45 Tewkesbury parish made from its plays and ale of 1600 paid most of the cost of constructing a new battlement on the church tower.[14]

The charitable purpose of these ales, and the collecting – perhaps coercing – of money from those attending, made it entirely appropriate that in many parishes Robin Hood games having mimetic elements took the place of religious plays. The Robin Hood game that accompanied the Whitsun ale at Yeovil was the principal parish fund-raiser until at least 1577. Robin Hood, Little John and a sheriff, accompanied by musicians, walked the streets of the town, carrying people on a cowlstaff, and demanding money from onlookers to avoid the same fate. The churchwardens' accounts mention costumes and props for this game, including a sword for the sheriff and arrows for Robin Hood. Yeovil's Robin Hood was not really an outlaw figure, as he was always played by one of the respected former wardens of the parish.[15] Other Robin Hoods might have been less respectable, like the ones who prompted William Dyke, a preacher of St Michael's parish in St Albans to complain of the Whitsun ale at Redbourn, where they had 'Maid Marion comyng into the Churche in the time of prayer and preachinge to move laughter with kissinge in the church'.[16]

One of the latest examples happened at Wells in Somerset in 1607. A Star Chamber case tells of the great Wells Show of that year, which was a kind of compendium of provincial traditions of entertainment, including

Robin Hood, morris dancing, a maypole, and shows and pageants by the city's six craft guilds.[17] Records of Robin Hood plays are most plentiful from the counties west of London – from the Thames Valley down through Somerset and into Devon – but they were popular also in the north. In Lancashire the authorities tried to suppress Robin Hood and May games at Burnley in 1579, and Bridgnorth in Shropshire had a Robin Hood play as late as 1588.[18]

Robin Hood is frequently associated with May games and summer games, and the distinctions between Robin Hood games and king games are often blurred. King games and summer games usually accompanied Whitsun ales, and centred on the choosing of a mock king or summer lord – and sometimes a queen or lady, as well, much as Perdita is chosen queen of the sheepshearing in *The Winter's Tale*. A fifteenth-century court case from Wistow, in the West Riding of Yorkshire, describes the parish summer game, in which a king and queen were chosen by lot, and led in procession by a minstrel and the youth of the parish to a barn, designated the 'Somerhouse'. There the king and queen held court on thrones, while others took the roles of knights and a steward, as the assembled parishioners engaged in plays or games for the rest of the day.[19]

In Hampshire some parishes held 'king ales' – as such games were known in that county – throughout Shakespeare's lifetime. Crondall and Weyhill held theirs into the 1570s, Stoke Charity theirs into the early 1580s. At Newton Valence in 1580 John Smith may have been swept away by the part he was playing, since a consistory court case charged that he had proposed marriage to Clarice Baker, when he 'was somer lord & the said Clarice was somer lady of newton'.[20] At St John's, Winchester, the wardens paid for 'payntynge of the clothe vpponn the somerloge' in the mid-1550s, and the king ale held in that lodge lasted until 1597.[21]

Latest of all in Hampshire was the parish of Wootton St Lawrence, where the wardens recorded king ales covering several days in 1600, 1601, 1603, 1605 and 1612. In addition to large sums spent on food and drink, the wardens also paid for liveries for the summer lords and ladies, and hired minstrels. Immediately following the payment for the lords' and ladies' liveries in the accounts for 1600 is an intriguing entry: two shillings paid 'to Whitburne for his play'. It seems most likely that 'for his play' meant that Whitburne was the leading performer in that year's king game, but the phrase does raise the question of whether these games included anything that might be called a play, in the sense of written dialogue. One doubts that there were written texts, though there may have been traditional dialogue, preserved through oral transmission, and certainly the games had mimetic elements that allow us to see them as manifestations of a popular dramatic impulse.

These late Hampshire examples show that many provincial people clung to their traditions despite the opposition of the reformed church. A 1585

diocesan letter of Thomas Cooper, Bishop of Winchester, expresses a view
typical of ecclesiastical authorities:

> Wheras a heathenish vngodly custome hath bene vsed before time in many
> partes of this land aboute this season of the yeare to have Church Ales,
> maygames, morish daunces, and other vaine pastimes vpon the Sabath Dayes,
> and other dayes appointed for common prayer, which they have pretended to
> be for the relief of their Churches, but indeede hath bene only a meanes to
> feed the mindes of the people and specially of the youth with vaine sightes,
> alluring them from Divine service, and hearing of the woord of God, and
> inducing them to the prophaning of the Sabath, to the provoking of Gods
> heavy wrath and Indignation against vs . . . [It] is a straunge perswasion
> among Christians, that they can not by any other meane of contribution
> repaire their Churches, and set forth the service of God, but that they must
> first do sacrifice to the Devill, with Dronkennes and dauncing, and other
> vngodly wantonnes.[22]

As Cooper suggests, parish officials may have believed that they had no
other way of maintaining the parish economy. Certainly the churchwardens' accounts of many parishes reveal that ales, with or without plays,
provided most of the parishes' income, and that the seat money or rates
that replaced the ales often made considerably less.

Whether they were concerned with community finances or just resistant to change, those who would continue the old traditions came into conflict with the reforming fervour of those the traditionalists called 'Puritans'
and 'precisians'. The early seventeenth-century records of Star Chamber
are full of disputes like the one from Rangeworthy in Gloucestershire,
where the constable tried to stop the parish Whitsun revel in 1613 on the
grounds that it was in fact 'a most disorderly Riotous and vnlawful assem-
bly'.[23] At Alton, Hampshire, in the same year, a like-minded constable was
beaten when he tried to prevent a group of parishioners from dancing in
the 'somer howse' to the music of an itinerant minstrel.[24] The Alton
dancers may have won a kind of victory, but only a temporary one.
Ironically, we learn most about seasonal festivity from court records of
this period – from Star Chamber, county quarter sessions and ecclesiastical courts – as they document the steady decline of such festivity from a
customary feature of the life of every parish, to infrequent and unusual
events found only in places far from London where Catholic recusancy
remained strong.

Lancashire was certainly one of those places, yet even there the growing
sabbatarianism of the civil and ecclesiastical authorities threatened to
eliminate all the popular pastimes of people in agricultural communities,
who had no time to participate in games and sports during the working
week. In 1617 petitioners from Lancashire complained to King James, who
issued *The Book of Sports* to declare the right of all his subjects to engage
in lawful recreations after divine service. James's declaration permitted

dancing, May games, Whitsun ales and maypoles, as well as athletic contests, though not interludes, bull- or bear-baiting or bowling.

One activity permitted by *The Book of Sports* that was especially popular in the north was the rushbearing; in fact, when James I visited Sir Richard Hoghton in 1617 at Hoghton Tower, Lancashire, the first entertainment offered was a rushbearing.[25] In its basic form, a ceremonial procession bringing bundles of fresh rushes to strew the floor of the church, the rushbearing has nothing dramatic about it, but often music and dancing was involved, and the most elaborate rushbearings included mimetic or representational elements. At Cawthorne, Yorkshire, in 1596 the people 'did arme & disguyse themselves some of them putting on womens apparell, other some of them puttinge on longe haire & visardes, & others arminge them with the furnyture of Souldiers, & beinge there thus armed, & disguised, did that day goe from the Churche, & so wente vp & downe the towne showinge themselves'.[26]

Despite the King's support, seasonal festivities and other pastimes with dramatic elements dwindled to a small fraction of their pre-Reformation numbers. As soon as it was issued, *The Book of Sports* became a focal point of contention between moderate and more radical Protestants, and between the Crown and Parliament as well. By 1625 Parliamentary resistance to the declaration succeeded in forcing the King to assent to an act outlawing Sunday sports. Charles I re-issued *The Book of Sports* in 1633, however, perhaps inspiring a late example of rushbearing at Hornby, Lancashire, in that year. The bearing of the rushes was accompanied by morris dancers, a lord of misrule, clowns and giants. The bearers carried crucifixes on their rushes, an indication that rushbearings were often associated with Lancashire's continuing resistance to Protestantism.[27]

Many at the time thought the re-issuing of *The Book of Sports* contributed significantly to bringing the nation to the point of civil war. The people of Rangeworthy had explained to the Court of Star Chamber that their Whitsun revel had not only been used 'for the refreshinge of the mindes & spirittes of the Countrye people' but also 'for preservacion of mutuall amytie acquaintance and love and decidinge and allayinge of strifes and discordes and debates between neighbour & neighbour'.[28] By the 1630s this traditional purpose of such seasonal festivities had all but disappeared; they aroused tensions that exactly mirrored the social and political tensions which divided the country. Archbishop Laud aggressively promoted Sunday sports as a means of combatting Puritanism, but even his support, and the threat that clergy might lose their livings if they did not comply, did little to reverse the disappearance of traditions of local dramatic activity outside London.[29]

From the fully dramatic plays of the mystery cycles to the limited mimesis of the rushbearing, we can see the richness and variousness of the dramatic traditions of regional performance. These forms of provincial dramatic activity had their own artistry, were effective as fund-raisers, and brought communities together in enactments of social unity. They also provide the national context for the drama of the London theatres, all the more so if there truly was a Lancastrian Shakespeare.

Notes

1 Audrey Douglas and Peter Greenfield, eds, *Records of Early English Drama: Cumberland / Westmorland / Gloucestershire* (Toronto: University of Toronto Press, 1986), pp. 17–18.
2 David George, ed., *Records of Early English Drama: Lancashire* (Toronto: University of Toronto Press, 1991), p. 87.
3 George, ed., *Lancashire*, p. 167.
4 James M. Gibson, ' "Interludium Passionis Domini": Parish Drama in Medieval New Romney', in *English Parish Drama*, eds Alexandra F. Johnston and Wim Hüsken, Ludus: Medieval and Early Renaissance Theatre and Drama 1 (Amsterdam and Atlanta: Rodopi, 1996), pp. 137–48.
5 John C. Coldewey, 'The Last Rise and Final Demise of Essex Town Drama', *Modern Language Quarterly* 36 (1975), 239–60.
6 James Stokes and Stephen K. Wright, 'The Donington Cast List: Innovation and Tradition in Parish Guild Drama in Early Elizabethan Lincolnshire', *Early Theatre* 2 (1999), 63–95; Stokes, 'Saints Plays in Lincolnshire: What the Records Tell Us' unpublished paper.
7 George, ed., *Lancashire*, pp. 167–70.
8 David Klausner, ed., *Records of Early English Drama: Herefordshire / Worcestershire* (Toronto: University of Toronto Press, 1990), pp. 308–9.
9 Douglas and Greenfield, eds, *Cumberland / Westmorland / Gloucestershire*, pp. 335–42.
10 Rosalind C. Hayes, 'Lot's Wife or the Burning of Sodom: the Tudor Corpus Christi Play at Sherborne, Dorset', *Research Opportunities in Renaissance Drama* 33 (1994), pp. 105–6.
11 *Ibid.*, p. 99.
12 *Ibid.*, p. 116.
13 John Wasson, 'A Parish Play in the West Riding of Yorkshire', in *English Parish Drama*, eds Alexandra F. Johnston and Wim Hüsken, Ludus: Medieval and Early Renaissance Theatre and Drama 1 (Amsterdam and Atlanta: Rodopi, 1996), pp. 149–57.
14 Douglas and Greenfield, eds, *Cumberland / Westmorland / Gloucestershire*, pp. 340–2.
15 James Stokes, ed., *Records of Early English Drama: Somerset* (Toronto: University of Toronto Press, 1996), pp. 481–3.
16 British Library Ms. Lansdowne 61, no. 25, f. 74.
17 Stokes, ed., *Somerset*, p. 480.
18 J. A. B. Somerset, ed., *Records of Early English Drama: Shropshire* (Toronto: University of Toronto Press, 1994), p. 404. George, ed., *Lancashire*, p. 6.
19 Barbara D. Palmer, ' "Anye disguised persons": Parish Entertainment in West Yorkshire', in *English Parish Drama*, eds Alexandra F. Johnston and Wim

Hüsken (Amsterdam and Atlanta: Rodopi, 1996), pp. 82–3; Sandra Billington, *Mock Kings in Medieval Society and Renaissance Drama* (Oxford: Clarendon, 1991), pp. 58–9.

20 Hampshire Record Office: M63M70/PW1, passim. Transcriptions from these records will appear in the *Records of Early English Drama* collection for Hampshire, being edited by Peter H. Greenfield and Jane Cowling.

21 Deposition Book of the Consistory Court of Winchester Diocese, Hampshire Record Office: 21M65/C3/8, p. 128.

22 Churchwarden's accounts for 1554–57, Hampshire Record Office: 88M81W/PW1, f. 14r, and passim.

23 Public Record Office: STAC 8/262/11.

24 Surrey Record Office, Guildford Muniment Room: Loseley Ms Cor 3/377, mb. 1d.

25 David George, 'Rushbearing: a Forgotten British Custom', in *English Parish Drama*, eds Alexandra F. Johnston and Wim Hüsken, Ludus: Medieval and Early Renaissance Drama 1 (Amsterdam and Atlanta: Rodopi, 1996), p. 22.

26 Palmer, 'Parish Entertainment', p. 86.

27 Elizabeth Baldwin, 'Rushbearings and Maygames in the Diocese of Chester before 1642', in *English Parish Drama*, eds Alexandra F. Johnston and Wim Hüsken (Amsterdam and Atlanta: Rodopi, 1996), pp. 34–5.

28 Public Record Office: STAC 8/239/3.

29 *The Kings Maiesties Declaration to His Subiects, Concerning lawfull Sports to be vsed* (London: Bonham Norton and John Bill, 1618); Ronald Hutton, *The Rise and Fall of Merry England: The Ritual Year 1400–1700* (Oxford: Oxford University Press, 1996), pp. 189–99; Christopher Hill, *Society and Puritanism in Pre-Revolutionary England*, 2nd edn (New York: Schocken Books, 1964, 1967), pp. 195–6.

Index